THE KEYS TO GROWING IN LOVE

THE KEYS TO
GROWING
IN LOVE

The Language of Love

Love Is a Decision

The Two Sides of Love

Gary Smalley &
John Trent, Ph.D.

Inspirational Press . New York

First published by Inspirational Press in 1996.
Inspirational Press
A division of Budget Book Service, Inc.
386 Park Avenue South
New York, NY 10016

Inspirational Press is a registered trademark of Budget Book Service, Inc.

THE LANGUAGE OF LOVE and THE TWO SIDES OF LOVE published by arrangement with Focus on the Family Publishing.
LOVE IS A DECISION published by arrangement with Word, Inc.

Library of Congress Catalog Number: 95-81979

ISBN: 0-88486-134-1

Designed by Hannah Lerner

Printed in the United States of America

Contents

The Language of Love

To Norma and Cindy, two faithful and loving wives,
who are like our favorite gold-leaf novel.
Each day, with each new page of life,
we discover a fresh way to love and be thankful for them.

And to Jim and Suzette Brawner,
world champions at using word pictures
to build a loving and lasting relationship.

Contents

CAN WORD PICTURES BE MISUSED?

**A TREASURY OF WORD PICTURES
AT YOUR FINGERTIPS**

Acknowledgments

We express our deepest thanks to the following people:

To Terry Brown, our faithful friend and ministry partner, for shouldering many extra hours of work while we were away writing this book.

To Steve Lyon, for his last-minute heroics; and to Penni Stewart, who also helped to bear the many extra burdens that came with creating this book.

To Lee and Susan Noble for providing a beautiful chalet where the original outline of this book came together.

To Doug Childress for his faithful friendship and wise words of critique and counsel.

To Steve and Barbara Ulhman for their love, help, and support.

To Diana Trent, for her brilliant work in researching quotes and proofreading this manuscript.

To S. Rickly Christian, Rolf Zettersten, Mark Maddox, Janet Kobobel, Nancy Wallace, Teresa Wilson, Irene Goslaw, Diane Passno, and the rest of the Focus on the Family team for their tremendous encouragement and support—especially Dr. James Dobson.

To Jim, Pam, Ryan, and Heather McGuire for their invaluable friendship and for providing an apple of great price.

To Dorothy Shellenberger, Ann Kitchens, Tim Kimmel, Ken Gire, Tom Rietveld, Ted and Lynn Kitchens, Karen Cavan, Troy and Myra Hutchings and many other special friends who faithfully read the early versions of this manuscript and gave wise counsel, correction, and advice.

And to Larry Weeden, our much-valued editor, for his skillful help in putting together the study guide for this new edition.

Authors' Note on the Revised Edition

Thank you for picking up *The Language of Love*. If this is your first time to read the book, you're about to discover the most powerful concept we've ever seen for adding life, power and depth to your words. If you read the first edition and are coming back to the book as a refresher or to share in a group, you'll find some important changes in this edition.

First, in a new chapter, you'll discover four ways in which emotional word pictures can deepen and strengthen your Christian walk. Word pictures can help to rekindle your prayer life, bring hope and encouragement to a hurting heart, and provide a powerful tool for evangelism.

Secondly, those of you who read the first edition will notice that we've changed some of the material in what is now chapter 4, "Unlocking the Gateway to Intimacy." When we first wrote this book, we wanted to support an observation we've made in working with thousands of couples and singles over the years. Namely, there are major, God-given differences in the ways the average man and woman communicate.

Men tend to share facts and speak a "language of the head." When the average man runs out of facts to talk about, he stops talking. However, most women have a strong natural ability and desire to share feelings, needs and hurts, a "language of the heart" that they long to have spoken in their homes.

In the first edition, we referred to right- and left-brain research as seeming to support those natural communication differences. All such references, however, have now been removed. Since the book came out, we have talked with several friends who have researched this area closely, and they have helped us to see that the validity of such research is not clear-cut. In addition, such research has been linked to negative psychological assumptions that we did not then— nor do we now—intend to support.

We sincerely apologize if we offended anyone by quoting such research. Our prayer is that the important message of this book will be judged by its scriptural support, for it was in the Bible's extensive use of word pictures that we first came to see this powerful communication tool. From Scripture's unshakable base we wrote this book and now offer you this expanded edition.

WHAT IS A
WORD PICTURE?

1
When Everyday Words
Are Not Enough

JUDY SAT AT the kitchen table, feeling more lonely and discouraged than at any other time in her life. Only a few hours earlier, she had come face to face with her worst fears. Now, try as she might, she couldn't stop wishing she could turn back the clock and undo what had happened. Slumped in her chair, she blinked back the tears and kept replaying the scene over and over in her mind . . .

It was early afternoon on a cool, fall day. Judy drove her new Buick past the rows of well-kept houses. Each was a monument to someone's climb up the ladder of success.

Judy fit perfectly into the upper-class neighborhood. Her blond hair and fair complexion were a tribute to her Swedish ancestry. And at thirty-nine, she still looked as young and trim as many of her friends in their late twenties. Her striking blue eyes flashed with satisfaction as she pulled into the driveway of her two-story, Victorian home. Columns of red brick laced with ivy, together with the manicured lawn, reflected just the right blend of formality and warmth. Her two children were off at school, so the house would be quiet. After a full morning of shopping and errands, she looked forward to a few moments to unwind.

Pulling into the garage, Judy lingered in the car. Closing her eyes, she let the last strands of a haunting love song carry her away to a moonlit beach. Finally, with a sigh, she turned off the stereo, opened the car door, and began unloading the trophies of her morning's conquest. Carrying a sack of groceries in one hand and her keys in the other, she opened the garage entry door.

What Judy didn't realize was that she was also opening the door to the most painful discovery of her life.

Crossing the floor to the kitchen, she put the groceries down on the island counter. When she turned around, her eyes were caught by a sheet of notebook paper taped to the refrigerator.

She recognized the handwriting immediately. It was her husband's. On the outside of the folded piece of paper he'd written, "Judy, don't let the kids read this."

Don't let the kids read this! she thought to herself. *If they'd seen this before I did, they'd have read it in a second!*

As she unfolded the note, she tried to shrug off the uneasy feeling that suddenly came over her. She struggled to convince herself that the message would concern merely their business or personal finances. *That's why he didn't want the children to see what was inside,* she thought. But her hands trembled as she began to read:

Dear Judy,

We both know we've been drifting apart for a long time. And let's face it, I don't see you or anything between us changing one bit.

You may as well know that I've been seeing another woman. Yes, we've been involved, and I really think I love her. I'm telling you all this because somebody is bound to see us together, and I wanted to tell you before someone else did.

Judy, let's make this as easy as we can on the children. It doesn't have to be a big thing with the kids unless you want it to be.

I don't love you anymore, and I really wonder if I ever did. I've already had my attorney draw up the papers because I want a divorce—now.

I've got to go out of town on a business trip. I'll be back in two weeks and will come by to pick up some things and say hello to the kids. One more thing. I'll be staying at an apartment I've rented until this is over.

Steve

Judy clutched the note in her hand as her eyes flooded with tears. Her mind flashed back to a moment in childhood when a slip of paper tore away another important person from her life. She was five years old when the War Department sent the unwanted telegram— two paragraphs regretfully informing her family that her father was the latest casualty of the Korean War.

All these years later, a few paragraphs scratched on a sheet of paper loosed another avalanche of emotional pain. She had again lost the most important man in her life, but this time the note bore no hint of regret. Memories and hurtful emotions collided within Judy's mind, leaving her inviting, once-tranquil world in shambles. In response to her tears and heart-wrenching sobs, her beautiful home offered nothing but silence.

Judy was devastated. But she hadn't reached bottom yet. The worst was yet to come.

From Darkness to Despair

The family went fourteen days without hearing from Steve. During that time, Judy somehow managed to survive the chilling, devastating force of her emotions. Fully a hundred times a day, Steve's handwritten words crashed through her mind. And with each remembrance, she was left to pick up more pieces from her shattered heart.

I've been seeing another woman . . . Yes, we've been involved . . . I want a divorce . . . . I'll be staying in my apartment until this is over . . .

Waiting for Steve to call or come by was a daily, emotional roller coaster. Each trip up the stairs, Judy passed walls lined with smiling family pictures. And each glance at them was a painful journey through nineteen years of marriage and the raising of two children.

Every opened drawer, every closet door left ajar, every corner of the house held its silent reminder of love lost. For almost half her life she had loved and shared herself with one man—someone who said he didn't care anymore, and may *never* have cared. But looking at her children's faces caused the most agony.

Night after night, in spite of her own inner hurt, Judy had to be both comforter and counselor to her son and daughter. She tried her best to put up a good front and explain what had happened. But how could she answer a seven-year-old boy's endless questions, especially when she didn't know the answers herself?

Mommy, why isn't Daddy coming home? Is he mad at me? Mommy, what have we done?

And how could she deal with her teenage daughter's angry fits that erupted every time her father's name was mentioned? In his note, Steve had written so offhandedly, "It doesn't have to be a big thing with the kids." But every tear Judy dried from her children's eyes ripped holes in his logic.

Each evening, after watching their sadness and confusion finally succumb to a fitful sleep, Judy would finally escape to her own bedroom. There, her mind crowded with lonely thoughts, she would cry herself to sleep in a queen-sized bed that suddenly seemed ten times too large.

As another evening crawled by, she wondered for the hundredth time, *Is there any chance we'll ever get back together?* No sooner had the thought drifted through her mind than the phone rang. It was Steve.

"Hello, Judy," he said in a detached, emotionless tone.

"Hello, Honey," she answered automatically, the words slipping out before she had time to think.

Honey? Why did I say that? she scolded herself. She wanted to be angry with him. She *was* angry with him. But now that he'd finally called, the anger she'd struggled with for days seemed to momentarily step aside.

Hearing Steve's voice made her yearn to see him again. She ached for him to put his arms around her . . . tell her that he still loved her . . . that it had all been just a terrible mistake.

But when Steve began to talk, all hope drained from her heart. His words came fast and cold.

"I'm glad you're home, Judy," he said. "I'm calling from the car phone and I'm on my way over to drop off some papers. I can't stop and talk now. We've tried talking for years, but it's never helped." His words carried the biting edge of a north wind in January. "I'll be there in a few minutes."

Before Judy could respond, the phone went dead in her hand. She shot up from her chair and hurried upstairs to tell the children their father was coming over. And as she went back downstairs and waited in the living room, thoughts cascaded down on her from nearly two decades of marriage.

They had always struggled to communicate with each other, even during their courtship. Over the years, arguments had accompanied far too many conversations. The fallout from their cold war of words had chilled their relationship and frozen a layer of insecurity deep within their children's lives.

For all Judy's married life, only one thing remained consistent. She had always longed for Steve to understand her feelings, needs, fears, goals, and wishes. *If only he could understand me; if only I could relate to him in a way he respected; if only we could both get beyond the arguments and angry words and communicate in-depth with each other; if only . . .*

Suddenly, the headlights of a car flashed through the living room window. Judy paused for a moment, quickly looked at herself in the hallway mirror, and straightened her skirt. Then she opened the front door and stepped out onto the porch. But as she stood watching Steve walk toward her, she noticed his car. The lights were still on; the engine was running.

Her eyes instantly opened wide, and she leaned forward, almost involuntarily. *Oh, no,* she gasped, blinking in disbelief. *He's brought the woman with him!*

The street light pushed back some of the darkness, and though Judy couldn't see clearly, there *was* a woman sitting in the front seat. Whoever it was, she refused to look up.

Steve walked up to the porch. He looked as handsome as ever, but his eyes lacked even a spark of warmth. "Here are some papers I want you to read," he said abruptly, thrusting a manila envelope at her. "There's a legal document you need to sign and return to me as soon as possible."

"Steve!" Judy cried, pushing the folder back into his hands. "I can't sign any papers. I don't even know if I *want* to sign them. We need to talk with someone first. Can't we go to a counselor or a pastor or—"

"Now listen, Judy." Steve's voice rang in the cool night air. "I'm not putting things up for a vote. We've talked for years, and nothing's ever changed. I've thought this through, and I'm not interested in hearing you say for the thousandth time, 'It'll work out.' Let's get this straight. It's *not* going to work out. This marriage is through. Over! Finished! I want out! It's time I got on with my life."

Suddenly, there was a sound behind them in the doorway.

"But what about *our* lives, Dad?"

Neither Steve nor Judy had heard their teenage daughter come down the stairs. She stepped to her mother's side. "Dad, I can't believe you're doing this! What are you trying to prove? We love you so much, and this is so embarrassing."

"Kimberly, you just don't understand," her father began, extending his arms toward her.

"Don't touch me! Don't ever touch me again!" Kimberly sobbed as she pushed him away. "I can't believe you're doing this to Mom and me. And what about Brian? You don't care about him, either, do you?" Her tear-stained face was a mixture of anger and terrible sadness.

"I do care. But I'm not going to stand here and argue like this. Anybody could drive by and see us. Your mother and I . . . well, we just can't talk anymore. We've *never* been able to talk. I can't explain it, but we just don't get through to each other."

"But Dad—"

"Look!" he said, his voice blasting like a rifle shot. "I'm not going

to get into this now! I've got to go; the car's running. I'll try to drop
by or call or something later this week."

He turned abruptly and stormed off the porch. But then just as suddenly, he turned back and said, "Say hello to Brian for me." With that,
he walked back to the car—and out of their lives.

Kimberly ran up the stairs to her room, crying. Judy stood frozen
at the front door, watching her husband and another woman drive
away. As the red taillights shimmered through her tears and disappeared into the darkness, she kept asking herself, *Why did this have
to happen? Why? Why? Why?*

The Language of Love: Moving Beyond Everyday Words

Judy and Steve faced an all-too-common problem that was ripping
apart their marriage: failure to communicate in a meaningful way.
It's not that they hadn't tried to talk. Over the years they had spoken thousands of words to each other. But their lack of communication skills kept their marriage in shallow waters. They were never
able to attain the depths of love and compassion for which they both
longed. As with many other couples, their relationship wasn't ruined
because of a lack of words. Their problem was that everyday words
were not enough to provide insight, intimacy, and understanding.

> If we're serious about having
> meaningful, fulfilling, productive
> relationships, we can't afford to let inadequate
> communication skills carry our conversations.

Our need to communicate with another person may not be as dramatic as Judy's was that night. But for all of us, our communication
skills directly relate to how successful we'll be in our marriages, families, friendships, and professions. And if we're serious about having
meaningful, fulfilling, productive relationships, we can't afford to let
inadequate communication skills carry our conversations. There's
got to be a *better* way of connecting with others in our lives—a way
that can guide us safely into the depths of love.

You may be a parent getting nowhere trying to talk with your teen-ager; a married person in a growing or struggling relationship; a friend groping for the right words to encourage an emotionally hurt neigh-bor; a boss who can't seem to motivate or explain an important con-cept to your employee; a worker trying to express an important point to your supervisor; a teacher struggling to get a class to listen and remember what is taught; a counselor attempting to maneuver behind a couple's defenses and bring change to their relationship; a minis-ter or public speaker who wants to challenge and stir people to action; a politician trying to sway the thoughts of a state or nation; or even a writer trying to capture a reader's heart.

No matter who you are or what you do, you can't escape the need to communicate meaningfully with others. And without exception, we all will run into the limitation of everyday expressions.

In a world awash with words, can we find a way to add new depth to what we say? Can a wife find a method to penetrate her husband's natural defenses and get her point across so he will long remember it? Can a man express himself more vividly or say the same old thing in a brand new way? Can men and women say more by using fewer words?

To all the above, the answer is a resounding *YES!* Largely unused in marriages, homes, friendships, and businesses is a tool that can supercharge communication and change lives. This concept is as old as ancient kings but is so timeless that it has been used throughout the ages in every society. It's a powerful communication method we call *emotional word pictures.*[1]

Unlike anything else we've seen, this concept has the capacity to capture a person's attention by simultaneously engaging a person's thoughts and feelings. And along with its ability to move us to deeper levels of intimacy, it has the staying power to make a lasting impres-sion of what we say and write. With fewer words, we can clarify and *intensify* what we want to communicate. In addition, it enables us to open the door to needed changes in a relationship.

This method can challenge the most intellectual adult, yet can be mastered by a child. In fact, we were astonished at how Kimberly, the teen in our opening story, quickly learned and dramatically ap-plied an emotional word picture when faced with the breakup of her parents' marriage.

Journey with us for the next several chapters as we discover the primary method that:

• ancient wise men used to penetrate the hearts and minds of men and women;

• Abraham Lincoln and Winston Churchill utilized to inspire their countries in times of great peril;

• Hitler used to capture and twist the soul of a nation;

• professional counselors employ to speed up the healing process in broken relationships;

• coaches and trainers use to inspire and motivate professional athletes;

• top sales managers utilize to train effective employees; and

• comics and cartoonists have mastered to make us laugh while challenging us to think.

And, most importantly, emotional word pictures *can enrich your every conversation and relationship.* That is, they will enable your words to penetrate the heart of your listener—to the extent that your listener will truly understand and even *feel* the impact of what you say.

Word pictures form a language of love everybody can speak. Specifically, it was this language of love that confronted the barriers surrounding Judy's husband. In the next chapter we'll examine the amazing results of how this irresistible means of communication met the immovable heart of a runaway father.

2
Words That Penetrate the Heart

DURING THE THREE weeks following the tearful scene on the front porch, Steve called a few times. He even came by the house twice—once to pick up his mail, the other to gather more of his clothes and personal belongings.

Whenever he called or visited the house, he would talk for a few minutes with Judy or the children. But his conversations were never more than skin deep. After skillfully dodging all meaningful questions, he would finally invent some excuse to end the conversation and get on to his next "important" commitment.

Not being home at night, Steve never witnessed the aftermath of his leaving. He never saw the confusion that grew into continual heartache for Brian or how his young son's schoolwork and self-confidence were affected. Steve didn't recognize the seething emotions directed toward him by his daughter, Kimberly, and how that anger flared at every person she had ever trusted.[1]

Nor did he watch his wife valiantly struggle to control her emotions in front of the children, only to retire at night and erupt with alternating fits of rage and brokenness. After crying herself to sleep, she would roll over in the middle of the night to snuggle next to him, only to awaken with her arms holding a pillow.

Judy, who hurt so badly herself, witnessed her son and daughter struggle through painful emotions. As she watched them suffer, not knowing quite how to help, a scene from her own childhood flashed back to her mind.

There had been a terrible rainstorm one summer day. She could see herself standing at the window, looking out on the backyard. As she watched, the wind and rain furiously lashed at the trees. After the storm, she walked into the yard and saw a nest of baby birds that had been blown to the ground. The emotions she felt for those tiny creatures crying out, floundering in the mud, and looking so helpless, frightened, and confused, were the same emotions she now felt as she watched her own children.

That's when she decided to seek counseling. Steve was adamant that he would never step into a counselor's office. Yet Judy felt she and the kids should go, if only for their sake. It was during those sessions that Kimberly learned about word pictures—and her first attempt to craft one broke through to her father's heart.

A Daughter's Life-Changing Words

More than two months after Steve's decision to leave the family, his stubborn heart met its match.

After a long, hectic day at work, Steve slowly scaled the two flights of stairs to the empty apartment that had once looked like freedom. He tossed aside yesterday's paper that was draped across an overstuffed chair, then flopped down to catch his breath.

Pulling out his briefcase, he began thumbing through various envelopes. He usually read his mail at the office. However, because the day had been so demanding, this was his first chance to leaf through the stack of letters that begged to be read. He found the usual collection of brochures and bills, along with a few interesting-looking business letters proudly sporting their embossed corporate logos.

But as he glanced at the pile before him, his eyes caught sight of a personal letter—one with handwriting that looked like his wife's. Looking closer, he saw it was actually from his daughter.

Through the years, Steve probably had been closer to Kimberly than to either his wife or his son. He'd always been frustrated by his wife's "unrealistic" expectations that he spend more time with his family than at work. And even at seven years old, Brian was already too much like Steve. Seeing his son was like looking in the mirror, and Steve was uncomfortable with the reflection. But it was different with Kimberly. When he talked to her, he didn't hear an echo of his own unhappiness. Her self-confidence and independence were traits he could respect.

Steve opened the letter, expecting to find a card or note. But what he found was far different. Inside was an emotional word picture his daughter had written—a story that would sink into his mind and heart, and hang on like the talons of a full-grown eagle:

Dear Daddy,

It's late at night, and I'm sitting in the middle of my bed writing to you. I've wanted to talk with you so many times during the past few weeks. But there never seems to be any time when we're alone.

Dad, I realize you're dating someone else. And I know you and Mom may never get back together. That's terribly hard to accept— especially knowing that you may never come back home or be an "everyday" dad to me and Brian again. But at least I want you to understand what's going on in our lives.

Don't think that Mom asked me to write this. She didn't. She doesn't know I'm writing, and neither does Brian. I just want to share with you what I've been thinking.

Dad, I feel like our family has been riding in a nice car for a long time. You know, the kind you always like to have as a company car. It's the kind that has every extra inside and not a scratch on the outside.

But over the years, the car has developed some problems. It's smoking a lot, the wheels wobble, and the seat covers are ripped. The car's been really hard to drive or ride in because of all the shaking and squeaking. But it's still a great automobile—or at least it could be. With a little work, I know it could run for years.

Since we got the car, Brian and l have been in the backseat while you and Mom have been up front. We feel really secure with you driving and Mom beside you. But last month, Mom was at the wheel.

It was nighttime, and we had just turned the corner near our house. Suddenly, we all looked up and saw another car, out of control, heading straight for us. Mom tried to swerve out of the way, but the other car still smashed into us. The impact sent us flying off the road and crashing into a lamppost.

The thing is, Dad, just before being hit, we could see that you were driving the other car. And we saw something else: Sitting next to you was another woman.

It was such a terrible accident that we were all rushed to the emergency ward. But when we asked where you were, no one knew. We're still not really sure where you are or if you were hurt or if you need help.

Mom was really hurt. She was thrown into the steering wheel and broke several ribs. One of them punctured her lungs and almost pierced her heart.

When the car wrecked, the back door smashed into Brian. He

was covered with cuts from the broken glass, and he shattered his arm, which is now in a cast. But that's not the worst. He's still in so much pain and shock that he doesn't want to talk or play with anyone.

As for me, I was thrown from the car. I was stuck out in the cold for a long time with my right leg broken. As I lay there, I couldn't move and didn't know what was wrong with Mom and Brian. I was hurting so much myself that I couldn't help them.

There have been times since that night when I wondered if any of us would make it. Even though we're getting a little better, we're all still in the hospital. The doctors say I'll need a lot of therapy on my leg, and I know they can help me get better. But I wish it was you who was helping me, instead of them.

The pain is so bad, but what's even worse is that we all miss you so much. Every day we wait to see if you're going to visit us in the hospital, and every day you don't come. I know it's over. But my heart would explode with joy if somehow I could look up and see you walk into my room.

At night when the hospital is really quiet, they push Brian and me into Mom's room, and we all talk about you. We talk about how much we loved driving with you and how we wish you were with us now.

Are you all right? Are you hurting from the wreck? Do you need us like we need you? If you need me, I'm here and I love you.

Your daughter,
Kimberly

A week after sending her father the letter, Kimberly stayed home with Brian and her mother rather than attend an evening high-school football game. Actually, the choice was easy. Nursing a broken heart, she just didn't feel like cheering and laughing with friends. For several hours she sat in her room watching television, trying to get involved in an old movie. Finally, she gave up hiding from her loneliness and went downstairs to rustle up a snack. She wasn't really hungry, but she thought a full stomach somehow would help to fill her empty heart.

She put her hand on the railing and slowly descended the stairs. But halfway down, something caught her attention, and she looked up. Standing in the doorway was her father. She hadn't heard the doorbell and had no idea how long he'd been there.

Heartbeats were measured in hours as their eyes met. Kimberly felt that if she looked away, he would disappear.

"Daddy?" she finally said in a faltering voice, her heart leaping.

"Kimberly," her father answered. Then, with emotion filling his voice, he asked, "How's your leg, Honey?"

"My leg?"

"I got your letter."

"Oh . . . well, it hasn't been doing too well."

"I'm sorry I hurt you so badly, Kimberly. You don't know how sorry I am," he said, fighting to control his voice. "Your letter came when I didn't know if I could ever return to the family. I felt I'd already gone too far from all of you ever to come back and try again. But your story showed me how much pain I'd caused you all. And to be honest, it made me face the fact that I'd been pretty banged up myself."

He looked at Kimberly and swallowed hard before continuing. "Is your mom upstairs? I'm not promising anything, but I think we need to get some counseling. There's a lot we have to work out."

It was Steve's handwritten note that had launched his entire family into deep, threatening waters. It was a second one—conveying an emotional word picture—that helped calm the waters and start their relationship back toward solid ground. While a word picture may not always carry such a dramatic and immediate impact, it can and did in this case. The result: Two days after Steve came home, he walked into our office for counseling with his wife. And not long afterward, he moved home for good.

What prompted such change in this man? In tears, his wife and daughter had pleaded with him to come back to the family. Yet their pleas hadn't touched him. It was an emotional word picture that finally penetrated his brick-walled heart and pried open his life to much-needed change.

Much More Than a Story

How could sharing a single story bring so much change to someone's life? Kimberly didn't understand how or why a word picture worked with her father; she was just thankful it did. As you'll soon discover, there are five powerful forces at work each time they're used.

In the following pages, we'll explore how and why this language of love is so effective. But first, let's briefly define this communication tool.

A concise definition would read something like this: <u>An emotional word picture is a communication tool that uses a story or object to activate simultaneously the *emotions* and *intellect* of a person.</u> In so doing, it causes the person to *experience* our words, not just hear them.

An emotional word picture
is a communication tool that uses a story
or object to activate simultaneously
the *emotions* and *intellect* of a person.
In so doing, it causes the person
to *experience* our words, not just hear them.

In short, <u>this communication skill brings to life the thoughts we want to express</u>. By looking through the pages of history and at current communication research, we find that the evidence is clear: Whenever we need to communicate important information with another person, word pictures can multiply the impact of our message.[2]

With this definition in mind, let's put word pictures under the microscope and turn it up to full power. By doing so, we'll see how many couples have moved to a deeper level of intimacy and understanding in a single hour than they have in months of everyday conversations.

HOW CAN
WORD PICTURES ENRICH
MY COMMUNICATION?

3
Igniting the
Power of Words

WE'VE ALREADY SEEN how a word picture dramatically changed one man's heart. But that's nothing compared to seeing this same power change men throughout an entire nation!

Altering a man's actions or attitudes has always been difficult, and many women feel their husbands wear armor plating that deflects everything they say. But in 1942, Walt Disney demonstrated that the effective use of a movie-length word picture could blast through such barriers. In his popular movie *Bambi*, he painted a picture that went straight to their hearts. And almost overnight he took thousands of men's fingers off the trigger, nearly bankrupting the deer-hunting industry in the process.

The year before the animated film was released, deer hunting in the United States was a $9.5 million business. But when one particularly touching scene was shown—that of a yearling who sees his mother gunned down by a hunter—there was a dramatic change in many men's attitudes. The following season, deer hunters spent only $4.1 million on tags, permits, and hunting trips![1]

It's often been said that one picture is worth a thousand words, and that certainly proved true with *Bambi*. But what does this mean to a man or woman who has a deep need to express important feelings, concerns, or information with another? It's high time to trade in a thousand everyday words for one effective word picture.

There are definite reasons this communication method has such a dramatic impact on people. In this chapter, we'll explore five of them, providing the mortar to bond for a lifetime with those you care about.

Five Reasons Word Pictures Work So Effectively

1. Word Pictures Have Been Time-Tested by the World's Greatest Communicators.

Your destiny may not lie in making front-page news. But if you want to leave a lasting impression on your own page of history, you'll do well to follow the lead of the world's greatest communicators.

Take Cicero, the silver-tongued orator of the Roman Empire. He believed word pictures are "lights" that illuminate truth. As he told his students, "The more crucial the message, the brighter the lights must be."[2]

In fact, he reported that a man was considered wise only if he could fit his thoughts within the frame of a word picture.[3]

Aristotle, one of the most respected scholars of early Greece, was a master at doing that very thing. For example, he once said of a fallen hero:

> He entered the combat in body like the strongest bull, in spirit like the fiercest lion. Proving the old adage true, "A soldier is to come back from battle with his shield . . . or on it."[4]

Centuries later, Benjamin Franklin challenged the heart of his young country by crafting his thoughts with this same communication technique. Word pictures filled his speeches and writings, but perhaps the best example of his skill at using them is the epitaph he wrote for his own tombstone:

> The body of Benjamin Franklin, Printer (like the cover of an old book, its contents torn out and stripped of its lettering and gilding), lies here, food for worms; but the work shall not be lost, for it will (as he believed) appear once more in a new and more elegant edition, revised and corrected by the Author.[5]

Prior to the Civil War, Harriet Beecher Stowe was enraged at the system of slavery down South. But who would listen to her? During the early years of American history, there was no platform from which a woman could speak. Yet an entire nation was greatly moved when she penned a book-length word picture called *Uncle Tom's Cabin*.

When her book was released, it inflamed those in the North. Her vivid description of the cruelest of slave owners fanned widespread opposition. Her message caused such white-hot fury that Abraham Lincoln felt the Civil War was inevitable.[6]

Nearly a century later, as a world war raged throughout Europe, another great communicator stepped forward. Winston Churchill always carried a look of utter defiance. It showed itself in the cigar shoved to one corner of his mouth and the warrior's glint in his eyes. But for a nation under siege, it was Churchill's picture-filled speeches that rallied the fighting spirit of his shaken countrymen.

Soon after the humiliating retreat at Dunkirk, Britain faced the discouraging news that Italy had joined ranks with the Nazis. But in typical style, Churchill went on the radio with these words:

Mussolini is a whipped jackal, who, to save his own skin, has made of Italy a vassal state of Hitler's Empire. Today, he is frisking up by the side of the German tiger with yelps not only of appetite—that could be understood—but even of triumph. . . . It shall do him no good. Dictators may walk to and fro among tigers, but they dare not be deceived. The tigers are getting hungry too.[7]

If Churchill was a master of motivating his countrymen, across the English Channel was his evil equal, Adolf Hitler. As we'll see in a later chapter, he held the soul of a nation captive with his gripping word pictures.[8] We'll also illustrate the tragic way some people still twist the language of love into a language of hate. In so doing, they use something intended for good to manipulate, intimidate, control, and destroy others.

Word pictures need not be lengthy to deliver a tremendous punch. Some of the great communicators in recent years have used this technique to spice up a single thought in a speech. In his 1961 inaugural address, John F. Kennedy spoke of the need to "let every other power know that this hemisphere intends to remain the master of its own house."[9]

Also, Martin Luther King, Jr. challenged a segregated society:

Let us not seek to satisfy our thirst for freedom by drinking from the cup of bitterness and hatred.[10]

And Ronald Reagan, called by many "The Great Communicator," salted his conversations with story after story and analogies, such as "Let's win one for the Gipper!"[11]

A look across the pages of history confirms that word pictures have rocked the world. Perhaps nowhere is that more evident than in one treasured book.

Without question, the Bible has had the most life-changing effect of anything ever written. It remains the most widely read, circulated, and translated book in history.[12] Of all the communication methods the biblical writers could have used, word pictures surface on nearly every page.

Consider, for example, one of the Bible's most familiar passages, the oft-quoted Psalm 23, which begins, "The Lord is my shepherd . . ." This psalm has provided hope for people everywhere as they crossed through their own personal "valley of the shadow of death."

It was spoken on the bridge of the Titanic as lifeboats moved away from the doomed vessel,[13] on a beach at Okinawa and in the jungles of Vietnam in the midst of fighting,[14] in a space capsule orbiting the moon,[15] and is still spoken every day in hospital waiting rooms where families pray.

What astonished us in our research was finding that throughout the Scriptures, Jesus' primary method to teach, challenge, and motivate others was word pictures. When discussing love, He launched into a word picture about a good samaritan. To encourage His disciples, Jesus told them that in His Father's home, there were many mansions waiting for them. When teaching lessons of faith, He spoke of faith the size of a mustard seed moving a mountain. And to describe the forgiving heart of a father, He shared a story about a prodigal son.[16]

We'll go into much more detail in chapter 15, but word pictures are also the most frequent biblical means of describing who Jesus is. For example, He is pictured as the Wonderful Counselor, Everlasting Father, Prince of Peace, the Word, the Light of the World, the Vine, the Lion of the tribe of Judah, and the bright Morning Star.[17]

We've looked at men and women who have conveyed their most important messages with this language of love. By standing in the shadow of these giants, you can gain their advantage—the power to change and enrich lives. But this isn't the only reason for using word pictures. There are four more that can provide a bedrock foundation for building lasting relationships with others.

2. Word Pictures Grab and Direct Attention.

A wise husband or wife can uncover the secret that advertisers have used for years to capture a person's attention. Advertisers know they have only a few seconds to make their pitch. By wrapping brief word pictures around their corporate slogans, they ensure their message outlives their commercial. Who can forget slogans such as: "You're in good hands," "Own a piece of the rock," and "Like a good neighbor"? Similarly, we don't drive cars; we drive Broncos, Blazers, Colts, Cavaliers, and Mustangs.

Studies show that when we hear a word picture, our brain works faster and expends much more energy than while reading or listening to conventional words.[18] To illustrate, read a page of your favorite novel and an equal amount from the encyclopedia. You'll find yourself reading the novel much faster, and for good reason.

Your response to a story is like driving into a layer of fog along the California coast. You're instantly alert, working hard to spot what's ahead. You strain to see the divider lines, and your eyes ache as they search for brake lights. Your mind won't let you relax until you emerge from the fog and can see clearly again.

In like manner, an emotional word picture creates a mist in your listener's mind. It forces him to strain mentally to see what lies beyond your story. And when the fog lifts, the person finally breaks out into a more clear understanding of what you wanted to express. For a weekly example of this, just watch the sleepy heads snap up in the pews when a minister uses a well-timed illustration in the middle of a sermon!

> Great communicators know that a
> word picture can give them an advantage
> from the moment they begin to speak.

It has been said that the first thirty seconds of a conversation are crucial.[19] Great communicators know that a word picture can give them an advantage from the moment they begin to speak. You can use this attention-grabbing advantage in your communication—even with hard-to-reach people.

That's what Kimberly found when she wrote to her father, a man who steered clear of confrontation. Her word picture held his attention fast—until the mist lifted, and he understood what she wanted to say.

3. Word Pictures Bring Communication to Life.

Another major reason for using word pictures is that they activate a person's emotions, which can lead to positive change. Up until the onset of puberty, children experience change primarily through straightforward teaching and instruction.[20] But once puberty hits, words alone have far less impact on a child. For adolescents and adults, life changes occur mainly through significant emotional events, such as a death, marriage, birth, loss of a parent, breaking off a relationship, winning or failing to win an award, or making a religious commitment.[21]

Word pictures simultaneously tap into a person's emotions, intellect, and will by creating a "theater of the mind" or "mental journey." As we read earlier, hunters who saw Disney's movie got more than they paid for. Many of them emotionally experienced the dark side of their sport for the first time. Instead of reveling in the thrill of the hunt, they felt the emotions of a youngster seeing its mother gunned down.

Studies have shown that word pictures not only activate our emotions, but they also *physically* affect us.[22] That is, when we hear a story about either a real or imaginary event, our five senses are triggered almost as if we experienced the event ourselves![23]

That helps explain why you can feel so drained after reading a thrilling book or why a suspenseful movie wears you out. In reality, you're safely curled up in your chair, far removed from the crazed tribe of cannibals. But physiologically you experience the same shortness of breath and the release of chemicals that pour into the hero's bloodstream.[24]

Not only does fear prompt this reaction, but so do love and other positive emotions. Many women are in marriages devoid of emotional warmth. Where do they turn for romance millions of times a year? To the picture of love painted in romantic novels. Reading about someone else's romance (real or imagined) causes these women to experience, at least in some measure, the longed-for feelings of love.

When Kimberly mailed her word picture to her father, she actually sent him a time bomb. Her words exploded inside him, forcing him to experience physically and emotionally the damage he had caused others. And, as mentioned earlier, awakened emotions can prompt changes in one's thinking. What's more, we plant within a listener a lasting seed that can grow into a changed life—even if that person rejects our words at first hearing.

4. Word Pictures Lock Thoughts into Our Memory.

We typically hear one or both parties in a struggling marriage complain, "Why can't he (or she) remember what I say?" Actually, frustrated spouses aren't the only ones who feel they're talking to deaf ears and forgetful minds.[25]

A constant complaint of ministers, teachers, and other educators is that people don't remember what they've been taught. In part, this is because so much teaching is done by straight lecture. There are certain advantages to this mode of instruction. However, after a few hours, the average person will remember only 7 percent of a half-hour speech!

As you might suspect, researchers have shown that people remember concepts and conversations far longer and much more vividly when a word picture is used. In fact, the more novel or bizarre the story or object, the longer the concept is remembered!

Corrie ten Boom, a Holocaust survivor and noted worldwide speaker, impressed this principle on us. "Don't ever step in front of a group without an object or story that illustrates what you're saying," she would tell us in her firm, heavily accented voice. "Every place I speak, I use one. And even when I've been away for years, people still remember what I've said."

In her travels, Corrie became a symbol of hope to anyone in spiritual or physical bondage. When she spoke before a group, she often held up a large piece of embroidery with the back side showing. Strings hung every which way, and no clear pattern could be discerned.

"This is the way our lives often look," she would say. "When I was in the concentration camp, it seemed there was nothing but ugliness and chaos. But then I looked to God to make sense of my world"—at that point she would turn the tapestry around, revealing to her audience a beautifully embroidered crown—"and at last I could see why He added a certain thread or color, no matter how painful the stitching."

Like the memory of a moon-lit walk, word pictures linger long after they've been spoken. When Kimberly sent her letter to her father, it made an immediate impact on his life. However, he told us later that it was its lasting impact—the way it stayed in his mind for days and continued to convict him—that broke through to his heart.

5. Word Pictures Provide a Gateway to Intimacy.

As powerful as these four reasons are to use emotional word pictures, they're overshadowed by the fifth: <u>Word pictures open the door to very meaningful and intimate relationships</u>.

In nearly every home, major problems can surface because men and women have markedly different ways of thinking and talking. But emotional word pictures help couples find common ground for communication.

Time and again we've seen dull, unfulfilling marriages transformed into vibrant, mutually satisfying relationships. It doesn't happen by magic or without consistent work. It happens because people discover the gateway to intimacy through the language of love. And we'll show you how in the next chapter.

4
Unlocking the Gateway to Intimacy

A NUMBER OF years ago, I (Gary) sat down to talk with an attractive woman who was in obvious pain. With tears streaming down her face, she sobbed, "I've tried to express what's wrong in our marriage, but I just can't seem to explain it. What's the use in bringing it all up again?"

After only five years of marriage, this woman had nearly given up hope of experiencing a loving, healthy, and lasting relationship with her husband. Opposed to divorce, she had resigned herself to a life that offered few of the wishes and dreams she once longed for.

I had heard this kind of story before. For years, I had regularly counseled with husbands and wives, spending countless hours talking to them about improving their relationships. Only now, I wasn't sitting in my counseling office. I was seated at my kitchen table. And the woman sitting across from me wasn't a counselee—she was my own wife, Norma!

That day, I made a decision to understand what was happening, or not happening, in my marriage. And I also decided to find the answers to several important questions. Why was Norma feeling so frustrated in her attempts to communicate with me? Why did I have such a difficult time sharing my feelings with her? And why was it such a struggle to understand each other—particularly when we discussed important issues?

> It isn't until we understand some of
> the ways God has equipped men and
> women differently that we will begin
> to maximize our communication.

It wasn't until we understood some of the ways God has equipped men and women differently that we began maximizing our communication. The bridge that spanned these differences proved to be word pictures.

Have you ever tried to express an important thought or feeling with members of the opposite sex, only to have them act as if you're speaking a foreign language? Have you ever asked, "Why can't he (or she) *feel* what I'm saying?" Join the club.

Throughout history, many women have found it difficult (some say impossible!) to communicate with men. And an equal number of men have given up trying to converse with women. I ran into this problem myself on a shopping trip when my wife and I were using the same words, but speaking a different language.

"Shooooooppping"

After that tearful session with my wife, I decided to commit myself wholeheartedly to understanding and relating to her. But I didn't know where to start.

Suddenly, I had an idea that I knew would get me nominated for Husband of the Year. I could do something adventurous with Norma—like going shopping! Of course! My wife loves to shop. Since I had never volunteered to go with her before, this would demonstrate how much I really cared. I could arrange for a babysitter and then take her to one of her favorite places in the world: the mall!

I'm not sure what emotional and physiological changes ignite inside my wife upon hearing the words "the mall," but when I told her my idea, it was obvious something dramatic was happening. Her eyes lit up like a Christmas tree, and she trembled with excitement—the same reaction I'd had when someone gave me two tickets to an NFL play-off game.

That next Saturday afternoon, when Norma and I went shopping together, I ran face first into a major barrier that bars many men and women from meaningful communication. What I discovered blew open the door to understanding and relating to Norma, and steered me toward emotional word pictures for help. Here's what happened:

As we drove up to the mall, Norma told me she needed to look for a new blouse. So after we parked the car and walked into the nearest clothing store, she held up a blouse and asked, "What do you think?"

"Great," I said. "Let's get it." But really, I was thinking, *Great! If she hurries up and gets this blouse, we'll be back home in plenty of time to watch the college game on TV.*

Then she picked up another blouse and said, "What do you think about this one?"

"It's great, too!" I said. "Get either one. No, get both!"

But after looking at a number of blouses on the rack, we walked out of the store empty-handed. Then we went into another store, and she did the same thing. And then into another store. And another. And another!

As we went in and out of all the shops, I became increasingly anxious. The thought even struck me, *Not only will I miss the halftime highlights, but I'll also miss the entire game!*

After looking at what seemed like hundreds of blouses, I could tell I was beginning to lose it. At the rate we were going, I would miss the entire season! And that's when it happened.

Instead of picking up a blouse at the next store we entered, she held up a dress that was our daughter's size. "What do you think about this for Kari?" she asked.

Taxed beyond any mortal's limits, my willpower cracked, and I blurted out, "What do you mean, 'What do I think about a dress for Kari?' We're here shopping for blouses for you, not dresses for Kari!"

As if that wasn't bad enough, we left that store without buying anything, and then she asked if we could stop and have coffee! We'd already been at the mall for sixty-seven entire minutes, which beat my previous endurance record *by half an hour.* I couldn't *believe* it—she actually had the nerve to want to sit around and discuss the kids' lives!

That night, I began to understand a common difference between men and women. I wasn't shopping for blouses . . . I was *hunting* for blouses! I wanted to conquer the blouse, bag it, and then get back home where important things were, like my Saturday-afternoon football game!

My wife, however, looked at shopping from opposite extremes. For her, it meant more than simply buying a blouse. It was a way to spend time talking together as we enjoyed several hours away from the children—and Saturday afternoon football.

Like most men, I thought a trip to the mall meant going shopping. But to my wife it meant *shoooooppping!*

Over the next several days, I thought back to our mall experience and my commitment to become a better communicator. As I reflected on our afternoon, I realized I had overlooked something important.

For years I had been confronted with unisex haircutters, unisex clothing, and coed dorms. Yet in the rush for equality of the sexes, I'd been lulled into overlooking an important aspect of healthy male/female relationships: recognizing and valuing the innate differences between men and women.

Of course, typical male/female differences don't apply to every relationship.[1] In some 15 percent of homes, the man may display more "typically" female tendencies when it comes to communication styles, and vice versa. This often occurs with men and women who are left-handed.[2] Yet male/female styles do predominate, even in homes where typical communication roles are reversed. In fact, virtually all relationships with role reversals experience as many differences as the most stereotypical couples.

With that in mind, let's examine several important ways men and women usually vary in the communication arena. We've witnessed many of them crop up around our house, and most likely you have, too. Interestingly, they're also the ones that physiologists have found to be common between the sexes.

The Little Buzzards Are Different, Aren't They?

In our home, we have our own version of the "Battle of the Sexes." On one side are Norma and our oldest child (and only daughter), Kari. The other consists of me, "the big kahuna," and our two sons, Greg and Michael.

Norma and I would testify before a live, televised congressional hearing that we didn't brainwash our children into adopting typical male and female roles and reactions. But from the time they first showed signs of life, they displayed the common differences between the sexes. It all began with how much more *noise* came from the boys and how many more *words* came from our daughter at the same age.

Gaining the Edge in Communication

Researchers have found that from the earliest years little girls talk more than little boys.[3] One study showed that even in the hospital nursery, girls had more lip movement than boys![4] That propensity keeps right on increasing through the years, giving them an edge at meaningful communication!

In our home, Norma noticed the same thing discovered by Harvard's Preschool Program in its research of communication differences between the sexes.[5] After wiring a playground for sound, researchers studied all the noises coming from the mouths of several hundred preschool boys and girls.

The researchers found that 100 percent of the sounds coming from the girls' mouths were audible, recognizable words. The girls each spent a great deal of time talking to other children—and nearly as much talking to themselves!

As for the little boys, only 68 percent of their sounds were understandable words! The remaining 32 percent were either one-syllable sounds like "uh" and "mmm," or sound effects like "Varooom!" "Yaaaaah!" and "Zooooom!"

Norma was comforted to discover that the propensity males had in our family to yell and grunt was caused by genetics, not environment. And after twenty-plus years of asking me questions and receiving monosyllabic answers like "uh" and "mmm," she claims this inability to communicate in understandable sentences remains constant throughout the male lifespan!

Young men clearly have more difficulty communicating than young women. Special education teachers are aware of that, since nine out of ten speech pathology problems involve males.

But what about us adults? You'd certainly think grown men would have caught up with their wives when it comes to communication skills. But think again!

Studies show something that Norma and I have observed for years in our relationship. When it comes to the number of words each of us uses, her total count was quite a bit higher than mine. It's been found that the average man speaks roughly 12,500 words a day. In contrast, the average woman speaks more than 25,000![6]

In our marriage that meant when I got home from work, I'd already used my 12,500-word daily quota, while Norma was just getting warmed up! I was being paid to talk all day. I didn't want to come home and then talk all night! I wanted to park in front of the television set.

Not only did Norma leave me in the dust when it came to the number of words we spoke, but when we did talk, it seemed as if we were headed down two different roads. Let me illustrate what I mean.

For most men, "facts" are a major part of a conversation. For example, when Norma would meet me at the door, she'd often say, "Can we talk tonight?"

My first response was always, "About what?" Like Detective Joe Friday, most men want their wives to "Give me the facts, Ma'am, just the facts." Indeed, when the average male runs out of facts, he'll stop talking.

For years, Norma longed to discover my deepest feelings, especially when we faced an important issue or decision. But time and again, when the conversation moved beyond the nuts-and-bolts facts of the matter, I'd clam up or change the subject.

Like most women, Norma was far more in touch with her emotions than I was. I was good with giving her the bottom line, but the bottom of my feelings remained uncharted territory. The difference showed in our consistent failure to have meaningful conversations.

Two Languages in the Same Home

In many homes, the ways men and women communicate are so far apart that it's as if they're speaking two different languages—without an interpreter! What do we mean?

Over the past twenty years, we've interviewed several hundred couples and thousands of women all over the country. And we've found that most men speak what we call a "language of the head."

Call it "fact talk" or "head talk," it means the average man enjoys conquering five hundred highway miles a day on family vacations; favors mathematical formulas over Harlequin romances; remembers only the dictionary definition of love; and generally prefers clinical, black-and-white thinking. "Head talk" keeps most emotions bottled up, desiring instead to deal with facts like memorized batting averages and box scores.

On the other hand, most women speak what we call a "language of the heart." They're comfortable with both facts *and* feelings.

Call it "heart talk" or "feeling talk," those who speak this language enjoy looking at the fine-detail work of quilts, are better able to use their imagination, and show a particular interest in deep relationships. They actually *like* to pull over at rest stops and read historical markers, and they usually don't care what's happening on a football field unless they personally know the players or their wives. They tend to express the feelings of love, not just the definition, and would rather read *People* magazine than *Popular Mechanics* because the former is more relational.

"There's a Stuckey's Up Ahead."

These mental differences were always painfully apparent when we (the Smalleys) took family vacations by car. I had spent hours plotting out the trip as if I were getting ready to drive the Indianapolis 500. I knew we had to be *on the road* each morning no later than 8 o'clock and make *exactly* 487 miles a day. And based on the 12.3 miles-per-gallon we got in our gas-guzzling tank, I even calculated where we'd stop for gas. I was determined to let nothing stand in my way. I would compromise only when absolutely necessary.

The first sign my goals were in jeopardy came when I felt Kari kicking the back of my seat.

"Cut that out," I'd say, my eyes glued to the bumper of a car I was trying to pass. I'd already passed about fifty that day, and I felt like John Wayne galloping toward the fort.

"I need to go to the bathroom."

"You'll have to wait," I replied, glancing first at the diminishing car in my rearview mirror, then at the odometer, then the dashboard clock, then the map. "We can stop in the next town."

"But Daddy!"

"Just another twenty-five miles."

Five minutes later, the boys alleged they were starving to death.

"I'm so hungry my stomach hurts," Mike, our youngest, would moan. "Oooohhhh! Oooowwww! Daddy, my stomach!"

"Mommy, it's past lunch time and Daddy won't stop!" Greg pitched in, seeking a higher authority.

"I can't wait any longer!" Kari shouted, kicking my seat.

"Quit kicking the seat," I replied. "Seventeen more miles."

Norma, looking at me as if I were a prison warden, pointed out a billboard as we sped down the interstate. And then ever so quietly and with a hint of a smile, she said, *"There's a Stuckey's up ahead."*

In our family, mentioning the word "Stuckey's" is the same as shouting, "Oasis ahead!" to people dying of thirst. My choice was made for me: I *had* to pull over at the next exit. My only consolation was that Stuckey's was a "three-star stop." That is, I could accomplish three tasks there at once: pit stop, gas stop, and food stop.

Practically before the car came to a stop, I jumped out to pump gas. Quickly, I shooed the kids toward the restroom and Norma toward the lunch counter.

"Please hurry!" I shouted, cringing as a line of cars whizzed by— cars I had passed just minutes before. "We've got to get back on the road and *catch* those cars!"

Differences, differences, differences! Why does it seem that God has given women such an advantage in personal communication and intimate relationships?

While some men look at a woman's communication skills as a negative, they're actually one reason she's so valuable to him. In Genesis 2:18, we're told the woman was designed as a "helper" to complete the man. That word *helper*, in the language of the Old Testament, carries with it the idea of doing something for someone that he lacks the skill to do.

One kind of help the average woman brings to a man is the ability to share deep, meaningful communication.

Most men have the factual, logical "language of the head" down pat. They can come up with a lecture on the spot—but they're often *put* on the spot when they need to communicate words of warmth, love or encouragement.

If men are to be truly effective in their relationships both at home and at work, they need to develop the ability to speak the "language of the heart." And right there under the same roof are women who can help them learn those skills.

Wise husbands and wives will learn to speak each other's language, and they'll also teach their children to do so to help them enter marriage some day as effective communicators. Most boys do need training, as evidenced by the "backseat syndrome" that strikes the Smalley boys every vacation.

While on the road, listening to our daughter talk nonstop for an hour, Norma or I would always say, "Okay, Kari, it's time to let the boys speak. Boys, it's your turn to talk." After Kari quieted down, we were greeted by. . . silence. So Kari would start talking again.

Like the boys, I'm still playing catch-up to Norma and Kari in the quantity of words spoken. And there remain some "mysteries" when it comes to Norma and me understanding each other. But just because the females in our home have a natural communication advantage doesn't lead to frustration for us males anymore. If anything, we're taking lessons from them.

For men and women to communicate effectively, it takes both *knowledge* and *skills*. So far we have focused on the former—developing knowledge about the importance of communication and how innate male and female thinking patterns can short-circuit understanding. But what about the skills?

There is a way for a man to boost his communication skills instantly and for a woman to multiply hers. By using the power of emotional word pictures, a man can move beyond "facts" and begin to achieve total communication—feelings and facts—with a woman. This same skill not only will help a woman get a man to *feel* her words as well as *hear* them, but it also will maximize her God-given relational abilities.

Years ago, Norma proved this point to me. She illustrated a concern in such a way that her words immediately moved from my head to my heart.

Add Feelings to Facts.

When I was working on my parenting book, *The Key to Your Child's Heart*, I asked Norma if she would write one of the chapters. It was a section that highlighted one of her strengths, and I thought the project would be an easy and pleasurable experience for her. I thought wrong.

As the days passed and time drew near for the chapter to be completed, Norma hadn't even started. Several times she tried to discuss how much of a burden the project was, but I always steered the conversation back to the "facts."

I decided it was time to motivate her. I told her that writing a book was absolutely no big deal. She wrote excellent letters, I pointed out. She ought to think of the chapter as just one long letter to thousands of people she'd never met. What's more, I assured her that as a seasoned publishing veteran, I would personally critique each and every page and catch her slightest error. I thought to myself, *Is that motivation, or what?*

Her emotional, softhearted appeals to duck the assignment made little impact on me, because I was armed with the facts. But my logical, hardheaded reasoning didn't impress *her* much, either. We traded words as if we were swapping Monopoly money. Frankly, we should have saved our breath. We were at loggerheads until my wife, in desperation, gave me the following word picture.

"I know you don't realize it, Gary, but you're wearing me out emotionally and physically," she said.

"Who, me?"

"Come on, let's be serious for a minute. For the past several days you've been draining all my energy. I know you'll be upset by me bringing this up, but—"

"Me? Get upset?" I said, trying to keep things light. "If I'm draining your energy, tell me about it. It's no problem."

"Do you see those hills in the distance?" she asked, pointing out the window. "Every day I feel like I must climb them, wearing a twenty-pound backpack. Between getting the kids fed, dressed, to school, and to their athletic practices—and still managing our business office—I barely have enough energy to take another step.

"Now, don't get me wrong," she continued. "I work out to stay in shape, and I love walking those hills daily. But you're doing something that's like asking me to climb Squaw Peak every day—in addition to climbing those hills."

"I am?" I said, pondering her words. Several months earlier I had climbed Squaw Peak, a beautiful mountain near our home, and I knew firsthand how demanding its incline was. My mind shifted into the hyper-search mode to determine where Norma was headed with the story. "Okay, I'm stumped," I finally said. "What in the world am I doing to force Squaw Peak on you?"

"You added Squaw Peak to my day when you asked me to write that chapter for the book. For you, carrying around a twenty-pound pack is nothing. But to me, the weight of my current responsibilities takes all my energy. Honey, I just can't add another pound, climb the hills, and take on Squaw Peak as well."

Suddenly, everything she had been saying before was clear. To me, writing a chapter wouldn't have added an extra ounce to my pack or caused the slightest additional incline to the hills I climb daily. But for the first time I could *feel* the strain I'd unknowingly put on her.

"If that's what writing this chapter is like, then I wouldn't want you to do it," I said without a moment's hesitation. "I appreciate what you're already doing and don't want to weigh you down any more. You're far too valuable for that."

After the conversation, it was as if a cloud lifted from our relationship. But I didn't know what to make of things the next morning when I came down the hall for breakfast. Norma was sitting at her kitchen desk, furiously writing away.

"What are you doing?" I asked, dumbfounded.

"Writing my chapter."

"You're doing *what*? I thought you said it was like climbing Squaw Peak!"

"It was," she said. "When I knew I had to write it, I felt tremendous pressure. But now that l don't *have* to, I feel like writing!"

Bridging the Communication Gap

Who said word pictures will help you understand *all* the differences between men and women? But they do help us bridge the natural communication gap—and better understand what another person is saying.

Let's go back to what happened when my wife first expressed her concerns about writing a chapter. Like a typical man, I focused on the facts—the actual words being said—to the exclusion of the emotions she was sharing. I failed to read between the lines. This isn't a fault peculiar to me. Something similar happened to a couple we know, and scenes like it probably take place in nearly every home.

It had been a particularly trying day for Diane, and everything that could go wrong around the house, did go wrong. The moment her husband walked in the door that night, she nailed him. "Jack, you never help around the house," she complained. "I always have to take out the trash and do everything else. *You never* lift a finger to make my life any easier!"

After having his hair parted by her emotional words, Jack replied with a matter-of-fact voice. "Now, Diane. Are you sure I *never* help you? And do you *always* take out the trash? I took the garbage out just yesterday, and two days ago I mowed the lawn. And what about earlier this week when . . ."

What Jack didn't understand (and what can breed tremendous frustration between a husband and wife) is that Diane wasn't really talking about whether he took out the garbage. Rather, she was expressing her feelings about how she needed his support around the house. But like most males, Jack heard only his wife's literal words. The nonliteral, softhearted feelings behind her words zoomed right by him.

In addition to a woman's verbal skills, she has a built-in sensitivity that acts like a radar detector. It picks up the tone of voice used in a conversation, as well as the emotional or pictorial messages that are seen or spoken. If Diane had used a word picture to convey her message, she could have helped Jack *feel* what she was actually saying.

Remember, change occurs with adults when they *experience* an emotional event. When Norma first discussed not writing the chapter, her words only registered as black-and-white facts to me. Consequently, they had little effect. But when she used a word picture, it was as if she began talking in color instead. I immediately saw the shades of her feelings, and as a result, both my attitudes and actions changed.

If a woman truly expects to have meaningful communication with her husband, she *must* reach his heart, not just his head. And if a man truly wants to communicate with his wife, he *must* enter her world of emotions. In both these regards, word pictures can serve as a tremendous aid. They won't eliminate all the differences between men and women, but they can enable us to unlock the gateway to intimacy.

Where Do You Go from Here?

If you haven't won any creative awards lately, you may be wondering how to paint effective word pictures. Where do you find them? When is the best time to use them in your most important relationships? In the coming pages, these questions will be answered. You'll learn the seven steps to creating word pictures, along with four ways to use them most effectively in everyday conversations.

Also, you'll be steered to four inexhaustible wells from which you can draw word pictures that work best in your specific situation, and you'll be shown how to apply them to make an immediate difference in your marriage and family life. If you're looking for even more ammunition to improve your communication, at the end of the book you'll find a treasury of more than one hundred word pictures, which you can use at home, in business, with friends, or in church.

Word pictures are the most powerful method of communication we know. Yet when it comes to this language of love, there are people who refuse to listen and aren't able to love back. In a later chapter, we'll talk about why some people remain resistant to any attempt at meaningful communication. We'll also see how these same people often harness the power of word pictures to hurt, manipulate, and control.[7] But thankfully, most people don't fall into this hard-to-reach category. Most men and women are open to change and intimacy, particularly when they're approached in a way that reaches straight to the heart.

Beginning in the next chapter, you'll start learning how to communicate with such power. And your relationships will never be the same.

HOW DO I CREATE A WORD PICTURE?

5
Creating an Effective
Emotional Word Picture

Part One

WHEN IT COMES to cooking in the kitchen, most men act as if they are above reading instructions. I hate to admit it, but I (John) fall into that category. Basically, I feel that following a recipe is a sign of weakness.

In my few adventures in the kitchen, I've turned three-alarm chili into a twenty-three-alarm fireball, causing my wife, Cindy, and daughter, Kari Lorraine, to sprint to the sink and guzzle gallons of water. I've substituted cream of tartar for baking powder because "they looked the same to me!" I've even used peanut butter to "hold" a meat loaf together.

Despite my culinary creativity, most of my exploits have caused little damage other than heartburn and "panburn." But years ago, I nearly destroyed an entire apartment complex by ignoring a recipe.

It was Thanksgiving break, and my college roommates and I were spending the holiday in our apartment. Since we weren't going to be with our families, we invited a bunch of friends to join us for a home-cooked Thanksgiving feast.

As the day neared, we made up a shopping list, bought out the local grocery store, and began preparing for our sumptuous meal. From the beginning, I should have known we were in big trouble when my roommate couldn't figure out how to use the electric can opener. But the damage he inflicted on the can was a minor issue compared to what I did to the turkey.

Consider the facts. I knew I had an IQ of at least my age. (My wrestling coach told me that repeatedly.) At the very least, I knew I was more intelligent than the turkey I was supposed to cook. So why waste time reading directions on how to prepare it?

1 had picked a mammoth bird that looked more like a small ostrich than a large turkey. As I removed the wrapper, I noticed a bag full of disgusting things shoved clear up inside the cavity. I debated whether or not to remove it, but I figured the butcher put it there for flavoring. So I left it in.

My next step was to "dress" the carcass. I had seen my mother rub peanut oil over turkeys to give them that golden-brown look. So, naturally, I planned to do the same with my masterpiece. The closest thing I could find was 3-in-1 oil, but I was smart enough not to use that. There wasn't enough left in the can, anyway. So I wrapped a sheet of aluminum foil around the bottom of the bird and proceeded to the oven, which I had remembered to preheat. In fact, I'd turned the thermostat to "torch" nearly an hour before to make sure it was hot enough.

My next in a long line of mistakes was to set "Turkey Kong" directly onto the metal rack in the oven. No baking pan. No cookie sheet. Nothing to catch the fat and grease. Just a paper-thin layer of foil separating an otherwise-naked, twenty-four-pound bird from the red-hot coils inches below.

While I'd already done enough to lead to disaster, my most catastrophic error was deciding I had plenty of time to pick up a few friends who were coming to our holiday feast. I walked outside with a jaunty step, filled with pride that I could rescue two Thanksgiving orphans from cafeteria food. I nearly broke my arm patting myself on the back.

Making the leisurely, twenty-five-minute drive to their house without incident, I spent the return trip bragging to my captive audience about the great meal awaiting them. But rounding the corner for the final approach to our "banquet hall," I spotted the flashing red lights of several fire trucks at our apartment complex.

"Great!" I said. "A little drama! Let's go see what idiot burned down his apartment!"

As I soon discovered, the idiot was me. Black smoke was belching from the door of our apartment, which the firemen had smashed into toothpicks with axes. As if that wasn't embarrassing enough, they dragged out what was left of my charred, smoldering turkey and hosed it off on the grass!

Swallowing my pride, I drove my roommates and our invited guests to a local cafeteria for Thanksgiving dinner. And instead of eating turkey for leftovers, I ate crow for months.

That Thanksgiving was one of the most embarrassing moments of my life. But it illustrates an important point: We don't want your first attempt at using word pictures to go up in flames. We know that some of you are so excited to use this communication method that you're ready to "throw the turkey into the oven" without reading the instructions. But to avoid having to repaint your relationships after fire and smoke damage, you'd be wise to follow each step below.

The Next-Best Thing

We'd love to sit around your kitchen table, join you for coffee, and help you create a word picture. However, since the chances are slim we can do that, we'll do the next-best thing: We'll show you, step by step, how to tailor-make one to fit your needs. We'll do this by examining one of the most life-changing stories in history—the very one that generated the idea for this book!

Seven Steps to Creating Emotional Word Pictures

1. Establish a Clear Purpose.

To create effective word pictures, you must begin with an important preparatory step: deciding how you want to enrich your relationship. Do you want your words to:
A. Clarify thoughts and feelings?
B. Move you to a deeper level of intimacy?
C. Praise or encourage someone?
D. Lovingly correct someone?
Having a clear purpose in mind is like making a grocery list before you go shopping. The list helps guarantee you'll come home with what you need. In other words, shooting a gun without first aiming may work in Hollywood, but in real life you'll undoubtedly miss the target.

Why not take a moment right now and think about an important point you want to communicate with someone. Which of the four reasons will best help you deliver your message? To illustrate the need to have a clear purpose in mind, let's take a close look at a life-changing story.

Word pictures can help you
clarify thoughts and feelings,
move to a deeper level of intimacy,
praise or encourage someone, or
lovingly correct someone.

How would you like to be a royal adviser who was called upon to confront a warrior king—particularly one who had recently tried to cover up both an affair and first-degree murder? People who break "Watergates" of our day get rewarded with book and film contracts. However, in this adviser's day, exposing the truth was likely to get your neck broken. No word picture we know of better demonstrates the power to change a person's heart than the story of this ancient king.[1]

Solving a King-Sized Problem

There once was a young shepherd boy, named David, who was singled out to be a future king.[2] As a tender of flocks, he sometimes had to drive off wild animals and even lay his life on the line to save one of his sheep. But those years of leading a flock helped to develop many of the skills he later needed to lead a mighty nation.

When David finally ascended to the throne, he was known throughout the world as a fearless warrior who led his armies in countless victories.[3] He maintained the heart of a shepherd in the early years of his reign, but as his fame increased, he began walking on the dangerous edge of power. Anything he wanted was within his grasp.[4]

It was during this time, when his shepherd's heart had grown cold, that he walked onto the roof of his palace and gazed across the city at all he controlled, all he commanded. As the sun set and a refreshing breeze drifted down from the surrounding mountains, his eyes suddenly caught a reflection from a rooftop below. It was the last rays of sunlight, shimmering off a pool of water. Looking closer, he realized the reflection came as the water was stirred by a woman bathing.

Moving to a better vantage point, he scrutinized the beautiful woman. His pulse grew quicker; his breath, shorter. Then, his lust having devised a plan, he dispatched his guards to bring the woman to the palace. Soon enough, David learned that this striking woman, named Bathsheba, was the wife of one of his officers on the battle line.

However, that didn't deter David. His mind was not on a faraway battle but on a conquest near at hand. So he had her brought into his private chambers for a night of forbidden passion.

The next morning, the evening's entertainment was sent back home. There is every indication the king wanted their encounter to be a one-night stand—an act he could sweep under the carpet of his cold conscience. But several weeks later, the young woman sent a private message to the king. She was pregnant with his child.

In his early years, King David had been noted as an upright man. But by this time, his one error seemed to justify another. Perhaps he feared his grip on power would be loosened if people caught wind of the scandal. All we know is that instead of acknowledging what happened, his darkened heart devised another cunning plan.

He would send for the woman's husband, who was still away fighting, and bring him home on leave as a decorated hero. David was sure this soldier, like any average, red-blooded serviceman who'd been away from his beautiful wife for months, would fill his first night home with romance.

But Bathsheba's husband was several cuts above average. Since the men he commanded were still on the battle lines, far from their wives and families, he refused the privileges of marriage.

The king was stunned that the man's loyalty to his troops was more powerful than his passions. His mind quickly scrambled for a second plan, and a crude idea struck him. He invited him to the palace, got him drunk, and then sent him home. Yet once again, he refused to go inside. Knowing the wine would weaken his resolve, he slept on the steps of his house. Unbeknown to him, this put him in as much danger as being on the front lines. In fact, by spending another evening apart from his wife, he signed his own death certificate.

Several weeks had passed since Bathsheba first announced her pregnancy, and it took a few more to get her husband back from the battle. As a woman with a shapely figure, she couldn't keep the secret much longer. Increasingly desperate, David stooped the lowest when he grasped an evil plan that couldn't fail.

Through a top-secret dispatch, he sent her husband back to the front lines and into the thick of the battle. Then, following the king's specific instructions, the commanding general pulled back all his supporting troops to leave the soldier alone in the face of the enemy.

The plan worked flawlessly. With no protection on his flank and no one to stand with him, he battled bravely but futilely. Like a wounded stag encircled by starving wolves, he was slaughtered in the open, alone.

With Bathsheba's husband out of the way, the king brought his one-time lover into the palace as his new wife. Overnight, a thin veneer of legitimacy covered the dark secret. In time, David's fears of being found out relaxed. He slept much easier, knowing there had been additional casualties on the front and that many of the widows had also remarried. He desperately hoped the general who executed his evil sentence would guard the secret with his life. However, the truth somehow leaked out.

Powerful Words That Pierce the Heart

While King David's conscience had been in hiding, a court adviser named Nathan was given a divine charge. He was to confront David with an emotional word picture that would change the course of a kingdom and echo throughout the ages.

"Your Majesty," his adviser began, bowing low, "a serious problem in the kingdom has just come to my attention."

After listening to dozens of everyday reports from other advisers, David suddenly snapped awake. Like most kings, he didn't appreciate surprises—particularly serious ones affecting *his* kingdom.

"Sir, in your kingdom is a very poor family, who with all their resources could purchase only one suckling lamb," he began, weighing each word for its emotional impact. "And as this animal grew, the children took over the chores of feeding and brushing it.

"The lamb became a special pet and an important part of the household," he continued. "In fact, they were so attached to it that they gave it the run of the house. At night, when the winds blew, it even jumped onto the children's beds and helped keep them warm.

"In this poor family, the father farms land owned by a wealthy rancher," he said. "Recently, late in the afternoon, unexpected guests arrived at the rich man's house. A customary feast was in order. Yet the herdsmen were away with the flocks, and the only fresh meat at hand was one of the aging goats kept for their milk—far too tough a meal for the important guests.

"That's when the landowner looked down the hill and saw two children playing with a beautiful, plump lamb," the adviser said, pausing momentarily to clear his throat.

"Well, go on," the king replied impatiently. "Finish your story."

"Yes, Your Majesty," he said, maintaining his voice at its deliberate pace. "As I was saying, the rich man saw the animal, and an idea came to him. He could butcher the lamb and not have to send a servant all the way to his own flocks. And that's exactly what he did.

The lamb was slaughtered and prepared for his guests, without any thought given to the children or their parents."

Color rushed to the king's face, and his eyes flashed with rage. His feelings brought back memories, which in turn sparked deeper feelings. He, too, had raised lambs from birth, sheltered them from harm, loved them as pets, and felt heartbroken if anything happened to them.

"As you know, Your Majesty, children may have the heart for battle, but they are no match for grown men. With their father away tending his fields, their cries for help went unheard. And the little boy, clinging desperately to the lamb, was slapped away like a fly.

"That night, the little children huddled in their beds, weeping to hear the music and laughter from the rancher's house above. Their hearts broke to think of other people's appetites being satisfied by the pet which—"

"That's enough!" the king shouted. "Say no more!" He jumped to his feet, livid with anger. "That man deserves death! I tell you, today he is to make restitution to that family. He is to pay them back fourfold what they lost. I want four of his best lambs to be chosen from his flocks, and I want them taken to that family—immediately," he commanded, hammering out the words. "And then," he said, with a glint in his eyes that reflected the warrior's heart within, "I want that man brought before me this very afternoon!"

The large throne room had the acoustics of a Gothic church. When the king's angry words ceased reverberating from the walls, a heavy silence fell upon the room. Ears were poised with anticipation. Though the adviser never spoke above a whisper, the impact of his words crashed through the room like peals of thunder.

"Your Majesty" he began, "you are that man! The little lamb you took was another man's wife!"

The story hit the king so forcefully and unexpectedly that he was driven to his knees. His heart, encased by adultery and murder in steel-like silence, now lay shattered by the blow of one emotional word picture. For the first time, he was forced to face the evil he had done, forced *to feel* some of the emotional trauma he had caused others.[5]

You may not have to face an angry king anytime soon, but you probably are aware of someone with whom you need to talk. Like Nathan, you may need to confront a problem in a relationship. Correction may not be the easiest of the four primary uses of word pictures, and it often takes the most courage. But when done in love to change a destructive practice or situation, it is frequently the most important. On the other hand, perhaps you're looking for more clarity in your communication or greater intimacy in your marriage. Maybe you're searching for just the right words of love and encouragement for your children.

Whether your relationships need a major overhaul or you simply want to add a turbocharger to your communication, the solution is near at hand. As we've seen, the first step in creating a word picture is to consider its purpose. As we highlight the six remaining steps, you'll see how quickly and easily you can develop word pictures that can make history in your home.

6
Creating an Effective
Emotional Word Picture

Part Two

IF YOU'RE LIKE most people, you're probably postponing a conversation or two because you're not quite sure how best to express your feelings. Perhaps you're headed into your boss' office to fight once more for a raise, or you need to talk to your teenager about her dress code (or lack of one). Maybe you've got to explain to your wife, for the third time, that you need to switch vacation dates, or to discuss with your husband, for the third time, the family chaos that comes with making that switch.

If you have a needed conversation in mind, first isolate your communication goal. Then you're ready to take the second crucial step.

2. Carefully Study the Other Person's Interests.
The word picture used with King David showed an intimate understanding of his background and interests. That is, Nathan chose a story that tapped into David's experience as a shepherd and a defender of his people. By doing so, Nathan took a shortcut to the king's heart.

The same is true of Kimberly's word picture that helped bring her father back home. All her life, she'd watched him take immaculate care of his company car to impress new clients. By tapping into his lifelong love affair with automobiles, she effectively parked her story of a wrecked car right on the doorstep of his heart.

It may take some detective work to discover your listener's interests, but even the most hard-core television addicts, "couch potatoes," or "lounge lizards" give you clues about their lives. Your listener may be a person whose problem behavior can be short-circuited by linking your word picture with his or her favorite television program!

Research another person's past, and don't neglect the present. Discover what he enjoyed as a child; what he hates as an adult; the sports, hobbies, food, or music he prefers; the car he drives and how he keeps it; what he does for recreation; and what motivates him to work overtime.

The same thing is true if you're researching a word picture for a woman. Learn enough about her world to understand what makes her good days good and bad days terrible. If she works at home, what are her needs and frustrations? If she works outside, what does she do during lunch breaks?

Again, your search for clues—for men or women—may take minor investigative work and draw you into areas you know nothing about. But don't quit until you've uncovered an interest that can support a word picture.

For me (Gary), the search for the key to my youngest son's heart took me to a swinging place.

Breaking Old Habits

When Michael was thirteen, I felt I needed to talk with him about his eating habits. Frankly, he was eating so much junk food that I thought he'd be targeted as a cleanup site by the Environmental Protection Agency. With the goal of communicating that concern to him, I began hunting for one of his current interests. Since we'd just bought him a new set of golf clubs, I had a major clue to what that might be.

We live in Phoenix, and the *Arizona Golf Course Directory* lists 108 courses in the metropolitan area. The weather permits you to play at least 360 days a year, and it's close to being golf heaven. Yet like the person who lives next to the ocean but never goes in the water, I rarely get my golf balls wet in the lakes of the local courses. But that all changed when I saw Michael's new clubs and realized what a major inroad they were into his heart.

When I suggested that we go golfing, Mike jumped at the idea. He was more than thrilled to thrash me on the links, and he even tried to convince me to double his allowance if he beat me by ten strokes.

Once on the course, I noticed that Mike was continually slicing the ball. While he worked to improve his handicap, I was replacing the huge divots I plowed with each swing. We'd each played better, but we still had a great father-son time and finished the front nine holes in a tie.

As we waited on the back nine for round two, I again rehearsed the word picture that I felt sure would capture my son's attention. As we sat watching a foursome ahead of us tee off, I turned to Michael.

"Hey, big guy," I said, "have you ever heard of Jack Nicklaus?"

"Of course, Dad. Everyone who's picked up a club knows about the 'Golden Bear.' "

"Well, if he were playing with us today," I said, "would you listen if he explained how you could get rid of your slice?"

"You bet I would!"

"Well, Michael, I'm not Jack Nicklaus, but you know I love you and want the best for you, don't you?"

"Sure, Dad. But what does that have to do with my golf swing?"

As I looked at him, I could see his mind racing back and forth, trying to guess what I was getting at. "Did you know that in one area of your life I see you doing something that's like slicing every shot into the woods? It's such a problem, it could actually slow you down in life, cause you to have an earlier death, and even keep you off the golf course for good."

"What do you mean?" he asked, a puzzled look clouding his face. "What am I doing that's so bad?"

"Michael, every day I watch you ignoring the advice of experts in the field of medicine. These men and women are as good at what they do as Jack Nicklaus is at golfing. Yet every time I talk to you about your eating habits, I feel resistance, not a receptive attitude."

I picked up his driver and held it in my hand. "Eating so much junk food is like gripping your club the wrong way and refusing to change your swing. It's like having Jack Nicklaus standing next to you, showing you how to change your swing, but still refusing to take his advice.

"Mike, if Jack Nicklaus were here today, he'd point out things that would help you be the best. I mention this because I want you to enjoy the healthiest life you possibly can."

I could see in his face that my word picture hit home—all because I'd tapped into one of his major interests. Plus our conversation provided a springboard for further discussion about how his junk-food diet was slicing away his shot at a healthy life.

My purpose in taking Michael golfing was not to manipulate him. Rather, I became a student of his interests out of love. I wanted the best for Michael—not me. Before, my words of warning had been received, at best, as a lecture. But as we sat on the golf course that Saturday, Michael clearly saw and *felt* the concern behind my words. While I can't say he instantly corrected his eating habits, his attitude about discussing them did change immediately. And in the months ahead, I found fewer and fewer hamburger cartons and Snickers wrappers littering his room.

We know there are limits on how much you can research another person's interests. It may be quite impractical for you to take up needlepoint or professional wrestling, and you may have no inclination to study nuclear physics. But if you look long and hard enough, you'll discover the interests that enable you to enter the world of the person you're trying to reach . . . and move on to the next step.

3. Draw from Four Inexhaustible Wells.

Many people experience a common initial reaction when considering the use of word pictures: "Wait a minute, I'm not creative! It would take a miracle for me to come up with a story that works." Actually, you don't have to worry about how creative you are. Believe it or not, you've been hearing and using word pictures for years.

Every time you sing the national anthem, you're singing a word picture. Before every ball game and school function, Francis Scott Key paints vivid patriotic pictures with lyrics, such as "the rockets' red glare, the bombs bursting in air. . . ." And if you've ever listened to a country music station—accidentally or on purpose—you've heard nonstop word pictures, including "I don't mind the thorns, if you're the rose," "She done stomped on my heart, and mashed that sucker flat," and "Don't it make your brown eyes blue?"

Interestingly, the root meanings of many everyday words can be traced to word pictures. For example, the Hebrew word for anger originally meant "red nostrils."[1] That's because when someone gets mad, blood rushes to the face and their nostrils flare. Likewise, the original Hebrew meaning of our word *fear* is derived from the word for "kidneys."[2] If someone has ever jumped out at you in the dark, you *know* why this part of our anatomy was used as a word picture!

In addition to the above, you've probably been using dozens of "mini word pictures" for years without realizing it. For example, have you ever heard or said: "Be careful—he's a wolf in sheep's clothing," "She's just pulling your leg," "He's a sight for sore eyes," "I lead a dog's life," "We're stuck in a rut," "He proved it beyond a shadow of a doubt," "They're just keeping up with the Joneses," "He's always selling people short," "It looks like a long shot," "They're like peas from the same pod," "It's just not going to pan out," "She'd stand up to him if she had any backbone," "He was as red as a beet," "She was as white as a sheet," or "That was a close shave"?

Or have you ever said: "Their baby is cute as a button," "He doesn't seem to have both oars in the water," "She's as skinny as a beanpole," "He's a chip off the old block," "They're taking us on a wild goose chase," "Her lights are on, but no one's home," "She's got a chip on her shoulder," "My supervisor has a yellow streak a mile wide," "It was mashed flatter than a pancake," "He's nice, but the elevator doesn't reach the top floor," or "It's time to quit with all these examples and get the ball rolling"?

Do you *get the picture*—that creating word pictures might not be as difficult as you think? It's not hard to find a meaningful one to use if you know where to look. As you read through the next four chapters, you'll discover four bottomless wells that are full of emotional word pictures. One well is filled with nature and its wonders. Another is packed with everyday objects. A third contains imaginary stories, while the fourth plunges deeply into past experiences and remembrances.

Kimberly chose her word picture from the Well of Everyday Objects. In her case, her father's interest in automobiles led her right to this well. The royal adviser, Nathan, drew from the Well of Imaginary Stories, sparking David's memories of his life as a shepherd boy.

Chapters 7 through 10 will thoroughly explain each of these wells. But with the introduction we've had to them, we're now ready for the fourth step—an important stage that, if ignored, can prevent your communication efforts from reaching their full height of effectiveness.

4. Rehearse Your Story.

Over the years, we've learned that practice *does* make perfect. Rehearsing your story pays big dividends. Failing to do so robs it of its potential power.

We didn't know until long after Kimberly sent her letter, but she rewrote her father's word picture more than a dozen times. With each revision, she picked out some new aspect of a car wreck that illustrated the hurt and pain her family felt.

We're not suggesting you must write down all your word pictures in advance. We seldom do. In many situations, it's not practical or even possible. But time and again, we've seen tremendous benefits to thoroughly researching and carefully thinking through a story.

As former athletes, we also recommend that you work with a coach. If word pictures are as new to your friend as they are to you, at least get someone to be your cheering section! Practicing with another person boosts your confidence and provides additional insights that you'll find tremendously helpful when the big moment arrives. So if you're serious about having your words achieve your desired purpose, call for a backup. Doing so will help maximize the impact of your word picture and build a stronger bond between you and your friend.

As we trace back over the path to creating a word picture, we've taken four important steps. We've chosen a clear purpose for communicating, focused on an area of the other person's interest, drawn an object or story from one of four overflowing wells, and carefully practiced what we want to say. Now it's time to consider the fifth step: the issue of timing.

5. Pick a Convenient Time without Distractions.

We recently spoke at a two-day, marriage-enrichment conference. The first night, we briefly discussed emotional word pictures. The next morning, just before the opening session when we were to talk in detail about the concept, a woman stormed up to tell us our "wild idea" didn't work.

"I went home and tried your dumb word-picture method with my husband last night, and I can tell you for a fact it doesn't work," she charged, beginning to pick up steam. "You ought to make a public statement this morning, telling everybody to forget about using it. In fact, *give me that microphone.* I'll make the announcement myself!"

Luckily, the microphone wasn't on yet, and we were able to calm her down enough to discover what went wrong. As we listened to her story, we realized she didn't understand any of the steps to creating word pictures—particularly step five, choosing the right time and setting. She had merely gotten excited about the concept, loaded both barrels of her verbal gun, and blasted away at her husband the second she walked in the door.

This woman certainly had legitimate concerns about her marriage. She was distraught that her husband had decided, at the last moment, to stay home and watch a football game instead of attending the marriage seminar. When push came to shove, he cared more about who won the game than the respect he'd lose in her eyes. So when she caught the scent of how word pictures could improve a marriage, she took off like a hungry park bear and smashed down every door in trying them on her husband.

"Why don't you tell us exactly what happened," we said.

"Well, my husband was watching another of his dumb football games when I got home last night," she began. "It was even a game he'd taped from the week before! I was so mad I thought up a word picture on the spot.

"'Edward,' I said, turning off the television and standing in front of it, 'do you know what you make me feel like when you're watching your dumb games? Do you?'

"I told him, 'I feel like a crumb on the kitchen table that is lying there from dinner. As if that's not bad enough, you come by on your way to watch TV and brush me off onto the floor. And if that's still not bad enough, the dog comes along and licks me right up! Now, what do you think of that?'"

"What happened next?" we asked.

"He just looked at me as if I were drunk. Finally, he shook his head and said, 'What do *I* think of that? I think that's a *dumb* way to feel, that's what I think! Now, turn that television set back on, and get out of my way!' And with that, he went right back to watching his game!"

The woman had created a word picture with great expectations. We suspect that at the very least, she thought her husband would instantly fall to his knees and beg her forgiveness for ignoring her in the past, and then smash his television set into a thousand pieces with the remote control unit.

Yet that didn't happen. They moved even further apart. Why? She had nailed down the first step in creating a word picture: clarifying her purpose. That is, she wanted to hammer her husband with words and nail him right where he sat! She was in such a hurry that she couldn't even wait until halftime. In effect, she'd tossed the turkey into the oven without reading the instructions. Consequently, her results went up in smoke.

She erred because her timing was wrong. She conveyed her message at the worst possible moment, and she hadn't taken the time to tap into his interests or draw from the well that best pictured them. After all, his primary interest was obvious. It was twenty-one inches diagonally, and his face was glued to it. This man was a TVaholic and a football fanatic. A world of sports word pictures could have tackled him and thrown his insensitive actions for a loss. It's no wonder her words never reached his heart. He couldn't relate to a crumb falling off the table.

Another mistake was that she took absolutely no time to practice her word picture. Granted, it can sometimes be as hard to hold back our words as it is to stop an onrushing lineman. Nevertheless, she needed practice to get her words in shape and a friend to encourage or coach her. That would have involved more effort, of course, but it would have been better than having her words slammed back in her face. By neglecting to practice and plan an effective game strategy, she lost her offensive weapon and was knocked from contention before she was able to score.

> Picking the right time and place
> to convey a word picture
> is a key to its effective use.

With all the athletic imagery we've used, it's obvious the woman could have chosen a sports-related word picture. Though she may have known nothing about football, she could have sought out a coach and learned enough about the game to meet her husband on familiar turf. But there's more to effective communication than selecting the right field of interest and then practicing. Picking the right time and place to convey a word picture is also a key to its effective use.

Again, take Kimberly as an example. There was never a good time for her to talk with her father. He slammed the door to serious conversation on his few visits and took his phone off the hook every night. So she delivered her message in the mail. Kimberly knew he reserved an unhurried time to go through his letters. And by choosing the right moment and setting to present her word picture, her planning paid off—as it did for Nathan, who waited until the opportune moment to confront King David.[3]

If your story is to be most effective, it must be given at a well-thought-out time and place. The rewards of a highly crafted word picture don't come by blurting out our thoughts of the moment. They come from engaging our minds before we engage our mouths.

6. Try and Try Again.

In the case of both Kimberly and Nathan, the very first word picture they used won the desired result. However, in some cases it may take more than one before the other person genuinely hears our thoughts and feelings. The better we become at steps two and three (becoming a student of someone's interests and choosing from one of the four wells), the more our first word pictures will hit their marks. But if they don't, don't panic. Reload and try again!

In another of our books, *The Blessing,* we relayed the story of a woman who couldn't stand the house she lived in.[4] Even though she and her husband easily could have afforded a nicer home, she couldn't convince her husband to move, despite years of trying.

Whenever the discussion came up, he'd explain away her feelings and make his own case for staying put. Even a word picture she devised fell on deaf ears. But instead of quitting, she went back to the drawing board, picked out another of his interests, and tried a second one. And then a third.

What we didn't mention in our previous book was that it took four attempts before she finally caught his attention. The earlier tries may have failed because he didn't understand them, or perhaps the timing wasn't right. Maybe his wife simply didn't capture an interest that lay close enough to his heart. Whatever the reason, her fourth story about a fish in a rusty barrel hooked him.

He was so moved by what she said that he promptly got up from his chair, called a Realtor-friend, and put the house on the market. Then he pulled out his checkbook. "Is this enough to start construction of the home you want?" he asked, handing her a check—that would clear the bank with room to spare—for $150,000.

The woman's persistence with word pictures got her a new house. Naturally, we won't claim that similar perseverance will enable you to move into a nicer home. But we can assure you that you'll get results if you don't quit. We've seen persistence pay off in other ways: for a woman who landed a job with a company that had turned her down twice before; for another woman who gained an extra five days of vacation time after repeated requests; for the parents who finally convinced a teenager to spend more time with his younger brother; and for a teacher who eventually helped a shy grade-schooler begin reaching out to her classmates.

We live in an instant society, where we expect all food to be microwaveable and all prime-time shows to conclude with a happy ending in twenty-five minutes and ten commercials. But real life doesn't always work that way. There are times when you can't get another person to understand what you're saying on the first try, or when you're still at loggerheads despite your initial hard work to craft the right picture. But don't give up! In the real world, a key to communication is being lovingly persistent.

Granted, it's frustrating not to get instantaneous results when we use a word picture. But some people could be pummeled by a hundred of the most powerful word pictures and not feel a single blow. In fact, we've devoted a later chapter to that small group of people who seem totally unaffected by them.[5] But please don't race ahead and label your "resistant" person as being in this camp without giving persistence every chance to pay off.

We must stress that over the years we've seen very few people who are so emotionally, mentally, and spiritually callous that they cannot be reached by word pictures. We've even seen "impossible cases"—where a husband or wife has insisted his or her spouse was beyond hope—be changed dramatically through the language of love.

So don't be discouraged if you run into an occasional "What a dumb way to feel!" In almost every case, your loving patience will enable you to reach new heights of communication with your friend, associate, or relative. While up there, put the seventh and final step into practice.

7. Milk Your Word Picture for All It's Worth!

What in the world do we mean by "milking" a word picture? Try thinking of it in these terms: Once you've gotten one light turned on with your word picture, flip on every switch in the house! For example, we once worked with a woman who was extremely frustrated about her personal life. After working for years in a career she loved, she married and had children relatively late in life. She had a strong marriage and deeply loved her twin baby daughters. But sometimes she battled with her emotions over her decision to resign her job to be home with her girls.

"I know I shouldn't feel this way," she said. "Still, I sometimes feel like a bird in a cage. I really love it inside, and I know how important it is for my baby birds to have a secure place in which to grow. But at times I feel like breaking open the cage and flying out!"

Her word picture conveyed a great deal of insight about her frustrations, and we could have let it stand on its own. But suspecting there was more to the story, we asked a series of follow-up questions that "milked" her word picture for additional meaning: "If you flew out of the cage, where would you go?" we asked. "How long would you be gone? Is your husband in the cage with you, or do you see him flying free somewhere else?"

When we asked this last question about her husband, it was as if we had opened the floodgate to some emotional dam she had been building inside. Suddenly, months of frustration spilled out.

In a rush of words, she explained that her husband was an only child whose sole premarriage experience with youngsters was watching other people's children from a distance. Though he had been eager to start a family, deep down he felt insecure as a parent. As a result, he unconsciously avoided being at home. The more time he spent at work, the less he was able to provide physical and emotional support for his wife and twins. And within only a few months, his lack of care had begun taking its toll on their relationship.

Had we not taken the time to milk her word picture, we might have let her go with a few encouraging words, such as "Thanks for being so honest with your feelings. Probably every young mother occasionally feels as if she's in a cage, particularly when her twin daughters have just had their shots and are teething as well!"

But milking her story helped us (and her) clarify her concerns, better understand her husband's fears, and catch a problem that could have led to a major breakdown. She later told us that one of the first things her husband did after hearing her expanded word picture was to ask, "Honey, what could I do to open the cage and help you get out and exercise your wings?"

By bringing more issues and feelings to the surface, you, too, will discover new depth in your relationships and additional benefits in your conversations. It's possible if you milk your word pictures for all they're worth.

At this point, we have examined all seven steps to creating and using word pictures:
1. Establish a clear purpose.
2. Carefully study the other person's interests.
3. Draw from four inexhaustible wells.
4. Rehearse your story.
5. Pick a convenient time without distractions.
6. Try and try again.
7. Milk your word picture for all it's worth.

You should now have a good grasp of how to use this dynamic communication tool in your most meaningful relationships. But knowing how to create effective word pictures isn't enough. You must also know where to find them. An inexhaustible source is near at hand in the four bottomless wells mentioned earlier. They provide an unending supply of word power, as one husband found when he drew from the Well of Nature to stop his wife's steady stream of nagging and critical words.

FOUR INEXHAUSTIBLE WELLS FILLED WITH WORD PICTURES

7
The Well
of Nature

JIM KNEW HE needed help with a problem that was crippling his marriage and causing problems with his children. Yet who would have thought that an object from the Well of Nature could have brought such dramatic changes?

This husband crafted one story that halted his wife's criticism. In fact, his word picture was so powerful that we have used it in counseling many other couples and have seen it deeply affect their lives.

By drawing from the inexhaustible Well of Nature, you, too, can utilize all the created world around you to increase your word power. Animals, weather, mountains, water, and hundreds of other natural elements can provide the entrance ticket to another person's heart, just as Jim discovered.

Turning the Tide of Criticism

As a high-school teacher and football coach, Jim rarely saw his house in broad daylight. That had its advantages. By going to work before dawn and coming home after dark, the peeling paint and overgrown weeds conveniently disappeared.

Though Jim's annual sacrifice for gridiron glory caused the house to suffer somewhat, he tried to make sure his family didn't. Each night possible, he carved out time for horsey rides and snatches of conversation with the kids. However, there seldom was enough time left over for his wife, Susan.

> By drawing from the inexhaustible Well
> of Nature, you can utilize the world around you
> to increase your word power.

After the kids were in bed, he would hole up alone in the den to spend long hours studying films of the next week's opponent. And morning always came too soon. In fact, the interval between setting the alarm clock and being jolted awake seemed to be measured in nanoseconds.

Before long, the lack of time spent with her husband began grating on Susan. By nature she never strayed more than three steps from her daily planner. (One look at it and any "Big 8" accounting firm would have hired her on the spot.) Her every move was charted by the hour, and she couldn't understand why Jim couldn't do the same thing. Indeed, the fluctuations of his schedule rocked her carefully structured life—especially each fall when the football season showed up on the calendar.

Every year that he coached, her frustration level soared higher than the football field bleachers. The more his schedule varied, the more critical she became. Like an uninvited guest who doesn't know when to go home, her disapproval wouldn't budge.

Jim tried everything to dislodge her bitter attitude toward the demands of his job: lectures, logic, even a few screaming threats. After all, he was a football coach and had played ball himself at a major university. He knew how to be loud. But he also recognized that his left-brain lectures and tough-as-nails approach failed miserably to change her behavior. In desperation, he finally resorted to the word picture technique he'd heard us discuss at a conference for educators.

The following night, Jim returned home from practice. The moment he entered the house, he spotted their four-month-old golden retriever. Cracker was a beautiful puppy that his wife loved dearly. As the dog scampered up to him wagging its tail, he realized he'd found a key to his wife's emotions.

For the first time, he felt he had something *new* to say instead of expressing the same stale thoughts again and again at different volume settings.

So far, he had followed the playbook step by step for creating an effective word picture.[1] He'd carefully chosen a clear communication purpose and had picked something close to her heart. What's more, he waited to practice his word picture—drawn from the Well of Nature—the next day after school with a close friend. Then, armed with his new communication tool, he prepared to share the story with Susan.

The children were in bed, and Jim had just turned off the late-night news. He knew that an important part of getting his word picture across was picking an unhurried time to express the message. And with three sons, the house would never be quieter. Predictably, Cracker was stationed at her favorite place in life, curled beside Susan's feet.

"Honey," he said, "let's have a talk."

"It's late," came her cool reply. "I don't know if I'm up to talking about anything right now."

"It won't take long. I just want to tell you a story about how I've been feeling lately."

Rarely did Jim offer to express anything even remotely resembling a feeling, so Susan nodded and sat back in her chair.

"Honey, I guess I've been feeling . . . well, sort of like Cracker probably felt when she was living with your grandfather over on the farm before we got her.

"I've got hunting blood in my veins, and I want to run, explore, and roam so badly!" he continued. "But I've been left in the fenced backyard, and spend most of my time walking in circles while chained to a tree.

"Well, one day I'm left unleashed and curiosity gets the best of me. So I dig a hole under the fence and sneak out. Like a shot out of a gun, I dash far into the woods. The problem is, I'm so excited about getting to run free that I don't realize I'm getting farther and farther from the house.

"All of a sudden, I look around and my heart sinks. Without realizing it, I've gone so deep into the woods that I'm lost—really lost. I search like mad to find a path back home. But every trail leads to a dead end or takes me farther from where I want to be. I spend the entire day trying to find my way back to Grandpa's, but instead I run into nothing but trouble.

"In the morning, I get chased by a pack of coyotes; in the afternoon, I'm nearly run over by a logging truck; about dusk, I fall into a dirty stream—the only water I can find to drink. By the end of the day, my paws are cut and bleeding, and I'm wet, exhausted, and scared."

With a quick glance at Susan, he could see that her attention was riveted to the story.

"Late that night, I finally stumble onto another trail. After having walked through the darkest woods I've seen, I suddenly spot some familiar landmarks. Sure enough, I recognize a trail I know will take me right back to Grandpa's house. Despite how tired and sore I am, I start running down the path. My legs carry me faster and faster. My heart pounds when I finally see the driveway, and I struggle the last few yards to the fence.

"I want to see Grandpa so much and to feel safe and warm again. I look around for the hole I had dug that morning and squeeze under it. Then, with my last ounce of strength, I crawl over to the back door and scratch on the screen. As tired as I am, I yelp and bark for the door to be opened. I can hardly wait for somebody to hold me, dry me off, and feed me.

"Just then, the back porch light goes on. I'm so excited, thinking, *At last, I'm with my family. Somebody's finally going to comfort me instead of chasing me. There's going to be fresh water to drink, food to eat, and . . .*

"Instead of any of that happening," Jim said, pausing a moment to let his words sink in, "the screen door is thrown open, and I'm knocked back down the stairs. Before I can get up, a stick about three feet long whacks me on the side. I'm already hurt and tired from being lost all day, but now I feel even more pain and confusion as I'm chased around the yard, being hit again and again. All the while, I hear an angry voice yelling, 'If you *ever* run away again, this is nothing compared to what's going to happen to you!' But all I can do is think, *I've worked so hard to get home, and now I'm being whipped!*

"He finally catches me, puts me on a long chain that's fastened to an iron post, and leaves me until morning in the cold and dew without anything to eat or drink. It's supposed to be a lesson, I'm sure. But it rips my heart out and makes me think running away wasn't so bad after all."

Jim paused again, and the room was as quiet as an empty church. "Susan, you probably don't realize it, but that's how I feel most evenings when I come home. You see, I really enjoy coaching and teaching, but by the end of the day I'm worn out. If it isn't something one of my students has done or another teacher has said, it's having a bad practice or losing a game.

"It's rough working all those hours with so little in return. During the day, I'm always thinking that I can hardly wait to return to my own backyard—back to the kids, back to you, back to those I want so much to hug me, tell me they love me, and assure me everything is all right. I need you to tell me that you love me and that you're proud of me—even if I'm not a perfect husband and father.

"But Susan, most evenings when I walk up to the door, instead of getting hugged, I get hit with sarcasm or critical words, such as 'You have time to do everything you want, why don't you have time to fix the one thing *I* want fixed?' or 'I asked you to bring home *wheat* bread, not *white*. Why can't you ever remember what I tell you?' or 'If you've got time to coach *everybody else's* kids, why aren't you spending more time with *your own?*' and on and on and on.

"Your words are like whips that sting me over and over. When I try to respond or get things on a better footing, you hit me with your critical words in the bedroom, chase me into the kitchen, and follow me outside. And if I raise my arm to ward off a blow, you strike my hand or elbow.

"Susan, I'm so covered with welts from what you've said to me that I just want to spend more time in the woods at school. It's lonely there, and I have to dodge a few coyotes and logging trucks. But at least I'm not hit by your critical words.

"Honey, I know you've got legitimate reasons to be upset about my schedule during the season. I don't like having to work so much, either. But this problem is really beginning to affect our relationship. I can see it having a negative impact every day, and the kids notice, too.

"I don't know how else to tell you, but when it comes to our marriage, I feel like little Cracker returning to something other than 'home, sweet home' after being lost all day in the woods."

Jim surprised himself at the amount of emotion that came out in telling the story, but he was even more shocked by his wife's reaction. Susan was so moved by the story that she wept uncontrollably for almost half an hour.

Later, Susan told us, "For years, I'd known I was overly critical of Jim and said a lot of hurtful things. But until he told me the story, I had no idea how my words affected him. He even felt bad for telling it to me, and afterward he hugged me and told me he was sorry for bringing it up. But I was so touched by his word picture that all I could do was cry.

"I'm not exactly sure why I *felt* his story so intensely, but it changed me," she continued. "That night I decided my attitude toward Jim was wrong. Even though I had previously rationalized it in my mind, I knew I was hitting him too often and much too hard with my words.

I was angry because I couldn't see him more. But all my complaining was pushing him farther away from me, not drawing him closer.

"It's still a struggle for me to flex so much during the football season, and each fall we still have to talk through those frustrations," she said. "But I made an important decision that night. Whenever Jim comes home, no matter how late he is or how frustrated I am, he'll never again be met with a stick."

Cracker never realized she was serving as "man's best friend" simply by lying at Susan's feet, but Jim did. And in using the puppy as the basis of his word picture, he selected just one of thousands of illustrations from the Well of Nature.

Like Jim, you can draw from this well when it best suits another person's interests. Let's look at three other people who dipped into the Well of Nature to make a positive difference in their relationships. These examples will give you a quick, snapshot glimpse of how they used the language of love to confront an insensitive guest, rekindle lost love, and honor a special friend.

Confronting an Insensitive Guest

"Jayne, we're both from Minnesota, right? Remember what it's like to wait and wait for spring?" Beth said to her houseguest, who was staying with her temporarily until the movers could get her settled into her new condo. "Remember how tired you got shoveling snow from your driveway, knowing that people in Florida were basking in the sun? Can you remember how excited you were to see the barren trees budding after a long winter's sleep?

"Jayne, you probably don't realize it, but shortly after you arrived to stay in our home, I heard you say something that really hurt me. It made me feel as if I was living back in Minnesota and heard that spring would be postponed six months—that I'd have to endure another half-year of ice, snow, and freezing wind.

"Let me tell you what you said that affected me that way . . ."

Longing for Lost Intimacy

"Brian, can we talk a few minutes before we head out on our jog?" Claudia said, sitting on the edge of the bed as her husband tied his shoes. "You need to know that I've been feeling as if we've been running along side by side on our favorite jogging course—you know, the cedar-chip path that winds through all those beautiful homes and down through the park.

"Running that course is fun for both of us. We're able to talk while we jog, there aren't any big dogs roaming around, and the exercise is doing us a lot of good.

"But lately, I feel as if every time we start to jog, we run into a big detour sign that forces us to take a path other than our favorite. Instead of running past the pretty houses, we're dodging traffic on busy streets. And instead of jogging down to the park and back, we're struggling up gravel hills.

"Brian, I used to really enjoy running with you. But now I feel as if the path we're running on is covered with rocks. It's just a matter of time before one of us stumbles or falls or worse.

"I need to tell you why I think that detour sign went up and why we're headed down such a rocky road . . ."

Honoring a Special Friend

"Hey, Don. Have a minute?" Bob said, taking a few quick steps to catch up with his coworker. "I just want to thank you for last week. I know you think it was no big deal, but let me illustrate how much I appreciated your help by telling you a story.

"We're both golfers, right? At least we call ourselves golfers! Anyway, about three months ago when the boss gave me that new assignment, I felt as if I was put in charge of the course that would be used for the Masters' Golf Tournament. It was a tremendous opportunity, and I was thrilled at the honor. But you know as well as I that I'd never taken care of a golf course in my life.

"Well, Don, I feel you took time you didn't really have to teach me how to care for that course. You showed me how high to mow the grass in the fairways and the best way to cut the greens. You taught me when to water, where to place the sprinklers, and how much water to use.

"I put in the hours all right, but you helped me know where those hours needed to go. And when the tournament was over and all the pros were walking around raving about the course, you were the one I wanted to call and thank."

These are but a fraction of the ways you can use a word picture from the Well of Nature to go straight to a person's heart. Like those we've written about, we've seen many people draw from this well to make an important difference in another person's life.

We've known a single parent who turned her teenage son's attitude around by talking to him about a backyard tree; a father who brought everyone to tears at his daughter's wedding rehearsal with his story of a beautiful butterfly; and a son who explained to his parents how he felt about leaving for college, using the image of a small creek that had grown over the years into a strong river.

While the Well of Nature is a tremendous source for life-changing word pictures, there are three other wells from which to draw. In fact, we think one of the most exciting parts of this book is the overwhelming potential for meaningful communication found in these four wells.

In the next chapter, we'll watch Susan draw from the Well of Everyday Objects to gain the deepest desire of her heart: more time with her husband. And though it was never her intention, her word picture splashed over and changed our lives also.

8
The Well of
Everyday Objects

IN THE PREVIOUS chapter, we saw how Jim's word picture from the Well of Nature brought a dramatic halt to his wife's critical words. It's now time to read about . . . the *rest* of the story.

The day after Jim spoke with Susan, he couldn't wait to call our office and to boast about the changes in their marriage. For weeks afterward, we heard his glowing reports about how Susan was making an all-out effort to take the sharp edge off her words and tone of voice.

Just as we were preparing to recommend them for a congressional marriage citation for "Most Dramatic Turnaround," Jim showed up unexpectedly at our office when John was at a conference. Jim's eyes and nonverbal actions screamed that something was bothering him. I offered him a cup of coffee, which he politely but firmly refused.

"Gary, I'd like to talk with you a few minutes if I can," he said.

No sooner had I ushered him into my office and shut the door than he verbally pounced on me.

"Thanks a lot," he said. "You know your word picture method has really helped us. For the first time in years, I feel Susan understands me. She's made some dramatic improvements this past month. She's even telling me things she appreciates about me instead of criticizing me."

Jim paused, as if waiting for me to say something.

"Well, that doesn't sound too bad!" I replied, hoping this was all that was coming but knowing it wasn't.

"Yeah, well that's only part of the story," he said. "A week ago, Susan asked if she could share a word picture with me. What she said stunned me so badly it brought tears to my eyes, and I still haven't gotten over it.

"I don't know how I've missed the problem for so many years. But now I understand what's been at the heart of her frustration with me. It makes perfect sense! Now I can see why she's been on my case so much.

"Let me tell you," Jim said, shaking his head. "I've had some kind of a week mulling things over. That word picture stays with me night and day, and it beats me up emotionally whenever I think about it."

Straightening up in his chair and looking at me with a twinkle in his eye, he said, "I thought you were my friend, Smalley. Thanks a lot!"

By focusing on an area of Jim's interest and choosing the best time to talk, Susan turned the tables on Jim. The hunted became the hunter, and she had lined up in her sights a blind spot in Jim's life.

Jim went on to recount the word picture his wife had given him, drawn from the Well of Everyday Objects.

As I listened to the story, my eyes were opened to an overlooked issue in my own marriage. Like Jim, I wasn't consciously trying to cause any problems at home. However, I was consistently robbing Norma and myself of a richer, fuller relationship. I just didn't realize it—until I heard a word picture intended for somebody else.

It's been many years and hundreds of counseling sessions since Jim came by the office. But I can still remember what was said that afternoon, and for good reason. Susan's word picture still has the same corrective effect on my marriage that it did the first time I heard it.

Setting the Stage

It was late on Sunday afternoon, and Jim was out in the shop off the garage. Besides watching sporting events, he had two hobbies but not much time to spend on either one. The first was dining out at nice restaurants, which he would do nightly if they didn't have to worry about paying off their charge-card bills. His other love was lying in pieces before him.

Like most young boys, Jim had gone through a model-building stage. He had just never gotten over it. Spread before him was his most ambitious project to date: a wooden model of a mid-1800s clipper ship, complete with slotted planks, three-foot masts, hand-tied rigging, and full sails yet to be cut.

With all the stress of teaching and coaching, Jim found that dining out and model building were two great ways to unwind. Knowing he was most open to talking while sitting at either a restaurant table or his hobby bench, Susan approached him in the shop.

"How's this one coming?" she said, secretly hoping this latest model wouldn't end up in their bedroom like so many others.

"Great!" he replied. "This will look perfect in the bedroom! I've got just the place picked out for it."

Wisely, she decided a discussion about which room would become a harbor for the clipper ship could wait until another time—and another word picture.

"Honey," she said, "I wanted you to know again how much I appreciated the story you told me a while back. It really made sense, and I'll try to be more encouraging."

"Are you kidding?" Jim said, looking up from his ship. "You've been great these past couple of weeks. I know you're really trying hard, and I appreciate it."

Compliments from her husband had been on the endangered species list for some time. His flattering words surprised her so much, they not only warmed her heart but also caused her to blush. They gave her more courage, too, to go on with the word picture she had been practicing all week with another coach's wife.

"Thanks, Honey. It means a lot that you can see I'm trying. You know I came from a pretty critical family, and it's easy for me to get that way with you.

"Jim, when you were telling your story, I not only understood it, but felt as if I *lived* it. All my life I wanted to be loved and hugged by my father when I came home, but all I ever got was anger or neglect. I don't want our home to be that way. I know I won't be perfect, but I promise I'll really work on what I say to you."

"That's great!" Jim said with a big smile, bending over his model ship and thinking word pictures were the greatest thing since chocolate ice cream.

"But Jim," Susan continued, "could I talk to you about something?"

"Sure, fire away."

"I'd like to share a word picture of my own that expresses how I'm feeling about our relationship."

Inside Jim's mind, a little alarm sounded. He glanced over at the portable phone, hoping it would ring to his rescue. He even glanced around for the boys, who were always doing something semidestructive to the house or each other. Running after them had saved him from more than one serious conversation. But Susan had picked her time well.

Reluctantly, he shrugged his shoulders. "Sure," he said, leaning back on his bench, and fell into a life-changing word picture.

More than Leftovers

Ignoring "that look" on Jim's face, Susan took a deep breath and began speaking. "Honey, you're a really hard worker. That's why you always stay up late grading papers, watching game films, or doing something else important. What that all means is that by the time you come to bed, you're worn out.

"Because you get so little sleep, you can barely get out of bed the next morning. But there's something that always succeeds in getting you into the shower and out the door, and that's your three-cheese omelet and a cup of coffee."

Jim had to smile. The deli, where all the varsity coaches met, served an outstanding breakfast.

"I'd like to tell you a story I made up about your day," she began. "After a few hours' sleep, you head off for breakfast and have the time of your life with the other coaches. You talk about some new trick play you're going to run in the next game; what the new school board superintendent will decide about overtime pay; or how much better the game was when you all were playing. Things like that."

It's all true so far, Jim had to admit.

"I'm not exactly sure what you order, but I bet you have your favorite omelet, with sliced avocados on the side, accompanied by homemade, honey-wheat bread smothered with butter and preserves. Oh, and I almost forgot, you probably top it off with a tall glass of ice-cold milk and a small glass of fresh-squeezed orange juice. Am I pretty close?"

Susan was making educated guesses based on the hundreds of breakfasts she had seen him eat. She could see by his enthusiastic response that his mind was drifting back to his favorite breakfast place.

"When your meeting is over, you all slap each other on the back and then argue about who's paying the bill. But before you go out to the car, you do something different: You ask the man behind the counter for a paper sack. Then you return to the table, pick a few pieces of egg and toast from your plate, and drop them into the sack. You put the sack into your Nike tennis bag—the one you carry instead of a briefcase—and head off to school."

Until the part about the sack and crumbs, Jim had been right with her. Now his mind was racing to figure out what significance a paper sack could have in her word picture. However, before he could ask any questions, she went on.

"All morning you teach history, which you enjoy. And before you know it, it's time for lunch. Because your office is over in the field house, you and the other coaches go off campus to a nice coffee shop. There, you order a turkey tenderloin pie, its flaky, homemade crust filled with chunks of white meat, the freshest of vegetables, and a creamy white sauce. Of course, it wouldn't be lunch if you didn't have their fifty-item salad bar on the side and a huge glass of brewed ice tea.

"You all have a great time talking sports and telling jokes. Then, just as you did after breakfast, you ask for a small sack when you're finished. The waitress brings it to the table, you drop in little bits of leftovers, and then place it inside your Nike bag before heading back to school.

"After a long afternoon of teaching algebra, it's back to school for football practice. Afterward, it's late in the afternoon, and you've still got things to talk about, so you guys all drop by the ice-cream parlor next to the mall.

"You have a brief struggle with your calorie-counting conscience, but when the waitress comes, you order their chocolate tower sundae— the one with four scoops of premium ice cream and ladles of hot fudge and butterscotch toppings. On the side you get a small cup of crushed almonds and a diet Pepsi. Of course, you get the diet drink because it cancels out the calories in the ice cream," she said with a grin.

"Of course," Jim said, grinning back. That was one of his standard jokes when he bellied up to the ice cream trough.

"And for the third time, you gather up what's left on the table. You scrape off some whipped cream and toppings, and some of the melted ice cream and nuts. Then you dump it all into a sack and put it in your tennis bag."

Not only was Jim getting hungry listening to her story, but he was puzzled trying to figure out what she was getting at. *Why did I have to tell her how to create word pictures in the first place?* he grumbled to himself. Finally, he couldn't stand the suspense any longer.

"Are you trying to tell me I've got so many food stains on my old Nike bag that it's time to buy a new one?" Jim asked with a hopeful smile. "Or are you hinting that you want me to take you out for dinner tonight?"

It was a feeble attempt to speed things up or at least break some of the tension building up inside him. Unfortunately, his smoke screen didn't work.

"Now, come on. Let me finish," Susan said. "I'm almost through. All day, while you've been at work, I've been wanting to have you near me. I think about getting to go somewhere together where we can sit and catch up on everything. But it's not just me. The boys love you so much, and want to be a part of your life, too.

"Well, after waiting for you all day, we finally hear the garage door open. We're so eager for you to spend time with us that we line up at the back door. Maybe you'll even take us out to a nice dinner where we can all talk and laugh and get to know each other better.

"And then the door opens, but you don't stop to talk to us or fill us in on the things that happened in your day. You just walk by and hand the boys and me a doggy bag each. And then you walk over and turn on the television set or come out here to your hobby bench. Instead of getting to enjoy a real meal together with you, we're left standing at the door, holding these soggy, smashed doggy bags.

"It's not that I don't want you to have a hobby, Jim. That's not why I'm telling you this. You need time to unwind and relax, and I want that for you. But all day, the kids and I have longed to be with you. We've waited to find out what's going on in your life—and for you to ask what's going on in ours. But you've already spent the day with people who are most important to you—your players and the other coaches. So instead of giving us your best when you come home, all we get are leftovers.

"I think that's the reason I've felt so cheated in our relationship over the years and why I've been so critical of you during football seasons. Growing up, I remember how my mother was always so hungry for meaningful communication with my dad. And now I'm standing at the door of my marriage, just as she did, waiting to enjoy a satisfying meal with you, hoping for time to talk and laugh and get to know you, longing to communicate the way you do every day with the guys. The boys and I all want that, but all we get are doggy bags. Honey, don't you see? We don't need leftovers. We need *you*."

The last thing I had expected to run into that afternoon was a word picture, particularly one that stopped me dead in my tracks. When Jim finished telling it, he wasn't the only one with tears in his eyes. I knew I couldn't escape the message it carried for my life as well.

Because of my travels and all the hours spent helping other people, my schedule was probably twice as crowded as Jim's. Just like him, I was giving my wife and children table scraps on nights and weekends. Deep inside, I knew it. And Norma and the kids knew it.

That evening when I went home, things began to change around my house, as they had in Jim's. I told Norma the word picture I'd heard, and her response confirmed we had a problem. I had been handing out scraps to my family instead of a nourishing meal of emotional attachment.

In the weeks that followed, I couldn't walk in the door at night and head toward the television without realizing I was handing out little brown bags. I hated to admit it, but my couch-potato days were numbered.

Something else also changed as a result of that word picture. I called my supervisor at the time, telling him I needed to cut back my travel. Having been deeply challenged to spend more quality time with my family, I was prepared to look for another job if my company couldn't change my job description. In particular, I would find a job that didn't rob my family of me.

> Everyday objects, when tied to
> another person's interests, can supercharge
> communication with meaning.

Leftovers are just one of the thousands of everyday objects found in this second of four wells. Each of these objects, when tied to another person's interests, can supercharge communication with meaning.

They can also provide tremendous inner strength and encouragement, as another man found. For him, an everyday object conveyed hope to live in a hopeless situation. What's more, it gave his sons a lifelong respect for him and their country.

A Picture of Hope in a Pit of Despair

From the moment his landing craft ground to a halt, Jerry felt as if he had arrived at the very gates of hell. All around him was black, volcanic ash that stung his eyes and wouldn't brush off his skin. And the terrible sights and smells of death were everywhere.

Iwo Jima meant nothing to Jerry when he first heard the words. But time took care of that. Soon enough, as a nineteen-year-old in the Fifth Marine Division, he realized the two words meant every nightmare he ever had would come true before his eyes.

The landscape was pockmarked with craters as a massive flotilla of warships pounded the island in advance of the Marines' landing. However, the enemy had had nearly four months to choose its positions, so the nonstop bombardment generally had no effect. With so much time to prepare for the American invasion, they had every inch of beach covered with rifle, machine gun, and artillery fire.[1]

Jerry's first hours on the beach were spent trying to dig a foxhole deep enough to escape the murderous fire raining down. However, the volcanic sand filled his hole as quickly as it was dug, leaving him exposed to the constant enemy fire. As the day became more hot and humid, Jerry threw off his poncho and field jacket. But the temperature dropped so radically after dark that he shivered all night in the cold.

It was a miracle, earned by blood and raw courage, that he and the other Marines ever fought their way off the beach. Nonetheless, their advance came at tremendous cost. Bodies from both sides lay torn and twisted beyond recognition, mute testimony to what was ahead.

While we talked with this veteran of three beach landings, his eyes filled with tears as he thought back to those horrible days. Time has dimmed some of the horrors he saw and heard, but five words a fellow Marine said to him are still as vivid as brilliant sunlight.

The date was February 21, 1945—two days after the landing. Jerry had taken cover in a small crater formed by an exploding artillery shell. The shelling from back in the mountains had kept everyone awake almost all night. The morning had dawned with falling rain and a restless fog drifting in the distant, higher slopes. But when the skies cleared and the Japanese could pick out their targets, the artillery bursts were joined by small-arms fire.

Jerry had already given up all hope of coming off the island alive. Of the fourteen men in his rifle section, only he and five others hadn't been wounded or killed. In just two days, he had already seen far too much death. But its cruel hand was just beginning to strike: More Marines would die on Iwo Jima than on all the other battlefields of World War II combined.[2] So many had died or been wounded around him already that he felt he had as much chance of living as keeping a soap bubble from bursting in the wind.

That's when his corporal crawled up next to him and flashed him a grin. "You still alive, Jerry?" he said in his Southern accent, offering Jerry a swig from a priceless canteen of water. "We're gaining on 'em, you know."

"How do you know that?" Jerry answered back with a thin smile. "Nobody came running up to me with a white flag last night."

"Look here, son, I have it on good authority. Tomorrow you'll see our boys on top of that hill. We're going to make it." Then he looked up at the fog-tipped volcano and spoke the words Jerry has never forgotten: "You'll see the flag tomorrow."

From the time the Marines first sighted Iwo Jima from the decks of their ships, they had been looking up at the highest point on the island. It was the top of Mount Suribachi, an extinct volcano. It was only 550 feet high, but the way death rained down from its steep, ragged slopes, it seemed more like Mount Everest. To have the American flag up there would mean that—at least from this hill—death would have lost its frightening foothold. It would also be the best sight any Marine had seen since he had landed.

As events turned out, Jerry wouldn't see the flag for another two days. And his corporal would never see it. He was killed in action that night. But on February 23, 1945, the hill was taken.

As the Stars and Stripes flew above them for the first time, men all over the island stood and cheered, ignoring the risk of exposing their position.

When Jerry saw the flag, the words his corporal had spoken came back in full force. And those same words would give him strength to carry on during the next eight days until he was critically wounded and carried off the island.

"When I got off Iwo alive, I felt my life had been given back to me," Jerry said. "You never forget something like that. In the years since, whenever I've had things go wrong I remember my corporal's words. When things look their toughest, I just think back and say to myself, 'Hang in there, Jerry. You'll see the flag tomorrow.'"

Over the years, in his times of deepest trial, Jerry remembered the words that always lifted his spirits. He often used them with his sons, too, as they grew up. He would tell them, "You'll see the flag tomorrow," if they lost an important game, failed an exam, or broke up with a girlfriend. The phrase was always said with his arm around his sons, and it always gave them new hope for another day.

Jerry has never discussed with his sons all the horrible details of his eleven days on Iwo Jima. But he has told them enough so that they carry around a piece of that forsaken island in their minds—the emotional word picture he took off "the rock." They remember five hopeful words that spoke of a better day ahead and offered the courage to wait for it.

In the late '60s, it became fashionable at many schools to burn American flags. But Jerry's sons, who were college students during that time, never would have considered such an act. The flag flew too proudly and stood too personally in their lives. It not only symbolized for them a proud country but it also was an intimate symbol of hope, courage, and endurance.

They couldn't look at a flag without seeing what was behind it. In fact, they still can't. The flag isn't just a pattern of stars and bars to them. It stands for their father who lived, and the many men who died, on battlefields such as Iwo Jima.

Using everyday objects to form a word picture (like a doggy bag, an American flag, a watch, a chair, and so forth) can make a vivid, lasting impression in your listener's heart.

Take a moment right now to reflect on your relationships. Is there someone you need to encourage who's facing a difficult time? A word picture can help. Is there someone who's getting further away from the family, and you want so much to bring him back? A word picture can help. The Well of Nature and the Well of Everyday Objects are two places to seek help or hope. You can also look for pictures in the third well, the Well of Imaginary Stories.

Read on to learn how the president of a company dramatically changes a pushy saleswoman.

9
The Well of Imaginary Stories

SALES HAD BEEN strong for another quarter. Jay Campbell sat at his desk, smugly satisfied as he glanced at the glowing reports he had been handed that day. As the founder and president of his company, he'd seen it grow by leaps and bounds, particularly because of its relationship with one major firm that consistently ordered huge quantities of its products.

I may even take the afternoon off and try and get in some golf, he was thinking to himself when his secretary buzzed him.

"Excuse me, Sir, but it's Mr. Devlin calling," she said. "I thought you'd want to know."

Less than an hour ago, in his firmest CEO voice, Jay had told his secretary to hang out the "I'm-in-a-meeting" sign. However, like all experienced executive secretaries, she knew certain names removed any sign posted on the door.

Mr. Devlin was the president of Valco, the major company responsible for most of those glowing sales. So Jay's initial irritation at being interrupted was quickly replaced with his usual grudging respect for his secretary's wisdom.

Punching the button next to the flashing light, Jay picked up the receiver and said, "Hi, Mark. What are you doing this afternoon?"

"What am I *doing*?" The voice on the other end of the phone spat out the words. "I'll tell you what I'm doing. I'm trying to calm down after telling one of your saleswomen to get out of my office, and I'm not doing a very good job of it!"

"You had to do *what*?" Jay said, all five of his senses snapping instantly to attention. Pictures of plummeting sales figures exploded in his mind as the voice continued its red-hot tirade.

"This woman from *your* office took an hour of my office manager's time, trying to force her to place a new order. And that was after she'd already been told no. Then, when I came out and told her to leave because she was taking up so much office time, she told me I was *rude* for not listening to her pitch about a new product!

"Listen, Jay. I don't care how much money you could save us. When I tell somebody no, I mean no! And I'm telling you, if that woman ever comes back in our office again, you can cancel our current agreements and forget about our purchasing anything from you in the future."

Click! The phone on the other end of the line sounded like a door slamming.

Jay had been chewed out in his time. There had been his father's angry words when he had given his pet turtle a bubble bath, his football coach's screams when he fell asleep during the game films, his drill sergeant's four-letter blasts about everything he did. Even his wife could lay down the law at times. But to have his most important customer chew him out because of how one of his sales agents had acted—*that* was too much.

Fuming, Jay paced the office, thinking about the problem he had on his hands. Without hearing a name, he knew who had made the sales call. After all, there was only one woman on his sales force.

Sally was the most productive salesperson he had. The last four months she'd been the volume leader, hands down. She had great skill and determination in closing the sale. But lately she'd become so pushy that she closed as many doors as she opened. Jay liked her enthusiasm and hard-driving nature, and didn't want to fire her. But he realized he had come close to losing an account that was the lifeblood of his business. He knew he would have to confront her that very afternoon.

In preparation for the meeting, Jay turned to the Well of Imaginary Stories for help. After choosing the right word picture, based on one of the most embarrassing things he felt could ever happen, he mentally practiced it a few times and waited for Sally's return.

Sally didn't know it, but his words were about to grab her by the collar. In fact, his imaginary story would shake her world so forcefully that simply mentioning their conversation in the future would instantly cause her to back off from being too pushy.

"Come on in," Jay said when Sally peeked her head into his office. It was only on rare occasions that she was summoned into the president's office. This time his note on her desk had read "Urgent."

"I came as soon as I got your note, Mr. Campbell," Sally said. With relief, she noticed he was smiling as he rose from his chair.

"Please, come in and close the door. Take a chair over here," he said. "There's something I'd like to talk to you about." As she sat back, he launched into his word picture.

"Sally, when the company first started, I was the one doing all the sales calls. And during that time, do you know what I used to think would be the absolute worst thing imaginable?"

Jay didn't wait for an answer but went right on with his story. "Picture this. I'm in the boardroom of one of our top clients, all excited about making a presentation. I've got all my charts and graphs ready. Without a doubt, I'm 100 percent prepared to knock the ball out of the park and sign a contract on the spot.

"Well, the chairman of the corporation is sitting next to me. He says a few kind words of introduction, and then it's my turn to stand up and present our product to the entire board.

"I throw myself into the presentation. I'm talking loudly and gesturing like crazy when my hand suddenly hits the coffee pot in front of me, knocking it right into the president's lap! I'm talking about an entire pot of scalding coffee.

"You can imagine the scene. He's screaming and jumping up and down. Everyone else around the table is trying hard not to laugh, but you can tell people are cracking up on the inside. So I grab a handful of paper towels and try to help dry off the president. But because of where the coffee spilled, drying him off is pretty embarrassing in itself. Finally, thoroughly disgusted with me, he grabs the paper towels and tries to dry himself off.

"The whole time, I'm working to calm him down so I can salvage my sales presentation. I point to the charts and graphs I've worked on so long, showing how much money they'll save with this new product. But he's not interested in hearing about it anymore. He's having a difficult time sitting next to me, much less listening to me."

The picture her boss acted out while he was telling the story was so comical that, in spite of herself, Sally was laughing right along with him.

There was a long pause after the laughter subsided. Sally finally asked, "Mr. Campbell, did you bring me in here just to tell me this story?"

"Well, in a way I did, Sally," he said, his voice and manner becoming serious.

"You see, this morning you poured scalding coffee right into someone's lap."

Another long silence stood between them before Sally looked down and said in a faltering voice, "What do you mean?"

Deep inside she knew what he was talking about, but she felt justified in working so hard to get that office manager to hear all of her presentation. After all, she had worked so hard in putting it together, and in her heart she felt the manager was wrong in not taking the time to listen.

"Sally, this morning when you were at the Valco office making your presentation, you were so excited you knocked a whole pot of scalding coffee into their business manager's lap.

"I know you do a great job of presenting our products. You also work hard at overcoming sales resistance. But for all your good intentions, you almost lost us our key client because you were far too pushy. Their business manager made it clear she wasn't interested in buying anything else at this time. Yet you still took an hour, trying to force her into a decision she couldn't make.

"To top it off, when the president came out and asked you to leave, you scalded him, too! In fact, telling him he was rude for not letting you finish was like opening the lid and just dumping hot coffee all over him. He called me to talk about it after you left."

Jay moved over next to her chair and looked her right in the eye. "Sally, pouring scalding coffee on people will only ruin relationships and lose accounts that take years to establish—not get you a sale. And I must say that I'm concerned about you as an employee and as a person. You see, people talk, Sally. I know you're having trouble in relationships with the other sales reps. I know there's always competition and petty jealousy, and I'm not trying to take away any edge you might have. But you're ruining your relationships around the office by pouring coffee on people. And while I'm not trying to be too personal, I imagine you're probably doing it to your friends outside the office as well.

"If you scald people once, they may chalk it up to an accident. But if you keep doing it, you'll be the loneliest person in the world. If you want to sentence yourself to loneliness in your personal life, that's your decision. But if you keep scalding our key clients, it will cost you your job."

Others had tried to talk to Sally about her over aggressiveness—both at work and in her personal relationships—but she had always rationalized it away as jealousy. Every time she would excuse herself by saying, "They don't understand the situation" or "There's nothing wrong with having strong opinions."

Sally came from a family whose anger and fighting had become ingrained in her. Hearing "no" from a customer ignited all her old emotions, causing her to overreact and snap into her verbal attack mode. She had never been willing to look at her overly aggressive nature, because it would have forced her to look at too many painful memories at the same time.

For years, no one or nothing could crack her ironclad defenses. But a significant conversation did—when her boss caught her broadside with an emotional word picture. It was as if he had ripped up a sixty-foot billboard from beside the freeway and planted it right in her front yard. This time, she couldn't miss the message that she was too pushy.

Jay was to tell us later, "Sally is still my top salesperson, and she's still pretty aggressive. Only now she's a lot more sensitive with our customers. In two years, to my knowledge, she hasn't scalded anybody else—including anybody at Valco."

This businessman didn't realize it, but he had not only saved Sally her job, but he had also given her a tremendous gift. Her attitude had been revolutionized and redirected with her coworkers and friends.

Her boss' ultimatum, wrapped in a word picture, did more than scare her. It changed her. His clear picture grabbed her emotions so forcefully that she couldn't get overly aggressive with someone and not imagine herself holding a pot of scalding coffee.

> Imaginary stories unlock the
> limitations that are often a part
> of everyday words.

In this third well, Jay tapped into a source of word pictures that is limited only by a person's imagination. In fact, imaginary stories unlock the limitations that are often a part of everyday words.

As we mentioned earlier, people love to listen to a story. When the tale begins, it's an open invitation for them to try to guess its outcome. It also locks in their attention and leaves a lasting memory of what we say.

Imaginary stories can use everyday objects or items from nature, as we've seen in the two previous wells. In addition, they can picture an event, a situation, or an occupation and thereby pull the listener into the scene.

Already, you have thousands of options for word pictures available in these three inexhaustible wells. However, pictures from the

fourth well may capture a person's heart more quickly than anything else.

In the Well of "Remember when . . . ," you'll see how a word picture has been a tremendous help to the two of us as we work together
on books and conferences. "Remember when . . ." calls to mind something terribly embarrassing and instantly changes our attitudes and
actions.

10
The Well of
"Remember When . . ."

WHILE EACH OF the three wells we've looked at can maximize our communication, this fourth well has an important advantage over the others: the ability to draw on a picture already lodged in a person's memory. And by causing someone to remember a past event, we also trigger vivid feelings he or she experienced at that time.

In a recent study, doctors tried to find the areas of the brain that controlled memories.[1] Working with volunteers, the doctors electrically stimulated portions of the cortex and found their subjects would suddenly remember such things as a smell of something they'd eaten or a particularly enjoyable experience. After a while, the doctors noticed an unexpected side effect in the volunteers: When a certain memory was sparked, the *feelings* accompanying that earlier event were also recalled.

In a personal way, I (John) have seen this phenomenon with my father and other combat veterans. My father spoke to us in detail about his war experiences only one time. That was back in 1969, the day before my twin brother, Jeff, and I were facing the draft for the Vietnam War. For almost two hours, he told story after story of World War II. He did so because if we were drafted, he wanted us to know that war was not like the movies portrayed it.

Many veterans experience an unpleasant side effect to remembering the horrors of war. In recounting the graphic mental images, they once again feel the fear, anger, and hurt. No wonder they avoid talking about war. But what effect does this finding have on meaningful communication?

> When you link a present message to a
> past experience or event, you take a direct path
> to a person's emotions, thereby multiplying
> the impact of your message.

When you link a present message to a past experience or event, you take a direct path to a person's emotions. That's because your words mix with past feelings, thereby multiplying the impact of your message. The end result is that the words you want to convey are electrified with incredible vividness and clarity.

As a rule, men are much less in touch with their emotions than women are. So as men face the task of unearthing past events and memories in the counseling process, they also face a flood of emotion. In large part, that's why so many men are initially resistant to seeking personal or marriage counseling. If they can overcome this threat, linking memories with feelings does have its positive side. That's especially true in the area of meaningful communication.

For example, let's say you've gone through a major difficulty with someone. By using a word picture from the Well of "Remember When . . . ," you can instantly tap into the emotions that were part of that experience. By drawing on them, you create an emotional bond that brings a deeper level of understanding to the conversation.

Do you need to straighten out a problem? To move deeper in a relationship? To clarify an important point in a conversation? To thank someone for a kindness? Then your memory of a past experience together can hold the key to finding and using an effective word picture.

Over the years, one especially graphic word picture drawn from the Well of "Remember When . . ." repeatedly has kept us on track at the office and has prevented us from making spur-of-the-moment decisions that could prove disastrous.

"Remember When We Were at Forest Home?"

If you're ever within earshot of our office, it won't be long until you hear one of us say, "Remember when we were at Forest Home?" When these words are tossed into the midst of a conversation or decision we're facing, they always bring new light—and more thought and reality—to the subject. This happens because the phrase represents a powerful word picture to us, stemming from one of the most embarrassing, humiliating moments of my (John's) life.

Located in the beautiful mountains of Southern California, Forest Home is one of the finest conference centers in the country.[2] Because of its incredible food, outstanding program, and the natural beauty surrounding the camp, it's jam-packed during the summer.

Several years ago, we were asked to bring our families and speak there. Since Gary was a veteran public speaker, he was asked to address the entire group of more than 450 people each morning. And I was asked to speak at an afternoon elective session—a tremendous honor because it would be my first time at Forest Home.

For months I worked to perfect my message. I'd been told to expect from forty to sixty people, and I came loaded with facts, files, and footnotes. Deep inside, I knew this would be a major step forward in my speaking career. Little did I know it would also be a banana peel upon which I would slip and fall face-first!

During Gary's first morning talk, he was illustrating a point about helping people accept and value each other's differences. In doing so, he explained that we often use an excellent personality test—called the Performax[3]—to help couples relate better together. That's when it happened.

In a moment of inspiration, he told everyone assembled, "This test can be so helpful in a marriage or a family that John can give it to all of you this afternoon. Instead of doing his regular elective, I'm certain he'll switch and give each of you the Performax!"

The idea sounded even better after he had said it aloud, so with more volume and intensity he continued, "That's right, folks. Dr. Trent is a qualified instructor in the test. A bonafide expert! I don't know what you've got planned for this afternoon. But whatever it is, cancel it. I guarantee you, the time you spend with John will be the most important hour of the entire week!"

I froze in my chair at the rear of the auditorium. My brain kept replaying his words. I couldn't believe my ears. Fear instantly gripped me. I wanted to jump up and yell, "Gary, wait a minute! What are you saying? I've prepared for months to do something else! Besides, there's no time to order the reams of tests and handouts I'd need for a group this size!"

As Gary continued to talk, I could tell what his motives were. Not only was he thinking that people would be greatly helped by going through this test, but he also was trying to drum up support for my afternoon elective and make me an instant Forest Home success!

Before I had the courage (or the intelligence) to jump up and say something, Gary closed his presentation with another moving appeal for every man and woman to attend my session. He laid it on so thick that anyone not attending my elective would have been labeled an introverted, psychopathic slug.

Though numb all the way to my toes, with a Herculean effort I stumbled forward to see if Gary had been stricken with mental illness. Perhaps that's what caused him to say what he did. On my way to the platform, mobs of people kept walking by, slapping me on the back and saying things such as, "Hey, I can't wait until your session!" and "Our family was going on the Jeep rides today, but we're canceling to hear you speak!" By the time I reached Gary, I'd already received ten times more positive feedback than I'd ever gotten for a message. And that was before I'd spoken my first word at Forest Home!

Like a presidential candidate sweeping up delegates in state after state, I was caught up in the tremendous momentum created by people's expectations. And when I finally talked to Gary, he got me even more pumped up.

"You can do it, John!" he said. "You don't need the actual test to hand out. Just explain what it says and wing it. I know it'll go great! Now goooo get 'emmmm, Big Guy!"

By the time Gary was finished with me, I was ready to sprint to the podium and lay it on them right then. The hour and a half between lunchtime and my elective seemed like forever. I figured my presentation would change lives, restore marriages, and cure every parenting problem known to humanity.

I also envisioned the camp director coming up afterward. There I would be at the podium, trying to look humble as I basked in the thunderous applause of a second—no, third—spontaneous standing ovation. He would shake my hand, offering me a lifetime invitation to speak at Forest Home each summer as he led cheers for my talk.

As I waited for everyone to return from lunch, I paced back and forth, thinking about what I'd say when presented with my "Speaker of the Year" award. Instead, I should have been panic-stricken about the terrible trouble I was in. With Gary's communication skills and years of experience, he no doubt could have "winged it" that afternoon. And the people would have gone away feeling it was the best hour of their week. I made the mistake of thinking I could get the same result.

I'd prepared for months to entertain and instruct a small group in a classroom setting. But soon I stood watching in horror as more than 500 people crammed into the main auditorium. All but a handful of people had canceled their afternoon activities of horseback riding, golfing, family outings, or napping just to hear about a test that could change their lives.

Not only were all the Forest Home campers and staff there, but many people had also called their friends in nearby towns. Cars jammed the parking lot, from which rivers of people flowed toward the auditorium to hear this "incredibly important" session. Instead of an average-sized elective, I was speaking to one of the largest crowds of the summer!

Sitting in the front row were the camp director, staff, and my wife and daughter. Many in the packed meeting room had skipped lunch and been sitting for almost an hour to save seats for friends and family.

The excited chatter of the crowd was replaced by an expectant hush as I walked up to the podium and looked over the sea of faces. Like the anticipation for the opening snap of the Super Bowl or the first number of a singing legend's final concert, there was an air of electricity in the room—electricity that would soon turn into a massive shock. It was my once-in-a-lifetime opportunity to fulfill my destiny as a public speaker and stand where the "big time" speakers had stood before. But suddenly I realized I was in big trouble.

The hush that came over the crowd when I started my message quickly became a death-like silence. The harder I tried to explain what the test was like—if *we had it to pass out*—and what was in the packets—*if we'd been able to run them off*—I could sense the mood and facial expressions of the crowd changing from questioning . . . to disbelief . . . to shock . . . and finally to intense dislike.

All around the edges of the auditorium, people began getting up and walking out. A few even began stomping out from the front rows. For an hour, I was emotionally abused by the remaining sets of eyes. And I knew each pair of eyes had a mouth that would tell all its friends and family across the country that fun outdoor activities had been canceled to sit inside and be confused and bored by me. After more than an hour, I finally finished my explanation of the test and told everyone they were free to go—unless, of course, there were any questions.

Agreeing to speak on this subject without being prepared was my first big mistake. My second was that I shouldn't have bothered asking for questions. The only question asked was why the camp director ever invited me to speak. As people stormed from the building, they looked at me the way people of Paris looked at the Nazi scum who had held their city captive for years.

As soon as I stopped, I knew I had finished more than my talk. I was finished at Forest Home. More than that, I was finished everywhere else in the free world. After news of this fiasco got around, I couldn't get an invitation to speak at a Toastmaster's Club even if I held them at gunpoint!

My wife put on her bravest, most supportive, wifely smile. But she was the only one smiling. If I'd been living in the Old West, I no doubt would have been torn from her arms and hung from a limb of the closest tree.

As I headed back to our cabin to pack my bags, I prayed the earth would open up and swallow me in one giant gulp. Then I suddenly remembered something that multiplied my misery.

This was only the first day of camp!

I *couldn't* pack and leave. Dinner was in an hour and a half, and I'd have to walk in and face everyone!

And then there was tomorrow's elective!

Words cannot describe the feelings of embarrassment and humiliation that fell on me like a two-ton weight. I could imagine the cutting words and snide remarks people would make—or at least think—during the rest of the week.

Waiting for the camp to end made the time between December 26 and the next Christmas seem like a heartbeat. Instead of the forty to sixty people who normally would have attended my elective the rest of the week, I spoke to row upon row of empty seats. The few people who did come were my loving wife, my daughter who was too young to object, and a few women in Mother Teresa's range of sympathy and compassion.

The week finally ended, and our car crawled out of the parking lot and inched back to Phoenix. Deep inside, I felt that what the atomic bomb had done to Hiroshima, my elective at Forest Home had done to my speaking career.

Several years have passed since that day of infamy in Southern California. Surprisingly, there were several positive results. First, Forest Home must have continued an active cover-up campaign, because invitations to speak haven't stopped coming in.[4] In addition, Gary felt so bad about what happened that we had several long talks that further strengthened our personal and working relationship. The discussions made me realize that the afternoon of agony was equally my fault. I should have put down my foot and explained my feelings.

We also acknowledged that we're both capable of doing the same kinds of things to each other.

In addition, I learned a tremendous lesson about optimism versus reality. There are some hills so steep that the little train huffing, "I think I can, I think I can, I think I can" had better realize it *can't*, pack its bags, and take the bus.

Finally, both Gary and I have gained one other major benefit through that experience. Years passed before I was invited back to Forest Home, but nearly every week we have used the phrase, "Remember when we were at Forest Home." It's our way of reminding each other that we should never again do something if we're not prepared to do an excellent job. It means "Slow down," "We don't have all the facts," "Maybe we're being unrealistic or too optimistic," or "We need to think this through before saying yes."

This one word picture says all these things and more. Because we've been drawn back to the memory of an event we shared together, the feelings return as well. And the mixture of words and feelings—the interaction of right brain and left brain—brings instant impact to our conversations. These benefits are ours—all because we've drawn time and again from the Well of "Remember When. . . ."

In the previous chapters, we've seen how powerful word pictures can be, how they're created, and the four wells from which to draw them. Nonetheless, some may say, "These are all great stories. But I'm still not exactly clear on how to personally use a word picture with my spouse or children."

As you turn the next page, you'll be stepping onto a bridge supported by five major pillars. These five pillars are what we feel support a successful and fulfilling marriage. We'll now look specifically at how a husband or wife can personally apply word pictures within a marriage to build intimacy as well as to span major and minor differences.

HOW CAN
WORD PICTURES
HELP MY MARRIAGE
AND FAMILY LIFE?

11
Pillars That Support
a Fulfilling Marriage

Part One

A FEW YEARS ago, we caught a plane to speak at a conference in southern Missouri. We'd heard on the news that high winds and torrential rains had been pelting the northern part of the state for several days. However, it never dawned on us that on the way to our destination—miles farther south—we'd come face to face with the dangerous aftermath of the storm.

We landed in the late afternoon in clear weather, then caught the shuttle bus to pick up our rental car. Aside from a few scattered clouds, it looked as if we had picked an ideal, early spring evening to drive the final leg of our trip. Heading out, we predicted the drive would take two hours.

The storm that had lashed out in fury north of us, however, left widespread havoc and danger in its wake. Fields had been turned into small lakes and were dumping their unwanted burdens into already swollen streams. Soon, every major tributary and river was choking from days of rain and mud—and roaring downstream toward a bridge we would soon have to cross!

The last rays of sunlight were fading to darkness when we came up over a hill and looked down on a small bridge less than a half-mile away. Suddenly, the brake lights of the car ahead of us flashed a brilliant red. The vehicle fishtailed as the driver wrestled it to a stop.

We quickly slowed and edged up to where his car had come to rest sideways in the road. That's when we saw what we had nearly driven over. Ahead of us, the raging waters were too much for one of the supports of the bridge. Several pillars had carried the bridge's weight for years. But in the past hour, the center support had shifted, causing the entire bridge to sag at a reckless angle.

We got out and looked at what had once been a calm, backwoods river, realizing how close we'd come to calamity. For the man ahead of us, a few yards were all that separated him from plunging into the debris-choked waters. Had he not stopped, he and his car would have certainly been swallowed.

In a dramatic way, we learned a lesson about bridge building that night. That is, a bridge is only as strong as the pillars that support it. And what's true of a bridge is also true of a marriage.

Building a Bridge of Intimacy That Won't Wash Away

We've counseled hundreds of couples over the years. In all our interviews, we have yet to meet one husband or wife who, when first married, didn't want to build a strong bridge of intimacy. However, after a few years many husbands and wives stand alone, stranded— one on one side of a problem-clogged river, the other on the opposite bank. Between them is their dying dream of intimacy—crumbling, twisting, and falling into a flood of bitterness.

Would you like to avoid that kind of anguish in your marriage? Would you like to build a solid support of meaningful communication that can withstand whatever storms may come? We've seen that intimate, fulfilling marriages have at least five major pillars of support. If they are driven deep and encased in the cement of unconditional commitment, these pillars can weather any trial or disappointment. But if any one of the five begins to crumble, the entire bridge that carries the marriage's dreams can sag dangerously.

A marriage built on the pillar of security can best withstand the inevitable storms of life.

Security: a Warm Blanket of Love . . . and the Best Birthday Present of All

The first structural support for a meaningful relationship is found in one word: security. A marriage built on the pillar of security can best withstand the inevitable storms of life. Conversely, insecurity can do major damage to a marriage, causing its entire structure to shake and crumble.

What do we mean by *security?* For us, security is the assurance that someone is committed to love and value us for a lifetime. It's a constant awareness that whatever difficulties we face, we'll work to solve our problems together. Security means we're fully committed to the truth and we'll be truly open to correction.

In our marriage book, *If Only He Knew,* we write about how love, at its roots, is a decision—not a feeling. In that regard, one of the most loving things any spouse can do is decide to build security into his or her marriage.

To discover how word pictures can help meet that goal, let's examine a special gift that a woman named Charlotte gave her husband. For years, she had seen doubts and unreasonable fears smash against the pillar of security in their relationship. Yet in five minutes, she finally sent those feelings of insecurity downstream.

Putting Insecurity Out the Door

Alan, Charlotte's husband, had been married once before. Back in high school, he fell head-over-heels for his wife-to-be and never lost that feeling until her untimely death at age thirty-two. For nine years afterward he felt like a shell—until one spring day when he met Charlotte, a cute, petite blonde with bright eyes and an energetic manner. Her constant smile and radiant personality made him feel ten years younger. For him, the relationship uncovered forgotten hopes, unearthed hidden feelings of love, and rooted out his deep loneliness.

After a lengthy courtship, they were married in Charlotte's home church. Alan tried his best to be an encourager and a loving support to his wife. He was patient when she was overly excited, consistently praised her for large and small accomplishments, and cared enough to point out areas where she needed to grow. He even helped her pursue a lifelong dream—to take a sabbatical from full-time work and get her college degree. He did this by moonlighting to pick up the economic slack. Not only did his after-hours efforts enable her to study without financial worry, but they also paved the way for the words "high honors" to appear on her diploma that hung in the hall.

In many ways, Alan was a model husband. Yet, try as he might, he never felt totally secure in their relationship. He didn't struggle with a lack of commitment, because he had vowed to love her for life. For her part, Charlotte had never given him the slightest reason to doubt her faithfulness. She consistently went out of her way to express her love and commitment.

Nonetheless, deep in his heart Alan carried a great fear. After losing his first wife to cancer, he was frightened the same thing would happen to Charlotte. And since she had a bright, perky personality and was ten years his junior, he felt sure she would leave him one day for a younger, more handsome, *college-educated* man.

Every time he walked down the hall of their home, he couldn't help thinking how her crisp, framed diploma made his old, faded trade-school certificate look small and cheap. And try as he might, he couldn't help feeling that one day his fears would become a reality. He would have only old pictures and a new layer of emotional pain to compound the nine years of past hurt.

Like a splinter pushed deep beneath the surface, his nagging insecurity remained a constant emotional irritant—until his fiftieth birthday. It was then that his wife gave him the gift of an emotional word picture that caused his doubts and fears to melt away in moments.

In the weeks leading up to his birthday, Alan avoided any mention of that day of infamy. He had turned forty without the usual traumatic thoughts. But fifty? Could he really be that old?

When the dreaded day finally came, part of him was glad Charlotte didn't say anything about his birthday before he left for work. The other side poked at him with long fingers of insecurity, trying to scratch and pry at his tender spots of fear and doubt.

Of course she didn't say anything about your birthday this morning, the inner voice would whisper. *She's as embarrassed as you are about your age. Can't you see that? What do you really have to offer her now that you're fifty?*

These thoughts caused Alan to stay late at the shop that day. And when he finally punched out, the same feelings slowed his steps to his car and made him take the long way home.

Even driving slowly, he beat Charlotte home from work—as usual. Things looked as they always did when he pulled into the driveway. The paper boy had missed his usual three-point attempt to hit the front porch, and a stash of letters begged to be taken into the house. And as certain as sunrise and sunset, his aging retriever, Casey, stood on the porch. He wiggled with excitement and wagged his tail as if trying to shake it off.

Alan loved that dog. Casey was his last living link to the years of happiness with his first wife. Through the many dark days after she had died, when he'd sit each night on the back porch and cry, his silent, brown-eyed friend would nuzzle up next to him. Alan was sure the dog could sense his pain, and Casey's warm presence was a tremendous comfort to his broken heart.

On his way inside, Alan stopped a moment to pat Casey's head and watch his dog smile in ecstasy as he scratched beneath his chin. Then, after retrieving the mail and paper, he opened the door and reached for the light. But before his hand could flick the switch, another light flashed on and a host of his family and friends jumped from their hiding places.

"Surprise!" they shouted. "It's about time you got here!"

That evening, there was much kidding and fun, yet it was a sensitive time as well. For each person also wrote a tribute to Alan, testifying how his loving spirit had touched his or her life over the years. But Alan told us later that Charlotte gave him the greatest present of all—a gift that helped not only to dissolve the unfounded fears and insecurity in his marriage but also to replace them with a rock-solid trust.

It started when she gestured for everyone to give her their attention. "It's my turn to give Alan his present," Charlotte said. "And it comes in two parts."

First, she handed him a box containing a new watch. There were applause and oohs and ahs all around as he held up his new timepiece.

"It's something I know you've been needing. And whenever you look at it, I want you to think about me," she said, with a twinkle in her eye. "But I have another gift for you—a little story I'd like to tell while our friends and family are here.

"I've never told most of you about my background, but I guess I've always been like a hyper, cocker spaniel puppy—one that's always bouncing around and getting into something it shouldn't," she began.

There were nods and smiles of understanding all around the room. Everyone present knew that even on an off day, she was a nonstop whirlwind of activity. Basically, everyone thought of Charlotte as a party waiting to happen.

"But I grew up in a home where being a cocker spaniel wasn't acceptable. I always was disliked for being me and was made to feel I should have been something different. I was never brushed or combed, and every time I'd jump up for some attention or get into something I shouldn't have, I'd be knocked down and put on a choke-chain leash.

"I'm not going to go into it all, but by the time I was in high school, things got really bad. At one point, I was told I was a mongrel who'd never be worth anything. I was even put in a car and driven down to the local animal shelter and thrown out on its doorstep.

"I ran away before the people in the pound could grab me. But for years after that experience, I wandered around the streets, never really believing anyone could love me just as I was, a cocker spaniel.

"But then one day, Alan saw me walking by—matted hair and all— and he gently picked me up. I don't know how, but he believed that a purebred was beneath all that dirty, matted hair. And then he took me home, washed and brushed my coat, and even gave me a beautiful ribbon to wear.

"All my life, I'd been made to feel I was a mutt. But when I could see how much he believed in me and cared for me, I began to think I might have a pedigree after all."

Charlotte paused for just a moment to push back her hair. A quick glance around the room indicated she had everyone's attention— especially Alan's.

"Over these past six years, I've been loved and protected. I've even found that I have a lifetime friend to live with. There are days when the puppy in me still comes out, and I run around and accidentally knock things over. Even then, I'm still loved, not beaten and thrown outside," she said, turning toward Alan with her eyes dampened.

"After years of feeling like a mixed breed, I finally have a home where someone feels I'm a purebred champion. I finally have somewhere to go where I don't have to worry about changing and being something or somebody I'm not.

"Alan, 1 know you're the one with the birthday and presents, but I feel I've gotten the greatest gift of all. That's because every day, I get to live with a man who says to me in a thousand different ways, 'I will never, ever take you away or put you back on the street again.' Honey, I love you with all my heart."

Charlotte had spent less than an hour thinking up and practicing her word picture, drawn from the Well of Nature. She knew Alan loved animals, especially Casey. She had originally thought her story would be just another way of adding a special touch to a surprise party. But it meant much more to Alan. It touched him so deeply that six years of insecurity and unfounded fear were swept away.

When it comes to building a bridge of intimacy in your marriage, is your own pillar of security solid? If you were to question your spouse—without any pressure or nonverbal threats about how secure he or she feels in your relationship, what would the answer be?

Why not ask your spouse to choose, on a one-to-ten scale, how secure your actions and attitudes make him or her feel? If "one" equals total insecurity and "ten" is complete security, how high would you score? Have you ever asked your spouse what it would take during the next six weeks to move closer to complete security or what you could do to maintain it if you've already achieved that goal?

A bridge between husband and wife can't stand up to raging waters if the pillar of security is made of sandstone. By using word pictures to strengthen the self-esteem of your spouse, you not only will help him or her discover new levels of confidence, but you'll shore up your marriage with pillars of granite as well.

Of course, we realize it takes more than this language of love to build security in a marriage. Word pictures must also be linked with everyday actions that promote trust, truthfulness, and confidence. Other books we've written, including *For Better or Best, The Blessing, The Gift of Honor, If Only He Knew,* and *The Key to Your Child's Heart,* offer detailed instruction on developing specific traits that instill lasting security in a relationship.[1] If these nuts-and-bolts skills are lacking in your marriage, these books will serve as how-to manuals for your rebuilding effort.

Nonetheless, though actions may speak louder than words, the latter are still critical to a healthy marriage. Simply put, our spouses need to *hear* they're appreciated and *told* they're loved. Of all the ways to express praise and support, word pictures are the best, for they immovably plant words of security in a person's heart. And remember, they can build security in more ways than one.

In Alan's case, his wife used the language of love to praise him, and her expression of encouragement worked beyond her wildest dreams. In several previous examples, we've also seen that correction can be accomplished most effectively with an emotional word picture.

Remember Jim and Susan, each of whom told a story that brought the other to tears?[2] While tears shed over angry or insensitive words can erode security in a marriage, they can also act like glue to bond love and commitment.

Some of us need to stop right now and closely examine our everyday actions. We need to take an objective look at how well we're doing at building up or breaking down security in our marriage. This examination may prompt us to get more knowledge and skill with which to build security, or it may steer us toward a marriage-enrichment visit with a pastor or other counselor.

Once we've worked to establish this first pillar, we need to examine the second major support needed to hold up a healthy marriage. It involves something for which word pictures are custom-made: meaningful communication.

Meaningful Communication: Talking Heart to Heart

The word "communication" is derived from the Latin *communis*, from which we get "common."[3] Expressed another way, if a husband and wife are ever to communicate effectively, they must find common ground that spans their differences.

In chapter 4, we discovered enough natural differences between the sexes to choke a horse—or a marriage. Yet we also found that one of the most effective ways to bridge these differences is emotional word pictures. For this and all the other reasons we've given earlier, we should use word pictures in communication to:

- increase the clarity and vividness of our conversations
- rivet a person's attention
- capture someone's emotions
- cause others to remember our words
- replace black-and-white conversation with living color—and much more.

Word pictures are essential to creating intimacy and resolving conflict. Only by mastering this language of love can you achieve clear and powerful speech.

Security and meaningful communication are inescapable necessities if a bridge of intimacy is to last. In the following chapter, we'll examine the remaining three pillars that support a meaningful relationship. Set deep in the soil of your marriage, they'll carry years of weight without calamity.

12
Pillars That Support
a Fulfilling Marriage

Part Two

To HELP SPAN more of the inevitable differences and disagreements over a marital life cycle, three additional pillars are necessary. In the most successful marriages we've seen, each couple has decided to keep an important flame alive—a flame that can be ignited and fanned by an emotional word picture.

Emotional/Romantic Times: Creating Moods That Bond

Keeping the flames of romance burning may not seem as important to a relationship as security or meaningful communication, but it is. This third pillar can help stabilize a home, particularly through difficult times.

We're not implying that a couple must spend each weekend night over a candlelight dinner. (In many homes, the kids would have blown out, squirted out, or eaten the candles long before the meal was finished!) But we are saying that wise couples never lose sight of the importance of romance to their marital well-being. Take Rick, for example.

When he was old enough to date, his mother pulled him aside and explained the importance of romance. After having seen a lifetime of sensitive things his father had done for his mother—and the payoff in the close relationship they enjoyed—he took her advice.

In high school, he went the extra mile to open the car door and get corsages for special occasions. He made a point of remembering birthdays in a big way and sending cards for special accomplishments. After graduation, when he looked into the deep blue eyes of a girl in his freshman English class, he knew his practice was about to pay off.

During the four years of dating that followed, his constant stream of notes, cards, flowers, and creative dates with Nancy were a romantic introduction to a lifetime of love. When it came time to propose in their final year of college, he did so in an unexpected way.

He was accompanying Nancy to her parents' home for Christmas break. He realized she was beginning to expect he might pop the question any time, but he had other plans.

He had picked up her engagement ring the day before their departure and was bubbling with excitement as they checked in at the airline ticket counter. But then he froze in fear as they neared the security gates. He knew the ring in his pocket would set off the metal detector. The screaming alarm would force him to empty his pockets, and all his planning would be in vain.

Fortunately, the metal detector kept his secret, and they made their way to the departure gate. But even after boarding, Rick remained as nervous as an expectant father. Almost as soon as he sat down, he excused himself to go to the lavatory. But in reality, he went back to the galley. Trembling all over, Rick stepped up to the closest flight attendant and awkwardly pushed a black jewelry box into her hands. But he was so nervous that she became frightened and tossed it right back! Finally, after assuring her it wasn't an explosive, he talked her into serving Nancy a plate with her engagement ring on it instead of dinner.

Each of the flight attendants did a tremendous job of keeping the secret. Not once did they give Nancy any special attention that might have aroused her suspicions. They went about their duties, getting all the passengers seated, and after takeoff they came slowly down the aisle serving the meal.

Nancy occupied the middle seat between an elderly woman at the window and Rick on the aisle. The flight attendant served the older woman first, then Rick, and then there was a long pause. When Nancy finally realized something was wrong and looked up, she saw the entire crew surrounding her. Grinning from ear to ear, they placed a handmade, aluminum foil basket in front of her. Inside was the small jewelry case, which she opened with a cry of surprise.

"Yes, I'll marry you!" Nancy said, beaming as she hugged Rick. The elderly woman, along with all the crew, cheered. And then suddenly the intercom crackled to life as the captain congratulated Rick and Nancy and invited everybody on the flight to their wedding! The entire plane burst into spontaneous applause and laughter, and Nancy cried and laughed at the same time.

Whenever the story was told in years to come about how they got engaged in midair, Rick would chuckle and say their relationship had been downhill ever since. As the years passed, however, their marriage grew stronger. In fact, it was equaled only by the success Rick enjoyed in the oil business. During those years when his business flourished, he continued to go to great lengths to keep a spark of romance alive.

He would arrange for baby-sitters and would "kidnap" his wife for special dates. Or he would take a teddy bear with an "I love you" note taped to it, wrap it in aluminum foil, and stick it way back in the freezer alongside the foil-wrapped leftovers and meats. Sometimes it took months, but sooner or later Nancy would dig back into the freezer, looking for something to defrost for a meal. But instead of finding a chicken or roast, she'd find a frozen teddy bear with her husband's love note.

To many of their neighbors, they were a model couple that put Ken and Barbie to shame. Then, in a state where oil prices never dipped, the market crashed virtually overnight. Over the course of almost twenty-five years, Rick had accumulated a fortune. But in less then twenty-four months, he saw the fruit of his labors slip away to creditors and foreclosures.

Things got so desperate at one point that Rick had to do the unthinkable—something he never dreamed could happen. To make the monthly payment on their house, he had to sell her diamond engagement ring for needed cash.

Rick was finally forced out of the oil business altogether. They lost everything they had. For the first time since their marriage, he wasn't the joker he had always been. With so much pressure and pain because of the loss of his business, his endearing acts of romance dwindled to a trickle.

But when things looked the worst, Rick landed a promising job in another industry. Slowly, the family's outlook began turning around as his new company recognized and appreciated his business skills. But it wasn't until nearly two years later, when Rick and Nancy were out at dinner celebrating a new promotion at work, that she saw the Rick of old again. What he did that night was so romantic and meaningful that she was soon flying higher than the 36,000 feet where their commitment began.

"Nancy," Rick said as they looked out the window of the restaurant at the twinkling city lights far below, "don't you think the lights look like diamonds tonight?"

She nodded and smiled. "It's good to be back."

When he had been in the oil business, they had frequented this same downtown, high-rise restaurant. They had even hosted an anniversary party here for his parents several years before, treating over eighty people to a sumptuous meal. But that was years ago, and this was the first time they had been back since losing their business.

Nancy drank in the view from their perch high above the city. Indeed, the lights did dance below like glittering diamonds.

Just then the waiter arrived with their main course. He and his helpers had been just as attentive as in years gone by. She enjoyed watching their skills. They were always nearby to fill a glass or take away a dish, but never so close that they intruded on a conversation.

She had ordered her favorite dish, and it was set before her just as she remembered it—covered by the bright, silver warming dome that the waiter would whisk away with a flourish. Only this time, when he lifted the silver cover to expose her meal, all that was on her plate was a small, black jewelry box.

It took time for her mind to take in what was before her. After all, it had been almost twenty-five years since their engagement. Almost afraid to touch the box, she slowly reached out and carefully opened it. The engagement ring she had received years before was a beautiful, one-carat diamond. Now she was staring at a magnificent, two-carat stone, surrounded by a host of miniature diamonds.

Rick took his wife's hand in his own. "Nancy," he said, his voice filled with emotion, "you are like this diamond—beautiful, exquisite, precious. There are many facets about you that I love—your warmth, your faithfulness, your kindness. In each situation we encounter together, one of your facets catches a ray of light and sends back a splash of color to me. Even during the hardest of times, you look for the light, the good, the encouraging thing to do or say, and you take that light and reflect it to me in beautiful rainbows. You are the most priceless treasure God ever gave to me.

"The happiest day of my life was when 1 gave you your first diamond. The darkest day was when I had to ask for it back. Every time you look at this new diamond, I want you to remember that it represents the way I feel about you. Happy anniversary, Sweetheart—a little early."

It was almost eight months until their next anniversary, so his present definitely came as a surprise. Once again, a roomful of strangers were told they had just been "engaged," and broke into spontaneous applause. But just when Nancy reached the height of her emotions, she was hurled back to earth by the reality of the price tag.

"Rick," she said shakily, as if waking from a dream. "I'm so touched, but . . . where did you get the money?"

"I knew you'd ask that," he said with a wink. "I sold one of the kids."

"Seriously, I want to know," she said, a hint of fear creeping into her voice. Even though there were no longer wolves at the door, she knew they could ill afford to go into debt for a ring, especially one so beautiful.

"Well, I got the money from my dad."

"You did *what*?"

Throughout their darkest financial times, Rick had never turned to his father for help. His dad had been a successful businessman and would have given them everything he had. But Rick preferred to find his own way through their problems and so he had refused his dad's help.

"You know the gun set I get when Dad dies—the one he never uses? Well, we had a long talk a few weeks ago, and since neither of us hunts anymore, I cashed it in for the ring. Pretty good swap, don't you think?"

Rick's father had been an avid hunter and had a shotgun collection worth several thousand dollars. It was a personal treasure he planned to pass down to his son. In her mind's eye, Nancy could see the two grown men acting like children, plotting to get her this ring. Rick had come by his practical joking and romantic bent naturally—inherited straight from his father.

Knowing they had both given up something precious to buy the ring was almost too much for her to take. She kept staring at the diamond, knowing it stood for a love far beyond the price it would command in any jewelry store.

Rick's words penetrated straight to Nancy's heart because he used both an object as well as a verbal picture to communicate his love for her. His words, together with the visual symbol of his love, created a lasting image in Nancy's mind. Each time she watched the rainbow colors sparkle in her diamond, she heard Rick's affirming words, and they warmed her anew, creating confidence and strength in their marriage. The ring and Rick's words would always be a priceless reminder of how much he valued her, and of the special way he built romantic times and thoughts into their marriage.

Of course, most of us don't have a gun collection to swap for a diamond that could spark a romantic evening. But there's a priceless treasure we can give our spouses for only the cost of the air we breathe. It's available merely by drawing an emotional word picture from one of the four wells. For when it comes to generating romance in a relationship, men and women have seen their words turn to gold for centuries.

For example, consider King Solomon and his bride. Listen to the word pictures he used to capture her heart:

Your eyes behind your veil are doves . . .

Your lips are like a scarlet ribbon . . .

Your temples . . . are like the halves of a pomegranate.[1]

She offers him a word picture with language of love all her own, saying of her fiancé:

Like an apple tree among the trees of the forest,

is my lover among the young men.

I delight to sit in his shade,

and his fruit is sweet to my taste.[2]

Or listen to Romeo and Juliet, creations of William Shakespeare. Their words of love—again captured in word pictures—have been immortalized for generations. Romeo says:

But soft, what light through yonder window breaks?

It is the East, and Juliet is the sun.[3]

See how she leans her cheek upon her hand.

O, that I were a glove upon that hand,

That I might touch that cheek![4]

Or consider Juliet's bittersweet picture of her love for Romeo—a love she felt would last beyond his death:

Give me my Romeo, and when I shall die

Take him and cut him out in little stars,

And he will make the face of heaven so fine

That all the world will be in love with night

And pay no worship to the garish sun![5]

In one of the most romantic relationships of modern times, Elizabeth Barrett Browning and her husband, Robert Browning, sent word picture after word picture to each other. A perfect example of hers begins with the oft-quoted words, "How do I love thee? Let me count the ways."[6]

Instead of counting all the ways, we know what some of you—particularly males—may be thinking: *Wait a minute! That's poetry! Do you mean to say I've got to make my word picture rhyme to build romance into my marriage? That's going too far!*

If we were saying that, not one man in a hundred would pick up this book or devise a word picture. Remember, poetry and fine arts come more from the heart than from the head. So we're not asking the typical fact-oriented male to become a Shakespeare to build romance in his marriage.

> ### The greatest lovers of all time were those who used word pictures to win their mates.

However, the point is still valid. The greatest lovers of all time were those who used word pictures to win their mates.[7] So whether you use a word picture like Rick's—with straightforward, everyday speech—or a poem like Shakespeare's, in either case you're crafting lasting bonds of love.

Remember, if Solomon was wise enough to realize that a woman gains love and security through romantic words, so should we. Security, meaningful communication, and emotional/romantic bonding—all three provide strong support for an intimate relationship, and all three are best accomplished with the language of love.

In addition, to the three pillars we've looked at, there are two more. Both can help support a bridge of intimacy that can take a couple safely above the rough, dangerous waters of inconsistency and emotional distance.

Meaningful Touch: the Silent Language of Love

Study after study has reached the same conclusion. An essential part of an intimate marriage is found right at our fingertips. Among many others, UCLA researchers have concluded that meaningful touch is crucial to the formation and preservation of an intimate relationship. In fact, research has shown that a woman, in particular, needs eight to ten meaningful touches each day just to maintain physical and emotional health.[8]

Since most husbands are left brained, and touching—like romance and meaningful communication—is a right-brain activity, it's safe to say that many women's needs are unmet. The result is that outside the bedroom, a woman must often look to her children, relatives, or supportive friends to make up for a lack of meaningful touch from her husband.

Many husbands don't understand that by depriving a woman of nonsexual touching, they are opening the door for another man to provide that missing fulfillment.[9] That door never needs to be left open. Men need to realize that more than 80 percent of a woman's desire for meaningful touch is nonsexual.[10]

For example, holding hands while waiting in line, giving an unrequested back rub for a few moments, gently stroking her hair (in the right direction!), and hugging her tenderly are all ways to build intimacy in a relationship.

Consistent, gentle touching is one of the most powerful ways to increase feelings of security, prime the pump for meaningful communication, and set the stage for emotionally bonding and romantic times. But what does meaningful touch have to do with word pictures? A great deal. A gentle hug, for example, can be one of the most powerful *nonverbal word pictures* of love.

Communication studies show that nonverbal messages are actually more powerful than verbal ones![11] Because of the incredible emotional weight of meaningful touching, the nonverbal picture of a hug left in a person's mind can solidify a relationship—just as it did for a man who called us one day on a radio talk show and told his remarkable story.

We were on one of our favorite radio call-in programs in Southern California. With his sensitive style, the host asked us to explain a relationship principle and would then encourage listeners to call with their problems, questions, or comments.

We had just finished explaining the significance of meaningful touch when a man we'll call George phoned us.

"When I was fifty-one years old, I suffered a major heart attack," he said. "I was rushed to the hospital, and because the attack was so severe, my wife called my father to come to my bedside.

"To my knowledge, my dad never told me he loved me. Nor did he ever say he was proud of me. He was always there and always supportive in his quiet way, but I still left home questioning whether he really loved and cared for me.

"But as I lay in that hospital bed, with the doctors telling me I might not make it, my seventy-year-old father was flying across the country to be at my side. He arrived the day after my heart attack, and when he came into my room, he did something I'll never, ever forget. He pulled up a chair next to my bed, sat down, and then took my hand in his. I couldn't remember him ever hugging or kissing me, but as I lay there in intensive care, with tubes running everywhere, he stayed for several hours, much of that time just holding my hand."

Up to that point, we thought we were hearing just another dramatic example of the powerful, symbolic picture that meaningful touch can leave behind. We weren't expecting what he said next.

"It still hurts to a degree that my father never said he loved me. But by reaching out and holding my hand, he expressed what he could never put into words. And it was just what I needed to know, because two days after he flew out to be at my bedside, he died of a stroke."

We adjusted our headphones to make sure we'd heard him correctly.

"I was the one expected to die, but I recovered and my father died," he said. "But when he came to my hospital room, he left me something for which I'll always be thankful. When he held my hand, he shouted the words he could never speak—words of love that I saw in his eyes and felt through his hands."

By definition, a word picture involves actual *words*.[12] But for this man, his father's touch spoke volumes and left behind a dramatic image of love and acceptance. And that word picture healed years of insecurity and doubt.

In a marriage, you can also leave lasting pictures of love for your husband or wife. Your gentle acts of touch, no matter how small, can impart an indelible image of commitment and unconditional acceptance that supports an intimate marriage for a lifetime.

Security, meaningful communication, romantic/emotional experiences, and meaningful acts of touch—all four are pillars upon which a fulfilling marriage is built. And all four, when strengthened by word pictures, can help span the differences and disagreements that can wash away a couple's marriage vows.

There is one final pillar upon which all the others depend—the pillar of spiritual intimacy. Without it, a couple can miss God's power to transform hearts and lives. Listen to the beautiful word picture, intended as a musical chorus, found in the Bible, the most inspiring source of word pictures:

> Blessed are all who fear the Lord,
>   who walk in his ways . . .
> Your wife will be like a fruitful vine
>   within your house;
> your sons will be like olive shoots
>   around your table.[13]

What an incredible description of the rewards that await husbands and wives who are energized by faith in God! We're so convinced of the importance of this marital support that we've written an entire book about it. *Joy that Lasts*,[14] describes how to find fulfillment—more than our cup can hold. Such a life can free us from our selfishness to build the bridge of intimacy that will last forever.

Those who enjoy an intimate, secure, romantic marriage have learned about bridge building. And as we've mentioned, word pictures are a key tool in the process. They're also crucial with our children. From experience with our own children and with families across the world, we've learned that word pictures aren't an elective—they're a requirement. To show what we mean, let's turn our attention to how word pictures can aid moms and dads. Without a doubt, parents who master the language of love possess a key that can open their child's heart.

We've watched with amazement the many times our children have responded to emotional word pictures of praise, discipline, and love. That's why we discuss in the next chapter how to use them to balance two crucial parenting skills.

13
Gaining Higher
Ground as a Parent

IN THE PAST fifteen years we've seen two aspects of parenting consistently generate the most frustration and disharmony in a home. They top the list when it comes to counseling letters we receive, and keep us busy nonstop during coffee breaks at conferences.

What are these two parenting concerns? The first is a ten-letter word that has become a dirty word in many homes—discipline. Discipline problems can cause an unhealthy pendulum swing between a permissive and restrictive parent. It can leave the mother feeling like a policewoman in the home; the father like a broken record.

Isn't there a better way to raise a child than raising our voices? Isn't there an alternative to giving Lecture #202 which the kids have memorized? They even correct you if you skip part of it!

We wholeheartedly recommend several books on the subject of discipline.[1] Yet, when it comes to this crucial area of parenting, there's one tool that is often overlooked. This tool, a word picture, grabs children's emotions and delivers a message of lasting conviction to their hearts.

Does that sound too easy? The next time you're tempted to apply the "board of education" to your child's seat of learning, try a word picture first. It can pack a tremendous emotional wallop.

That's exactly what I (Gary) discovered years ago with my oldest son, Greg. Though I didn't realize it at the time, the story I shared with him instantly stopped an unwanted behavior and still helps to shape a positive relationship between us.

Getting Back on the Team

When Greg was twelve, a problem surfaced between us that I couldn't ignore. It dealt with his reaction whenever I flew out of town for a speaking engagement.

On the day I was to leave, everyone in the family would help me pack. Then, at the door, they would always send me off with a "Go get 'em, Dad!" or "We'll miss you!"

However, when Greg entered the sixth grade, I noticed that he no longer was a vital part of the going-away party. Instead of lingering at the door with the rest of the family, he would walk away. Soon, his behavior wasn't limited to avoiding me on my outbound trip. For several hours after I returned, he would often keep his distance.

As time passed, he went to great, creative lengths to give me the cold shoulder. Even when I tried to catch him for a moment of conversation, his words were frigid "Later, Dad," he would cut me off. "I've got to go over to one of my friend's now."

As a counselor, I realized his actions largely reflected his feelings about my traveling. But I also realized I couldn't abandon my monthly trips and still feed my family. Plus, allowing him to ignore me at home and letting his anger build up when I left wasn't doing either one of us any good.

Furthermore, I didn't want him to develop a pattern of ignoring others when he was upset with them. Nor did I want him perfecting a negative habit that could easily carry over into his friendships and, later, his marriage. Most of all, I missed his friendship and didn't want this problem to become a permanent wedge in our relationship.

So I decided I would practice what I teach. On the next flight home, I came up with a word picture for him. I knew it would be effective, because I had seen others work over the years in hundreds of adults' lives. But I had never tried to use them as a corrective tool with my children.

After the conversation I had with my son, word pictures became a permanent part of our parenting plan. In the years to come, I would use them with each of my children—and still do. With word pictures, I saw more positive change in less time than from any lecture I had ever given.

If you're a parent who wants some extra ammunition for dealing with a problem situation, word pictures can help. I know, because the imaginary story of an all-star basketball player kept my son's attention, right to the final buzzer.

It had been two days since I had returned home from my latest business trip. Sure enough, Greg was playing emotional hide-and-seek, but didn't want me to find him.

As was my custom, I would often wake up one of the children early Saturday morning, and then we would go out together for breakfast. This morning, it was Greg's turn.

When I first woke him, I could tell by the look in his eyes and the way he shrank back from my touch that he was still upset. But when I mentioned going to his favorite breakfast spot, I put a choke hold on any ideas he might have had to avoid me.

Later, as we sat at the table enjoying stacks of pancakes and syrup, I began sharing my word picture.

"Greg," I said, looking him in the eye, "I need to explain something to you, and I'd like to start by telling you a short story. Are you up for it?"

"Sure, Dad, fire away," he replied, swallowing a mouthful of pancakes.

"Let's say you were a star basketball player on the junior high squad."

It was the time of year for the college basketball championship. Like me, Greg was a rabid fan and remained glued to the television from the opening tip-off of the Final Four. With popcorn bowl in hand, he watched nearly every game of the NCAA tournament.

For years, I'd shot baskets with him and watched him practice, practice, practice by himself on our backboard at home. I knew the goal of his backyard heroics was to be good enough one day to be the star of the varsity team.

With all this in mind, I had selected and practiced a word picture that I thought would grab his interest. I certainly hit the bull's-eye as I continued.

"For half the season, you've been the high-point man on your team and the leader in assists as well. Your fellow players and the fans love you so much that every time you go out on the court, they yell, 'Greg-O!' 'Greg-O!' 'Greg-O!'"

My chanting his name in the restaurant brought a quick smile to his face as he devoured another pancake.

"Then one game, you twist your neck pulling down a rebound, and it's really sore the next day. In fact, it gets so stiff that Mom takes you out of school and into the doctor's office.

"After looking you over, the doc says you must wear a plastic neck brace and can't play or practice for the next three weeks. Sitting out of the games is the hardest thing you've ever done. You can only watch your teammates from the stands and dream about playing alongside them.

"Twenty-one long days and nights later, you're finally ready to throw away the neck brace and get back on the team again. But something happens your first day back at practice.

"Instead of the players crowding around, cheering and telling you how glad they are you're back, they ignore you! The guy who took your place is especially cool. Even the coach acts like you never were that important to the team and doesn't put you into games like he did before your injury."

From the moment I mentioned basketball, I could see in his eyes that I had picked the one subject that captured his interest more than what he was eating. I had done the impossible. He had actually put down his fork to listen to my story.

"If something like that happened to you, Big Guy, how would it make you feel?"

"I'd feel terrible, Dad. I'd want to get back on the team."

Returning his look, I paused before saying, "Greg, do you realize that at least once a month you're treating me like this coach treated you in my story?"

"No! I'm not doing anything like that," he said emphatically. "I love you, Dad. I'd never try to make you feel terrible."

"Greg, I know you don't realize it, but every time I leave on a trip, you act just like those guys on the team. For several hours after I'm back home, you reject me and don't want to let me back on the family team.

"If my boss tells me I have to go out of town and miss three days at home, you often keep me out of the game when I get back. Like the guy in the story, it hurts to be sitting on the bench—especially when I don't understand why you won't let me back in the game.

"Greg, I want to be a part of your life. I want to get back on your team when I come home. It hurts being rejected by you, and it's not doing you any good to build up anger against me."

That morning at the table, I saw the light of conviction and understanding dawn on my son's face. He was so caught up in the emotions my story generated that he said he was sorry for ignoring me. Even more spectacular, he assured me things would be different from that moment on. He still wasn't crazy about me traveling, but he said he would never again purposely ignore me.

To be honest, as we drove home and I listened to my son's promises about the future, I couldn't help thinking, *This all sounds great, but he's only twelve! There's no way he's going to remember this.*

However, the first test of my doubts came all too soon. Only a few weeks had passed when I was packing my bags. But this time, along with the rest of the family, Greg helped me get ready. And like everyone else, he even hugged me before I left.

I walked outside feeling surprised, relieved, and thankful for my son's change of attitude. Just as I reached the car and started to open the door, he called to me from the front porch. With that classic grin of his, he said, "Have a great trip, Dad. And get ready to be rejected when you get home!"

When I got back from my trip, he didn't ignore me. And he never has since. As the result of one shared breakfast and a word picture used to sweeten the conversation, we dealt with a problem that could have mushroomed into an angry, distant relationship between father and son. Once again, I saw the personal value of using word pictures with children.

> An emotional word picture
> can help sharpen and extend your
> parenting skills by maximizing
> your words. It also helps you whittle
> many problems down to size.

An emotional word picture can help sharpen and extend your parenting skills by maximizing your words. It also helps you whittle many problems down to size.

A Second Parenting Frustration: Losing Perspective in Tough Times

Dr. James Dobson, a noted psychologist, has written an excellent book, *Parenting Isn't for Cowards.*[2] We love the title and the book, primarily because it talks openly about the courage it takes to be an effective parent—especially during tough times. In particular, the book discusses the kind of courage it takes during the uphill years with two-year-olds and teenagers, and the struggle parents face with letting go as their children grow up.

If there's a subject we get asked about as frequently as discipline, it's facing those two difficult stages. That being the case, how can a word picture help parents gain the patience and encouragement to face a problem age or to "hang in there" during a difficult time?

Let's listen to the word picture one young woman used to give us an answer. For years, this woman dreamed of being a mother. Yet the very day her dream came true, it was also shattered. It wasn't until she put her feelings into a word picture that she finally got a handle on her emotions and expectations.

Her word picture has given her the hope and courage to continue being the best parent she can be, even when she's tempted to collapse inside. Here's the moving word picture she expressed to us:

"I had always dreamed of owning a beautiful vase—an expensive one, hand-crafted just for me with exquisite curves and intricate details," she began.

"I spent hours thinking of where it would best fit in my house and how proudly I'd display it. I'd picture it being the first thing a relative or guest would see. It would capture their eyes and generate their praise.

"Finally, the day came when I was to pick up my precious vase. Neither the years of waiting nor the pain of its price tag could dampen my joy—until I was handed a crushed vase.

"Instead of the work of art I'd seen in my mind for so long, I was given a vase that was shattered into a thousand pieces. My heart was broken into as many pieces, and I cried long after my tears had run dry.

"For days, I felt there must have been a mistake. Surely someone else deserved a broken vase, not me. But slowly, painfully, I pulled myself together. That process began the day I held the broken pieces in my hands and vowed to put them back together. Although I realized the vase would never be perfect, I knew that I could love it, cracks and all.

"Little by little, the pile of pieces started to take shape. As the days went by, I gathered more love and patience to glue them together than I ever thought possible. In time, I began to see a masterpiece growing from what had been a mess.

"But that doesn't mean things have been easy. Two groups of people keep coming back time and again.

"The first group is larger and louder than I ever imagined. Every time these people walk by, they go out of their way to step on some of the broken pieces. They crush and grind them into the ground with their cruel words and contemptuous stares—until the pieces seem beyond repair. I always feel so helpless and frustrated when they parade by. I wish they'd leave and never come back, but they always return. With them around, I'm again tempted to see only broken pieces and smeared glue; not a priceless vase.

"The second group is much smaller, but has a heart twice as large. Seeing the shattered pieces, these people kneel beside me and gently help me pick them up. One by one, they carefully help me fit each piece into place—almost as if it were their vase. Unlike the first group, these people leave me filled with renewed hope and love.

"If you haven't realized it yet, the vase I'm talking about is my precious, handicapped child.

"I had always wanted a baby. But I was devastated when the doctor said she'd never be 'normal.' My husband and I asked God to give us a special love for our daughter, and He has. Of course, there are days when I tire of picking up the pieces. But somehow the work is easier now. So much love and commitment have already gone into cementing her life together that I can't imagine loving anyone or anything more."

For this young woman, picturing her precious child as a priceless vase helped her think through her feelings of love, hope, anger, confusion, and grief. It also gave us a graphic picture of what was going on in her life.

When the parenting task gets tough, emotional word pictures can flesh out hidden feelings and give parents an entirely new perspective. It can help lift their eyes above their circumstances and give them a vice-like grip on their feelings.

The first two hurdles that trip parents are those of discipline and maintaining a positive attitude during tough times. Like an expert coach, word pictures can help you get over these barriers in winning form. In addition, word pictures can assist parents four other ways.

Not only can they help you get over the hurdles, but they can help you raise blue-ribbon children as well. They provide a legacy of love your children can carry with them for a lifetime.

14
Building Blocks to
Successful Parenting

OVER SEVERAL YEARS, we researched and wrote a book on how parents can most effectively communicate love and high value to their children. In writing the book, entitled *The Blessing*, we learned a great deal about the skills of unconditionally loving and encouraging children.[1] Unfortunately, we also unearthed far more than we ever wanted to know about children who grew up with critical disapproval.

When we wrote the book, we knew the failure to communicate love and acceptance was an issue in many homes. Yet, we had no idea of its magnitude. Since *The Blessing* was released, we've heard from hundreds of people who, as children, never felt loved or valued by their parents. As a result, they often left home and walked right into alcoholism, substance abuse, chronic depression, workaholism, and shattered marriage and parent/child relationships of their own.[2] These problems are all echoes of their unhappiness from childhood.

In an attempt to run away from a family in which they didn't feel loved, many adolescents have also dashed right into the arms of cult members and damaging sexual relationships. They have left far behind the moral, spiritual, and religious values of their parents.[3]

We know that as a concerned parent, you would never want to see any of these problems crop up in your child's life. But then, neither did the parents of those we've received letters from—each of whom is now living in emotional pain.

Many parents thought they were making deposit after deposit into their child's love bank, only to have that child leave home feeling like he or she had a zero balance deep inside. In fact, the majority of letters we receive are not from physically abused children or from alcoholic homes. Often the most tragic stories are from boys and girls who grew up in families that were loving in many ways—yet their love wasn't communicated in a manner that was understood and accepted.

How could this happen? What makes the difference between a home that sends a child out into life feeling valued, loved, and blessed, and a home that doesn't? Often it lies in what was said by the parents—or not said.

Children desperately need to know—and to hear in ways they understand and remember—that they're loved and valued by Mom and Dad. How can you communicate the high value and acceptance you have for your children in a special way? How can you share words that protect and provide for them? How can you better understand them, and have them understand you?

Again, we know of no better way for you to leave a legacy of love for your children than to use emotional word pictures.

> ## Word pictures can help a parent say "I love you" in a manner a child can't miss.

Providing a Legacy of Love for Your Children

As we mentioned in the previous chapters, the reason many people don't build intimate marriages is because they lack the necessary knowledge and skills. The same thing is true with effective parenting. It, too, takes knowledge and skills—knowing what breaks relationships down and being able to build them up.

You've already seen how word pictures can help in the important parenting areas of discipline and positive attitude. In the pages that follow, we want to share with you four additional ways in which word pictures can help a parent say "I love you" in a manner a child can't miss. They're reflections of the pillars that hold up an intimate marriage, which we discussed in chapters eleven and twelve.

But before we launch into the various ways word pictures help parents, we must face another problem. For in many homes, it isn't a lack of skills that's the issue. It's the lack of time.

"I've Got All the Time in the World . . ."

If a common cry for many children is, "Please say you love me," an equally common response by many parents is, "I've got all the time in the world to tell you." Really? We wish that were true!

What would you do if you walked into a doctor's office one day and were told you had Lou Gehrig's disease? How would you react to the black-and-white words that you would be dead in twenty months or less?

If you had spent almost all your waking hours learning skills to build a career, how could you begin to switch your focus to building an intimate relationship with your wife and children? If you knew that, in a short time, all your family would have was a memory of you, how could you leave a legacy of love for them to embrace? Most of all, how could you leave your wife and children words that would warm their hearts, even when you were no longer able to pull them close and wrap them in your arms?

If you were a friend of ours, whom we'll call Steve, you would really have to answer these questions. They're all things he's heard and thought. They're all real-life questions he's facing now, even as we write this book.

Steve has three children and a loving wife. And he's dying of amyotrophic lateral sclerosis, a rare and fatal disease best known for bringing down Lou Gehrig, the "iron man" of baseball.[4]

I (John) met Steve at a family camp where I was speaking. Unlike those who had come for vacation, he came with another purpose in mind. He didn't have long to live and wanted his life—and his words—to count.

As I spoke about practical ways to build value into relationships, Steve took detailed notes. After the presentation, we sat down and talked about an idea he had—an idea to capture his love and prayers for his family through word pictures.

He won't always be able to look into his children's eyes. Yet, over the years, their eyes can read and reread a series of letters he's working on right now—a collection of word pictures that will be waiting for them to open at important times in their lives.

He won't have the chance to be one of the proud parents seated at his children's high school graduation, but his words will be there.

He'll miss the excitement of packing up his son's and daughters' car as they head off for their first day of college, but his message of encouragement will be there.

He'll never have the opportunity to walk his daughters down the aisle on their weddings or receive the phone call that he's just become a grandfather, but his pictures of love and support will be there.

That's because he's writing word pictures now that will carry his prayers, wishes and hopes for them in the future—where his voice won't reach.

By the time this book finds its way into your hands, Steve may already be in the hands of God. Yet his family will always have his personal legacy of love—word pictures that are so vivid and real they will seem to become flesh, complete with arms to hug and hold his wife and children. Through these words, his presence will bless and encourage his family for a lifetime.

Moms and dads, what's your reason for not speaking the words your children need to hear so much? Are your other activities really so important that you can't speak or write down words your children can treasure for a lifetime? We may not have a medical clock ticking behind us. But for each of us, it's later than we think.

With the light speed at which children grow up and with the very real uncertainties of life, this is no time to withhold words of love and affection. There's too much at stake in their future for you to put off learning the skills that can make a lasting difference in their lives.

For whatever reason, let's all stop procrastinating and start looking at four ways emotional word pictures can carry our message of love straight to their hearts, beginning with the pillar of security.

Word Pictures and Parenting

1. Children Need Security in Words and Actions.

A few years ago, we counseled with a husband and wife who were constantly fighting. Try as we might, we couldn't seem to help bring an end to their heated arguments.

Whenever we think we're getting nowhere with a couple, there's something we do that always puts things in a new perspective. That is, we ask the couple to bring their children to the next session.

Over the years, we've discovered that children are God's little spies! Mom and Dad may be able to snow us and walk around issues. But when we invite the kids, in an unguarded moment they'll walk you right up to what you most need to know.

When we sat down with this couple at our next session, we were joined by their handsome eleven-year-old son and darling six-year-old daughter. And while we didn't realize it at the time, we were about to be given a tremendous lesson about the importance of security in a home.

"What bothers you the most about your parents' arguing?" we asked their daughter.

She looked quickly over to her parents. When her mother nodded, the little girl said, "Every time Daddy gets mad at Mommy or us, he takes off his wedding ring and throws it away."

Her father quickly explained that he wasn't literally throwing away his wedding ring. He was just "venting" his anger. When something set him off, he would pull off his ring and make it ricochet off a few walls. He then explained away what he was doing as a "healthy expression" of anger. After all, he said, we were counselors and would know how damaging it was to hold anger inside.

What he didn't realize was that his actions had become a word picture of instant insecurity to his daughter. By ripping off his ring, he conveyed a symbol to her that was projected in technicolor on a forty-foot screen in her mind. His action represented all the fear this little girl had that he would hurt or desert the family.

Every time this precious little one saw her daddy's wedding ring get thrown across the room, she saw her future sail away with it. Instead of building the security that she so desperately needed, her father created for her a world of constant fear. This fear, brought on by lack of security, ate at her stomach so badly that she had already been diagnosed as having childhood ulcers.[5]

For more than a year before they had come in for counseling, her father's wedding ring was a word picture for desertion, loneliness, fear, and anxiety. That began to change only when he was confronted with the damage he was doing.

We began "milking" the young girl's word picture (a skill we discussed earlier in the book)[6] by asking her father questions, such as:

"What causes you so much frustration around the house that you pull off your ring and throw it?"

"When you were growing up, did you see your father—literally or figuratively—pull off his wedding ring?"

"How close do you think your wife is to pulling off her ring?"

"How do you think it makes the kids feel when they see your ring go flying?" and

"What would it take, beginning right now, to put the ring back on your finger and always keep it there?"

Through the word picture of a ring, we spoke to an entire family about the subject of security. Because we tied into a word picture in their home, our words grabbed the father's emotions like nothing we'd said in all the previous sessions.

While not every story has a happy ending, this one did. At the conclusion of their time in counseling a few months later, this family did two things.

First, they took the time to share a word picture with their children about a wedding ring that had been scarred and dented, but now had been repaired and brightly polished. And they assured their children that the ring would stay on both Mom's and Dad's fingers, no matter what they faced in the future.

This wise couple knew they had not built a foundation of security for their children, and willingly admitted they had caused their children physical and emotional damage. That's what brought them into counseling. There they opened up to needed changes when their daughter pointed out a word picture to them.

Their little girl now has a very different picture in her mind of Daddy's ring. No longer does it stand for anger, frustration, and fear. Instead, it shines with the love, courage, and resolve needed to work through problems. His words, together with his actions, repainted the faded picture of an unstable home into a masterpiece of security.

On a one-to-ten scale, how's the security level around your home these days? If it's slipped into the threes and fours, you're communicating a word picture of insecurity to your children.

When it comes to parenting, kids don't bloom and grow if their roots are constantly ripped out. Insecurity in a home pulls out roots; security provides the depth and shelter for them to thrive.

If you're a single parent, you have ten times the reason to assure your child that you won't leave him or her, and word pictures can help. In any separation or divorce, children get a massive dose of insecurity. To combat the negative damage of such feelings, you must provide a constant source of security. In a later chapter, we'll share a treasury of more than 100 word pictures to help you do that very thing.

We've seen how important security is, both for our children and marriage. Now let's look at how we can use word pictures to build character in our sons and daughters.

2. Children Need Instruction and Friendship.

It's clear that with young children, the greatest way to bring change is through instruction that builds character. Educators have known this for years. That's one reason that figurative language and word pictures are a key to teaching younger children.

From preschool on, children learn and remember lessons better if they are communicated with a story or object.[7] In fact, one early sign of a learning disability for a grade school child is his or her inability to understand figures of speech.[8] It isn't only modern-day research that supports this use of word pictures to instruct children.

Since ancient times, a parent's goal revolved around "training up a child in the way he should go."[9] As the primary shapers of a child's character, parents do well to spend time instructing young children in ways that would provide a healthy platform for later life.[10]

How do children best understand abstract concepts, such as honesty, truthfulness, discipline, and love? Whether it's an educational concept or a spiritual truth, children (or adults) learn best when a word picture is part of the instruction time.

Parents with young children can find a ready-made application of the research studies and history we've already mentioned in this book. That is, word pictures are a key to building character and helping us communicate our point. In large part, that's because emotional stories take on the qualities of real life, especially with children.

This is one reason television viewing should be so closely monitored. It's also one reason a word picture, drawn from one of the four wells, can be so powerful.

We know of one mother who used her microwave oven to teach her son a much needed lesson about anger. She took a clear plastic mug, filled it with water, and set the microwave on high for three minutes. As she and her son watched the calm surface of the water be transformed into raging bubbles, she talked with him about handling his frustration.

She asked her young son what made him boil over inside at times. Then they talked about how he could push the "pause" button and talk to her when things began frustrating him. That way she could help him with his frustration in its early stages, instead of hearing about it when he was boiling over with emotions.

Another mother drew upon a biblical proverb—a type of word picture—to talk with her very unmotivated child. The proverb says, "Go to the ant, you sluggard; consider its ways."[11]

After a good deal of thought, this wise woman made her son do just that. She bought him an ant farm and got him excited about capturing, feeding, and watching the nonstop activity of a colony. Every day, her son observed how the ants all worked together and stayed at a task. In so doing, he saw living examples of character traits his mother wanted to build into his life.

In an appropriate time and way, she used a word picture with him. She talked about how he could be a better "ant" with his household chores and schoolwork, and how what he did or didn't do around the house affected everyone else. To her immense surprise, he began making tangible changes in his behavior.

In these homes and hundreds of others, the parents have used word pictures to bring lessons to life for their youngsters. They know that when a child has a picture of a desired behavior—instead of just words—he learns a lesson faster and remembers it longer than the most inspired lecture they can give.[12]

Mastering word pictures with young children is crucial. That's because their little minds are still in the "input" stage where they're most open to change through instruction. But soon, with the onset of puberty, a youngster will move to the "I've-already-got-the-answers" stage. Adolescence requires a different approach to accomplish change.

Using Word Pictures with Adolescents

Teenagers usually go through an "individuality crisis" just about the time their parents go through the midlife "identity crisis." What's the result of this emotional mismatch? As a man once said, "What we have here is a failure to communicate!"

If the goal of parents with young children is character building through instruction, their goal with adolescents is building through friendship.

Discipline takes on new meaning when you're looking up at your son, instead of down at him. And when your daughter's friends all drive cars, it's hard to keep her around the house long enough to hear your hour-long speeches. By a child's teen years, parents often reap the results of the character instruction—both good and bad—they sowed earlier. But if that's the case, how do you change a teenager's behavior? Again, word pictures hold a powerful key.

Researchers point out that for adults (teens are adults in their thinking process, if not always in their judgment), the best way to change someone is through a significant emotional event.[13] Think about this for a moment.

When are adults most teachable? When a significant event impacts an important relationship.

We've seen a husband who wouldn't crack a marriage enrichment book devour dozens of them when his wife walked out.

We've seen a woman who never wrote a letter home suddenly write nonstop notes after receiving the news her mother was dying.

And we've seen teenagers listen to words of praise, instruction, and correction with the greatest effect, when expressed by a parent who is also their friend. It's a wise father or mother who doesn't rely only on grounding or grabbing away car keys, but who can grab a child's emotions in a heart-to-heart conversation.

If you're like many parents and have declared war on your teenager, we can assure you there will be no winners—only prisoners. And if a teenager is a captive in his own home, watch out when he breaks the chains and goes off to college or work.

If you're more interested in your son's behavior than his character, he'll pick up the inconsistency. If your daughter senses you're more concerned that she doesn't embarrass you than that she does what's best for her, you'll get resistance. And if you don't know what it takes to develop a meaningful friendship with your child, then your first priority should be to get the necessary knowledge and skills.[14]

You can force a two-year-old to sit down on the outside . . . even if he or she is standing up on the inside! But you can't force-feed words and ideas down teenagers' throats and expect them not to react and regurgitate those words later.

In a home where a parent and child can't be friends, teens will listen to their peer group instead of you. If you want to be the one who has your son's or daughter's ear, then try learning their language. Try speaking the language of love. The music they listen to does. Their peers do. Even the Bible they read does. If you want to make inroads of friendship with your child, then you will, too.

Whether we have young children in the instructional stage or the friendship-building years, word pictures help us as parents. A brief look at the remaining two reflections from the pillars of marriage can help as well.

3. Children Need the Love That Meaningful Touch Can Bring.

In the chapter on building an intimate marriage, we noted that meaningful touch can greatly impact any relationship. In a very real sense, it leaves a word picture of commitment and caring in another person's mind. But is this also true with children?

We recently heard from a young, single-parent mother who had read one of our parenting books. In one of the chapters, we stress the symbolic picture that touch gives a child, and it convicted her right down to her socks.

This young woman, whom we'll call Julie, had become pregnant out of wedlock. Believing life was sacred, she opted to carry her baby to term and not kill him. She had initially decided on adoption, but at the last minute she decided to keep her newborn son, Jason.

After the excitement of having a newborn wore off, problems began to develop. As the baby grew older, so did her resentment of him. Instead of a joy, he became a burden. Instead of an object to love, he became a symbol of her frustration with life.

But she began to head down a different path when she started going to a church near her small apartment. Members took her under their wing and helped her in every way. Yet she still felt deep resentment toward Jason that she couldn't seem to shake. That emotion manifested itself in one particular way—she didn't want to touch him.

Touch is the first way babies know they are loved. Long before they can understand words, they clearly read the nonverbal language of love, expressed through meaningful touch. But that was missing from the pages of Jason's little life.

What changed Julie? What made her open to going against her feelings and reaching out for her son?

As he grew older, she began noticing problems in his life that she couldn't ignore. After reading in our book about the incredible power of meaningful touch, she talked with a group of close friends about the repulsion she felt toward her son. Wisely, they encouraged her to talk further with a counselor.

Within a few sessions, Julie was confronted with many reasons why she withheld meaningful touch: guilt from the past; a lack of touch in her own home; the fact that Jason looked very much like his father—the man who had gotten her pregnant and then laughed at her plans to keep the baby.

Finally, she decided to give her son a picture of the love she had for him—through physical touch. But her first attempts didn't go quite as she'd expected. When she reached out to hug him, he ran away! She'd only touched him before when she was angry. So when she put her arms around him he fled, crying in confusion and fear.

However, after several weeks, Julie's determination to offer this powerful picture of love won out. And the transformation in Jason's attitude and actions was dramatic. Not only did her son become more sociable and less anxious around others, but his schoolwork and attention span in class also improved! All because she began giving him a powerful, nonverbal word picture of her love for him.

On a scale of one to ten, how high would your children rate you for touching them in meaningful ways? Have you asked them lately? Have you ever asked your spouse that question?

Even with teenagers who cringe when their mom or dad hugs them ("Oh, Mom, stop that! One of my friends might see you!"), they still need that picture of love. You may have to get a little creative (Try wrestling on the carpet!). But you build love and value in a child when you're not afraid or don't neglect to touch your children in meaningful ways.

4. Children Need Times of Emotional Bonding.

We realize that "romantic/emotionally bonding" times that are so important in a marriage have definite limits with a child. However, if you drop the word "romantic," you should have all the emotional bonding you can with your son or daughter!

The best way we know to bond within a family is by going camping. It's not the act of camping that provides closeness, but what happens when we camp with our kids. You guessed it: catastrophes!

For some reason, the memories of a camping trip—where you forgot all the food but the marshmallows; where the tent collapsed for no reason—twice; where you had a blow-out on the way up and a blow-up on the way back home—all can become great bonding experiences.

You'll never forget the time you went out for ice cream and had your little one's cone drop on his shoe! And how can you forget the time you took the older one surfing for the first time and then paid for the stitches when the board sliced open his chin? Such experiences not only bond us (after the stitches have healed, of course), but travel right to a child's heart.

By this point in the book you've seen the "whys" and "how-tos" of using word pictures in your important relationships. Soon we'll close the book by giving you 101 word pictures that you can begin to apply immediately. Yet before we reach this treasury of word pictures, there's something we can't overlook.

Misusing word pictures is a danger we'd rather ignore, but can't.

Over the years we've seen dramatic examples of the good that's come from using the language of love. But we've also seen great emotional destruction come when it's misused or twisted into a language of hate.

We don't relish the look. But we feel it's important to pull back the shades and expose those who would exploit the dark side of emotional word pictures. These are people who emotionally (or physically) hurt others time and again. They repel any word pictures you give them, and turn theirs on you like an attacking pit bull terrier. They are the kind of people who can't seem to love back.

HOW CAN
WORD PICTURES
HELP MY WALK
WITH GOD?

15
Using Emotional
Word Pictures to Strengthen
Your Spiritual Life

SINCE THIS BOOK was first published, one of our greatest joys
has been to receive letters that tell how a word picture has benefited
someone. An especially encouraging report arrived a while back that
described one of the most unusual uses of a word picture we've ever
heard.

Broken Bottles . . . Shattered Lives

Imagine you're ministering to those at the very bottom of society's
ladder. Seated in front of you are several rows of dirty, downcast,
skid-row alcoholics. While a few might be at your rescue mission out
of a pure desire to hear about God's free gift of grace, most are there
because they know that once you finish your sermon, they'll get a
free, hot meal.

Like many on the homeless trail, these men have heard the gospel
message countless times, from countless preachers, in countless
shelters across the country. And while familiarity with the gospel
might put words of faith in their mouths, their minds are on physical, not spiritual, nourishment.

Interested in getting up and trying to motivate *this* crowd?

That was the situation facing Chaplain Bill one cold November
night. He knew the challenge before him, and it frustrated him. How
could he break through to those men's hardened hearts with the light
of God's love? How could he tell the old, old story in a way that
brought a new response of faith?

Chaplain Bill always worked hard on his talks. But in preparing to speak to his castaway congregation this week, he had come across a new communication tool he couldn't wait to try.

Bill had just finished reading the first edition of the book you hold in your hands. With a strong inner conviction, he believed a word picture was just what he needed to break through the barriers that the hard edge of life had put on his "parishioners'" lives. So he prepared to do something he'd never done before in a sermon.

Standing before the men, Bill pulled something out from behind the podium as he began to speak.

An Unlikely Picture of Unconditional Love

"Okay, men, what's this I'm holding?" Bill asked with a mischievous grin.

Slowly, he drew something out of a brown paper sack. As the hidden item came into view, a chorus of laughter swept across the room.

"You've got yourself a bottle, Rev!" one man shouted.

"I've seen a few of those!" another said with a laugh as the familiar green glass of a cheap wine bottle was brought into sight.

"That's right, men," Bill said, looking out on his smiling audience. "I've got a bottle here. Now, let me tell you a little about myself, and then I want to tell you a story about this bottle—and what happened to it."

The crowd was unusually attentive as Bill continued. "Instead of finishing high school, I joined the Navy at seventeen. After ten years in the service, I made petty officer and was doing real well. I had a fine wife, a good job, and a family. I even had a house I was paying on. But then my wife was killed in an accident, and I was left alone with the two young kids.

"It was like my heart died when she did, and I took to drinking hard. In less than two years, I had turned myself into such a problem the Navy discharged me. Then I lost my kids to the state because I was neglecting them due to the drinking, and things just got worse from there.

"You see, my life was a lot like this bottle here. I always thought I was going to be something special. Maybe I'd be used to hold some special medicine, or I might be made into a fine piece of china to set in some rich person's house. But when it came right down to it, I ended up just a plain, green bottle, sent down a conveyor belt and filled with cheap wine.

"I was packed with a bunch of other bottles and shipped to a big city. There I sat on a dark, dusty shelf for a long time. And while that was bad, something worse finally happened; an old wino pulled me off the shelf and carried me out back into a dark alley.

"Three of his drinking buddies met him there, and they all passed me around and finished me off. Finally, that old wino staggered to his feet. Swaying side to side, he drew back and heaved me into a brick wall, smashing me to pieces.

"That's where my life was, men," Chaplain Bill said. "And for a long time, I lay there in that alley, so shattered and mixed in with all the other broken bottles that I knew there was no way the pieces of my life could ever come back together."

Shifting his weight and looking the men in the eyes, he continued, "But I was wrong."

Chaplain Bill told us that by this point in his weekly sermon, he's usually preaching to nodding heads and frozen smiles or hearing snide remarks about getting on to dinner. But not that night. "No one was saying anything," he said, "and the eyes of every man in that room were riveted on me." He went on with his story.

"For what seemed like a lifetime, I lay in that alley, all out of hope. Then suddenly, I saw a dark shape coming toward me. Whoever it was actually kneeled down in that dirty, smelly alley and began sifting through all those broken pieces.

"How He did it, I don't know, but that Man found all my shattered pieces, one by one. And starting with my heart, He pieced me back together. It's been five years since He found me in that alley, and He's been polishing away at the cracks ever since."

Choked with emotion as the memories flooded back, Bill finished his talk with an invitation.

"I know what you men are like on the inside," he said. "I was just as broken up as you are—just as hopeless, just as filled with doubt that anything or anyone could ever piece my life back together.

"But there's someone who can make you whole—the same Man who sought me out and found me in that dark alley." Holding up the bottle, Bill continued, "His name is Jesus, and you can know Him as your personal Lord and Savior. You can have Him put the pieces of your life back together, like He did for me—and He can do it tonight."

Bill's sermon was over, and the response he got staggered him. With smells of dinner wafting up from the kitchen below, no one stirred from his seat. The usually rambunctious crowd was quiet as the men thought through what the chaplain had said. And while such services often yield no visible results, that night there was rejoicing in heaven—two men came to know the One who made them and who alone could put their lives back together. Several others rededicated their lives to the Restorer of their souls.

Why did a word picture work so well in communicating spiritual truth to those men? Actually, it shouldn't surprise us that word pictures are so powerful a tool. The pages of Scripture are filled with them, and emotional word pictures can help strengthen our spiritual lives in four major ways.

1. Word Pictures Can Draw Us Closer to God.

Imagine living in a small, rural town, and in all your life, you've never driven more than a few miles from home. If you were asked to put yourself in the shoes of the president of the United States, with all his traveling and international networking, understanding who he is and what he does could seem impossible. But read a newspaper, turn on the television, or subscribe to a news magazine, and suddenly the whole world of public events is at your doorstep. You can even see pictures of the president's travels, and you feel closer to him as a result.

Words and pictures can help us bridge the distance between a politician and an everyday citizen. Yet for all time, finite people have struggled even more in trying to bridge the immense gap between themselves and a God who is all-powerful and all-knowing.

The psalmist wrote of God, "The Lord has established his throne in heaven,"[1] and through the prophet God Himself proclaimed, "My thoughts are not your thoughts, neither are your ways my ways."[2]

How dare we draw near to such a powerful God? Thankfully, He took the initiative in revealing Himself to us. We see the invisible God most clearly in the visible expression of His Son. And throughout the Scriptures, emotional word pictures provide the best means of getting to know Him and communicating His love to others.

Consider parents who want to bring God's love up close to a child. Where will many of them turn? To Psalm 23, where they can read to their little lambs, "The Lord is my shepherd, I shall not be in want. He makes me lie down in green pastures."[3]

Those same fathers and mothers, when faced with the inevitable tragedies of life, will often turn to the same passage to catch a glimpse of their loving Shepherd: "Even though I walk through the valley of the shadow of death, I will fear no evil, for you are with me; your rod and your staff, they comfort me."[4]

Word pictures have always made God more accessible, more real, and more understandable to our finite minds. Perhaps that's one reason Jesus employed them so much.

Our Lord's primary teaching style was to use *parables.* Word pictures filled His messages to the crowds and disciples alike. On any given day, you could hear stories about the good Samaritan, the fig tree, the lost coin, and the lost sheep. At other times, He would issue great challenges by talking about different types of soil, buried or invested talents, and the need for His followers to pick up their own crosses and follow Him.

Jesus also described Himself as the Good Shepherd, the Door, the Way, and the Truth. He was called the Cornerstone, Bread, and Living Water, to cite just a few examples.

The Picture Behind the Verse

While many of Jesus' word pictures are well known, others go overlooked. And perhaps the most neglected word picture Christ used in describing Himself comes just before one of the most familiar verses in all the Bible.

The first verse many people memorize after becoming Christians is John 3:16: "For God so loved the world that he gave his one and only Son, that whoever believes in him shall not perish but have eternal life."

But do you know what John 3:*14-15* says?

Jesus had been speaking to Nicodemus at night, answering the fearful Pharisee's questions regarding salvation. He heard from Jesus that he would need to be born again. When Nicodemus couldn't comprehend the necessity to be born physically *and* spiritually, Jesus called to his mind a word picture that would explode with meaning for this learned teacher of the Law.

"Just as Moses lifted up the snake in the desert," Jesus said in 3:14-15, "so the Son of Man must be lifted up, that everyone who believes in him may have eternal life." Then, to further explain that word picture, Jesus went on to say the often-quoted words, "For God so loved the world . . ."

A snake lifted high in the desert? What was Christ referring to? How would that word picture help Nicodemus understand who Jesus was and what He had come to do?

While we may struggle to connect the two verses, Nicodemus instantly would have seen Christ's allusion as a crystal-clear picture of who He was claiming to be. That's because this religious leader had surely studied Numbers 21:4-9 and the story of how many people were saved by looking up to a snake hung on a pole.

When the nation of Israel was wandering in the wilderness, the people began to grumble about Moses' leadership. They even questioned God's wisdom in leading them into the desert at all—and that's when they crossed the line.

God judged the critical Hebrews by sending fiery serpents among them. Once bitten, the individual would die, and that led to a massive cry from the people for Moses to plead with God for a way of escape. Moses did intercede on their behalf, and God gave him a most unusual remedy to their life-and-death dilemma.

Moses was directed to cast in bronze a likeness of the lethal snake. Then that bronze serpent was to be placed on one of the poles used to carry the tribal banners—a long pole with a crossbeam attached. Now, when any of the people were bitten by the deadly vipers, all they had to do was to look up at the serpent—on a cross—and they would be healed.

Look up at a snake on a cross and be healed? As simple as it sounds, I'm sure some people who were bitten by the snakes felt it was just too silly a request, or not complicated enough, or it didn't involve enough effort on their part. But as they soon learned all too well, those who put their faith in what God said and looked up would live, and all those who didn't would die.

Now can you understand the word picture behind the most familiar verse in the New Testament? Jesus was telling Nicodemus, "I'm like that snake Moses lifted up in the wilderness. Every person has been bitten by sin and will die, yet God has provided a way of escape. For when I take on the sins of the world—and become like that snake on the cross—those who look up to Me will be saved."

What clearer picture could Christ have given about our need for salvation and the only way of escape? Yet still today, there are those who think God's plan is too simple, not scientifically demonstrable, or doesn't involve enough human effort—and all those people stay poisoned by sin and chained to the terrible consequences, because they refuse to look in faith to Christ on the cross.

Whether it's the well-known word picture of a Good Shepherd or the powerful imagery of a bronze serpent, God has always shared bits of His character and personality through emotional word pictures. And those same pictures can also help us remember the truths of Scripture.

2. Word Pictures Help Us Understand and Remember the Truths of Scripture.

How could the Infinite communicate His truths to finite human beings? The problem is similar—though on a much greater scale—to meeting with a doctor (perhaps a specialist) and having him explain your condition in technical terms. He's probably literally speaking Latin for all you know. Yet when he asks if you understand, you nod your head and say, "Mmm," knowingly. But inside you're thinking, *What was all that? Am I going to live another eighty years or die tomorrow?*

When it comes to understanding some of the great truths of the Bible, we can feel just like that. We know we're *supposed* to understand, so we look at each other and say, for instance, "Wow, isn't justification great?" But on the inside, we're as confused as if we were in that Latin-loving doctor's office.

God knew, however, that emotional word pictures can cut through the fog and help us understand His Word in a deeper, more intimate way. In fact, *God uses emotional word pictures to communicate almost all His most important truths.*

God consistently uses emotional
word pictures to communicate
His most important truths.

You may have heard your Sunday school teacher or a Bible college professor use the word *reconciliation* to describe one of the aspects of our relationship with Christ. But if you're like most of us, that word doesn't seem to have much personal impact.

Watch how Ephesians 2:14-15 makes that truth come alive, however. Talking about how Gentiles are now able to share a relationship with God that was once reserved for Jews, Paul said, "For he himself is our peace, who has made the two one and *has destroyed the barrier, the dividing wall of hostility.* . . . His purpose was to create in himself one new man out of the two, thus making peace" (italics ours).

What a powerful picture! For centuries, the Jews were privileged to be God's chosen people, standing on one side of a "wall" that separated them from the rest of humanity. To symbolize this separation, the Jews even built a literal wall around the inner and outer courts, of the Temple, allowing only Jews to pass into the inner court, where God's presence dwelt in the Holy of Holies.

Try as the Gentile nations might, they could never find a battering ram big enough to break down that wall and become full participants with the Jews in God's blessings. But when Christ came, through His death and resurrection He tore down the dividing wall so that *everyone* could have a loving relationship with the Father.

Like East and West Germans celebrating the fall of the Berlin Wall, we realize through Paul's dramatic picture that something we once could not have (peace with God) is now ours for the taking. That's reconciliation, made clearer than any theological definition.

Our security as believers is also made clear by yet another word picture. In Ephesians 1:13 we read, "And you also were included in Christ when you heard the word of truth, the gospel of your salvation. Having believed, you were *marked in him with a seal*, the promised Holy Spirit" (italics ours).

In biblical times, when a king wanted to make sure his letter went undisturbed to its final destination, he poured a spot of molten candle wax on the end of the scroll, then stamped in his seal with a signet ring. The only way to open the letter was to break the seal. Thus the letter was safe, because any tampering would be obvious and would bring down the king's wrath.

What a picture of how God has provided "safe passage" for us who believe in Him! As New Testament believers, we can know we are sealed by the Holy Spirit and don't have to pray like David of old, "Do not . . . take your Holy Spirit from me."[5]

Even the book of Romans, held by many to be the jewel of Paul's theological teaching, is filled with word pictures. To explain how all are bound up in sin, both Jew and Gentile, he quoted a series of Old Testament word pictures: "'There is no one who does good, not even one.' 'Their throats are open graves. . . .' 'The poison of vipers is on their lips.'"[6] Regarding our dedication to Christ, Paul wrote, we are to "offer your bodies as living sacrifices, holy and pleasing to God"[7]—that is, we're to lay our lives and talents on God's altar.

Throughout the Scriptures are moving word pictures that carry home God's truth and help us remember what's being taught. For example, try reading Isaiah 53 (the gripping picture of the suffering Messiah) without experiencing—and remembering—the emotions wrapped around the many word pictures there.

"He was led like a lamb to the slaughter, and as a sheep before her shearers is silent, so he did not open his mouth."[8] "We all, like sheep, have gone astray, . . . and the Lord has laid on him the iniquity of us all."[9]

Word pictures can draw us closer to God and bring more clarity to our knowledge of Him. Yet with the positive emotion word pictures carry, they're also a powerful tool God uses to bring us comfort and encouragement.

3. Word Pictures Are a Primary Way God Gives Us Hope and Encouragement.

To see how word pictures can deepen our love for God and help us experience His love, there's no better place to turn than to the many prayers found in the Psalms.

When David was fleeing for his life from his son Absalom, for example, he prayed, "O Lord, how many are my foes! How many rise up against me! . . . But you are a shield around me, O Lord."[10]

On another occasion, David was celebrating his deliverance from Saul and praised God using a word picture: "The Lord is my rock, my fortress and my deliverer; my God is my rock, in whom I take refuge. He is my shield and the horn of my salvation, my stronghold."[11]

In our own lives, we've seen that using a word picture can help turn a stale prayer time into a meaningful conversation with God. For example, I (John) have often turned to Psalm 1 and used the word picture there as a pattern for prayer.

The psalm reads, "Blessed is the man who does not walk in the counsel of the wicked. . . . But his delight is in the law of the Lord. . . . He is like a tree planted by streams of water, which yields its fruit in season and whose leaf does not wither."[12] That picture can become a clearly guided prayer: "O Lord, I ask that You keep my feet in the path of wisdom today, and that You would send my roots deeper into You than ever before."

As for me (Gary), my entire life and view of prayer were changed through experiencing the word pictures Christ gave of the widow seeking protection, and of the man who woke his neighbor at night to get food for an unexpected guest.[13]

Besides being the tool that both David and Solomon used to express their fears, doubts, praise, and sorrow, word pictures are also one of the primary ways in which God ministers His love to us.

Pictures of Love, Hope, and Support

Have you ever gone through a difficult trial and doubted God cared for you or that He would protect you during that tough time? Listen to the word pictures God chose once to reassure us of His love:

"He who dwells in the shelter of the Most High will rest in the shadow of the Almighty. I will say of the Lord, 'He is my refuge and my fortress, my God, in whom I trust.' Surely he will save you from the fowler's snare and from the deadly pestilence. He will cover you with his feathers, and under his wings you will find refuge; his faithfulness will be your shield and rampart."

Like a young child standing in her daddy's shadow, a soldier retreating to an armed fortress for cover, or a young eagle seeking the warmth of its mother's wings, we see in those encouraging words from Psalm 91:1-4 pictures of God's love and care for each of us.

Have you ever been so alone that you doubted even God was there? Let's look at a snapshot from a trip someone took centuries ago down the dimly lit road of doubt.

"Where can I go from your Spirit? Where can I flee from your presence? If I go up to the heavens, you are there; if I make my bed in the depths, you are there. If I rise on the wings of the dawn, if I settle on the far side of the sea, even there your hand will guide me."

Those reassuring words from Psalm 139:7-10 show us that no matter where we go or how lonely we feel, we can never lose God's presence or His ability to lead us through whatever situation we find ourselves in.

Have you wondered if God really deals with the Castros, Khadafis, and Saddam Husseins of the world? Gaze at this picture from the hand of the prophet Isaiah:

"Do you not know? Have you not heard? . . . He brings princes to naught and reduces the rulers of this world to nothing. No sooner are they planted, no sooner are they sown, no sooner do they take root in the ground, than he blows on them and they wither, and a whirlwind sweeps them away like chaff."[14]

Whether the issue is depth to our prayers, help for our doubt, or aid in our fears, Scripture uses word pictures time and again to bring comfort and encouragement.

Even on the last night of Christ's earthly life, He employed word pictures to make sure the disciples knew of His Father's care and provision for them. While they were in the Upper Room, not only did Jesus promise the presence of a great Counselor who would come alongside them, but He also told them, "In my Father's house are many rooms; if it were not so, I would have told you."[15]

So far, we've seen that word pictures can draw us closer to Christ, help us grasp and remember key biblical truths, and give us hope and encouragement. But one more fact stands out as an important reason for Christians to use them regularly. Just like Jesus, we need to be able to translate the gospel into a picture that can span even the greatest differences.

4. Word Pictures Provide a Powerful Tool for Evangelism.

A welder used his welding tools as visual aids in helping a co-worker come to know Christ. Both men understood how important a good welding job would be on a key stress point of a building. By explaining about how Christ is the only one who can weld our lives together without having the seams come apart, the welder led his friend to the Lord.

An airplane mechanic used an "unsafe plane" illustration to confront a fellow worker with his sins and lead him to the Savior. Time and again, the everyday objects, stories, and remembrances drawn from the wells we write about in chapters 7-10 have been used for deeper communication between people—and between them and God.

Just ask those on the mission field how important it is to use word pictures in communicating spiritual truth. They'll tell you stories like Don Richardson's, which he captured in his exceptional book, *Peace Child*.[16]

Don was laboring among the Sawi tribe of Indonesia, struggling to communicate the gospel. Yet to this savage band, known for their human sacrifice and even cannibalism, he seemed to be going backward rather than forward.

They had accepted him warily into their midst because of the tools, medicine, and farming skills he brought, but they weren't interested in what he said about Jesus—until he told them about Judas.

When he recounted the story of Judas's betraying Christ around the tribal fire one night, suddenly the tribesmen became agitated and even cheered and shook their spears. Little did Don know that in their culture, treachery was admired. Tricking an enemy into thinking you were his friend—and then killing him—was considered one of the greatest warrior skills!

Don was totally frustrated that in all his months of labor, the only reaction he had gotten from these men was cheers for Judas, not praise for Jesus. But that's when God opened his eyes to an enormously effective word picture.

This culture had a custom Don had heard about. If war broke out between neighboring tribes, they had one sure way to restore peace. The chief of one tribe was to take a young child from among his people and give it to the chief of the opposing tribe. Then, as long as that child lived—*that peace child*—there would be a truce between the tribes.

At last, Don had his entry point into this culture that so needed Christ. And that night around the tribal fire, he told the natives about how God and all people struggle because of sin, and of the war inside them as a result. Then he told them about God's Peace Child—Jesus Christ—and how He lives forever to make peace between God and humanity.

In Don's stirring book, you can read about the evangelistic fervor that broke out in that tribe, and in neighboring tribes, when the people received a picture of God's love they could understand.

It's not only on the mission field that word pictures can help spread the good news, either. For years, Campus Crusade for Christ has used its "The Four Spiritual Laws" booklet as a witnessing tool, complete with drawings and even an explanation of the Christian life showing the "locomotive" of facts pulling the "caboose" of our feelings. This small tract, basically an extended word picture, has helped thousands find Christ.

From evangelism to discipleship, from encouragement to correction, word pictures help us strengthen our own spiritual lives. And perhaps as an added benefit, they can help us pass that life on to others.

As we close this chapter, we'd like to tell you about a final word picture used by one of the greatest preachers of all time. Charles Haddon Spurgeon died in 1892, but even now, one of the best compliments a preacher can get is for someone to say he preaches like Spurgeon.

While the printed messages of other great orators are gathering dust, Spurgeon's sermons are still read—and *preached*—today. And it should come as no surprise that his sermons were full of word pictures aimed at his listeners' hearts.

Several books of his works remain in print, but a story about him recounted on Paul Harvey's radio program just before one Easter is our personal favorite.

It seems that Spurgeon was struggling with his Easter sermon one year, and even as late as the Saturday before, he was walking the

streets of London, trying to capture just the right phrases and illustrations.

That's when he saw a young boy walking by who was one of the
city's many street children. This rough, ill-clothed lad was carrying an old, bent bird cage, and inside was a sorrowful-looking field
sparrow.

Intrigued by the sight, Spurgeon stopped the boy and asked him
about the bird.

"Oh, this?" the boy answered. "It's just a sparrow, and it's *my* bird.
I found it."

"What are you going to do with it?" the great clergyman asked.

"Well—" the boy said. "I think I'll play with it for a while, and
then when I'm tired of playing with it—I think I'll kill it." He made
that last comment with a wicked grin.

Moved with compassion for the bird, Spurgeon asked, "How much
would you sell me that bird for?"

"You don't want this bird, mister," the boy said with a chuckle.
"It's just a bleeding field sparrow."

But when he saw the old gentleman was serious, suddenly his mind
took a step toward extortion.

"You can have this bird for—two pounds." Two pounds at that time
would be worth more than a hundred dollars today—an astronomi-
cal price for a bird worth only pennies. "That's my price. Take it or
leave it," the boy said defiantly.

Spurgeon did pay the price, and then he took the bird to a nearby
field and let it go. . . . But he wasn't finished with the cage.

The next morning, at the great Metropolitan Tabernacle where he
preached, an empty bird cage sat on the pulpit as people took their
seats.

"Let me tell you about this cage," Spurgeon said as he began the
sermon he had stayed up late rewriting. Then he recounted the story
about the little boy and how he had purchased the bird from him at
a high cost.

"I tell you this story," he said, "because that's just what Jesus did
for us. You see, an evil specter called Sin had us caged up and unable
to escape. But then Jesus came up to Sin and said, 'What are you going
to do with those people in that cage?'

"'These people?' Sin answered with a laugh. 'I'm going to teach
them to hate each other. Then I'll play with them until I'm tired of
them—and then I'll kill them.'

"'How much to buy them back?' Jesus asked.

"With a sly grin, Sin said, 'You don't want these people, Jesus. They'll only hate You and spit on You. They'll even nail You to a cross. But if You do want to buy them, it'll cost You all Your tears and all Your blood—Your very life!'"

Spurgeon concluded, "That, ladies and gentlemen, is just what Jesus did for us on the cross. He paid the ultimate, immeasurable price for all who would believe, that we might be free from the inescapable penalty of death."

How about you? Has there been a time in your life when you responded to what Jesus did for you on the cross? Has there been a specific moment when you know you trusted Christ as the only way out of the cage of death?

Our prayer is that all who pick up this book will find the word pictures in Scripture to be a light to their path—a guiding light leading them out of the cage of death and into the wonderful freedom and everlasting life of a deep, personal relationship with Jesus Christ.

CAN WORD
PICTURES
BE MISUSED?

16
The Dark Side of
Emotional Word Pictures

W E HAVE DEVOTED almost all of this book to the benefits of using emotional word pictures. Frankly, our heart's desire would be to quit right here, without looking beyond their positive side. But no matter how powerfully word pictures can launch emotional arrows right to a person's heart, they are powerless with certain people who seem to wear three-inch-thick, tungsten steel armor.

Not only will such people deflect word pictures—even those offering praise or encouragement—but they'll also often pick up the same arrow, turn it into a flaming dart, and shoot it back at us.

With all the power word pictures have for good, they also have an evil twin that can't be ignored. Mastering word pictures can be extremely advantageous to a relationship. But put in the wrong hands, they can be very dangerous.

As we began our historical research of emotional word pictures, we noticed a disturbing pattern. Namely, some of the most destructive people throughout the ages have, in large part, brought about that damage through word pictures.

Such individuals are often infamous for the human carnage they've caused. But some of the most damaging individuals we've known have never fired a gun or incited a riot. They've simply used the power of words to break down and destroy marriages, families, friendships, and businesses. These people may have never pulled the trigger. But their words have shoved a loaded gun into another person's hand, then pointed it at that person's temple.

Mastering word pictures can be
extremely advantageous to a
relationship. But put in the wrong hands,
they can be very dangerous.

Without a doubt, the use and misuse of word pictures have shown us the absolute truth of the statement, "Life and death are in the power of the tongue."[1]

A faithful doctor tells a patient not only the advantages of taking a medication, but also explains its dangers and possible side effects. In like manner, we'd be remiss not to discuss the potential harm when the language of love is twisted into a language of hate.

At their best, word pictures share praise and correction, improve insight, and develop lasting intimacy and better understanding. They are at their worst when used to control, suppress, hurt, or manipulate others. We've labored diligently to convey the life-changing tool of emotional word pictures. But now we want to warn you. There may be those who will turn this tool against you and use it as a weapon.

The fact that some people can misuse a word picture's innate power to affect lives should not deter us. A concerned husband can get behind the wheel of a car and rush his expectant wife to the hospital; but put an angry alcoholic behind the wheel, and you have a weapon that can kill.

We still drive cars, because of their power for good. But we are aware and cautious of their power to hurt and cripple. The same thing is true with emotional word pictures. We should be delighted to find a tool that can breathe new life into our communication and relationships. But in the wrong hands, like those of *der Fuhrer*, Adolf Hitler, this tool can also convey words of death.

Words of Life, Words of Death

The years before World War II found Germany in troubled economic and political times. With its economy at a standstill, the elected government faced growing discontent from the working classes.

In that unsettled time, one man saw his chance for power. Hitler had grandiose ideas, but he needed a rallying point to gather a following. His restless mind had to find some symbol that could carry him into the spotlight for which he longed and lived.

An obscure man who was prone to fits of depression, he failed to enter the front doors of political power. But he opened wide the back door with a word picture, pulling his countrymen to himself and his radical views.

The twisted picture he painted was of the Jews, a race he described as "evil and slanderous"—a "corrupt" people who had "crept into Rhineland" and stolen the power and wealth from the German worker.[2] The word pictures he so insidiously crafted and so often used were then sold daily to the working class struggling to buy bread in long depression lines. In so doing, he spread unfounded anger and resentment in crowds of unemployed or underemployed workers. These fears and frustrations were like sparks on dry tinder. Hitler then gleefully fanned the flames into hatred. Listen to one of the hundreds of scathing denouncements he used to incite and inflame the nation:

> The Jewish race is a parasite living on the body and the productive worker of our nation. . . . Only when this Jewish virus infecting the life of the German people has been removed, can one hope to establish a co-operation between nations which shall be built upon a lasting understanding.

> The Jews are fond of saying, "Workers of the World Unite!" *Workers of all classes and of all nations, I tell you, wake up and recognize your common enemy![3]* (Italics ours.)

With his symbol of hatred in hand, Hitler was surrounded by a growing legion of followers that shouted down any political or religious leaders who opposed him. The struggling German working class swallowed his reason for their economic and social distress. And the corrupt picture he painted of the Jews became the scapegoat for all Germany's problems.

Hitler's ability to twist people's minds and souls—especially the minds of the young—was, in large part, due to his skills as a communicator. Unfortunately, he's not the only one to wield negative power over others' lives. His evil clones and counterparts have marred every generation before and since. Take Jim Jones, for example.

Echoes of Evil

Have you ever wondered what Jones said to prompt hundreds of people to leave their country of birth and join in a death march to Guyana?

In the early days at his church in Los Angeles, his pulpit would rock with word picture after word picture.[4] He used them like chains to bind and enslave hundreds of men and women to his teachings. Listen to the picture-filled sermon he gave that later proved tragically prophetic:

In my mind, we are at battle. We are a mass of people, so many that it actually dims the rising of the sun.

And this mass is marching and singing. They have enemies who are ordered to fire on them. Their bodies are splintering into the sky. But the people keep coming and will not be stopped.[5]

His control over his followers was so powerful that more than nine hundred people followed Jones' words into darkness. They have not been the only ones to die. Charles Manson's followers did their share of killing. Like Jones, he, too, led a band of fanatical followers on a tirade of death. And he, too, was a master of word pictures.[6]

Cult leaders across time have drawn on mental pictures and mystical symbols, such as Satanists' upside-down cross, that are actually word pictures for their hidden teachings. The same is true of contemporary cults, which have adopted such religious symbols as the cross, rainbow, and oasis to promote their own brand of counterfeit Christianity.[7]

Political and cult leaders have long used word pictures to strangle physical and spiritual life from people. Tragically, there is a much less conspicuous group that does every bit as much damage: men and women who practice their destructive art from within regular homes in average neighborhoods. These people emotionally cripple, crush, and control their spouses and children. The more we read about and talk with them and their victims, the more we see that they, too, are masters of word pictures.

These are people who, in many ways, can't love back. And through their words, they actually endanger the physical, mental, emotional, and spiritual lives of others. Jackie's father is a perfect example.

A Case Study in Words That Control

Jackie grew up in a home that could more accurately be described as a nightmare. Because her family background was so damaging, it's no wonder she ended up in a psychiatric ward.

I (John) met her there years ago when I was in school. At the time, there was something about her I never could understand. I walked right past it then, but at the heart of her fears were two emotional word pictures. Each was a vivid image of cruelty and fear that helped cause her mental collapse and finally pushed her into darkness.

With an alcoholic father, fear and uncertainty were her constant companions. He had a nickname for her that he used constantly when he was drunk and angry: Demon Child. An on-again, off-again painter, her father was addicted to horror films and books, as well as alcohol. The lower he sank as a man, the more "manly" he felt by frightening his sensitive, impressionable daughter with horrible stories.

Most nights, with his cruel laugh chasing her down the hallway to bed, she would lie awake for hours. She was afraid to go to sleep, lest some of the horrible things he said were inside her body decided to come out. Even when she got older and professed she didn't believe in demons, she still couldn't shake the negative scars his word picture left on her self-image. Over the years, as she grew to a young woman, his words burned like sulfuric acid poured on her soul. And then one night, that pain was multiplied a hundredfold.

In a drunken fit, he barged into his daughter's bedroom and robbed her of what little remnants of innocence and childhood she had left. As if the incest wasn't bad enough, he left her a second, terrifying word picture on his way out.

As she lay in bed, fighting back tears of shame and pain, she was told that if she ever revealed to anyone what happened, a curse would be on her. He said the most horrible things would happen to her— perhaps a week or maybe even a year later if she violated their secret. But one night, she would wake up to the footsteps and then the clawing of someone outside her window, coming to get her—someone who would kill her in the most terrible way.

As a child, it never occurred to Jackie that her father was insane. And so, like many other times before, she choked down this latest dose of fear and shame. But she never closed her eyes until morning sunlight bathed each corner of her room.

Jackie did her best to go on with her life, and tried not to let her anguish show. Outwardly, she looked as peaceful as a cemetery, but a war was raging deep within. There seemed to be no place to rest, no place to hide. With no earthly source of comfort, she even tried praying. But as she knelt beside her bed, pouring out the terrible burden on her heart for the first time, she was suddenly overcome with fear.

In telling God her problems, had she just broken the secret and loosed her father's curse? Would the stranger kill her? By night she was stalked by the thought of someone standing outside her window with a knife; by day, by the words, "Demon Child."

On the edge of sanity, she finally told her mother the terrible secret she had been hiding. For a moment, she felt relieved that her horrible burden had been shared with someone else. But then her mother suddenly slapped her and accused her of lying. That pushed her over the edge. Gobbling down a handful of sleeping pills, she sought shelter in the darkness of death.

She survived that first suicide attempt and stayed in a psychiatric ward for two months before returning home to her parents. But within six months, word reached me that she had taken her life. Jackie died a frightened child, more afraid of the dark side of her father than of death itself.

We realize Jackie's story is extreme. It's probably the most graphic example we know of the tongue's destructive power. While the damage in many homes is less life-threatening, there are severe emotional and physical tolls, nonetheless.

Everyday Examples of the Dark Side of Word Pictures

We know a salesman who can't keep a job, in large part, because he can't rise above his father's words from the past. They were spoken after the first and only baseball game his dad came to watch. He may have intended them to "motivate" his son to do better, but they had a dramatically different result.

"You're pathetic," he said, after his son struck out and made two errors in the two innings he played. "You're just a fourth-string player. Don't bother asking me to take off work again until you're first string. In fact, don't bother asking me at all. *You'll always be fourth-string.*"

This certainly wasn't the only cutting thing his father ever said to him. He made a career of speaking damaging words. But the picture of being a "fourth-string" person has stayed with his son for years—the way all word pictures do. And now this grown man can never seem to be "first string" in anything—including as a husband and father.

But he isn't alone. We know a housewife whose mother repeatedly gave her the following word picture:

"Diane, when they're lowering me into my grave, then you'll be sorry you didn't come by more often to take me to the store and tell me what that husband of yours is doing. You'll be sorry you neglected me like a dog at the pound."

Every insensitive demand her mother made was punctuated by the guilt-causing sentence, "One day you'll be sorry, Diane, as they lower me into my grave." Her mother jerked her around like a kite on a string.

Even when Diane would stamp her foot down and try to stand her ground, she would slip into periods of anger and depression. If she didn't run to do some senseless errand for her mother, she would walk into days of terrible guilt for not "loving" her mother as she should.

"You're a bum!" "What an air-head!" "If your brains were gunpowder, you couldn't blow your nose!" Each of us is capable of occasionally saying negative things to our children or spouse that we would like to have back.

Such words, spoken in the heat of an argument, can hurt and punish. But over the years, the most damaging words we've seen aren't necessarily those that are spoken rashly. Rather, the most damaging ones carry a cold, hardened purpose and are used to manipulate, punish, and control.

But what kind of people gravitate to the dark side of word pictures? And why?

Before we express our feelings about the "whys" involved, let's look at the profile of "who" is involved—that person who can't love back and never seems to *hear* the word pictures we share. We're afraid this is the kind of man or woman who could take the communication tools found in this book and use them to emotionally crush others.

We don't claim that what follows is an exhaustive picture of such a person. But we have consistently seen a similar pattern emerge. If it can help you spot the misuse of word pictures, our warning will be well served.

Profile of a Person Who Consistently Uses the Dark Side of Word Pictures

In talking with a great many victims of hurtful homes, we've begun to see a common profile of the person who repeatedly shares hurt, not love. Often he can appear socially acceptable to others, but emotionally that person can be deadly to live with.

In all, we've seen five characteristics of those who twist word pictures into weapons for destruction. Before we look at this list, let us mention again that we are all capable of saying damaging things. To a degree, we may periodically see ourselves in each of these categories. But to persistently find ourselves (or someone else) practicing them as a lifestyle—or to adamantly deny they apply—should raise the warning flag that there may be danger ahead.

People who consistently use the dark side of word pictures jump on your faults but fight off any correction you give them.

At the heart of a person who would use words to punish others is a terrible need to keep the light of correction shining on someone else, not turned toward him or herself. People who tend to be the most destructive with their words are lightning-quick to see the faults of others. But they move at a glacier's pace when it comes to accepting any personal fault or problems in their own lives.

These laser-quick faultfinders rarely demonstrate their destructive talent on outsiders. Their skill is saved for use on those at home. As a result, the near-perfect image they present to those passing the house can confuse and torment those who live within. They can begin thinking that perhaps their home is actually "normal" and that they should be more happy and secure.

Such a person uses word pictures as weapons to constantly correct someone else, but you won't see him using them for praise. If you should dare to correct him, you'll meet the fury of a cornered snake. For if he gave one inch, by accepting one of your word pictures for correction, it would unlock miles of litter-strewn roadways in his life.

People who consistently use the dark side of word pictures often make you feel terrible with their words, and somehow convince you it's your fault.

There is something remarkably consistent about people who misuse word pictures. They are somehow able to slide in the blade of hurtful words and then retract it without ever leaving evidence to incriminate themselves.

For example, take the man's father who called him a "fourth-string" person. We confronted him with his persistent, negative word picture, and he explained it away as a positive, motivating factor in his son's life.

"Years ago, the best coach I ever had told me the same thing! He told me I'd never be better than fourth-string, and I went out and proved him wrong. That's all I want for my son. I know he can do it. I just want him to finally prove to his family and friends that he's a success!"

Sounds pretty good.But not if you press his words. While the veneer might look as solid as oak, his imbedded barbs are as rotten as soaking driftwood. Somehow, when his "fourth-string" speeches were communicated over the years, they didn't carry the altruistic meaning he claimed. Instead, his words made an incision that was so quick and clean, it left his son wondering why he carried around so many emotional scars.

His paltry explanation did something else to his son. It left him hating himself for being overly sensitive, when all his father was trying to do was help him. This poor "fourth-string" son never saw the fire behind his father's words, but wisps of smoke often stung his eyes. Not only did his father refuse to see any fault in his own behavior, but he was an expert at hurting his son—and making him think it was his own fault.

People who misuse word pictures often do so to accomplish a good thing in a bad way. But because they always have the other person's "best interest" in mind, it excuses the emotional knife-marks left in their victims.

People who consistently use the dark side of word pictures often cover a trio of personal problems with words of darkness.

At the heart of most addictions—whether it be to sex, alcohol, drugs, or verbally hurting others—is a trio of personal problems.[8] Namely, fear, anger, and loneliness. It's hard to get a destructive person to come in for counseling. After all, they don't feel the need.

People who are addicted to hurting others include men and women who carry so many personal problems that they're uncomfortable with the warmth of a close relationship. Like a prisoner locked in a dungeon for months who cringes at his first glance at raw sunlight, they stay in the shadows. They are more familiar with speaking and hearing words of darkness than words of light, which make them feel out of place.

People who are filled with pictures of fear and anger, covered with deep-seated loneliness, are prime candidates to misuse word pictures. With their words, they re-create for others their own terrible world of darkness.

People who consistently use the dark side of word pictures often lack the skills of empathy and encouragement.

The housewife's mother who consistently used guilt to motivate her daughter had another characteristic common to those who misuse word pictures. She demanded instant empathy, understanding, and encouragement from her daughter, but was unable to give these things in return.

She wanted her needs met—now! But never once did she see the toll it took on her daughter's marriage to drop everything and rush to meet a petty need. Such needs included getting her an extra half gallon of milk just before her daughter went out of town for the weekend. ("After all, the weekend is coming, and you know I can't get out to the stores myself, and they're all so busy anyway, and you're not going to be here for days, and . . .")

Watch out for those who demand empathy for themselves, but who can never see the glaring needs for comfort and encouragement in your life. As with this punishing mother, they can latch hold of a word picture and use it to control, manipulate, and enslave.

People who consistently use the dark side of word pictures often don't respect legitimate boundaries around your life.

As with anyone who commits incest, Jackie's father smashed down the healthy boundaries between parent and child. He would not only walk into her room unannounced or interrupt her conversations at any time, but he also respected no boundary to her person as well.

This father is a dramatic example (although not an uncommon one, unfortunately) of those who destroy protective fences. Such people often use word pictures to erase any barriers they feel separate them from smothering another person.

The housewife's mother would destroy her daughter's marriage because it represented a fence between her and getting her selfish needs met. And Jackie's father wouldn't even allow the natural barrier of sexual protection to stand in his home.

If you awaken to a word picture crashing down on you, the blow is often inflicted by someone who wants to destroy a perceived boundary between you and them, no matter how healthy it might be.

These five characteristics are the most common and most destructive ways we see word pictures being misused. Please let them be a warning. For the damage that we or someone else may cause can last a lifetime.

A great concern of ours is that people will take this list and go off on a witch hunt. That is certainly not our intent. All of us can be less encouraging than we should be, less open to correction, less sensitive. Yet, if a person has all of these characteristics and manifests them consistently, don't expect to make tremendous headway in confronting them. Do expect them to turn the power of word pictures against you. And do expect them to seek unhealthy control over your life and the lives of others.

After the Darkness Comes the Day

In the society and world we live in, there will come a time when we run into evil people. If this chapter succeeds in warning you of the negative power of their words and word pictures, then our purpose has been met. If it's done nothing but scare you away from using word pictures, we've missed our mark.

In C. S. Lewis' excellent children's series, *The Chronicles of Narnia*, his main character is a magnificent lion named Aslan. In one of the stories, this mighty lion befriends several children.

Two of them have already met Aslan, and the third is about to, but is fearful of the result:

"Is he—quite safe?" Susan asked. "'Course he isn't safe. But he's good," said Mr. Beaver.[9]

That's the way we feel about word pictures. History and experience have shown us that they are too powerful to be tame or safe. But they can be used for good.

We don't want to close the book on a negative note—and we won't. For there is warmth, love, and life that can come from our words and word pictures. In the next chapter, we've personally chosen more than one hundred of the most powerful word pictures we've heard to share with you. Each may be used in your family, business, or friendships . . . or to stimulate your creativity in designing your own.

A TREASURY OF
WORD PICTURES AT
YOUR FINGERTIPS

17
101 Life-Tested
Word Pictures

RESEARCHING THIS BOOK has been a particular joy. In large part, that's because it has involved sitting down over coffee with various couples or staying long after a conference has ended to talk with someone. In many everyday encounters and by letter, people have expressed to us that word pictures have made a very real difference in their lives.

We wish we could include the several thousand word pictures we've been fortunate enough to gather over the years. They're a collection of irrepressible gladness and inconsolable sadness. They're the words of an aged father writing a "blessing" to each of his children and the grief expressed by a grandmother who was far too busy for her children when they were young. They come from a husband who, for the first time, found the words to praise his wife, and from a wife who wrote the book on encouragement.

We've also gathered hundreds of word pictures—springing from business, family times, friendships, and spiritual life—that can challenge a person to think deeply about his or her relationships. We've been moved to tears in reading one word picture, and have erupted in laughter at another. They show the finest qualities of human character and all its frailties.

We hope you've enjoyed learning about this everyday concept with its extraordinary capacity to change lives. And we hope you'll be further encouraged by the sample of word pictures we've selected in the pages that follow.

In closing, we hope to hear from you about a word picture that has made a positive difference in your life. You've been given a powerful tool, and we'd love to know how it has been used for good. What's more, we'd like to leave you with a word picture of our own.

It represents our deepest desires and brightest hopes that this communication concept will enrich your life and most important relationships:

Like the finest apple trees in the land, may all your relationships grow and prosper and bring forth much good fruit. May you stay planted beside life-giving springs of water, and may your blossoms bring forth a fragrance of love and encouragement to others. May God shelter you from storms and keep you forever in His sunlight.

Gary Smalley   John Trent

Today's Family
P.O. Box 22111
Phoenix, AZ 85028

Capturing the Joys and Struggles of Marriage

The Joys . . .

1. My husband treats me like a roomful of priceless antiques. He walks in, picks me up, and holds me with great care and tenderness. I often feel like I'm the most precious thing in our home. He saves the best hours and his best effort for me, not the television.

2. With the kind of job I'm in, I often feel like I'm walking on a desert trail on a hot, summer day. After struggling through the heat and cactus all day, I come to the end of a path and there's a beautiful pool of cool water. At last I'm at a place where I can drink and be refreshed. That's what it's like being with my wife. In forty-four years of marriage, I still feel that being with her is like coming upon an oasis.

3. I'm a ship with brightly painted banners riding the warm, gentle, Caribbean breeze of my husband's love. All through my childhood, I was forced into an unsafe ship and made to ride across the North Atlantic. I was nearly shipwrecked more times than I could count. But with my husband's love, I feel like I've traded ships and sailed around the world. Instead of the fierce gales of the Atlantic, I feel like there's always a steady warm trade wind blowing me to a safe harbor.

4. I felt like an acorn that was tossed into a pile of rocks. I never had the right amount of light or the proper soil, and so I grew into an oak tree that was bent and crooked. But in nine years of marriage, I feel that you've done the impossible. You've transplanted me to a place in the sun where I can at last grow straight and tall.

5. There have been times over the years when I've faced hailstorms that I thought would turn into tornadoes. But like the shelter of a storm cellar, I can always run to my husband to protect me from hardship. He's as solid as a rock, and I know he'll always be there when the storm clouds blow into my life.

6. I feel like the kids and I are a valuable piece of farmland with dark, rich soil that would quickly become overgrown with brambles and thorns if it weren't cared for properly. Fortunately, my wife is like a master gardener. Every day, in many ways, she lovingly nurtures and cares for me. Primarily because of her skills at planting and raising an intimate relationship, we've got a garden that's the envy of all our neighbors.

7. I love my husband because he always makes sure I know I'm the number one woman in his life. He reminds me of a beautiful English setter. His amber coat glows as he romps in the meadow near our house. I know there are other dogs in the meadow—beautiful show dogs, far prettier than I. But he always ignores them and comes back to me. His soft brown eyes tell me each night, "There is no one but you."

8. When I turned thirty and was feeling insecure, my husband gave me just the word picture I needed. When he found me pouting and feeling afraid that he would leave me for another woman, he told me, "Sweetheart, when you live with a brand new, gleaming white Cadillac convertible, there's no desire to rush out and drive a Volkswagen."

9. For me, life is sometimes like waterskiing. The towline is unexpectedly jerked, and I fall headlong. I try it again, only to be dumped once more and left in the water, shivering, exhausted, and alone. Just when I'm ready to give up, my wife lovingly speeds to my rescue. In an instant, she throws out a life line, and I pull myself from the water's icy grip. With her, I am warm, safe, and loved. My wonderful wife has rescued me again!

10. Before I lost my leg in an accident, I felt like any other apple in a barrel. But for a long time after my surgery, I felt like I was rotten inside and out, and totally worthless to anybody else. Yet, my wife has never viewed me any differently. She knows I don't look like everyone else on the outside, but on the inside I've never changed. To her I am unique and complete.

11. My wife's love is like a huge glass of ice tea on a hot summer day. It's cool and crisp and its refreshment restores my strength and quenches the thirst of my dry, dusty soul.

12. My wife and I are like an all-star baseball team. I'm able to field some of the hard-hit grounders, and sometimes I knock the ball over the fence. But if it weren't for her consistency in stepping up to the plate day after day, we wouldn't have a winning season.

13. When I met you, I felt a rush of excitement ten times greater than when the first client walked into my office. We've been married for eight years now, and I've got many clients I get to spend time with. But spending time with you is still the most valuable appointment that goes into my book.

14. I feel like a happy little fox that was running through the woods one day and met a nice male fox. We fell in love, and he's become my closest companion. Despite occasional brushes with hunters and bigger animals, he always protects me. Even when it means standing up to fight for me, he takes on everything that's faced us. In a few months, we'll have a baby fox to care for. My prayer is that that little fox will grow to love his or her dad as much as I do.

15. Life's problems sometimes make me feel like the captain of a sinking ship. Often, the closer the ship gets to going under, the more those around me dive overboard and leave me to save the vessel by myself. I'm thankful to have a first mate who stays by my side no matter what. If it weren't for her and the quiet, gentle strength she always uses to encourage me, I would have given up and jumped overboard a long time ago.

16. When I come home from work, I often feel like a fighter pilot whose jet has been riddled with bullets. It's so great to come home to my wife! Like a dedicated ground crew, she works overtime to bring me back to full strength and gets me ready to soar into battle again. I couldn't do it without her.

The Struggles . . .

17. Sometimes I feel like our miniature poodle. She was once the object of our deepest affection, but now she gets pushed aside. She continually seeks our love but to no avail. Just sitting near us would make her happy, but she's often sent in the other room by herself. I continually seek my husband's love, yet he pushes me away. I wish I could get some attention or even an occasional snuggle.

18. When I was first married, I felt like a beautiful, handcrafted, leatherbound, gold-trimmed book that had been presented to my

husband as a gift from God. At first I was received with great enthusiasm and excitement—cherished, talked about, shared with others, and handled with care. As time has gone by, I've been put on the bookshelf to collect dust. Once in awhile he remembers I'm here. But if only he would take me off the shelf and open me up! If only he'd see how much more I have to offer him!

19. I feel like a little boy's beloved dog. For seven months of the year, he takes wonderful care of me. We play, take long walks together, and shower one another with affection. But when the baseball season starts, he leaves me to play with his friends. He sometimes forgets to feed me and rarely has time for me. He's so busy that he gives me just enough food, water, and attention to make me yearn for more. The sheen in my fur and spring in my step go away, and I dream about how wonderful it will be to have him back again. I just hope I can wait.

20. I know I can be a roaring flame of enthusiasm, but my wife often hoses me off with her words, and I wind up a dying ember. If she would only fan the fire with some encouraging words or a tender hug when I get home from work, I'd burn as brightly as ever.

Expressing the Joys and Challenges of Parenting

The Joys . . .

21. When I see my daughters and how well they're doing in life, pride swells within me like the snow-capped Rockies above a beautiful mountain valley. It's a feeling like I'm on top of the world. My children have moved away now, and most of the time the mountains stand at quite a distance. Yet, even from afar, looking at them fills me with wonder and thankfulness.

22. Experiencing my daughter's birth was like God leading me to a beautiful sandy beach and showing me an ocean full of future blessings that my daughter will bring. It's all been too wonderful to comprehend, too beautiful to believe.

23. My children are like stars in a desert sky. Each has a brilliance all its own and a unique place in creation. Like those stars, my children glimmer in their own special way and burn brightly with love for others. I hope that for as long as they live they will shine with the love I see now.

24. When my children go out of their way to call and come by, it's like getting an unexpected gift. You expect a present at Christmas.

But nearly every week, I get a card, a call, or a visit from one of my children. It's like getting Christmas presents all year long.

25. I feel like a nesting hawk, carefully feeding and protecting my children. With a keen eye and fine-tuned senses, I gather food and watch carefully for predators who seek to get at them. Tiring at times? Sure. Yet, I've never felt more important and useful. I cherish the demands of guarding and loving them.

26. When I come home from a busy day, I often feel like a woman stranded in a barren desert. Exhausted and thirsty, I long for a quiet, cool, peaceful oasis. My husband and son give me that place of rest and refreshment I need so much, by both their pleasurable company and their sacrificial willingness to help with duties around the home. I feel like I have two angels that are also my great friends, good helpers, and loving encouragers.

27. I love my family. When life makes me feel like I'm trying to bail out a sinking ocean liner with a paper cup, they lovingly pitch in and help. That doesn't decrease the amount of water pouring into the ship, but it sure helps get it out faster! I don't know how I ever lived without them!

28. My family is like a soft, overstuffed recliner, complete with every option and extra the manufacturer has ever made. Their words are warm and soothing like a heating element; their hugs like massagers that ease the aches and pains of life. With them around, I can tip way back but never fall to the ground. After spending time in my recliner, I've got the rest and loving support to keep going. My family is like a soft cushion of love.

29. Because of my children's constant affirmation, I feel like a beautiful, well-groomed show horse. My coat shines and my beautiful mane dances as I parade about. I often go out for a run with other show horses, and many of them feel abused and misused by their children. I'm so thankful for the kids I've got, and the way they reflect even more love than I give them.

The Challenges . . .

30. For years when my son was young, my life was like spending a wonderful time in the quiet waters of a nearby beach. But lately, I feel like there has been a storm that caused the waves to pound the sand with boiling anger. I've been desperately searching for gentle swells and a safe place to swim. But if I'm not careful, no matter what subject I share with him or what I say, I get smashed by the waves and dragged out to sea. I'm so confused. I wish the storm would go

away and we could get back to the quiet waters of friendship and respect we once had.

31. When I begin a difficult day at work, I feel as if I'm building a pyramid of dominoes. Early in the day, I'm able to stack the base securely and begin building. As the day progresses, the pyramid gets higher and more difficult to build. Yet, I'm able to keep it from falling. Finally, I get to the end of the day without tipping any of them over! But the moment I arrive home, one small problem with my children seems to topple the whole stack. I'm ashamed to admit it, but seeing my day falling around me makes me feel like not even coming home.

32. I feel like I'm a book in my father's office library. We are always admired but almost never read. Occasionally we're used as paper weights or to prop open a door. But day after day, I mainly sit on the shelf, my pages yellowing and cracked, my binding coming undone. I need my father to do more than just admire me at a distance. I need him to take me off the shelf and to see what's inside me. He's never taken the time to turn the pages and really get to know me. And that hurts so much.

33. Sometimes I feel like a teddy bear. My family hugs me, tells me they love me, and always comment on how much fun I am to squeeze (I'm a little overweight). I love being hugged, but I can't seem to verbalize my love back to them. I was raised with so much criticism. Maybe it's my personality or the pressures at work that make it hard to say I love them. Maybe it's time for some changes.

34. I feel like a bear that's a month overdue for hibernation. I yawn and wrestle with waves of slumber sweeping over me. I want to crawl inside a nice, warm den and sleep for the rest of the season. But I can't because my newborn cubs aren't ready to hibernate, and I must watch them. If only they'd lay down and hibernate for a week—or even for a few hours—so that I could get some rest!

Telling Someone How I Feel Today

I'm Feeling Great . . .

35. Today, I feel like a path that seems to be straightening out. The brilliant sunlight shines down on it, making the way sharp, clear, and easy to follow. There is more direction and definition to the path than there has been in years, and fewer rocks to climb over.

36. I feel like a tree branching out in every direction—sometimes

uncontrolled; at other times, graceful and elegant. Though my branches sag on occasion, they are full of dense, bright foliage. I've even learned to rejoice when my branches must be pruned. I've found that while it may be painful, God is always a tender, compassionate gardener. He prunes me not out of spite, but so I'll grow and see how much I can count on Him in any situation. I'm thrilled because I feel my roots of faith growing deeper every day!

37. I feel like a green tree progressing through the seasons. Winter sometimes brings cold, harsh people who hurt me. But spring always returns, and with it comes new green leaves. I keep growing!

38. At work lately, I feel like a brightly decorated Christmas tree that gets tons of praise and encouraging comments on Christmas Day. Losing the forty pounds was worth all the work it took!

39. I used to feel like a valuable old chair that was scratched and painted numerous times, and then abandoned in a garage. But wonderfully, God has stripped off the old paint, polished and cared for me, and put me in a special place in His living room. He has given me life again!

40. I feel like a salmon fighting its way upstream, with an occasional stop in a calm eddy of friendship. Those cool waters always refresh me for the next part of my journey into the mainstream of life. With these pools of friendship along the way, I know I can continue to swim for as long as I have to.

41. I feel like I'm living in the country during springtime. The air is fresh, the buds are blooming, the meadowlarks are singing, and I feel great!

42. I feel like a helpless caterpillar, cut and bruised from the pain of life, but I've finally been wrapped in a healing cocoon of love. I can already tell that the wings of a monarch butterfly are beginning to emerge. Soon I'll be healed and more beautiful than ever. I can't wait!

43. I feel like a car. I'm a good basic model but I don't really have many extras. I know that some cars have more flash, but I know I don't need that. I'm sturdy and dependable, and it's great knowing I'm unique!

44. I feel like a beautiful old car that was in need of repair. An expert mechanic has been working to correct the problems. Though much of the work has been painful, I can tell the car rides better already! Change is never easy, but I feel that my time in counseling has helped rebuild my engine and get me back on the road.

45. This conference has made me feel like an empty barrel that's now full of crystal-clear water after a much-needed spring rain. Many

people around me need this water to refresh them, and finally I'm ready to give it to them!

46. As I reflect on my seventieth birthday, my travel through life has been like a trip to a faraway land. It's been full of excitement and uncertainty, which is sometimes scary but never boring. Through it all, I've met many new, interesting people and seen God's faithfulness displayed in ways I never thought possible. I've had a great life!

47. I've just seen an amazing miracle in my dad's life. For years, he's been too busy to spend any time with us kids or his grandchildren. But now that's all changed. Whenever I see him holding my son, I feel like I'm riding on Space Mountain at Disneyland! It's a little scary, but it's so exciting I hope the ride never ends!

48. I feel like a beautiful Clydesdale horse, strong and powerful. I've been carefully cared for and nurtured since birth, and now I'm fully grown and ready to hitch up to life's challenges. I know my parents have equipped me to handle the heavy loads that are going to come in college, and I feel I'm up to the task.

49. I was born with a physical handicap, and when people express doubts about my ability to do something, I feel like a bumblebee. They look at me and say, "Aerodynamically, there's no way you can fly!" But my parents look at me and say, "The way you were made, you can't help but fly!" I've been buzzing around ever since!

50. I feel like a quaint log cabin nestled snugly in a forest that's blanketed by a carpet of silent, virgin snow. A stream gently bubbles its way through the woods, guided by the delicate silver moonbeams of a starlit winter sky. A warm fire glows within, its gentle plume rising into the calm stillness of the night air. I am content and at peace with all around me.

51. A special teacher in my life has taken me from being an ugly duckling to an elegant swan. She saw in me potential I didn't know was there, and patiently encouraged me when all others had given up. Now I swim in life's waters without fear. Thanks to her, I never lose what I have become even though things are turbulent at times.

52. Today I feel like a sunrise. As I pop up over the horizon and cast my light on the land, I'm excited about what the day will bring. As I ride the sky, life explodes in a flurry of activity, and I beam with the challenge ahead. I'm so worn out by evening that I let the moon take over so I can get some sleep!

53. I feel like a glass-smooth lake, reflecting the morning's glory. All around me, life is occurring just as it should. Hundreds of birds rise from their roosts, calling to each other about another day's flight.

A beaver begins his busy day, preparing for the winter that lies ahead. And a doe with her gangly-legged fawn bows gently to the water's edge and drinks in quiet, cool refreshment. All my life I've been too busy to enjoy any of these beautiful things going on around me. Finally, I'm at peace with myself and can enjoy life's beauty.

54. I feel like the guy on the doughnut commercial. With working and taking care of three kids, it's always "time to make the doughnuts." But there's still nothing as sweet as doing just what I'm doing!

55. I just got back from vacation, and instead of feeling like a horse pulling a cart, I feel like I'm a sleek jet—like those in the movie *Top Gun. My* engines are running all out, and I'm climbing to new heights and challenges. As I speed above the clouds, life suddenly seems more simple and more in focus. I can see for hundreds of miles. After only two weeks off, I feel like I'm soaring over those things that seemed so insurmountable when I was stuck on the ground, pulling a cart. I think I've convinced myself I need to take some more time off!

I'm Struggling . . .

56. I feel like a hamster in a maze of hills and dark holes, weary from wrong turns and dead ends. I'm scared I may never make it to the light. People sometimes look down to watch what I'm doing. Some encourage me; others make fun of my plight. I often do tricks to try and amuse them, but I'm always afraid of being rejected. And I never ever feel like I'm one of them.

57. I feel my life is as boring as a VCR tape on constant rewind—the same thing gets played over and over again. At times like that, I want to fast forward to the end and put in a tape with a new job, new house, and new car.

58. One day, I feel like I'm alone on a desert road, with nothing in sight. The next day, I'm on a beautiful path that's lined with trees, flowers, and grass. The sun is shining. It's beautiful! I'm torn between these two feelings—of contentment with being single and still wanting to be married. At times, I really do feel fulfilled, and I enjoy my life as a single. But the very next day, it's as if I'm in an endless desert with no hope that someone will rescue me.

59. As a single, I often feel like I'm standing outside a warm, cozy house full of my married friends who are laughing and enjoying one another. I feel cold and alone. It's not that they won't let me in. I know it's me who has put the lock on the door, not them.

Telling Others How Much They Mean to Me

60. Returning home to you from a trip is like taking a quiet drive in the country after having driven a taxi in New York City for a week. No one is cutting me off or yelling at me. There are no red lights to frustrate me nor any crummy drivers to swerve into my path. Coming home is like driving on a country road where people actually wave because they like me and are glad to see me, not because they're mad.

61. Marrying you was like getting a release from life's prison of loneliness. For thirty-six years, I spent every night in solitary confinement. I now spend each night in a garden of love, with the one I love sleeping next to me.

62. You're as beautiful and delicate to me as the most expensive piece of Waterford crystal. Looking at you is like looking at a work of art, skillfully crafted by masters. Your every facet is unique and perfect in its own way. You sparkle in a rainbow of light, and every day I catch a new reflection of why I love you so much.

63. Being with you is as fulfilling as the first and only time I received a standing ovation from a class of students. As a teacher, I work so hard and rarely get any praise. But when that class showed its genuine appreciation by standing to applaud, it made all the work and long hours seem worthwhile. Honey, your encouragement and loving words make me feel like I come home to a standing ovation. Even when I haven't put in the time and don't deserve it, you support me like the best class I've ever had.

64. Your love is to me what going to McDonald's is to the kids—especially when they get to order all the chocolate shakes and French fries they can eat!

65. Your quiet, gentle spirit is like a delicate, beautiful flower. Sometimes, I get frustrated when you don't open up and share your feelings with me. But I've learned that if I'm patient and wait until you're ready, you'll bloom and share with me in a beautiful way.

66. My marriage is a lot like a raft trip. There are times when I take us down an uncharted section of the river, and we overturn and everything gets soaked. But I never see you complain. I know I tend to go off on a new idea without looking at a map, but you never hold it against me. I know I'm blessed to have you.

67. Though I'm just like millions of other women, when I'm with you I feel like a prize painting hanging in a place of honor in a lovely mansion. I'm the object of your undivided attention and the admira-

tion of all who enter the room—all because you treat me like a priceless work of art.

68. Your love, so solid and enduring, is like a mountain rising out of the plains. I can always look to it, receive comfort from its presence, and know it will always be there. Its beauty moves me. And it's a monument to how much I love you!

69. When I woke up this morning, I got to thinking about your love being like a snowflake. It's gentle, soft, and unique in its every expression. And like an evening snowfall, your love blankets me when I awaken.

70. When I think of our marriage, I feel like Cinderella. Never in my wildest dreams did I think you'd ever want me. Yet, the slipper fit. And life with you, my Prince Charming, has been all I envisioned in my little-girl dreams!

71. My husband's love is like a huge ice cream sundae, *without the calories!* It is sweet and pleasing, and no matter how much I want, there's always more than enough!

Conveying Thoughts on Friends and Relationships

72. When I'm with my friends, I think about the time I climbed Mt. McKinley. I would have never made it to the top of that peak without the help of other climbers. In the same way, I thank God for the mountaintop friendships I have. They have helped me so much!

73. When I'm with you, I feel like I'm sleeping on a warm, comfortable waterbed. I can rest at night, always knowing that you'll be there for me. Your understanding gently rocks me to sleep, and the time I spend with you always leaves me refreshed and ready for a new day.

74. My friend is like a charming easy chair with big soft cushions. I'm always comfortable and secure with her. She's there for me whenever I need her. I know I can relax, take my shoes off, lean back, and just enjoy being with her. I'm so thankful for such a wonderful friend!

75. Dating you is like wearing designer jeans. Your label makes me really proud to be with you. You're such a quality person! And I don't even have to take you to the cleaners!

76. The surprise party you gave made me feel like a movie star who was recognized by a group of fans at the mall. It's a little uncomfortable to be surprised and to be the center of so much attention. But it also feels great!

77. The other day, I felt like a puppy at a pet store—admired by all, cared for by none. I wanted so much for someone to hold me and spend time playing with me. And then you stopped and sat down with me, even though you were way too busy to do so. Thanks for taking the time to love and care for me.

78. My friends and I are like a circus of happy clowns. We do some of the craziest things! We perform so people can enjoy life's all-too-rare moments of laughter. What's unique about us is that when the performance is over, we can take off our masks and accept each other for who we really are. These guys are true friends; I hope we're together for a lifetime!

79. I've got a special friend who acts like a flashlight to me. When I'm lost or in the dark, sure enough—I see his light, piercing through the darkness, coming toward me. Then he leads me home to safety. At times, he even points his light on a problem area in my life that I've been trying to keep in the dark. I've learned to appreciate that.

80. I have a special friend who has an amazing ability to help me overcome my faults. She's like a skilled surgeon, with a keen eye for diagnoses and a sharp mind to wisely discern how best to solve the problem. When it's time for surgery, she soothes the pain with an anesthetic of genuine love and concern. Then, when the surgery is over, she gently closes the wound with tender stitches of compassion. But what I like about her the most is that, like any good surgeon, she constantly checks up on my progress and assures me I'll be better because of the operation.

81. The four of us are like a beautiful set of clothes. Each of us, by him or herself, isn't that glamorous. Yet, God has styled us in such a way that people who see us together admire our beauty and style.

82. When I'm with my friends, I feel like we're on a giant surfboard together, riding the waves of Oahu's north shore. Sometimes the ride gets rough, but we're there to help each other stay aboard. We often catch a great wave and enjoy the thrill of riding it together. When one of us falls off, we all dive in after him. We really care about one another, and it's great to know that even if a shark attacks, someone will be on hand for the rescue.

83. I feel like a seed that contains every God-given ingredient needed to grow. Yet, I'm dependent on others to provide the water, soil, and sunshine so I can sprout and develop. It's been so long since anyone provided me with the help I need that I'm a little afraid to trust others. But I'm not going to give up. I know that one day I'll find some friends here at school who can help me grow.

84. I feel a lot like an old sewing machine. I've been faithfully running for years, but I'm not as fast as I used to be. I squeak more often these days. That's why it's such a blessing to have friends who give me the oil of encouragement and support. With them, I know I have many years of faithful service left!

85. I'm like a mirror, trying to reflect God's image to others. Sometimes that's hard to do. It's so wonderful to have friends who will still love me in spite of my cracks!

Telling Others That I'm Hurting

86. I feel like a carpet that no one notices. I wish people would take off their shoes and appreciate my plush, soft comfort, but they don't. Instead, I get stomped on and ignored.

87. I feel like a computer operator who has spent months devising a special program, only to have the night janitorial crew accidentally pull the plug and lose my work. I've spent six months trying to design a great relationship with my girlfriend, only to find that someone else has taken her and pulled the plug on us. It's going to take a long time for the hurt to go away and to reprogram new friendships.

88. I feel like a daisy transplanted in a vast field of Texas bluebonnets. Those who admire the field don't realize I'm different. Before this, I was plucked from the ground, placed in a pot for awhile, and then planted again. I'm now wilting for lack of water and care, and no one hears my cries for help. Others' roots choke out any chance I have to grow again. Will anyone help me?

Expressing How I Feel about My Job

I Feel Great about What I'm Doing . . .

89. Our company is like the heavyweight champion of the world. Thousands of contenders are trying to knock us off. We're a bit like Rocky and Apollo Creed. It's between rounds; we're in the corner. We're bruised, battered, and bloodied. But we're going to stay in the ring. We're not going to give up. We're still going to be champions when this is over. No matter whom we face, we will never, never, never give up!

90. I feel like a hunting falcon. My company has trained me well.

My skills have been honed razor-sharp. I have total confidence I can do a good job. Let me at 'em!

91. I'm like a baseball team in late September that has a great chance for the playoffs. I've had ups and downs this season, but things are looking good right now. I've gotten my second wind, and I'm going for it!

92. My boss made me feel great yesterday. He compared me to the center on a football team. It's not the flashiest position, but it's just as important as the others. In fact, much of the company's success depends on the center getting the ball to the quarterback. I'd never thought about it, but as the office manager I'm in the middle of the action. The plays all start with me. He said I deserve as much credit as the quarterback for the team's success!

93. As the newest supervisor, I feel like I've been on one of Christopher Columbus' ships for months. I've faced discouragement, fatigue, frustration, and potential mutiny. There have been times I wanted to jump overboard. But finally, I feel as if I've awakened after a night of terrible storms to see land on the horizon, shining in the bright morning sun. At last I can see that the changes I've made were right.

94. I feel like a Labrador retriever out with some duck hunters who are having a great day! Because I faithfully work hard for them, they shower me with praise and affection. I love this! Shoot some more ducks!

95. I'm like an old baseball glove. Though well-worn, I can still catch. With a helping hand, I can handle anything, even a red-hot grounder!

96. My boss told me that our company used to be like a bucket with a hole two inches from the top. No matter how hard employees worked, they could never fill it with water. But since they added me to the staff, the hole has been patched, and we're doing great. And for the first time in years, the bucket is about to overflow with profit!

97. I'm a mechanic. A few days ago my boss paid me a compliment that made me feel great. He said the work I do around the shop is like the oil in an engine. It makes everything run smoothly with a minimum of friction. Without it, everything would lock up. It's great to work for someone who appreciates me!

98. Our company just gave me a big bonus for landing a huge account. I feel like I'm playing a video game and scoring unbelievably well. The better I do, the more free games I win and the more excited I am about what I'm doing. This is great!

I Feel My Work Can Be Drudgery . . .

99. I feel like a beautiful Arabian racehorse that is only used to give kids pony rides. I constantly walk in a circle. Kids kick me when they get on and off. They drip ice cream on my back. My coat is dusty and matted, and my owner doesn't care one bit. The sun beats down on me. My once-beautiful mane is tangled. My head hangs low in shame. I know that the swift, noble blood of a racehorse is within me. If I only had the chance to be free from this drudgery, then I could show what I'm capable of doing.

100. I feel like a tube of toothpaste. By the end of the day people have squeezed everything they can out of me. My work has really helped the company, and I know I'm appreciated for that. Yet, nobody seems to care that I'm empty and gnarled up inside.

101. The Super Bowl is over and the players file into the locker room. Dirty uniforms are thrown on the floor, along with dirty socks and muddy cleats. The players shower and slowly file out, leaving me behind. Not only do I have to clean up the mess, but no one even knows I'm here doing it.

Love Is
a Decision

*The material in this book is based largely on the
"Love Is a Decision" Seminar, and its success is due largely
to the efforts of Terry Brown, our national seminar director.
This book is gratefully dedicated to*

Terry

*Without knowing it, thousands of couples' lives have been
enriched by his years of faithful, loyal service
in coordinating the many details for the seminar.
We thank God for this special servant and
for the unique way he enriches everyone who knows him.*

Contents

1
Planning on a
Great Marriage?

IT WAS JUST turning dark when I arrived at the home of a family I was staying with in Tampa, Florida. Exhausted after speaking at a seminar all day, I was looking forward to a restful, uneventful night.

I knew my hosts only slightly, but they lived in a beautiful home in a peaceful neighborhood. But then again, looks can be deceiving. In fact, I would never have expected either event that happened to me over the next few hours.

As I walked up to the front door, I reached into one pocket, then another. That's when I realized I'd left my key inside in my room, and I was locked out of the house. Ringing the doorbell wouldn't have done any good. My hosts had told me they wouldn't be home until late. So I decided to go around to the back yard and see if by chance a window or door had been left open.

As I rounded the back corner, I froze in terror. From out of the dark, a huge black form was racing toward me at breakneck speed. It was the biggest dog I'd ever seen in my life!

Ten feet from where I stood petrified with fear, the dog left the ground with a tremendous leap—and I knew I'd soon be on my way to the hospital. In milli-seconds I'd feel the pain of his teeth tearing into me.

I closed my eyes and braced myself for the collision . . . but nothing happened. At first I thought, *He's toying with me. This dog knows I'm about to die, and he wants to watch me suffer!* But after a moment more, I finally built up enough courage to open my eyes. Unbelievably, he was sitting happily at my feet, his big friendly tongue hanging out and his tail wagging. He was actually whimpering for me to reach down and pet him.

After my heart rate dropped from triple to double digits, I checked the house only to find it securely locked. It was getting late, and I was worn out. I was faced with either camping out on the back porch with my new-found canine friend or thinking of some alternative. That's when an idea hit me.

Another family I'd been introduced to lived in Tampa. Perhaps I could stay with them until my hosts returned. So I jumped into my car and drove across town to John and Kay Hammer's stately home—and into an even more surprising situation.

As I knocked on the door, I was greeted by Kay. "Hi, Gary," she said, flashing her million-dollar smile. She makes anyone she meets feel special and important. I explained my situation to her and John, and they insisted that I stay at their house for the night.

I met their charming children as they piled out of their rooms. Finally, after a little small talk in the living room, we all retired for the night.

My body must have known that my plane didn't leave until the next evening, because it overruled the alarm clock, and I slept late the next morning. By the time I got up, showered, and dressed, the kids and John had already headed off to school and work. Only Kay was left in the kitchen to play short-order cook for her unexpected house guest.

I'd already received one shock when Godzilla the Dog leaped at me, but little did I know I was about to be hit with a second shock that was even more disturbing. As we sat at the kitchen table, the smile quickly fell from her face and down into her teacup. She sat there, her head bowed, staring blankly at the table top. With very little prompting, Kay began pouring out an all-too-familiar story.

For years, this wife had felt neglected. Her husband gave the best of his week to his thriving business, and she and the children were left with emotional left-overs on the weekends. All the family responsibilities for raising four youngsters fell on her shoulders, and she was exhausted from putting out fires between her husband and the children.

At times she would plead with John to work on their disintegrating relationship, but her cries fell on deaf ears. Too consumed with building up his career, he didn't have time to worry about the way his marriage and family were breaking down.

Kay suffered through the "domestic" neglect that many wives do, but with one added heartache. She was a Christian with a genuine faith, but she knew that when her husband went to church it was more for social contacts, not spiritual growth. Slowly, as the years went by, his insensitivity had eaten its way to the very core of their relationship—and had begun to poison her heart.

The Ruin of a National Treasure

As I sat with Kay that day, I felt like I was watching the wreck of the Exxon tanker, *Valdez*. Here was a beautiful home and a stunning family. Yet with disharmony and heartache steering at the helm, their family relationships had been guided right onto the rocks, just as that ill-fated oil tanker had been.

Day after day, the poison of a ruptured marriage poured onto their lives, covering the natural beauty of a loving family with three inches of sludge. They had tried to clean up some of the disaster (which their relationship had become), but in many ways the damage was already done. The kids were feeling the tensions at home and beginning to reflect it in their lives, and any interest they might have shown in attending church was now falling dormant.

Kay had been listening to her friends—even to Christian friends—who told her, "Quit being a *doormat*, Kay. You've already gone through too much. *God will forgive you.* Get out of this mess of a marriage, and try again with someone else." She'd even gone to her pastor at the time and to a "Christian" psychologist. Both had told her that *with her husband* she could never hope to get the ship off the rocks—their marriage was dead in the water and unsalvageable.

"I'm not rushing you to leave, and I hadn't planned on telling you any of this," she said to me at the breakfast table, embarrassed by the tears that quickly came to her eyes. "But when the children come home from school today, I'm leaving my husband. We're all moving out. . . ."

I'd like to say that John and Kay's story is unusual, but, unfortunately, it isn't. In working with couples and families for almost two decades, I've seen many such disasters. They have ruined our greatest natural treasure—our families.

From every appearance, a few rags or suction hoses wouldn't begin to repair the damage that had taken place in the Hammers' relationship. In fact, the more I listened, the more I could see why certain "advisors" had told her the landscape of their life would never be the same. From a human standpoint, it certainly did look like the better option might be to pack up and move on than try to rebuild the impossible. But God allowed something miraculous to happen over the next few hours with Kay that transformed her relationship with her husband—and my life as well.

It's been almost fourteen years since that fateful morning at John and Kay's home. And today the Hammers are not only some of our closest friends, but members of our National Board! Their relationship has changed from oil-soaked blackness to a crystal-clear reflection of Christ's love. Even more, their deep friendship and love for each other is a testimony in itself and has turned back many, many couples from the brink of divorce.

> Without a clear action plan that
> points the way to deep waters of
> intimacy, and avoids the shallow
> rocks of marital ruin, we're
> inviting heartache into our homes.

What brought about the change in their lives? That's what this book is all about. The very verses and concepts I first scratched out on a sheet of notebook paper for Kay that day are the same things I've seen God use in the lives of hundreds over the years. I'll be sharing biblical principles that when applied to a relationship—even one washed up and on the rocks—can turn a mess back into a treasure. Learning specific directions for steering clear of danger can also keep a strong marriage or family from running aground. But change only begins at the place we all must start—at the same point the Hammers had to come to.

Planning to Have a Great Marriage and Family?

Whether it's a family, a school, a company, or a sports team, we cannot possibly guide our relationships safely through the waters of our day without a plan. That's the starting point. Without a clear plan of action that points out the way to the deep waters of intimacy and avoids the shallow rocks of marital ruin, we're inviting heartache into our homes. It's critical that we clearly plan our lives and not let chance set their course.

There may have been a time in an earlier day when society itself delineated boundaries clearly enough to substitute for a clear purpose at home. But that's simply not true today. We're asking for a natural disaster of our own if we don't have a specific sense of direction for our families. And that's what this book is all about. It's our best effort to give you a workable, biblically based plan of action for building loving, lasting relationships.[1]

Now we know that asking you to adopt a "plan" of action for your home sounds a great deal like work, but we can assure you that the effort spent on steering your relationship into safe waters is far less work than trying to get it off the rocks would be.

Can having a clear plan of action really bring that much change? In one case, taking the time to learn and practice a plan of action turned a group of defeated individuals into an undefeated team:

The Man Who Made History

When our good friend, Norm Evans, was picked by an expansion National Football League team, they were mired in last place. The owner knew a change was needed, so he hired a new head coach. But that was nothing new. He had already hired several coaches, and hadn't changed their fortunes yet. With the way the team was currently playing, this young "upstart" he'd picked would probably be history himself within a year.

As it turned out, this particular coach *would* go into the NFL history books—but not as a failure. Today, even with ups and downs, he has been in the league longer than any other active coach—and there's a reason. He built his men into a champion team by following a clear plan of action.

The year prior to this coach's arrival, the team had a record of three wins and ten losses. Morale was down, motivation was low, and the players' efforts on the field were lack-luster. Norm remembers standing along the sideline with the other players, wondering how they were going to lose each game they played.

Then the new coach arrived in town, and he wasted no time in getting down to business. His first official act was to call a team meeting—and it was one the players would never forget.

He walked into the room, folded his arms, and stood silently in front of them for several minutes. The moments seemed to stretch into hours. He looked from player to player, and from eye to eye.

Finally, he spoke in a clear, convincing voice and said, "Men, you're going to be champions of the NFL."

There was an awkward moment of silence in the room. Several of the veterans had to lower their heads to keep their smiles from breaking into laughter. *Sure, coach . . .* they thought. *Anything you say. . . .* But inside they were thinking, *Who's this guy kidding? We've always been losers in this league. Champions? We're not even challengers!* Then the coach laid out the reason he felt certain the team would be successful—a clear plan of action.

"*First,*" he said, "we're going to give you a great game plan each week that works. I'll guarantee that you'll know more about the person you're playing against than anyone except his wife. *Second,* you're going to *practice* that plan until it becomes a natural part of you. *Third,* you're going to *learn the game plan and practice it—and win.*"

Bit by bit, the next season saw the wisdom of his strategy unfold. The players learned a specific plan and then practiced it over and over until they felt a confidence in themselves and between each other that they'd never had before. Now they stood on the sidelines wondering how they were going to *win* games—not lose them. In just one short year, they were a different football team. How different?

It was exactly the reverse of the year before; they came out of the blue to win ten games and lose only three. And the next two seasons, the Miami Dolphins, under head coach Don Shula, won the 1972 and 1973 Super Bowls as the best team in pro football.

"That's a great story if you're a football team," you may say, "but the only similarity our marriage has to an NFL team is that we're always taking cheap shots at each other!" Can having a "plan" really make that much of a difference in a marriage relationship—or even with our children? It did for John and Kay.

Kay Hammer didn't know much about the pro football team in nearby Miami when we sat down that morning, but she still had something in common with them. For years, she and John had let circumstances and the emotions of the moment call all the plays in their relationship—and their lives were on the brink of a last place finish as a result. Yet like this pro team, things started to turn around in their lives once they began to follow a clear plan of action and to practice it consistently.

That morning at the Hammers' breakfast table, I scribbled out for her several biblical principles that I was only then beginning to understand and apply in my own home. The scriptural guidelines that broke through that day and gave Kay hope are the very same ones I'll be sharing with you in this book.

A Marriage Mended . . .

By applying these principles, Kay was able to see her marriage turn around in as dramatic a fashion as I've ever witnessed. Her marriage was doomed for the ashheap of divorce, but because of her willingness to follow a biblically based plan, it's alive, active, and growing today. The man she once couldn't wait to get away from is now her best friend . . . and the one with whom she wants to spend the rest of her life.

The secret doesn't just belong to John and Kay—it's available for everyone who desires to have a strong family and a fulfilling marriage. I look forward to the years ahead and get excited about what can happen in families all over this country. I'd love to see hundreds of thousands of husbands, wives, and children make a commitment to do whatever it takes to honor God by following a clear plan for family intimacy. I believe it can happen; in fact, that's the whole goal of our ministry! One of the places you can start is by putting a biblical plan for relationships into action.

To keep our relationships off the rocks, we need to follow two essential steps: we must gain *knowledge* and then *skills* at applying what we've learned. The more we *learn* and *practice* what we've learned, the more gifted we'll become at developing intimate relationships within our homes. In the chapters that follow, we're going to open God's Word and see what He says about making our relationships strong and fulfilling—beginning with the very foundation of a successful family.

Keys to Building Loving, Lasting Relationships

In the next two chapters, we're going to discover that to have any loving and lasting relationship, we must understand:

- *Honor is at the heart of all healthy relationships—and*
- *Genuine love is a decision . . . not a feeling.*

Are you tired of your feelings of love going up and down like a roller coaster? I'll share with you how you can develop a love that remains consistently strong from season to season, year to year. Contrary to popular belief, love is actually a reflection of how much we "honor" another person—for at its core genuine love is a decision, not a feeling.

Second, you'll see that love can best be put into action by mastering and practicing specific skills like:

- *Recognizing the incredible worth of a woman*

I'll spend an entire chapter helping men in particular see how incredibly valuable women are. In particular, we'll see how God seems to have designed within a woman the very talents that can make her an invaluable resource in the home.

- *Learning how to energize our mates in sixty seconds*

One key to loving relationships is the ability to step in when our loved ones are hurting or discouraged. In this section of the book you'll see a method Christ often used with His disciples and others that can help you reach out to those who are facing discouragement, frustration, or a loss of energy.

- *Keeping a major destroyer of relationships out of our homes*

There is a killer lose in many homes today. It can take the life out of a relationship. One thing that I shared with Kay was how to keep the destructive "tapeworm" of anger out of relationships, and how to re-open the spirit of a loved one who may be closed to you.

- *Understanding the tremendous value of a man*

While many couples don't realize it, a man is not a "second class citizen" when it comes to the ability to have strong, lasting relationships. In this section of the book, you'll discover how to tap into a man's God-given gift for nurturing which can form the basis of genuine love. In fact, you'll see in detail four specific skills with which each man comes "naturally" equipped. These can make a tremendous difference in his relationships. *These same four skills are ones a wife must also master to see her relationships deepen and grow as well,* and they include:

- *Providing security to see a marriage bloom and grow*

If a relationship was like a plant, then security would be the sunlight it needs to grow strong and true. In this section, you'll see not only the results of insecurity, but how to build—or re-build—trust and hope in a home.

- *Uncovering a crucial key to meaningful communication*

For everyone who has ever felt misunderstood, there is a way to communicate with our loved ones that provides the greatest understanding—and the least negative reaction. This communication method is used throughout the Scriptures for praise, correction, deeper understanding, and intimacy—and you'll see it strengthen your relationships as well.

- *Keeping courtship alive in your marriage*

Emotional, romantic times can be a constant part of a courtship—and nonexistent in a marriage. In this important aspect of intimacy, you'll see how to keep or regain the elements of courtship, even years after a wedding.

- *Opening the doorway to physical intimacy*

While many people don't realize it, one book of the Bible focuses specifically on the sexual act of marriage—Song of Solomon. Instead of this important area of marital life being a source of frustration, putting some biblical basics into practice can strengthen a couple's physical intimacy, so that this important aspect of married life is no longer a problem.

- *Discovering how to be best friends with your family*

I've spent years studying and personally interviewing "successful" families, and we've consistently found they share one major characteristic. They've all learned the secret of developing family intimacy in even the most difficult of times. We can use that same secret to draw closer to the Lord personally during difficult times as well.

Kay's life did change the day I spoke with her—or at least she had a dramatic change of heart. But her marriage didn't turn around over-

night. It took consistent prayer, time, and energy as she began to learn
a specific plan of action and how to put it into practice. Even so, the
specific skills I laid out to improve her marriage weren't what ultimately made the lasting difference in her life. Those skills made a
major impact on her husband, but in themselves they weren't enough
to bring the relationship back from the brink of disaster.

Am I saying that her personal force of will and effort to change
weren't enough—even when she learned several specific communication and relationship skills? That's exactly right. You see, if we
set out, in our flesh or with our own "will power," to guide our relationship into safe waters, I can guarantee that the day will come when
we'll fall asleep at the wheel and run aground.[2] If we want to see
lasting change in our lives and the lives of our loved ones, we must
learn to rely on the only Source able to guard us "day and night."

Without question, the most important section of this book —and
of my life—is found in the final two chapters. It is here that Kay
Hammer found the power to put into practice all the relationship
skills she learned—even when she didn't feel like doing a single one
emotionally. For it is only in learning to depend upon the Lord as the
Author and Sustainer of any truly successful relationship, that we'll
find the inner strength to make lasting changes. And these changes
can come—just as they did for John and Kay—by:

- *Learning the art of tapping into the unfailing power source behind a great marriage*

Most of us expect the "gifts" of life—including our spouse and
children—to be the "source" of our life and happiness. In this most
important section I'll show that while husbands and wives can make
great friends and lovers, they make lousy gods. Learning to plug into
the only consistent source of love, peace, and joy is the only way to
have the spiritual and emotional stamina to withstand the storms of
life. And finally, we need to learn how to . . .

- *Turn trials in our homes into lasting benefits for our lives*

"But what if things don't change around here?" "But you never met
my husband!" "But you never tried to live with my wife!" "But *your*
kids weren't born with a naturally rebellious spirit!"

In every relationship, there are roadblocks that can seem to stand
so high they block out any hope of our ever getting past them to in-

timacy and oneness. And yet in this last section of the book, *you'll see that even the problems we face can do nothing but benefit our lives.* Even more, they can provide a consistent source of deeper love and sensitivity to pass on to others.

Much of the material in this book comes mainly from the "Love Is a Decision" video and film series which, in turn, is based on much of what John Trent and I do in our conferences. It also includes concepts from other books Dr. John Trent and I have done together as well as books I have written individually. Therefore, if you've had the opportunity to read some of the other books we've written, you may recognize some of it as familiar ground. However, in this book's unique format, I've had the opportunity to rewrite and update almost all the major concepts we share at our marriage and relationships seminar. John and I are only able to do eight to ten "Love Is a Decision" seminars a year, but by providing this information for you in this way, I hope it will give you a comprehensive look at what we teach in a way no single book we've done before could ever do.

It's a scary thought that the twenty-first century is right around the corner. And with a new century breathing down our necks, it's unfortunate that most of us don't have a plan for next week, let alone a plan for the next century.

I hope you're different. I hope you'll work at learning and practicing a plan—any plan—that is based on the Scriptures and grounded in His love. If you do use this book as a guideline, it's my prayer that it will be one of the most sensible, down-to-earth books you've ever read. I also hope that once you've read it, you and those you love will never be the same.

I earnestly pray that spending time in these pages will cause you to fall more deeply in love with God and His Word. As a by-product, I hope that loving God and His Word more deeply will then give you practical tools for constructing a mirror image of God's love to reflect to your family. That building process begins in Chapter 2, where we'll discover that all relationships begin with an essential element to a fulfilling life.

2
The Foundation for All
Healthy Relationships

I T IS WINTER in Washington state, and a cold, wet wind is blowing. Smoke pours from the chimney of a small, two-story white house
that looks warm and cozy in the chill night air. In fact, if you were
to come close and peek through the kitchen window, you'd see a
scene reminiscent of a Norman Rockwell painting.

Inside are a father, a mother, and five children, seated around the
kitchen table having dinner. At first glance, it seems to be a portrait
of pure Americana. Like the crackling blaze in the nearby fireplace,
the scene gives the illusion of emotional warmth. But if you stayed
around for a bit, you'd see that looks can be deceiving. For inside is
an emotional chill that can cut to the bone like the northern air
whistling through the trees.

The American dream starts to disappear when the father reaches
over and pops the nearest teenager on the arm with the back of his
hand. The teenager fires back a smart remark, and the two begin their
nightly yelling match. The rest of the children all join in with a chorus of jeers—some angry, some laughing.

That is, all except the smallest child . . . the young boy sitting
across from his father. He sits wide-eyed, his little heart pounding,
watching everything that's happening around the table, wondering
why his mother looks so sad, and wishing things would be different tonight.

But at this home, it's always this way—the smart remarks, the challenging looks, the unbridled anger. In most homes, there is a soft side
and a hard side to life. But for this little boy, there's just one side of
life with his father.[1] The cold, rough side that recalls his Dad deck-
ing one of his older brothers in anger . . . but never his giving him or
his mother a hug.

Before turning away from the window, we see the father jump up from his chair and slap his napkin down on his plate.

"I never get any respect around here!" he shouts. "I'm leaving!"

"Yea, go ahead! *Get outta here!*" the kids shout back, laughing and taunting their father as he stalks out of the room. But for the little boy, it's been another night of conflict and confrontation at the dinner table, and another layer of painful memories to cover his soul . . . memories that are as vivid today as they were almost forty years ago. . . .

I hope this story doesn't bring back personal memories of a hurtful home for you; but it certainly does for me. For that little boy watching wide-eyed at the dinner table, getting all the wrong messages about family relationships, was me.

Over the years, I've thought quite a bit about what happened in my home growing up. Even as a child, I knew something was very wrong. There always seemed to be something missing from our family that kept us intimate strangers—always together but forever apart. For years, however, I had no idea what it was!

Have you ever wondered at times about the missing ingredient in your own relationships? Have you ever been so hurt that you've felt like throwing up your hands in despair? Have you looked at marital or family unity like candy inside a broken gumball machine—taking nickel after nickel after nickel—but never putting intimacy within your grasp?

Join the club. Most of us—even those from very loving homes and happy marriages—have experienced times when our most important relationships were difficult or unfulfilling. Why is it that the intimacy we want so often seems to be just out of reach?

At times, some of us have felt like John and Kay Hammer in Chapter 1—that the answer to all our family's problems is close at hand. Perhaps she's staring us right in the eye, or he's sitting across the table from us or even sleeping next to us at night. If only "that child or spouse" would change and begin meeting some of our expectations, finally our family life could be all it should be!

The Age-Old Mistake

It's easy for us to get excited about *another* person's need to change. For years, I was like a husband I once heard about. In his personal devotions he was reading Proverbs 31, the section in the Bible that gives a picture of a practically perfect wife. During the course of an average day, this far-from-average woman buys and sells land, feeds the poor, prepares scrumptious meals for the entire household, hand-sews each child's wardrobe, and basically leaps over tall buildings with a single bound.

The more he read about this godly woman, and the more virtues that piled up about her, the more frustrated this husband became with his own wife. Finally, his emotions reaching the boiling point, he picked up his Bible (making sure he kept his finger on the verse to mark his place), and stomped off to find the "source" of all his problems.

Finding her sitting at the kitchen table, he laid the Bible down in front of her and pointed his finger repeatedly at the verses he'd been reading in Proverbs.

"Honey, do you know about this section in the Bible?" It was less a question than a threat.

She glanced nonchalantly at the open Bible in his hand, recognizing the passage.

"Yes," she said, "I know about that section."

After waiting, unrewarded by any further response, he continued, "Look, I know you want to be a godly person, and if you knew about this section. . . ."

Lifting an eyebrow, she repeated more firmly, "Listen—I *know* about that section."

Then straightening up to his full stature, towering over her as she sat at the table, he said, "If you *know* about this section, how come you don't get up every morning and make me a hot meal?"

"Dear," she said, "if you want a hot meal, *light your cornflakes on fire!*"

By most people's standards this couple might be classified in the "highly strained" category. The story still points up a key problem in many homes. For years I felt that if only my wife Norma would change, every problem in our relationship would disappear. And during all that time, Norma was feeling exactly the same way I was— with one exception. She wanted *me* to change and then marital intimacy would finally be within reach.

But a funny thing happened on our way to changing each other. As much as I pushed Norma to change, and as much as she pulled me, neither one of us ever budged an inch—and neither did our relationship. For many reasons that we'll look at later, when our best efforts go into trying to change another person, we seem to reap the worst relationship rewards.

It's like the wife who noticed the new neighbors who moved in across the street. Every evening, she peeked through the curtains and watched as the husband came home from work.

She couldn't miss the fact that nearly every night, this man would bring home flowers or a little gift for his wife. She'd run to greet him as he got out of the car, and he'd hand her a gift. Then they'd hug and kiss until they had walked inside and closed the door behind them.

> God's Word contains the only genuine blueprint for successful relationships, both with Him and others.

One night, after weeks of watching this same gushy scene repeated over and over, the poor neighbor woman finally reached the breaking point. The moment her husband walked in the door, she said, "Have you noticed we have new neighbors across the street?"

As he dropped his briefcase on the floor and fell into the easy chair in front of the television, he replied, "Yeah, I've noticed we have new neighbors."

"But have you noticed what they *do* every night?"

"No, dear," he answered, "I haven't noticed."

She continued, "Every night when he comes home, he gives her a big kiss, he hugs her, and he almost always brings her a special gift." Then she added, "How come *you* don't ever do that?"

Her husband stared at her with a puzzled look on his face and said, "Honey, I can't do that. I hardly know the woman!"

This age-old tactic of trying to get one's mate, friend, child, or boss to change may win a few minor battles, but it never wins the war of unmet expectations. Nonetheless, it was the primary way I tried to improve my marriage for several years.

Looking back now, I deeply regret not having realized how fruitless this approach is. It causes so many more problems than it solves (unhealthy dependency and increased selfishness to name just two). And it forces each marriage partner to be a competitor—not a completer. There have been many times I've wished I could have those years back.

Had I been wiser, Norma and I could have been spared dozens of painful, unnecessary discussions. If only I'd been aware that God had a plan for family relationships—and a personal plan for each one of us—I could have stopped arm-twisting and started arming myself with His wisdom on the family.

The Knowledge and Skills
Necessary for a Great Relationship

God's Word contains the only genuine blueprint for successful relationships, both with Him and with others. Yet, for years, I had been looking at the wrong set of plans. As a husband, I based most of my actions on unhealthy family patterns drawn from my past. Instead, I should have been looking to God's unchanging plan for the family where the results would have been far less frustrating and much more fulfilling.

Over the years, in speaking and counseling with thousands of couples, I've discovered I wasn't alone in coming into marriage without the proper knowledge and skills to nurture a growing relationship. In fact, across our country, the average couple spends more than two hundred hours getting ready for the wedding service, and less than three hours in any type of premarital counseling or preparation.[2]

In every state in our country, it is far easier to get a marriage license than it is to get a driver's license! And yet statistics show time and again that even a small dose of training before marriage can positively affect marital satisfaction and outcome.[3]

In talking with hundreds of couples, I've found that my premarital preparation wasn't far from the norm. It consisted of one meeting with a minister who asked me two questions:

"Gary," he asked, "do you love Norma?"

"Well . . . yes," I said. (Norma was sitting right beside me . . . what else could I say!) But now I realize that I really didn't understand what it meant to truly love her in the way the Scriptures describe.

Then the pastor asked me a second question, "Gary, would you lay down your life for her?"

Again I said yes, thinking he was asking if I would throw myself in front of a truck for her, or step in front of a gunman to take the bullet meant for her.

The truth of the matter is, when I married Norma I knew the right words—but not the right answers. I didn't have a plan to go by, and after marrying a sparky, enthusiastic, godly woman, it took me about five years of applying the wrong information regarding relationships to knock the sparkle right out of her life.

Early in our marriage, I could tell we weren't doing well, so I decided to try a few quick-fix remedies. As I mentioned, I tried the "If you'd just change" tactic, and even resorted to the lecture method of teaching her what the Scriptures say about being a godly wife. I never used an overhead projector, but I probably would have if I'd thought about it. Many a night, 99 percent of my dinner table conversations were actually lectures aimed at drilling into Norma what the Bible said *she* should do to make "us" happy.

During all that time, I conveniently ignored the Scriptural words of wisdom that applied to the husband—probably because I had never taken the time to truly understand the concepts behind the words. And to go one step deeper, without realizing it, I was covering up my own weaknesses and feelings of inadequacy by pointing out hers.

The Death of a Dream . . . the Birth of a Genuine Love

Norma kept hoping that I'd "get with it," but I never did. As she saw her hopes for a warm, fulfilling family life slipping away, she felt resigned to a marriage that would never match her dreams.

After nearly five years of watching our relationship grow more and more strained, I came home one day, walked into the kitchen, and greeted Norma with the usual, "Hi, I'm home." But she didn't respond.

"Is anything wrong?" I asked.

I knew from the look on her face and her nonverbal expressions that I didn't need to ask the question. It was obvious that something was drastically "wrong."

Suddenly, I felt tired all over. I had been battling my conscience for years and spent untold energy to keep up a facade of closeness to those at the church. Here I was teaching and counseling each week on relationships, and in my own marriage I felt like a failure. After years of pretending, I knew I didn't need a quick "self-help" gimmick to get through to my wife. I needed the kind of total heart transplant that only God can give. And so I gently put my arm around her and asked, "Norma, what do *you* think is wrong in our relationship?"

"Oh, no, you don't," Norma said, pulling back from me, her eyes filling with tears. "You're not going to get me to share what I'm feeling and then turn it into another lecture on what I'm doing wrong."

"Honey," I said, trying to stay as soft as I could, "I can see how you'd feel that way, and I'm very, very sorry, but could you *please* just tell me one more time? I promise you, this time you won't hear a lecture."

Reluctantly, Norma did share with me the concerns that had been building up in her heart, and while it may have been her one hundredth time to tell me, I had never heard it the way she explained it that day. Little did I know that this single conversation would become one of the most traumatic—yet one of the most significant—moments in our lives.

Norma said several important things that afternoon, but there was one thing in particular I'll never forget. I now realize that the problem she explained that day is one of the most common reasons many couples and families struggle for years to find a healthy, meaningful relationship, and yet never quite reach it. She told me:

**"Gary, I feel like everything on this earth is far
more important to you than I am. . . ."**

"I feel that all the football games you watch on television are more important than I am, the newspaper, your hobbies, your counseling at the church. Gary, I can spend hours working in the kitchen, and you never say a word. I can even farm out the kids to a baby-sitter and have a candlelight dinner all prepared for you, and the phone will ring and you'll say, 'Oh, I'm not doing anything important. I'm just eating. Sure, I'll be right over.' Then you're gone, telling me to keep something warm for you in the oven.

"I'm not saying that your counseling isn't important, but many of those couples you talk to have struggled with their problems for *years!* Taking one night out to spend with your wife isn't going to bother them—but it's killing us!

"It's like I don't matter to you, but other people do. In fact, sometimes I feel that you're more polite to total strangers than you are to me. You'll say the most awful things to me, but never to anyone else, especially not people at the church. . . ."

She went on, but you get the point—and so did I. While it may have been a message that was on continuous play around our house, I was hearing the recording loud and clear for the *first* time.

Before talking with Norma, I would never have stood up in front of a group and said that my counseling or even the nonstop sporting events I watched on television were more important than my wife, but without realizing it, that's exactly what I was communicating to her.

Little did I know that for five years of marriage, I had also been violating a crucial biblical concept which lies at the heart of any strong relationship. Every time I ignored its power to build loving, lasting relationships, I was literally shutting the door to the kind of home and family I'd wanted all my life.

What is this biblical principle that I'd been ignoring for years—and that weakened my marriage as a result? It's a simple, yet incredibly powerful, principle, and it comes wrapped in a single word—"honor."[4]

Honor Is the Foundation for All Healthy Relationships

Without a doubt, the concept of honor is the single most important principle we know of for building healthy relationships. It's important for a husband and wife to begin applying it toward each other. And children to apply it toward their parents, and for parents to apply it toward their children. It even works with friend-to-friend relationships. The results of allowing "honor" to reign can be dramatic and life-changing.

Honor is not only the basis of all our earthly relationships, it's at the heart of our relationship with God (see Matthew 6:19-21, 33). Yet we know so little about it that it's almost as if there's an active cover-up going on to keep it a secret from us.[5] To give you an idea of this crucial concept, let's get a brief thumbnail sketch of what "honor" means in the Scriptures.

During biblical times, the word "honor" carried a literal meaning that has been all but lost by translation and time. For a Greek living in Christ's day, something of "honor" called to mind something "heavy, or weighty."[6] Gold, for example, was the perfect picture of something of "honor," because it was heavy and valuable at the same time.

For this same Greek, the word "dishonor" would also bring to mind a literal picture. The word for "dishonor" actually meant "mist" or "steam."[7] Why? Because the lightest, most insignificant thing the Greeks could think of was the steam rising off a pot of boiling water, or clouding a mirror on a cold winter day.

When we honor particular people we're saying in effect that who they are and what they say carries great weight with us. They're extremely valuable in our eyes. Just the opposite is true when we dishonor them. In effect, by our verbal or nonverbal statements we're saying that their words or actions make them of little value or "light-weights" in our eyes.

When the apostle Paul wanted the Corinthian believers to repent from their immoral life-styles and renew their love for Christ, he told them, "You were bought at a price [literally, with "honor"]. Therefore honor God with your body" (1 Corinthians 6:20).

Every angel in heaven and each of us who make up the heavenly hosts of believers will one day sing, "Worthy is the Lamb, who was slain, to receive power . . . wisdom . . . *honor* . . . glory . . . praise" (Revelation 5:12). In both these verses, honoring God means to recognize that nothing on earth or in heaven is as valuable, as weighty, as significant as He.

But how does the concept of honor specifically apply to a marriage relationship?

How to Bring Honor into Your Home

One of the most powerful statements in all the Bible for husbands is, "You husbands, in the same way be considerate as you live with your wives, and treat them with respect *(honor)* as the weaker partner and as heirs with you of the gracious gift of life, so that nothing will hinder your prayers" (1 Peter 3:7).

In 1 Peter 3:1-2 the apostle states the same idea about a wife's relationship with her husband. Do you want to motivate your husband spiritually? Then the apostle says for a wife to use the powerful shaping tool of "honor" by letting him see your genuine and respectful (or honoring) behavior. Finally, a verse that also communicates the mutual need for honor in a home or in any relationship is Romans 12:10. It clearly states, "Be devoted to one another in brotherly love. *Honor* one another above yourselves."

When I came face to face with the concept of "honor" in a home, I suddenly understood why a major part of my prayer life was being hindered. When it came to Norma, the person who from an earthly perspective should receive the "highest value" I could give, I put a hundred things ahead of her. Work projects were more important to me than my mate, and while it's to my shame to admit it, there were countless times that a mountain trout, a small white golf ball, numerous church meetings, close friends and acquaintances—and almost anything "interesting" on television—took the place of honor which should have been reserved for Norma.

If someone had stopped me on the street or at church and asked me if I loved my wife, I would have answered emphatically "Yes!" The problem was, you could never tell I loved Norma by her place of honor (her priority status) in comparison to a hundred more "important" things in my life.

So right there at our kitchen table, I pledged to change. I didn't realize all the implications of what I was doing, but I had a profound sense that things in the Smalley house would never be the same—and they haven't been.

First, I went alone before my Heavenly Father and asked His forgiveness for my incredible selfishness. I realized that at times many things, even good things like my ministry, had taken on more "weight" to me than my relationship with the Lord. That would have to change. I knew that the first step toward giving my wife honor had to be giving God the place of honor reserved only for Him in my life.

It was hard to admit, but I was coming to realize that the idea of honor was out of balance in my life. At that point, something interesting happened. Almost immediately, I noticed it was easier than ever before to pray and read the Scriptures.

Because I valued too many other things of this world more than my time in God's Word, I didn't naturally dive into the Bible and pray early in our marriage. In addition, I wasn't obeying the command of Scripture to give "honor" to my wife. Today, because of my decision to make God the "weightiest" Person in my life—and my commitment to give Norma the "honor" she deserves—one of the most natural things I do in the course of a day is to pray and spend time in His Word. We'll take time to focus on this important issue in a later chapter.

However, while I had come to grips with the concept of honor in my relationship with my Heavenly Father, like Peter, I couldn't stay on the mountaintop. It was time humbly to go back down in the valley to Norma and ask her to forgive me for the way I'd treated her.

"Honey," I said, "I know that we both want to give God first place in our lives. But from an earthly perspective, I want you to be above everything or everyone else in my life."

When Truth Needs a Track Record

Going to Norma was an extremely traumatic moment for me, and it would prove to be a major turning point in my life and in our marriage. But there was one problem. Norma didn't believe me that day.

I knew I had come face to face with the truth of God's Word, and that my life was going to be different as a result, but she just thought it was more empty words. So she threw out a half-convincing, "Yeah, okay," at my vow to honor her and got up from the table to continue preparing dinner.

It's not that Norma lacked faith in God or His Word. From the first time I met her almost twenty-nine years ago until today, I have always been blessed by her deep faith and commitment to Christ. What she lacked wasn't faith in God, but faith in her husband. She needed a track record of being "honored" from a husband who had never practiced it.

I have to admit that at the time, I didn't know exactly what it meant to put the concept of honor into action in our home, but I knew enough to realize that honor would have to be a daily—sometimes hourly—decision. And I had made that decision. I wasn't going to keep Norma on a starvation diet of praise and three full meals of criticism and unrealistic expectations anymore. I was going to consistently feed her with a nourishing meal of significance and high value in our home.

"Norma," I said, "I know you have every reason to doubt me, but I mean what I'm saying. I never understood this before, and I want to ask you to forgive me for making you think that everything else I'm doing is more important than you. No matter how I've acted in the past, that's not what I really believe."

Our evening discussion was over, and she wasn't dazzled by my promise of change. In fact, because of the five years she had lived with the "old Gary," it took her almost two full years of a consistent track record of honoring acts to finally believe the "new Gary" was for real.

> ## With honor as a permanent resident in a home, there is hope we can restore our relationship with God and with our loved ones.

Norma has never failed to forgive me when I asked her, and she forgave me that day. But she was right to question whether I would actually follow through on my promises. She'd been standing in fifth or sixth place in my life for so long, it was natural for her to be skeptical. It was hard for her to believe she was finally moving to the front of the line.

If you make a decision today to increase the honor in your home, don't be disappointed if your mate doesn't do back-flips until tomorrow or the next month. Remember, he or she has been watching your actions for a long time. They have all your past press clippings cut out and pasted in their memories. And if your previous track record has been less than spectacular—as mine was—emotional scar tissue may cause them to be calloused to your present promises for several months. Hype may sell hamburgers and automobiles, but it doesn't work on your spouse the way time linked with a track record does.

With honor as a permanent resident in a home, there is hope we can restore our relationship with God and with our loved ones. Feelings that have taken years to develop don't change overnight, but persistent honor has the power to win over even the hardest of hearts—particularly as a husband or wife sees affirming actions become a consistent part of a marriage.

Putting Relationships in the Right Order

For me, that fateful conversation with my wife at the kitchen table forced me to get my spiritual and family life in order. In fact, I actually began to prioritize my life from zero to ten, zero being something of little value, ten something of highest value.

I established God and my relationship with Christ as the highest—a ten. On a consistent basis, I began looking at my spiritual life and asking the question, "One to ten, where is my spiritual life with Christ?" "How highly do I value His Word?" "Prayer?" "Sharing my faith?"

Then I placed Norma above everything else on this earth, way up in the nines. With this relationship, too, I often asked myself (and Norma), "How am I doing at making you feel like you're up in the high nines, above every one of my hobbies and friends and favorite sports teams? What can I do to keep you believing you're a high nine?"

How about you? If you were to rate the "honor" quotient of your marriage relationship right now, where would it be? Where do you think your spouse would rate it? Have you asked him or her lately?

You're probably as convinced as I am that we need to give God the honor He deserves first, and then make honor a non-negotiable item in our home, but you may still have questions about how to honor those you love in a practical way.

Let's bring honor out of the cloudland of theory right down to the cobblestone level where we live. Let me share with you three ways to bring honor off the pages of Scripture and right into your home. Each has been life-tested in my home and in the lives of thousands of people at our seminars. It all begins with practicing the "ah-h-h-h-h-h" principle on a regular basis.

Three Ways to Honor Your Loved Ones

1. The "Ah-h-h-h-h-h" Principle

As I've noted, the most fulfilling relationships in life begin with honor. In fact, the Bible says that the "fear" of the Lord—the honor and respect we give Him—is the beginning of wisdom.

The fear of the Lord is being "awe-inspired." For Moses it happened as he beheld the burning bush (Exodus 3). For Elijah the Prophet it came as he listened for the still, small voice as God's glory paraded by (1 Kings 19). And for Peter the fisherman, it was the result of watching Christ calm a rolling sea with only three words (Mark 4:39). In each case, being in God's presence produced reverence and "awe."

In fact, the fear of the Lord is being so awed that you drop your jaw and inhale a gasp, catching your breath in an audible "ah-h h-h-h-h." It's a gasp of reverence mixed with a bit of wonder.

In short, honor is a reflex of the heart toward one who is deeply treasured. It's the conviction that you are in the presence of somebody so valuable it's "ah-h-h-h-inspiring." It's important to realize too that this life-changing attitude doesn't start with a feeling—it's a *decision*; and the *feelings* of "awe" eventually follow.

Picture it this way. Let's say you're a homemaker who has taken a well-deserved winter break from housework. It's spring now, and you've decided to pull the house back in order.

You reach into the pantry and take out a can of Johnson's Wax and begin to clean the parquet floor. You've been working an entire twenty minutes when the doorbell rings. Since you were just getting ready to take a break anyway, you cheerfully get up off the floor you've been scrubbing and head to the door.

As it opens and you look up, there stands the President of the United States in the flesh, flanked by two husky Secret Service guards.

"Hi," the president says. "I was just walking in the neighborhood and thought I'd stop in and ask you a few of your thoughts on my foreign policy."

As you stand there with your wet sponge dripping on your fuzzy slippers, how do you respond? Can you picture the president suddenly showing up at your door to ask a question? No matter what your political viewpoint, having the main occupant of the White House suddenly appear at your doorstep would be cause for a breath-catching gasp of reverence mixed with awe—the "Ah-h-h-h-h-h" response.

Now, I agree that having the president show up at your home for a foreign policy discussion is far fetched, but every day, we see examples of the "Ah-h-h-h-h-h" principle at work. If you've ever been called to jury duty, what does the bailiff say as the judge enters the courtroom?

"Would everyone please rise? The Ah-h-h-h-honorable Judge Wapner is entering the room." It's time to stand up and show ah-h-h-h-honor because someone extremely valuable is about to enter the room.

What do the Orientals do upon meeting someone important or upon signing an important agreement? They bow to each other as a symbol of honor. The gesture means that I have decided you're important and deserve special merit and respect.

Sometimes I walk in the house and see one of my kids sitting in the easy chair watching television. Just for fun, I'll drop to my knees and say, "Unbelieeeevable! I'm actually in the same room with Michael Smalley! I can't believe that I'm living in the same house with somebody as ah-h-h-h-h-mazing as you!"

My kids usually howl, "Da-a-ad." But basically, that is the way you build the "Ah-h-h-h" principle into your relationship. You decide that the people around you—your spouse, your children, your friends, and your parents—are worthy of honor. They are worth an "ah-h-h-h-h-h" on a consistent basis.

Have you ever wondered why the dog is considered man's best friend? As you'll discover in Chapter 5, it's because men, in particular, are extremely motivated by the "Ah-h-h-h-h-h" principle.[8]

Think about the way the average dog greets its owner. Whether you've been gone for two weeks on vacation or ten minutes to the mini-mart, he probably falls all over himself showing his happiness at seeing you. Nonverbally, dogs honor their owners with massive doses of love and enthusiasm. In fact, I'm sure that if the dog could gasp, "ah-h-h-h-h!" when he saw you walk in, he would!

That's probably one reason why men tend to dislike cats. You can call them and they just give you that "Garfield" look of disdain, as if they were saying, "Where do you get off thinking you're valuable enough for me to come running over to you? *I'm the one who gets honored around here!"*

In the book of Proverbs, we're told that even the smallest act of "ah-h-h-h-h" can have a positive effect on a relationship. There we read, "Bright eyes gladden the heart . . ." (Proverbs 15:30, NASB).

Have you ever appeared at a surprise party for a special friend and seen their eyes "light up" when they see you? That same feeling of "I'm really special to them" is at the heart of having "bright eyes." And where do "bright eyes" come from? From a heart that is looking at someone very, very special to us—someone we're delighted to see. Someone we're ah-h-h-h-honoring.

2. Remember That "Ah-h-h-h-h-h" Is in the Eye of the Beholder

When we honor someone, we make a decision that a person is special and important. Biblically (and thankfully), honor was not always something that had to be earned. It was given as an act of grace to someone who didn't deserve it.

An example of this is the verse, "While we were still sinners, Christ died for us" (Romans 5:8). Just like our Lord, we sometimes need to make our decision to honor someone apart from our feelings about that person.

It's amazing how a person's response to something or someone can change dramatically once they've made a decision that the individual is truly valuable. That fact was never more clear to me than after what happened at a special seminar we did that was filmed for a nation-wide television audience.

Jim Shaughnessy is a close friend who has been to several of our "Love Is a Decision" seminars, and he knows that I always teach a section on honoring those we love. Without me knowing it, he planned something for this special seminar that brought about the greatest natural "Ah-h-h-h-h-h" response from a crowd I've ever witnessed.

At most of our seminars, I use a three-inch piece of sparkling crystal cut in the shape of a diamond to give people a word picture of "honor." I usually begin by asking the audience:

"How many of you believe this cut stone is a $100,000 diamond?" A chuckle will ripple through the audience as people look at the crystal. Usually, I have to talk at least one person into raising his hand just so I can continue with the point I'm making. Truthfully, people should chuckle when they hear me put the value of that piece of crystal at $100,000. After all, it's probably not worth more than sixty dollars in any store in the country, but as far as I'm concerned I wouldn't part with it for one penny less than $100,000.

It's kind of like the farmer who crossed fifty pigs with fifty deer— and got a hundred sows and bucks! *It's we who set the value of something.* And that was a fact my friend helped me illustrate better than I could have ever dreamed.

Jim owns a very old Stradivarius violin. Just for the television special, he had it flown in—complete with its own "security guard"! As I began to talk about honor in the seminar, I brought out what looked just like any old, unstrung fiddle or violin.

"This violin is worth over $65,000," I said. I could see by the smiles and nodding of heads that people believed me about as much as they did when I would hold up my "$100,000" diamond. In fact, my holding up the violin didn't produce even one "ah-h-h-h-hdible" gasp in the entire crowd. After all, they could see with their own eyes that it was an old violin. Particularly those sitting close to the speaker's platform could see that it didn't even have any strings.

But as I talked about attaching honor to something, I told them a little bit more about what I actually held in my hand. After all, there are only about 600 violins like it left in the world, and when I angled it so that I could read the inscription inside, and then mentioned the word "Stradivarius," the effect was incredible.

A spontaneous, collective, breath-catching "ah-h-h-h" reflex rifled throughout the crowd. Just a few moments before, it was just an old violin, not worthy of any special honor, but by attaching that one word, "Stradivarius," to it, it suddenly was given a high place of honor by everyone in the room (especially by me as I hoped I wouldn't drop it!).

Remember, people make the decision that something is of high value. Does a Chevy pull up to a Mercedes at a stoplight and gaze at it enviously, wishing it could be a Mercedes? Of course not. Do you think that silver cries itself to sleep each night because it's not as valuable as gold? It doesn't care. *We're* the ones that attach value to a thing—or a person.

Someone came up with a great idea years ago. They decided to take all the old pieces of furniture sitting around in people's attics and garages and call them "antiques." Instantly, people lined up to pay exorbitant prices for all these old pieces of "junk." Then, after spending huge amounts that would make new furniture prices blush, they take home these worn relics and spend countless hours and extra dollars refinishing them!

What happened to all those old sticks of furniture to make them suddenly become antiques? Their value suddenly rose, and that happened for only one reason—we had decided they were more valuable to us. I was aware of this concept everywhere else in life, but I wasn't practicing it in my own home—the most important place for the "Ah-h-h-h-h-h" principle to take root and grow.

Let's say the husband comes home at night and the whole family meets him at the door. Instead of running past him to go out to play or to watch television, he is greeted with a collective chorus of *"Ah-h-h-h-h! Look who's here!!"*

Then, to his amazement, the wife and kids roll out a red carpet runner into the house and as he walks down it, the kids throw rose petals at his feet. Scurrying ahead of him, they usher him into his easy chair, prop up his feet, lovingly hand him his paper, and peel grapes for him, throwing them (at an angle) into his mouth to eat.

What would the average husband think if he was greeted this way when he walked in the door? He'd probably think he was in the wrong house! Honoring actions don't have to be exaggerated the way I've described above. But the attitude of honor does have to be present if our relationships are to grow and develop.

"Hold it," I can hear someone saying, "what if some people don't *deserve* our honor? How can I act in an honoring way toward them when they're not living up to what I want?"

Whether it is a husband or a wife who asks that question about the person they vowed to honor, it takes another question to answer it: Do you want your relationship to blossom instead of wither? If the answer is "blossom," then you can't avoid the issue of honor in a home.

You may be concerned that honoring an undeserving mate will make things worse rather than better. Or you may even be worried your mate will take advantage of you and use you because of your willingness to treat them with respect. However, before you react to what I'm saying and close the book, please try to understand how love and honor intermingle.

I know that God is the only being in life who is always worthy of honor, and yet in His Word we are told to honor others —all others. Children are to give "honor" to their parents. A husband should honor his wife and a wife her husband. We are to prefer "one another" in honor.

Remember, honor is an *attitude* that someone is valuable.

It is not an absolution of all a person's faults, nor a command to be less than honest with who they are. Let me give you an example:

I have a good friend whose father is an alcoholic. I know for a fact that this man "honors" his father by praying for him, encouraging him to accept Christ, and even inviting him to his home consistently.

But "honor" does not mean that he allows his alcoholic father to drive his three-year-old daughter around in his car. Neither does honor dissolve all healthy boundaries in their relationship. There is no swearing allowed, no smoking in the house, and no "teasing" the children. There are times when the father doesn't want to play by the rules—and doesn't come to the house as a result. But he knows and has even admitted—in spite of his complaints—that his son "honors" and even loves him.

"Honor" doesn't cast pearls before swine—but neither does it mean that you treat a person like a swine until he measures up to your standards.

If you're in the situation of having to "honor" a difficult person, you may want to go deeper into several books that John Trent and I have written on this subject and can also recommend.[9] Without exception, be sure to read and absorb everything I cover in Chapters 13 and 14 in this book.

The material in these chapters (on tapping into the very power source of love) will be especially helpful for you. There you will find the secret to really enjoying life in spite of difficult circumstances. The concepts found there are also absolutely crucial for working through the fear of "What if they won't change?"

There have been times when I have been motivated to honor Norma not out of my "feelings," but as an act of my will and in obedience to God's command that I do so. And consistently, once I put honor in its right place, positive, loving feelings will follow.

Is this some type of psychological trick or basis for manipulation? Hardly. It's actually a biblical principle:

In Matthew 6:21 Jesus said, ". . . for where your treasure is, there your heart will be also." In other words, when it comes to our spiritual life, what we treasure—what we place high value upon—is where our feelings reside. The same thing is true in my relationship with my spouse. If I "treasure" or honor a person, my positive, warm feelings about him or her begin to rise correspondingly.

I realize that it isn't always easy to keep one's thoughts and feelings at the "honoring" level. As a wife, you might begin to grumble

about the little things your husband does that irritate you. There's
the trash can that only gets taken out when you remind him for the
tenth time, or the way he remembers to fill up his car but always
forgets to check out yours. As a husband, you may be frustrated with
her weight or her discipline of the children or even with the way she
drives at night.

But if an attitude of dishonor is allowed to develop or turn destructive, it's a short step to attaching negative feeling to that *person*,
instead of his actions. When men (or women) begin a pattern of consistently dishonoring their spouses—even if it's only in their minds—
within a matter of a few weeks they can lose nearly all their loving
feelings for them.

That's when you begin to hear the comments, "Why did I pick this
guy?" or "Of all the fish in the sea, I got stuck with her!" That's also
where small acts of irritation—like squeezing the toothpaste tube
from the wrong end—can end up being "grounds" for divorce.

But the opposite is true as well. Time and again, when honor begins to take root in a home, within a matter of a few days or weeks,
your feelings will start to change. Your husband may seem like a
beat-up old violin, but the moment you begin treating him like a
Stradivarius, your world and his can change for the better.

There is a third way to keep honor inside your home. We must
concentrate on keeping dishonoring acts—even minor ones—outside
of our experience.

3. It's Worth the Hard Work to Keep Dishonoring Actions at Arm's Length

It takes time for honor to take root in our lives, and before it does,
all of us are capable of the type of thing I used to do. It violated this
crucial principle.

As is typical of all small children, every now and then they need a
little "motivation" to behave. Ours were no exception. When the
need arose for discipline, I'd often take my thumb and middle finger
and "flick" them on the head.

"Greg," I'd say, and flick him on the head, "turn off the television!"
or "Michael," flick, "stop bothering the dog."

One night we were in a restaurant, and the kids were acting up.
As usual, I reached across the table and flicked my daughter on the
head to get her to stop pestering her brother.

"*Gary*, " Norma said, in an icy tone, "we're in a restaurant. Is this
any kind of place to flick your daughter?"

Her reaction startled me. After all, flicking my kids had become such a habit, I never stopped to think it was dishonoring, so I turned to my daughter and asked, "Kari, how does it make you feel when I flick you?"

"Daddy, I don't like you flicking me." Without an invitation to comment, my two boys quickly agreed.

"Yeah, Dad. We don't like you flicking us *either*." Norma didn't say anything at this point because I had never flicked her.

Right there I decided to quit flicking the kids, but I knew that since it was a habit, I'd need some incentive to remind me not to dishonor them. So, after thinking about it for a minute, I said, "I'll tell you what, kids. I don't want to dishonor you any more by flicking you. Will you forgive me?" They nodded their heads.

"To show you how serious I am about wanting to stop, I'll make a deal with you. From now on, anytime I flick you I'll give you a dollar right on the spot."

Their immediate response after looking at each other, was, "Flick on, Dad, flick on!"

Let's start making a mental list of what we do that can dishonor our family or friends. Here's our current list of the top ten dishonoring acts we have reported to us all over the country. They're not in a particular "dishonoring" order, but all of them can be killers of meaningful relationships.

The Top Ten Dishonoring Acts in a Home

- Ignoring or degrading another person's opinions, advice, or beliefs (especially criticizing another person's faith)
- Burying oneself in the television or newspaper when another person is trying to communicate with us
- Creating jokes about another person's weak areas or shortcomings (Sarcasm or cutting jokes act like powerful emotional word pictures and do lasting harm in a relationship.)[10]
- Making regular verbal attacks on loved ones: criticizing harshly, being judgmental, delivering uncaring lectures
- Treating in-laws or other relatives as unimportant in one's planning and communication
- Ignoring or simply not expressing appreciation for kind deeds done for us
- Distasteful habits that are practiced in front of the family—even after we are asked to stop

- Overcommiting ourselves to other projects or people so that everything outside the home seems more important than those inside the home
- Power struggles that leave one person feeling that he or she is a child or is being harshly dominated
- An unwillingness to admit that we are wrong or ask forgiveness

I don't want my wife or children to feel any less loved than God would have them be in my home, and that means that honor must become an everyday activity in my life—like shaving or taking time out for meals. How about you? Are you ready to turn loose the "Ah-h-h-h-h-h" Principle in your home?

In this chapter, we've talked about the decision we all need to make to honor others—that people are worth our time and energy! Now, in the next chapter, let's look at the second greatest aspect of any healthy relationship: love. *You'll discover that love is the action we take to communicate how valuable another is* and, like honor, that love is actually a *decision*.

3
Love Is a Decision

IMAGINE THAT YOU'VE pulled up a chair next to me as I sit facing Kay Hammer, the woman whose story began this book. Like me, you can sense the tension around the table as it soon becomes obvious that the only thing standing between her and the door are the words that will be shared during the next few hours.

What do you say to a woman who was clinging to the end of her rope when it came to her willingness to hang on to her marriage? As you sit with me, you'd hear me tell her that she should try once more to hold her marriage together, but you'd also hear reason after reason why she should leave John. You would hear me tell her how important it is that God be given every opportunity to keep them together—and sharing the latest research that shows the life-long emotional pain that children and spouses suffer after divorce.[1]

Kay listened and agreed to stay with John after our conversation. But I never realized that things were about to get much worse for her and her husband, not better. In fact, he did something a few weeks later that even caused her Christian friends to say to her, "Kay, *leave* him. You shouldn't take that from anybody. . . ."

At first it took an hourly decision to stay, but with each day, Kay became more committed to do what we shared in Chapter 13 and especially Chapter 14. She made a decision to respond to her husband out of the fullness of her love for Christ—not the empty feelings she had about her marriage. And the difference in her attitude instantly began to show. But a severe test was coming of how much Kay was willing to seek God's love first, and then reflect it back to her husband. For a few weeks later, he ripped away the most important thing to her in a moment's notice.

Almost Too Much to Take

John couldn't help but notice the change that had come over his wife. Like many mates who see the first blush of change—he tested her to see how real it was.

For two years, Kay's life-line of support had been her Bible Study Fellowship group. These ladies had prayed for her and encouraged her on those hopeless mornings when she was ready to toss in the towel. As a group leader, the highlight of Kay's year was the annual "leaders' retreat" coming up.

She had already paid her money and arranged for babysitting for the children. Kay was less than twenty-four hours away from heading to the airport and the retreat when John came home from the office.

"Where are *you* going?" he demanded, looking around at the suitcases she'd packed.

"To the Bible study leaders' retreat," Kay said. "You know that I leave tomorrow."

"Well, I've changed my mind," John announced. "I don't want you to go. In fact, I think you're spending way too much time with this group. I want you out of that leadership program right now."

Can you imagine the choice she had to make? To stand against her husband and go to the retreat would be to play the same chorus of "I'll do it *my* way" that she had sung unsuccessfully for years. On the other hand, to follow his leadership—and cut herself off from her primary source of fellowship and spiritual support—seemed equally wrong.

What was she to do? This wasn't a situation where she could change the channel and have her decision go away. She could tell John was waiting for her response. What's more, she knew that this was a major test of her "decision" to show him honor, no matter what the circumstances. Just then the phone rang, and she was saved from having to respond to him on the spot.

It was a friend calling to ask if she and John could come to dinner that night with a noted pastor who was speaking in town—a man named Ray Stedman. John and Kay ended up going to the dinner, and as soon as she could, Kay drew Dr. Stedman aside and explained her situation.

"What should I do?" she asked. "What can I say to my husband that will get him to change his mind about my going to the retreat and being in leadership?"

Kay would never forget what this wise pastor told her:

"Kay," he said, "your first responsibility is to seek the Lord, then your family, and *then* a ministry. I'm not going to talk to you about a way to manipulate John to change his mind. If your husband tells you to get out of Bible Study Fellowship, then when I leave tonight you tell him that you're getting out!"

At the time, she thought someone had tossed four gallons of ice water right in her face. She sat with her mouth open wondering, *How could he say such a thing?* Yet as the evening wore on, she realized that what he said was right. For years, she had tried with varying degrees of success to manipulate her way in and out of things—and now she was being asked to change. It was like hearing an army trumpet sound general quarters. The pastor's words called out that she was in the midst of a spiritual battle—not just a battle with her husband.

When they got home from dinner, Kay's normal response would have been, "There is not enough money in this *world* that could keep me home from this retreat. We already agreed that I could go, and you're breaking that promise!"

But instead, her response was based on a decision that God was in control of her life. "If John doesn't want me to go," she said, "then God must not want me to go this time."

"Father," she prayed, "I don't understand why, but I feel like this is a test. So, Lord, please help me find a reason for my not going."

As she looked at her plane tickets lying on the piano, tears filled her eyes. Yet, in spite of the pain, with all her heart she knew what she was doing was right. It was one of the most difficult things she'd ever done in her life, but she walked up the stairs and told her husband that she would skip the retreat, that she would drop out of her leadership position.

We live in days and times where words like "sacrifice" and "commitment" are four-letter words. I realize that, to many people, Kay's decision to love and honor her husband's wishes might seem unenlightened or even terribly wrong. After all, *she had her rights.* But as Kay was to find out, it was in laying down her rights that she finally broke through to her husband.

In simple terms what Kay literally did was make love a decision. *Genuine love is honor put into action regardless of the cost.* It comes from a heart overflowing with love for God, freeing us to seek another person's best interests. Kay knew that only by loving God first and foremost could she ever hope to pull off loving John—especially after what he had done. Every "instinct" she had told her to lash out.

Yet in spite of her "instincts," her love would be based on a decision to honor her husband—not her emotions.

Let me admit that there are situations where either the husband or wife is emotionally unhealthy. In no way am I saying that we are to give a "blanket" yes to a spouse who commands us to do something against the law or in direct violation to God's law. (For a look at the balance between unconditional love and dealing with an emotionally destructive person, we recommend Dr. James Dobson's *Love Must Be Tough*.) But Kay believed this was her chance to prove to John what was more important: her husband or her retreat. Perhaps that's why she determined more than ever that her love for Christ would be the basis of her love for her husband. And that's what led to . . . the rest of the story.

The Rest of the Story

Several months passed, and John and Kay were invited to a large Christian conference held in the auditorium at Indiana University. At the conclusion of the seminar, the speaker did something unusual. He opened up several microphones for people in the audience to come up and share what God had been doing in their lives. That's when it happened.

Kay suddenly looked over and noticed that John was getting up from his seat and heading to the front of the auditorium. He waited his turn in line and then stepped up to the microphone.

"Ladies and gentlemen," he said to a group of over a thousand people. "*I just want you to know that I'm here tonight because my wife First Peter three'ed me into coming!*"

The entire place came unglued with laughter as his words sank in. Indeed, as the verse says, Kay's commitment to trust God had won over her husband "without a word" by her godly actions (1 Peter 3:1-6).

"I'm going to tell you all something Kay doesn't know," John continued. "We had this guy named Gary Smalley come to our house and I don't know what he told my wife—but things haven't been the same since. Basically, I'm here tonight because my wife has worn me out with her love.

"I've got to confess that there have been days when I actually sat in my office, thinking up something I was going to tell her to do when I got home *just to see if she would do it*—and she did! Watching the reality of this woman's love for God is the reason I'm standing up here tonight. . . ." And there was more to come.

John changed so much that soon *he* was in the leadership program of the *Men's* Bible Study Fellowship. And then came the day of *their* men's leadership retreat. Kay drove her husband to where the bus would take him and several others on a weekend retreat. John had never been on a men's retreat, and he was like a schoolboy going to summer camp for the first time.

> # Genuine love is honor put into action regardless of the cost.

While she never said anything at the bus station, Kay couldn't help thinking about the retreat she had given up months earlier. And as she drove off, the emotions of the moment finally hit her. She was thankful for the changes in her husband's life, but the hurt of being denied an opportunity to go to her own leaders' retreat brought tears to her eyes—until the phone rang.

Kay had barely gotten back home when John called.

"We're at a truck stop picking up some other people for the retreat," he said, "and I just had to call you."

With his voice choking with emotion, he said, "Kay, I've been thinking back to a time I told you you couldn't go to a retreat. Could you forgive me for asking you to give up something I knew was really important to you? I'm so sorry I asked you to step down from your leadership group. I never should have asked what I did, and I never will again. Can you find it in your heart to forgive me? . . ."

Kay has been to many retreats since the one she missed over thirteen years ago—but none have held as much meaning as the one she never attended. Later, she would say in reflecting on that unforgettable call, "*I gave up a retreat—but I gained back a husband!*"

Over the years, John and Kay have developed a rock-solid love for Christ and each other. This couple whose relationship at one time was dead in the water, held fast by the rocks of insensitivity and bitter arguments, now help countless couples fight back from the brink of divorce. And they do this by sharing the reality of their own story—and by helping others see that genuine love is a decision, not a feeling.

Moving Honor into a Home by Loving Actions

I realize that there are times when love needs to be tough and set firm boundaries with a loved one. But what turned around John and Kay's life was a principle that is true in any home. *The most effective way to open the door to needed changes in a relationship is to honor a loved one. And once we've made that decision to honor, love is the action we take no matter how we feel.*

Genuine love is honor put into action, regardless of the cost. It comes from a heart overflowing with affection for God, freeing us to seek another person's best interest.

In a nutshell, that definition is an outline of this book. We've already seen in Chapter 2 that honor is at the foundation of all healthy relationships. Now we've seen that out of our decision to honor flows loving actions *regardless of our feelings—regardless of the cost.*

Now in the chapters that follow, you'll learn the ten areas that took me all day to teach Kay, and that I've spent fifteen years refining and researching ever since. Each one is a *specific loving action* that expresses the honor and the decision to love that we've made.

The very first loving action that is so essential in any home or relationship is recognizing the incredible worth of a woman. Every woman has two tremendous tendencies that we'll uncover for you. What's more, you'll see that there are three questions any husband can ask his wife that can reveal her built-in marriage manual.

4
The Incredible
Worth of a Woman

ONE OF THE greatest joys I have in teaching the "Love Is a Decision" seminar is sharing with men how incredibly valuable women are. Why? One major reason is that I've spent time learning and asking questions from women. That includes twenty-five years of marriage, and interviewing over 30,000 women at conferences and in counseling sessions across the country. I've seen, first hand, the tremendous relationship skills that God has woven into the fabric of their lives.

But a few years ago, I had an experience that gave me a whole new appreciation for their incredible worth. For on a windblown afternoon, one woman's "intuitive" senses quite possibly saved my life, and the lives of several others as well.

A River Gone Wild. . . .

It was mid-May, and time for our annual "staff retreat" where we do more retreating than staffing. We did have one legitimate reason for spending the weekend fishing. We were in the process of interviewing Steve Lyon, now an invaluable associate on our staff, and we decided that spending a weekend quizzing him at our favorite fishing spot was just the place to get to know him—and a few trophy-sized trout at the same time.

We were on our way to Lee's Ferry, located just below Lake Powell on the Colorado River. Lying at the mouth of the Grand Canyon, it offers great fishing and some of the most spectacular scenery in the world.

Early the first morning, we waited at the dock for our two guides. Soon, a truck rumbled up, two figures bouncing in the front seat as it rolled to a stop. The door opened and out stepped a tall, weather-beaten man of about forty. Beside him was his wife, a petite woman only half his size. What I would discover later that day was that anything she lacked in size, she would more than make up for in fishing skill—and her natural female "instincts."

Beautiful canyon walls rose literally two and three hundred feet straight up from the edge of the water as we began a tour of the Grand Canyon at water level. It took our boats nearly an hour traveling upstream to reach the dam which stood as a towering marker to "the end of the line." We shut our engines down and quietly began to drift with the current, letting out line behind us as we trolled for speckled and rainbow trout.

The early morning passed with little success. Then lunch time rolled around and we beached the boats about halfway back to the dock. It had been a fairly calm morning, but by the time we got back to the boats, the wind had changed from a whisper to a stiff breeze. I remember thinking, *We won't catch a thing until these gusts die down.* But they didn't.

With each passing minute, the wind grew stronger and more steady. The once glassy surface of the river was beginning to roll as the water churned with a thousand tiny waves. But we were all seasoned campers and fishermen. *What's a little wind?* I thought.

As we got back in the boats, I noticed our two guides talking. I couldn't hear the words they were saying, but it was obvious they were in the midst of a heated discussion. Finally, the man shrugged his shoulders, nodded his head, and marched over to us with some unwelcome news.

"I'm sorry, guys, but we're going to have to pack it in for right now. I can't explain it, but my wife really feels strongly that this isn't just a minor front coming in—and I've learned to listen to her on these waters. So we're heading back."

It was a good thing we listened to her when we did. Almost instantly the wind began to howl, and the waves were beginning to form whitecaps. Within minutes, we lost the ability to communicate from boat to boat as the fury of a desert windstorm drowned out even the most desperate attempts to shout instructions.

We were all on our own to make it back. By now the wind was blowing with such a galelike force that if we had turned sideways to the current, we would have easily been swamped by the angry swells. The only hope we had of making it back on top of the water was to point the boats directly downstream into the wind, meet the waves head on, and speed full throttle to dock and safety.

For thirty minutes (they seemed like a life-time), our three boats fought a river gone wild. A major storm had turned the narrow Canyon walls into a wind-tunnel. I had no idea at the time what was going on in the other two boats, but I knew that prayer kept ours afloat.

Finally, after stopping to bail out water at one point, all three boats had docked safely with all hands accounted for. I learned later from my two sons, who were in the guide's wife's boat, that she had handled herself beautifully. In fact, she was the first one back to the dock. At one point, a gust of wind caught the front end of the boat and began to flip it over backwards, but her cool-headed reaction, at the very least, saved everyone from an icy swim. At most, she saved my sons' lives.

I walked away from that trip with another reason why women are so incredibly valuable. I know for a fact that if our guide hadn't listened to his wife, we would have been in major trouble.

It's struck me several times since that incident how much I've profited from learning the valuable character traits and natural talents that God has built into my wife. Far from an attempt to erase all differences between the sexes, I feel strongly that God placed the differences there for a purpose.

In this chapter, we'll look at several areas of natural, complementing strengths in men and women. I hope one result for every man will be that he finds new reasons for treasuring and valuing his wife, and I hope that one result for every woman will be to find yet another reason to thank God for the natural gifts she brings to those she loves.

Meeting Our Missing Part

It was a wise and loving God who said, "It is not good for the man to be alone" (Genesis 2:18a). But was a woman designed merely to provide a man with companionship—or does it go deeper than that?

Most people are familiar with the passage that talks about God creating woman and His words, "I will make (him, Adam) a helper suitable for him" (Genesis 2:18b). The Hebrew word for "helper" actually means "completer." The word is used throughout the Old Testament to talk about God being our "helper," the One who "completes what is lacking," or "does for us what we cannot do for ourselves."[1]

One of the things that should increase the "honor" a husband gives to his wife is realizing that God created her to help him in areas he isn't naturally equipped to handle. In other words, a wife is designed to bring strengths to the relationship that the husband does not naturally have himself.

Over the years, I've noted a number of ways in which men and women are different, but there are four areas in particular, I've seen a woman's natural gifts act like missing parts needed to complete a man. That first missing piece comes with a special language that a woman speaks which cannot only strengthen a marriage—it can literally be a life-saving gift to some husbands.

1. Two Languages in the Same Home

One study of little four-year-old boys and girls recorded every noise that came out of their mouths over a period of time.[2] The study concluded that 100 percent of the sounds made by little girls had something to do with literal words. They spent a great deal of time talking to each other, and almost an equal amount of time talking to themselves.

For little boys, however, the figure was only 60 percent words. The remaining 40 percent were simply noises and sound effects (like Bzzzzzzzz!, Zooooooooom!, Baaammmmm!). In short, the tendency in even little girls is to use more words than little boys, and that early difference in language skills holds up throughout each age level.

Not only are women more verbal, but they often speak a different language than men do. I'm not talking about homes where English and Spanish, or Japanese and English are spoken, but about a much more common family environment where "Womaneise" and "Maneise" are spoken!

In roughly 80 percent of all homes, men primarily relate to their wives using what we call a *language of the head* while women tend to speak a *language of the heart*.

Typically, men tend to be logical, factual, and detail-oriented. In general, when a man runs out of facts to talk about in a conversation, he often stops talking! Usually, men don't have as much of a need to share as deeply or consistently as do their wives. Nor do they have the need to speak the same number of words their wives do. Some studies have shown that the average woman speaks roughly 25,000 words a day, while the average man speaks only 12,500! What this can mean in a marriage is that a woman is often left holding her cup out for meaningful conversation day after day and drawing it back with only a few drops to nourish her.

On the other hand, women often speak a *language of the heart*. In most cases, they love to share thoughts, feelings, goals, and dreams.

A woman's natural skills at communicating often will make her wonderfully sensitive to small things others are thinking, saying, or feeling. And her desire for deep relationships usually exceeds what the average man desires.

It's almost as if men are two-humped camels. They can take a little conversation and then go for days across even the most difficult terrain without any need for more "watering" words, but a woman covering the same distances needs a daily allotment of water to survive and flourish—and often double that ration of "watering" words during difficult periods in her life.

Why should a man be interested in having his wife help him learn to speak her "language of the heart"? For one thing, it can actually help him live longer.

In his provocative book, *The Language of the Heart*, Dr. James J. Lynch presents compelling evidence that effective communication skills can do wonders for a person's cardiovascular health.[3] Whether we realize it or not, each time we engage in conversation, whether we are under stress or not, our blood pressure increases. However, when the conversation is stressful—*and especially when we hold our words inside*—our blood pressure can go to extremely high levels. This can be a dangerous situation, especially for people with a history of heart problems such as hypertension.

When a man learns to bridge both worlds—by speaking the language of the head and the language of the heart—it can make tremendously positive changes in his own life and the lives of those with whom he lives and works. Not only that, it can decrease the unnecessary stress that accompanies poor marital or business conversation. In the end, our hearts will thank us for the decreased workloads, and those around us will be thankful for the increased depth and feeling we have added to our communication.

But how does a woman actually help her husband bridge the "language" barrier in a home? If a man opens his eyes to several natural characteristics of his wife, he'll see that her natural strengths can complete him because. . . .

2. Women Tend to Relate on Multiple Levels

When most women are asked to describe the mental capacity of men, their response is, "He has a one-track mind." In a sense, that's pretty close—and not just in the area of sexual relationships. We men usually do concentrate on one thing at a time. It's as if our minds are like the inside of a battleship, with many different decks and com-

partments. When we leave one deck, we close the water-tight door
to the last compartment and busy ourselves with what's close at hand.

> Many a wife knows that if she
> leaves the house for an hour
> with her husband "in charge"
> of the kids, she's likely to come
> back and not see them anywhere
> in sight.

That's one reason why a wife, when she asks her husband if he
thought about her at work that day, is likely to hear:

"Did I think about you today? Well . . . I mean . . . I'm sure I *must*
have thought about you sometime!" Take heart, ladies; it's probably
not that he doesn't love you, it's just a reflection of his tendency to
"compartmentalize" his thinking. A man tends to remain in one
world at work that centers around the office or job-site, and when he
leaves that one, he enters another that revolves around the family.

A woman's mind, though, is like the war room on that battleship.
It's the nerve center, equipped with fancy electronic devices that
allow it to monitor all the vital signs on every deck of the house at
the same time. Because of the way her mind has been designed, its
radar is constantly on and sweeping in all directions.

What this means is that the average woman misses very little about
her environment, no matter how crowded it is. That same "radar"
system that is so sensitive in Norma is what alerted our fishing
guide's wife to the coming windstorm. And it's also the same system that makes it very difficult for the average woman to relax completely if her husband is watching the kids.

Many a wife knows that if she leaves the house for an hour with
her husband "in charge" of the kids, she's likely to come back and
not see them anywhere in sight. Then when she asks her husband
(who's now in front of the television set) where they are, he's liable
to say, "Oh, I don't know . . . they're around here somewhere. . . . I
think they went down to the pond to play," as he turns back to his
game.

She, on the other hand, usually knows exactly what's going on with
the kids, no matter what time of day it is, or what part of the house

they are in. It doesn't matter if she lives in a three-story Victorian mansion. She can be in the basement when her radar goes off, but she knows the kids are in the attic fighting.

Greg and Mike literally thought that Mom had the house wired when they were out. Invariably, they'd be as quiet as church mice doing something they shouldn't, and still Norma's radar would go off, and she'd catch them.

A woman misses very little about her environment, which is probably the basis for that mysterious gift some have called intuition. We feel strongly that it's more than a natural "hunch." It's just one more way in which a woman can complete her husband—and another reason a man should honor and value his wife.

3. Women Have the Unique Skill of Personalizing Their Environment

Another tremendous strength a woman has is to become personally involved with everything around her. For example, have you ever wondered why the average wife doesn't care that much about watching a football game with you? Most of the time, it's because she doesn't *know* any of the players. There's nothing "personal" going on down on the field. (Now, this may not be true when she is in the stands sitting with you and some friends, but for many women, the battling going on down on the field is not as interesting as who you meet coming and going to the game.)

One way to get a woman to be more interested in a sporting event is to "personalize" it. Take a few moments and share some information with her about one of the players ("Honey, see that guy who just caught the ball? He's the guy I told you about who's been really struggling with his wife and kids . . . "). Then she'll feel more a part of the game and what's going on because she has an emotional tie to it.

How strong is a woman's need for an "emotional" attachment to someone? One indication is the fact that in this country alone, over ten million romance novels will be purchased this year, and 97 percent of them will be bought by women. Why? At least in part because these stories offer a picture of intimacy and deep personal relationships that, unfortunately, many find too infrequently in their own lives.

If a man isn't aware of his wife's tendency to "personalize" almost everything around her, it can lead to friction in a home. That's because for most women, the cat is not just an "animal," but their first baby. The wallpaper isn't just "something to cover the walls," but a reflection of who she is.

As you may have noticed, many men tend to take certain things in their surroundings for granted. For example, the car they drive. Recently, a story appeared in *Reader's Digest* that I really enjoyed.

There was a man with several daughters who owned an old, decapitated convertible. For years, every woman in the house urged him to get rid of the "pile of junk" and even refused to ride in it with him in public. Then one day it happened. He walked out from work, and the car had been stolen.

The man's wife and daughters were celebrating that night that his eyesore of a car had been stolen when the phone rang. The party was over—the police had found the car.

"We found your car only about ten blocks from where they took it," the policeman said. "We don't know who did it, but they left a note saying, '*You can have it back. We'd rather walk!*'"

For a man, a car can often be in the worst of shape because "It's just transportation" to him, but for a woman, if her car isn't washed it can often leave her feeling incomplete. Why is that? In part, it's because it's usually easier for a man to separate himself from his surroundings than it is for a woman.

This is especially true of the house or apartment you live in. To a man, the home is a place of rest. To a woman, it's an extension of herself.

That's why a woman may feel "trashy" if the trash hasn't been taken out; she may feel dirty if the floors aren't cleaned and the carpet not vacuumed; she may even feel broken down if the fence isn't fixed or the door is falling off the hinges. Each of these things is a part of her; when they aren't right, she feels as if something's not right with her.

Why is this something that can benefit or "complete" a man? In part, it's because a woman's natural sensitivity to her surroundings makes her alert to the things that surround us—and especially the people in her world.

It's like having a quality control expert in the home who can spot lurking problems with her "early warning" system. In addition, her heightened awareness of those around her rarely causes her to make a crucial relationship mistake many men make at the office—and at home.

4. Women Are Generally More Concerned about People Than They Are about Projects.

For the most part, men are conquerors. That means at least some of the time they tend to be less concerned about people and feelings than they are about "getting the job done." This is quite natural for men, because we tend to derive our sense of worth from what we do. The better "job" we do, the better we feel about ourselves.

Women, on the other hand, primarily derive their feelings of worth from those to whom they're related. If a woman is married, she looks to her husband more than any other earthly individual for her personal sense of value and worth.

That natural concern for deep and loving relationships that a woman has can certainly be shared by a man—but it can also be more easily set aside by him as well. Take hunting for example.

The average man can load up his high-powered rifle, go hunting, and blow away one of God's beautiful creatures. Then he can cut off its head, stuff it, hang it on a wall, gather his neighbors around, and triumphantly say, "I did that!" He's conquered something!

But generally women have already made much too deep an emotional attachment to Thumper and Bambi in the movie theater to execute one of their real-life counterparts out in the wild. When those sweet little animals die, a part of the woman is hurt as well.

You can even see this difference between the sexes when men and women go shopping. When the average man hears the average woman say, "Honey, let's go shopping and find a new blouse for me," he hears the word "shopping." But what she usually means is "Shooooopppppppiiiiinnnng!"

Once a man hears her words, "Let's get a blouse," he is like a bloodhound who has just had an escaped prisoner's scent held in front of his nose. Once he's gotten a "whiff" of what he's going to the mall to hunt for, then it's off to sniff out a new blouse (any blouse), bag it, get back home, and lie on the porch as quickly as possible.

Since men are often more "conquer"-oriented than women, they usually tend to concentrate on the completion of a project—regardless of the personal costs. But because a woman's sense of value is so closely tied to all the relationships around her, she's often gifted in helping a man be more sensitive to what's really important beyond the immediate goal.

Take Brian, for example. For several Saturday mornings, his goal was to get up as early as he could, mow the yard, do his chores, shower, and get in front of the television set just before kickoff of the first football game of the day. As he attacked his objective of getting the yard done and getting in front of the television, he wasn't always concentrating on how to build a strong relationship with his six-year-old son, Mark.

Mark would get up with his father each Saturday and desperately try to help him with the yard. But try as he might, he could never keep up with his father on any of the chores. That was especially true when it came to "helping" his father dump all the grass from the catch bag into the trash can.

"Son, that's enough," Brian would finally say in frustration after having to pick up yet another pile of spilled yard clippings. "I don't need that kind of help right now. Why don't you go inside and see if you can help your mother? *Now.*"

Brian's wife watched each week as little Mark would walk out the door to help his Dad with his chest sticking out—and walk back in a short time later crest-fallen. As a loving wife, she brought what was happening to his attention.

At an appropriate time, she used a word picture[4] to explain to him the way he was killing his son's spirit in his "quest" to quickly mow the yard. He was sacrificing his relationship with his son for a football game that could easily be video-taped and played when his son was in bed. Fortunately, Brian was wise enough to accept her correction. He even expressed appreciation to his wife for what she said:

"Thanks, Honey. Now that you mention it, I've got to admit that I have been pushing Mark aside these past few weeks. I'm not sure why I get so caught up in getting something done my way, but I'm going to learn. My son is a lot more important to me than how quickly I get the chores done—no matter what game is on."

In Brian's home, a sensitive woman received extra honor that night because of her willingness to point out his steamroller tendencies to put projects in front of people. But that's not the only reason he's thankful for the woman God has given him. There's one more reason that outshines them all. Namely, in every marriage, right under a man's roof, is one of the most priceless things God has given him— one that he can tap into almost any time to help him in his responsibility to develop a close-knit family.

The Incredible Worth of a Woman: She Has a Built-In Marriage Manual

Do you know the main reason why men are held back from a promotion at work? Is it a lack of technical skill? Rarely. A lack of education? Occasionally. But the primary reason men fail to be promoted is their lack of relationship skills.[5]

What most men don't realize is that they have the world's greatest instructors in relationships living right under their roofs. A wife is a gold mine of relational skills. If a man wants to take advantage of the "missing part" of the nature that has affected every "Adam" since the beginning, all he has to do is look into the eyes of his wife—and learn to *tap into her built-in marriage manual.*

In talking personally with women in over sixty cities (where we've done our conferences these past five years), I've always asked for—but never found—a woman who was an exception to this rule. Namely, I have never met a woman who by her God-given nature didn't possess a built-in relationship manual.

So here's how a husband can tap into this rich source of relational skills to improve his own marriage—and his skills with his children and others as a result. First, a man needs to realize that his wife comes equipped with two tremendous inner strengths:

1. She has a strong, innate desire for a good and healthy relationship; and

2. She has the natural ability to recognize a great relationship.

These two underlying qualities are the basis for three important questions that a man can use to pull out of a woman her built-in relationship manual.

Three Questions That Can Help a Man Tap into a Woman's Built-In Marriage Manual

Three simple but life-changing questions are all it takes. For the sake of argument, let's say Bob is going to ask Julie these questions:

Julie, I realize that one way God equipped you as a helper was to complete me in the relational side of life. So let's begin with our marriage . . .

Question #1: On a scale from one to ten, with zero being terrible and ten being a great marriage, where would you like our relationship to be?

Naturally, almost every woman (and man, too!) answers that they'd like to consistently be around a nine or a ten. After all, how many of us are into misery? Bob would then go on to question two:

Question #2: On a scale from one to ten, overall, where would you rate our marriage today?

In most cases, a man will rate the marriage two to three points higher than his wife will, so don't let the initial difference in perception shock you. Remember, the average woman is much more in tune with the state of the relationship than the average man.

Be sure and give her time to think and share. Use the "quick listen" method described in Chapter 9 to reassure her that you value her opinion and want to understand her as much as possible.

Whether you agree with your wife or not, it's important to honor her by giving her your full attention. The goal is to understand her and to be open to what she may say.

The next question is the crucial one. In fact, in some ways it doesn't matter what she answers to Question Two, for the most important question is this third one—the one that can flip open the pages to her natural marriage and relationship manual.

Question #3: As you look at our relationship, what are some specific things we could do over the next six weeks that would move us closer to a ten?

I have yet to find a woman who cannot paint the answer to that question in brilliant detail. However, I have met numerous men who can't even find the paintbrush!

In some cases, your wife may be reluctant to answer this question, fearing she'll hurt your feelings—or even worse, that you'll hurt *her* feelings by your defensive response. That's why it's important to patiently give her the time to talk and to consistently reassure her about the security of your relationship—no matter what she says or where she rates things. If she feels secure in your love, almost without exception she'll be able to open up with many helpful specifics on how you can more effectively steward the gift of the marriage and family God has given you.

For any of us who are serious about effectively loving those who mean the most to us, honor must characterize our relationships. Nowhere is that more true than for the man who is serious about being a Christlike lover to his wife.

Let me state something clearly. *Valuing his wife's differences, and even tapping into her built-in marriage manual, does not transfer leadership or responsibility away from the husband and place it onto the wife.* Biblically, there is no escape clause from the man being the head of the home—the man is the fact-finder when it comes to building a strong relationship. But to be the type of loving leader God intended, allowing a wife to fulfill her God-given function as a loving "completer" is a must. It can help a man replace insensitivity with sensitivity, and lording it over others with genuine love for them. It can also help men become the observant servant leaders they were always meant to be.

By appreciating the unique and wonderful way God has created a woman, we can add a richness and joy to our marriage that virtually everyone wants, but very few have. The secret is in learning to honor a woman as someone unmatched in God's creation, made especially by Him as a completer, to do things for a man he could never do for himself.

Yet what do you do when your "completer" becomes discouraged or loses energy in your relationship? Or what happens when you do? In the next chapter, we'll see a second loving action that can be a tremendous help to a home. It involves learning a practical method of energizing your mate in as little as sixty seconds.

5

Energizing Your
Mate in Sixty Seconds

My WIFE NORMA has always loved zoos. Regardless of what
type of zoo, or how many times she's been through it, she always
thrills at the opportunity to go again. On the other hand, having been
through dozens of zoos over the years, I rarely get excited about going
through another one. But one day on a speaking trip to the Midwest,
Norma picked up a brochure advertising a "Wild Animal Park" that
actually attracted my attention.

When she saw I wasn't immediately saying "no," her face lit up. Her
voice was full of excitement as she read me the brochure and said,
"Gary, I know you'll like this one. Will you come with me? *Please*."
Once again, we were off to one of Norma's favorite places in life.

Before we could actually go, there was one minor problem we had
to overcome. The brochure described this park as a "drive-through zoo"
and we didn't have a car. So with a phone call, I arranged with my close
friend and now ministry associate, Terry Brown, to borrow his car for
the afternoon. He graciously agreed and delivered to us his tiny Fiat
convertible within the hour, and we were on our way to the park.

As we drove up to the main gate, they said convertibles were allowed, but that we would have to keep the top up. The friendly park
ranger also gave us some advice on how to feed the animals, when
not to feed them, and a strong warning about the one place in the
park where we had to keep the windows rolled up. This area was
called a "danger zone" because of the very large or very wild animals
living there. Emphatically, we were told:

"If anything happens to your car in this section of the park, just
pull off the road and honk your horn and a friendly ranger will come
and rescue you."

It sounded safe enough to me, so we began our self-guided tour of
the drive-through zoo. Once inside, we quickly discovered that

the animals living there were particularly friendly. The giant birds tried to stick their heads inside the car looking for food. One giraffe did manage to stick his twenty-inch gray tongue inside the car and tried to slurp Norma's sandwich out of her lap. At this point I readily agreed with her that this was far better than a "regular" zoo.

Then it happened. Halfway through the park, we finally came to the well-marked "danger zone," and right when we were in the middle of no-man's land, Norma asked, "What's that coming out from under the hood?" Well, it was steam from our overheating radiator, and it was beginning to form an unwelcome white cloud!

"Oh no," I groaned. Glancing at the temperature gauge for the first time, I noticed that it was way beyond the "hot" reading on the gauge and nearing the "melt down" zone.

Great, I thought. *We've only been gone an hour and already I've ruined my friend's car.*

I started to pull over, but Norma cried out,

"You can't pull over here! Didn't you see that sign? *This is a danger zone!*"

"But honey, I can't wreck this man's car. I've *got* to pull over!"

"But not here!" she pleaded. "What if we're both trampled to death or eaten alive? Who'll take care of the children? . . ."

"Now, don't worry," I said as gently as I could. "It says right here in the brochure that if we have any trouble in a danger zone, all we have to do is honk the horn and a friendly ranger will come right over and rescue us!"

Norma frowned, but with the way the car was acting, it was obvious we didn't have any choice. So we pulled over, and I started honking the horn. . . . and honking. . . . and honking . . .

I honked for forty-five minutes, and no friendly ranger ever came and rescued us. Basically, the guide at the gate had lied to us. We could have been eaten, trampled, or both. But what happened between Norma and me during this time illustrates one of the most important principles I've ever discovered when it comes to developing loving, lasting relationships.

"Don't Look Now, but. . . ."

While all my honking didn't alert a single ranger, it did notify every furry resident of the "danger zone" that we were there—and that we might have (or become) lunch. First, the wild burros ambled up and began nibbling at the top of my friend's convertible. I finally had to get out of the car and yell and chase them away to convince them that hay would be better than our fabric top. I had just gotten back inside the car when I made the mistake of looking into the rear view mirror.

"Norma," I said in my calmest voice, "don't look now, but you're never going to believe what's coming!"

An entire herd of huge, shaggy buffalo were walking out of the woods and soon surrounded our little Fiat. One of them, on my side of the car, wandered over, knelt down, and put his head right up against my window. With those great big brown eyes and a huge head about four inches from my face (the steam coming out of his nose began fogging my window), it was obvious he was saying nonverbally, "Got anything in there for me?"

Then he started pushing on the window, rocking the car as he did. During the whole ordeal, neither of us looked up, hoping our ignoring them would make them go away.

"Listen to that thing breathe!" I said.

"That's not him breathing," Norma said. "*That's me!*"

Finally, our hairy friends wandered off, and our car cooled down enough for us to drive to the main gate for help.

As funny as it seems now, that hour trapped in the car together was actually a very tense situation. In fact, if it had been several years earlier, one or both of us might have responded in a very different way. We could have easily used that tense situation to explode and so weaken our relationship, rather than relying on an important principle that could strengthen it.

Norma could have said to me, "Gary, I can't handle this! I don't care if this thing explodes, get this car moving!" or I could have easily said to her, "Be quiet! You're going to see a wild animal inside this car if you don't hush up!"

Either of us could have done and said things to each other in the "heat of battle" that we would have later regretted; and if we had blown up, it would have drained away the positive feelings and energy we'd stored up in our marriage for weeks as quickly as the water draining from our radiator.

On this trip, however, things were different. They were different because we had finally begun to understand and practice an incredibly important concept in the Scriptures.

We never know when we're going to find ourselves in a frustrating situation with someone we love. During these times, when a high-intensity predicament is threatening to drain the positive energy right out of our relationships, most of us take one of two roads. We either choose to react and blast those near us or we choose to respond in a way that actually helps to strengthen our marriage. It all begins with learning how to energize your mate during a stressful situation in as little as sixty seconds.

Energizing Your Mate in Sixty Seconds

What is the biblical principle that kept our emotions in check during this difficult time? It's really an incredible power that is right at our fingertips—the ability to be gentle and to tenderly touch each other.

> What is the biblical principle that kept our emotions in check during this difficult time?— The ability to be gentle and to tenderly touch each other.

For years I had known intellectually that "a soft answer turns away anger" (Proverbs 15:1), and that a key fruit of the spirit was "gentleness" (Galatians 5:23). But I had never applied either principle in my most important relationships. Now, if softness as a way to energize a person sounds too easy to you, how often do you feel gentle in the middle of catastrophe?

Most people's basic bent during times of stress is to lash out or lecture—or both—especially if the predicament is somebody else's fault. But tenderness, above and beyond the call of our human nature, is a transformer, an energizer of those around us.

Since I wasn't fortunate enough to have a father who knew how to be tender to his wife, I wasn't aware that softness during stressful times was even an option until several years into my marriage. And that's when I learned that one of a person's greatest needs is to be comforted, especially during those moments in life when the roof falls in.

A Creative Way to Add a Skylight to Your Home. . . .

One afternoon I was very late coming home from boating with my son Greg. I had taken the car, which left Norma with only our mini-motor home for transportation. She waited and waited, but when I was several hours later than I had predicted, she decided to take our mini-motor home to the grocery store.

Granted, our motor home is not the easiest thing to handle in the world. I'd already had my share of close calls when it came time to park or back the vehicle out. But Norma re-defined the word "close-call" as she tried to back the camper out of the driveway.

She had almost made it out from under the carport when she turned the wheel the wrong way and sheared off an entire section of the roof. And if that wasn't bad enough, the falling roof bounced off the hood of the camper, scraping away paint and leaving a deep dent in its wake.

When I pulled into the driveway an hour later, I couldn't believe my eyes. Looking at the gaping hole in the roof, my first response was to look at the sky to see if the tornado was still around, but one look at our mobile home told me that it was Mother Norma, not Mother Nature, who had caused this catastrophe.

I instantly felt like ordering her out of the house and asking her questions like, "Where did you get your driver's license? From a gumball machine at Shop-Mart?!"

Instead, I sat in my car, frozen, with my hands on the steering wheel, praying, "Lord, you have to give me strength. Every fiber in my body wants to lecture my wife now and not be gentle with her. This is one of those pressure situations, and I know I have a choice. Lord, help me figure out what I'm going to do." Turning to my son Greg I asked him, "What do you think I ought to do?"

Greg said, "Dad, why don't you do what you teach?"

"That's a good idea," I said.

But all the while I was praying for the strength to be tender. Being tender at such a moment is definitely not natural. You have to take off the comfortable old nature of lectures and anger, and put on the new nature of tenderness. This can be excruciatingly difficult (Ephesians 4:22-24).

Finally, I got out of the car and walked toward the piece of roof lying in the driveway, but just as I got up to the camper, Norma came flying around the side of the house.

I fought off the voice ringing in my mind, *Lecture her! Lecture her!*

and I did what didn't feel "natural" at the time. I simply held her in my arms and gently patted her on the back. I hadn't spoken one word when finally, Norma pulled away and said, "Oh, look what I did! I wrecked the motor home and knocked off the roof," she said. Then she added, "And I told the neighbors across the street what I did, and they're watching to see how you're going to respond."

Thankfully, I hadn't given the neighbors anything to gossip about by exploding at Norma. I just put my arms around her again and gently called her by my favorite affectionate name for her:

"Norm, listen. You know I love you. You're more important to me than campers and roofs. I know you didn't do this on purpose, and you're feeling really bad about it."

At that very moment, I could feel Norma relaxing. What's more, I immediately felt better myself as my own anger drained out of me to be replaced by feelings of tenderness. While it's hard to explain, I could tell that instead of being pulled apart, we were actually growing *stronger* as a result of the trial.

After a few more minutes of talking and holding her, Norma went on with whatever she was doing, and I went out to the garage to lay my hands on the few tools I had. After taking a deep breath, I said to Greg, "Well, I'd better get at it."

Just then, from out of nowhere, a friend from my church pulled up into our driveway. This wasn't just any ordinary friend. He was a local contractor pulling up in his pickup filled with hammers, saws, lumber, nails, paint, and a long ladder. He jumped out and said, "OK, Gary. Let's get at it!"

"Where did you come from?" I asked in disbelief.

Apparently our good neighbors across the street weren't only watching my reactions to Norma. They had also been calling everyone around town to talk about our hole in the roof. Ironically, my friend had been one of the first to hear the news. With his expert help, and without exaggeration, we had our impromptu skylight patched and re-painted within two hours.

As I went to bed that night with Norma snuggled up next to me, I was amazed that I had actually done something right for a change, during a stressful situation. What would I have normally done? I could have zapped the life right out of her emotionally with angry words and lectures, and it would have taken days for us to feel our way back to each other.

If I hadn't known about the power of gentleness, I'm sure I would have acted as I had in the past and blown up. This time I didn't, and

amazingly, it made all the difference. The old Gary Smalley might
have lost it. The new one followed a biblical blueprint for turning
away anger, and it made even a stressful event a time of closeness.

I learned an important lesson that day; it's one I've seen repeated
time and time again in my life and in the lives of others. Simply put,
that lesson is:

> Remaining tender during a trial is one
>   of the most powerful ways to build
> an intimate relationship (James 1:19, 20).

The power of tenderness is outlined and illustrated from one end
of the New Testament to the other. However, from my perspective, Ephesians 4 does the best job of explaining it. In this section
of Scripture:

• Verse 15 introduces the concept of gentleness by challenging us
to grow up in all aspects "into Jesus Christ." We're to grow up in love
and to become mature. That's what each of us wants I'm sure—to be
mature, caring people who can encourage those around us.

• Then verses 22 and 23 tell us that to become complete in Christ,
we're to take off our "old self," which is the opposite of godliness,
and then put on our "new self." Now the question is, what is it we
take off and what do we put on in its place?

• While there are certainly many aspects of our fallen nature that
need to be exchanged for godly characteristics, verse 29 gives us one
specific we can begin to put into practice today. Without pulling any
punches, it says we are not to let "any unwholesome word proceed
out of our mouth." Unwholesome words popping out of our mouths
are a reflection of our old nature, and they need to be replaced with
their opposite—words that are tender, gentle, and nurturing.

The verse continues with the encouragement to speak only words
that are "good for edification according to the need of the moment,
that it may give grace to those who hear." These are words that build
up or strengthen others, words that bring energy and life to people.

Let's look at several practical ways to energize your mate, children,
and friends on a daily basis by learning to replace angry, deflating
lectures with tender, strengthening words.

Lectures and Tenderness Don't Mix

Let's say a woman is losing emotional energy and reaches the end of her rope. In frustration, she might say to her husband:

"Oooh, I've had it around this house. *Look at this mess.* Nobody ever picks up anything around here. I've got to have some help!"

Now that's a clear sign of a woman who is losing energy. The problem is, her husband may hear only the words, "I need help," and not the feelings or issues behind her frustration. Once a man hears the words, "I need help," his natural desire is to solve the problem at hand. Instantly, he's capable of taking over and saying something like this:

"Honey, I'm really glad you brought this up. You know, if you could just get organized around here, you wouldn't be so frustrated. It's about time you got a system of housework like we have at the office. And by the way, are you still taking those vitamin pills we spent all that money for? Are you getting your rest on a regular basis?"

Or worse yet, we men are capable of hitting below the belt and saying something like, "*Honey, do you think your being disorganized is an indication that you're not spending enough time in God's Word on a regular basis?*"

Lectures are so natural. Particularly when they make us conquering males feel like we're solving a problem. The real problem, though, is that we've missed the deeper message *behind* her words. In fact, if we do give her a management-effectiveness course on cleaning the house, she tends to resent us, not applaud us. That often leads to a man saying something like:

"Well, what's wrong with you? If you don't want my help, then why did you ask me!"

The problem is, *she never was asking for help in the first place!* At least not the type of help that comes from lectures and object lessons. It only sounded that way because he focused on the words alone. Like many women, this wife was sharing her underlying feelings, her hurt, and her need for support, but what she expressed was her frustration. What a woman needs during times of expressed frustration is not a husband's mouth, but his shoulder. She really needs to be comforted and encouraged. She needs energizing—with a nice dose of meaningful touching tossed in.

We need to understand that when someone is going through a trial, they sometimes express that emotional draining of energy through their anger, discouragement, hurt feelings, or anxiety. The last thing a friend, spouse, or child who's hurting wants from us is a lecture, especially one that's delivered in harshness and anger.

Not only females resist or react to lectures or harsh words. Let's say it's been a very frustrating day at the office and a typical man walks in complaining, "This job doesn't pay enough for what they make me go through." In most cases, he's sharing his frustration—not issuing an invitation to be criticized. Not many men would enjoy hearing their wives say, "Yeah, they *don't* pay you enough, all right. You need to get a real job that pays more so we can make ends meet. In fact, I'll tell you what kind of job you *ought* to get. . . ."

The same thing is true with children. Teenagers rarely appreciate coming home after flunking a test and being met with angry, challenging words. I'm not saying that you can't confront a person in love over areas of error in his or her life, but at the *moment of vulnerability*, and particularly in the midst of the crisis itself, what a person needs first is tenderness.

Tenderness acts as a firebreak to an advancing forest fire. Fire-fighters get ahead of the fire, then clear a wide trail free of all "flammable" material. The fire may roar up to the firebreak, but it can't jump across and keep burning. That's one tremendous benefit of tenderness.

It takes work to "strip" an area clear of emotional kindling—particularly when a fiery trial is closing in on us. But we can head off the negative emotions that are coming and keep from getting "burned" if we do. Or, as we mentioned, we can add more fuel to the already burning fire—in the form of lectures.

> Kindness is communicating that
> someone is valuable through our
> actions.

To use another word picture, lectures act as an electronic suction device that can suck out all our energy, leaving us emotionally, spiritually, and physically drained. I've sat in numerous counseling sessions where a man was criticizing his wife or vice versa, and you can almost hear the suction machine roaring, pulling the life right out of their relationship.

Lectures may seem right, and occasionally they are an appropriate response to a person, but tender, honoring, "edifying" words can head off an argument before it breaks out in our relationship.

Making Tenderness a Habit in Your Home

Okay, I hear what you're saying: "I'd like to be more tenderhearted. But it's still a little abstract. How about several concrete suggestions on how to practice this new gentle habit?"

Ephesians 4:32 is your instruction booklet for becoming a tenderhearted person. In these verses are two powerful ways to be tenderhearted. The first is, "Be kind . . . to one another," then, "forgiving each other, just as God in Christ forgave you."

In other words, when it comes to being tender, kindness, gentleness, and forgiveness are like battery packs. They are what gives tenderness its punch. Let's look at each of these steps more closely.

Have you ever wondered what being "kind" to someone really means? *Kindness is communicating that someone is valuable through our actions.* There are ways to be kind—like visiting friends at the hospital or going to their home after the loss of a loved one. In these cases, kindness is usually best spoken without a word—by a hug, or a gentle act or touch. Our presence alone says, "I'm so sorry; you're very special to me; I'm praying for you." Combine a "kind" act with a tender touch, and the results can be life-changing.

Recently John Trent and I were on a radio program in California talking about the importance of being "tenderhearted," when a man called in and told us an incredible story about the power of silent tenderness.

A few years back, the caller had had a major heart attack. Though he was only in his early fifties at the time, it was so serious, the doctors at the hospital told his wife to notify the family he probably wouldn't live for more than a few days.

When his seventy-year-old father was called, he flew cross-country to be at what he thought was his son's deathbed. The fact that his father had come at all was a tremendous encouragement to his son. In all his life, he had never once heard the words, "I love you," from his father. Deep down, he always felt he was loved, but for years, he had longed to actually hear the words that would prove he was valuable to his father.

"My father never did come right out and say he loved me," he said. "But after he came out to see me in the hospital, I knew he did—and all because of one thing he did when I was lying in that hospital bed."

"What was it he did?" we asked, glued to our headphones.

"When I was in the hospital," the man continued, "my dad walked in and without saying a word, he took my hand and gently held it for over half an hour. He was tender with me for the first time I can ever remember. He still couldn't bring himself to *say*, 'I love you,' but I know now he really did."

We all teared up just listening to the emotion in his voice as he told us his story. As powerful a story as this was, it was "the rest of the story" that hit us the hardest, for the man went on to tell us that he miraculously recovered from his heart attack. But three days after he had come to visit his son in the hospital, the seventy-year-old *father* passed away!

This man shared with us and the entire listening audience, "If my father had never shown me his love by that one tender act, I don't think I would ever have truly known how much he loved me, but that one act of gentleness spoke more to me than anything he could have said. . . ."

His father's actions communicated kindness in its purest form. Without words—simply by his gentle touch—he shouted out the concept of tenderness in words that will forever ring in his son's heart.

Tenderness and Timing

Often the time to give someone a gentle word of encouragement or a meaningful touch is obvious. Sometimes, though, especially for people like me who do not come from a "high touch" background, it's hard to recognize the not-so-obvious times we need to be tender. What do we do then?

I'll never forget what one woman told me:

"If my husband would only put his arms around me and hold me when I'm feeling blue, and not give me a nonstop lecture or pep-talk about 'counting it all joy,' it would transform our marriage."

"Have you ever *told* him what you need?" I asked.

"Are you kidding? He'd be embarrassed and so would I," she laughed.

"This may come as a surprise to you," I said, "but he probably doesn't know how to be tender with you. He's been trained to lecture. Perhaps he needs some training in what genuine tenderness is."

"That makes sense to me," she said. "Many times when I'm crying and upset, he'll ask, 'What do you want me to *do?*' And I just flare up and say, '*If have to tell you what to do, then that would ruin it!*'"

A husband should ask his wife, and a wife her husband, to define "tenderness" in their own terms. How he should hold her for her to feel safe and loved—when is the best time for her to be soft and sympathetic with him? A wife or husband shouldn't expect his or her mate to be a mind-reader when it comes to meeting the very important needs in this area.

Most of us aren't good emotional mind-readers anyway, and too few of us come from comforting backgrounds so we don't know the nonverbal signals that say, "Please hold me." While attempting to talk about being tender may seem awkward at first, just being willing to talk about this much needed area tends to bring energy and life to a relationship.

Using Tenderness as an Important Protective Tool for Your Children

We've talked about the need both a woman and man have for tenderness—a willingness to decrease our lectures and increase our tender expressions of love, but if gentleness is a key to marital growth, it is equally powerful when practiced between parent and child.

I know a man who had a very strained relationship with his teenage daughter. Recently, she had been dating a boy he did not care for, and her father had been extremely cutting in expressing his feelings. In fact, every time he brought up the subject (and everything they talked about seemed somehow to lead into it), their exchanges became loud and dishonoring.

At our seminar, he realized for the first time how important tenderness was, and how little of it he was showing to his daughter. He decided that he had to begin putting on the new nature of encouraging words. He still disapproved of the boy his daughter was dating— but he didn't have to blast his daughter at close range every night with angry words just to vent his frustration.

That very night at the seminar, he prayed to be more gentle with his daughter—and the opportunity to put his prayer into practice came to pass. After he got home from the seminar, he walked upstairs to get ready for bed. He passed by his daughter's room and heard her crying as she talked over the phone. It was the boyfriend he disliked so much calling, and it was obvious that they were breaking up over the phone.

Inside, this father felt like jumping for joy. He couldn't think of anything better than what was happening, but something stopped him as he began to enter his daughter's room and pull out the standard "I told you he was a jerk" lecture. As he heard his daughter crying as she hung up the phone, he remembered his vow to God to bring tenderness into his home.

He walked slowly into her room and gently sat down on her bed. She lay with her head buried in her pillow. When she realized he was sitting next to her, she instantly bristled—figuring she knew what was coming, but her father said nothing. Instead, he quietly held her as she cried. When she finally stopped, she looked up at him and said, "Daddy, thank you for just being here with me."

As my friend walked out of his daughter's room, his emotions hit like a sheet of ice water. He realized that he had been so distant from his daughter for so long, it had been years since she had called him "Daddy."

The Master's Use of Tenderness

Our children, our spouse, our close friends, and each of us have a physical and emotional need for tenderness, expressed as words or as meaningful touches. Kindness comes from *honoring* that need in the lives of our loved ones and demonstrating that *love* by doing all we can to fulfill it.

The main reason I've mentioned tenderness and kindness as the second act of love is its great importance in communicating value to others. One of the loudest cries we hear among men, women, and children is the desperate plea for tenderness and gentleness from people who love them.

Jesus was the master at using tenderness to express high value to others. Remember how He greeted the children who came to Him? Mobbed by onlookers and protected by His disciples, Jesus could have easily waved to them from a distance or just ignored them altogether. He did neither. Jesus touched and blessed the children (Matthew 19:13).

His tenderness in dealing with others was graphically displayed when a leper came to Him, described in Luke as a man "with leprosy. . . . Jesus reached out his hand and touched the man" (Matthew 8:3).

To touch a leper in Jesus' day was to flirt with contracting the most terrifying terminal illness known to the biblical world. To have leprosy was to die shunned and untouched, driven away from civilization until finally, mercifully, you died. People in Jesus' day would literally not get within a stone's throw of a leper—and Jewish law allowed stones to be thrown at a leper if he or she did come any closer.[1]

Yet even before Jesus spoke to the leper, He reached out His hand and touched him. Can't you imagine the people around Jesus recoiling from the sight? *No one* would touch a leper. Yet Jesus, in His wisdom, knew the man's heart, and his need for both spiritual cleansing and physical tenderness (see Matthew 8:1-3 and Luke 5:12).

When Tenderness Is Tied to Forgiveness

I've mentioned several aspects of being "tenderhearted." The first is kindness, and the second is meaningful touch. There is a third element of tenderness, though, that can have incredible power in relationships, namely forgiving one another.

It was years before I discovered what "forgiveness" means in the original language, but its meaning has always stayed with me. The literal picture behind the word "forgiveness" is untying a knot.[2] In the confines of everyday life, we can all get tied up in knots because of what others (especially our spouses) have said or done to us.

Part of forgiving someone is actually helping them become untied from their frustrations. No matter if the offense was big or small, forgiveness is saying, "I want this person free! Released! Untied!" For those who want to give encouragement and energy to their spouse or someone else, it can have incredible results.

A doctor friend of mine told me a story about a man who was dying in a nearby hospital. He was very, very ill, and the doctors could give him only hours to live. To all around him he seemed to have given up the fight, but that afternoon, this man's brother appeared in his room. The brother was the same one with whom he had never gotten along and who had always been rough and unkind to him growing up.

"I . . . I just come to ask if you will forgive me for the way I have treated you," the man's brother blurted out. Then he did an extraordinary thing. The rough brother took his dying brother's hand and told him he loved him.

At first when the brother sat and held the sick man's hand, it was rigid and stiff from the years of resentment he'd harbored against his brother. But remarkably, in the moments that followed those extraordinary words, his hand relaxed and the strength of his grip increased.

A moment before, he had felt so weak he did not think he could make it through the night. Yet after that visit, the sick brother steadily recuperated. The doctor couldn't pin-point any single thing that led to his rapid recovery. He told me that there could have been a number of physiological reasons for the man's strange and quick recovery. However, he felt sure that his brother's appearance and this man's recovery were not accidental. Namely, his brother's touch—and especially his words of forgiveness—were an important part in giving this man the energy to have a fighting chance to live.[3]

Are you still hesitating at knocking down old walls of anger and putting in a doorway of tenderness to your home—a door that opens to energizing words, gentle touching, and courageous forgiving? Then start this way.

Begin by spending time listening to your spouse, your child, or your friend—without any lectures. Then, the next time they show signs of losing energy in the midst of a discouraging or pressure-packed time, walk over and, without a word, put your arm around them or gently put your hand on their shoulder.

If you must say something, just say something like, "I can see you're really hurting, and I want you to know that I'm very sorry," or "I'm not sure if I can help you in what you're going through, but I love you, and if you're up to it, you can tell me how you're feeling." Particularly if tenderness hasn't been a hallmark of your relationships, you'll be amazed at how quickly being soft with people in this way can bring positive results.

I often tell people it doesn't take great wisdom to energize a person, but it does take sixty seconds. That's the amount of time it takes to walk over and gently hold someone we love. A few seconds invested in being tender can not only help our relationships—it can become catching in a home as well. But the amazing part of tenderness is that it works wonders even when we're not near our loved ones.

Once, while I was on a speaking trip, my schedule put me out of town on Mother's Day. I called Norma on that special day, telling her how sorry I was not to be there.

"How's your day been?" I asked.

"It's been a horrible day. Mike and Greg have been terrible to me, and everything's gone wrong." Resisting the temptation to tell her "exactly" what to do to make things "right," I simply listened. Soon, she slowed down, and I could tell she felt a bit better.

So I said, "Oh, I wish I was there with you." I said, "I'd just give you a great big hug, ummmmmmm! In fact," I said, "put your arms around yourself and give yourself a big hug for me. Ummmmmmmm!"

Now I didn't expect her to say, "Oh, you're such a wonderful husband. Thanks for being so tender." Wives usually don't say that when they're hurting. You've got to do this by faith because there may be times when they say, "Aw, you don't mean that!"

Just as I was getting off the phone, I heard the sound of a door opening, and Norma gasping in delight, "Ohhhh, Greg! They're so beautiful!"

"What's so beautiful?" I asked.

"Greggy brought me flowers for Mother's Day!"

"Hey, that's great," I said. Then it dawned on me.

"Say, Norma. Let me talk to Greg a minute."

Once my son was on the phone, I asked him where he got the flowers.

"Oh, I ordered them from a florist."

At that time he was only about thirteen years old, so I said, "But how did you pay for them?"

He said, "Oh, I just used your charge card, Dad."

Let's just say, I tried to remember all about showing tenderness to my son when I got home.

Tenderness is catching when it's communicated in a home—whether it's shared by an encouraging word, a gentle touch, or with an act of forgiveness. And the result between loved ones is energy—and another important way to build a loving, lasting relationship.

It takes practice and relying on God's strength to put on this important aspect of our new nature, but it's worth every ounce of effort we put into harnessing the power of tenderness to energize our loved ones.

As I mentioned earlier, energizing your mate by being gentle and tender is an important act of love, but it doesn't stand alone. It's just one of several ways we can put honor into action and show others how much we love them.

In the next chapter, I'm going to discuss an unbelievably powerful emotion that all of us have, yet few of us master. It's as much a part of our human makeup as our instinct for survival. It shapes the course of human events just as a roaring river carves canyons in sandstone. In addition, it has the potential to make our lives more meaningful and our relationships more fulfilling—or it can literally destroy the very things that are most precious to us.

Understanding it, like understanding the importance of tenderness, is absolutely essential if we want to honor God and others. Let's discover the secrets to mastering what may be the most powerful of all human emotions.

6

A Closed Spirit: Overcoming a
Major Destroyer of Relationships

L ATE ONE NIGHT, while I was sound asleep, the phone rang.
It was a man calling long distance who had gotten my number from
a close friend. As I was struggling to wake up, he said, "Gary, I'm
sorry to call so late, but my wife has left me. Actually, she's thrown
me out of the house! She's so hostile toward me, it shocked me. I
really didn't see it coming. We've been married almost twenty-five
years, and now she's put me out on the street!"

As he continued, he asked, "Could you help me get back together
with my wife?"

He sounded so desperate over the phone, I decided to help him if I
could. So I asked, "Before I know if I can do anything to help you, I
need to talk to your wife."

He immediately shot back, "That's impossible. She's not talking
to me. She's not even talking to anyone who knows me. Gary, I don't
think you understand. She *hates* me. You have no idea how much
she hates me. She has a court order against me right now so that I
can't even get into my own home!"

Having talked with many people in similar situations, I replied,
"Well, I'll tell you what. I've never been turned down yet by a woman
I've called. This could be the first time, but I'm willing to give it a
try if you are."

After a brief pause, he said, "Well . . . I have nothing to lose, but
please call me back the minute you talk to her and let me know what
happens."

The next morning, I did call his wife. When she answered, I said,
"Hello, I'm Gary Smalley. Your husband called me last night and
really wanted some help, but I told him that in order to do anything
for him, I would need to talk to someone who knows him as well as

his wife. I was wondering. Could you just spend a couple of minutes with me, helping me understand your husband and why it was so difficult to live with him?"

Instantly she said, "Ohhhhh, I hate that man so much! I don't want to talk about him. In fact, even thinking about him upsets me."

I said, "It must have been horrible living with a man like that."

"You have no *idea* how horrible it was to live with that guy," she steamed. "He was so controlling, it was like I had to get *permission* to go to the bathroom!"

"How did you endure that kind of treatment for so many years?" I asked, trying everything I could just to keep her on the phone!

"I don't know how I managed, and now you're getting me to talk about him—and I don't want to talk about him!"

In the end, she did share several specific things this man had done— beginning with their honeymoon. Many were small, inconsiderate actions that had piled up hurt feelings until molehills became mountains.

After talking with her for only five minutes, I thanked her profusely for sharing her thoughts and time with me and hung up. Immediately I called her husband.

"Did you talk with her?" he asked.

"Yes," I said, "and you're right. *You are in big trouble!*"

Over the years, I could number in the hundreds the husbands who have called or written with a similar story. In each case, the man never "realized" that he was in such bad shape until his marital world came crashing down around him.

While there are unique situations with each person that has called, I can think of one common element in every case. In fact, it's one of the major destroyers of families—*unresolved anger*. Anger, though, is such a "normal" human emotion. How can it be so devastating to a relationship?

Opening the Door to a Major Destroyer of Families

Recently, a close friend told me about a rock star who brought home a cute little lion cub to raise on his ranch in Tennessee. Of course, he had to hire a lawyer to convince the local zoning board to give him a special permit to own a wild animal as a "pet," but with money being no object, he managed to get that detail taken care of quickly enough.

For several years his "tame" lion was quite a hit with his house guests. It never acted like a dangerous predator, only like a big, play-ful pet. Then one day without warning, a parent's worst nightmare became this man's reality.

His little two-year-old son was playing near the lion cage. The parents heard his screams for help from inside the house, but there was nothing they could do. The lion had broken out of his cage and brutally mauled the little boy before running off into the woods. In a terrible tragedy, the man's son died before they could even get him to the hospital.

I'm sure this man loved his son, and having raised the lion from a cub, he probably never consciously thought that it would one day rob his child of life. But all the reasoning in the world on why it was "safe" to keep a wild animal around the house couldn't erase that animal's nature. For centuries, people have learned the hard way about the dark side of a lion's nature. By allowing a predator into his home, the man was setting the stage for a potential tragedy.

I can't think of a single person I've met who would willingly ex-pose a child or spouse to the fury of a full-grown lion, but I know of many husbands and wives who are letting another deadly killer walk right through their front door without a fight—*unhealthy, unresolved anger*.

Anger can rip the heart right out of a relationship. Without exag-geration, every hour that anger is allowed to stay in a person's life, it acts like an emotional time bomb ticking down to detonation. Like a terrorist bomb placed in an innocent looking shopping bag, it cares nothing for whom it hurts or eventually kills.

"But everyone gets angry. Even Jesus got 'angry' at the people in the temple," some may say. While this is certainly true, there is a major difference between righteous anger (that can have a "correc-tive" effect on error), and the kind of unhealthy anger that grows wild and, unchallenged, leads to destructive conflicts.

Like that rock star's lion, anger inside a person can never be made a "tame" emotion. Even "righteous anger" can become corrupted if a person is not very, very careful.

The man who called me in the middle of the night learned a cru-cial skill needed in any healthy relationship. In his case it proved to be a life-saving skill. He realized that by letting anger build up in his wife's life—anger that he was directly responsible for provoking—he had *closed her spirit* toward him.[1]

Like that innocent looking lion cub, he had let his insensitive acts pile up until they finally broke full force on the relationship. What he learned, however, actually helped him begin to repair the damage. He learned how to reopen his wife's closed spirit by getting the anger out of her life—and it made a dramatic change in his situation.

> . . . we'll never be successful in
> our most important relationships
> until we learn how to drain the
> anger out of another person's life.

Unfortunately, my late night friend is not unique. Parents can sometimes leave anger in a child's life when he or she is young, closing the child's spirit to them tightly. These same parents then see that deep-seated anger turns into resistance and rebelliousness in their teenagers. Employers can even close the spirit of their employees and soon meet resistance and a stiffening will in them.

Even though anger is potentially destructive, it can be dealt with, even in cases that may seem humanly impossible. That's what we're going to talk about in this chapter. We don't have to live in continual disharmony with others. We can literally be in harmony with those around us the majority of the time.

But we'll never be successful in our most important relationships until we learn to drain the anger out of another person's life. It's absolutely crucial that we learn how to "open" a person's closed spirit and get back in harmony with them again. That begins as we learn the skills of putting unresolved anger out of our homes.

Putting Unresolved Anger out of a Home

First, let me define what I mean by unhealthy anger. *Selfish anger is the negative emotion we feel when a person or situation has failed to meet our needs*, blocked our goals, or *fallen short of our expectations.* It's what we feel when we've placed our needs, wants, and desires ahead of anyone else's. Then we become frustrated if those around us don't react the way we want them to. Let me illustrate more clearly what I mean by "negative" anger by giving a hypothetical example from my own home.

If I walk through the door one night and blast Norma for being five minutes late with dinner, I'd be absolutely wrong. It certainly isn't a sin for her to have dinner ready a few minutes late, and so to "let her have it" only demonstrates I was more interested in my own stomach than her welfare. That's the real problem with anger; it puts "me" ahead of everyone else and shows its displeasure whenever "I" don't get my way.

To clarify even further, there are two things we need to keep in balance. *First*, there is a "righteous" anger that stands up against sin. In Ephesians 4, there is a clear command to be angry over the things that would grieve God's heart (often the kinds of things that fill our newspapers and evening news). ". . . *But in your anger do not sin*" (Ephesians 4:26). Biblically, two wrongs never equal one right. Even if we become righteously angry over some anger-producing situation in our life or the lives of others, we are never justified in reacting in a sinful way.

Second, try as we might by logical reason, we will not always be able to avoid an immediate emotion. If someone accidentally steps on our foot or cuts in front of us on the freeway, our instantaneous reaction may be anger. There's nothing wrong or sinful about anger at this point. But when we let anger remain in our lives, or when we take its energy and direct it toward another person to hurt them, we move from a normal, healthy feeling to a destructive one.

Apply what Martin Luther used to say to negative thoughts: "You can't keep the birds from flying over your head . . . but you can keep them from building a nest in your hair!" We may not be able to keep anger from cropping up as an instantaneous and instinctive reaction to some pain or problem, but we can make a decision to keep it from staying in our lives and poisoning our attitudes or the attitudes of our loved ones.

Putting Healthy Limits on an Unhealthy Emotion

Let's go back to the couple with whom we started this chapter. From the time they were first married, this husband never placed any boundaries around his anger. Whenever his wife blocked any of his goals, or slowed him down in any way, he blasted her without regard to the emotional impact of his words.

One could say that his wife should have been more "spiritually mature" and should not have been hurt by his angry outbursts, but in real life, after a constant stream of angry words and actions over the years, she began to wilt under his treatment. This wife didn't realize that it is possible to be free from anger on our own, as you'll see in Chapters 13 and 14, and her husband didn't realize two things about anger in a home that can cripple a relationship.

1. Anger Eats Away at a Person's Health

Inside the brain, the decision you make to harbor negative feelings toward others can set off a series of physical events you would do well to avoid. When a person becomes angry, his body goes on "full alert." When the inner brain gets the message that there's a stressful situation out there, it doesn't ask questions—it reacts. Your body can easily release as many chemicals and disrupt as many bodily functions when you are angry with your spouse as if you're being attacked by a wild animal.[2]

After several years of living with an angry man, the woman in our story began manifesting several of the symptoms of a person with deep-seated anger locked inside them: early morning awakening, depression, tension, grinding teeth, an unexplainable sense of dread, jumpiness, and increased irritability.[3] None of these negative outworkings of anger is physically helpful. In fact, unresolved anger actually pulls a person's resistance to illness down.

When a person's body is constantly tense and on edge (for unrighteous anger never fully lets a person relax—even in his sleep), this tension will inevitably begin to wear the person down. That's when really undesirable things begin to happen physiologically, such as clinical depression, colitis, bleeding ulcers, anxiety attacks, lowered resistance to colds and flu, and heart and respiratory failure. Several researchers even believe that some types of cancer result from the mega-doses of stress that unhealthy anger carries with it.[4]

Perhaps all these physical manifestations of anger are behind the first commandment with a promise, "Honor your father and mother, so that you may live long . . . "(Exodus 20:12). Anger, however, doesn't just contribute to a poor grade on a health report card. It can also keep us "in the dark" when it comes to loving God and others.

2. The Greatest Problem of All

In 1 John 2:9-11, the apostle says that continual anger toward another results in losing the ability to live in God's light. Being angry with our brother pushes us into darkness—completely isolated from the light of His love. When we live with anger—or provoke it in the hearts of others—we pull a veil of darkness across our eyes that blinds us to the damage we're doing to others.

In part, this is why so many angry men or women don't "wake up" to the damage they've done to a home until the very walls of the family are falling down around them. The anger they have spewed out at members of their family has doubled back and blinded them to God's love and that of others.

Walking consistently in darkness prevents us from being lovingly sensitive toward others. It also kills any interest we have in studying God's Word and puts an icy chill on our desire to pray. Further, it robs us of any desire to please and honor Him or to experience His joy, contentment, and peace.

I've met a number of people who, after years of attending church and seeking God, have still not found peace. And after getting to know them better, the major reason for their failure in many cases is deep-seated anger.[5] They are unwilling to forgive or seek forgiveness, and as a result they hide pockets of darkness inside their lives—black holes in their souls that can expand throughout the years.

Anger does tremendous damage to a person physically and spiritually—and that's not all. It also goes to the emotional heart of a relationship and can bury any feelings of warmth or attachment in its icy darkness as well.

How can we tell that anger has begun to attack our relationship, pushing it into darkness? Our loved ones will begin to withdraw from us on every level—physical, emotional, and spiritual. That withdrawal is something I call a *closed spirit*. Left unchecked, this spirit can drain every bit of sparkle and vitality out of our families and leave them empty, wounded, and alone.

Recognizing a Person's Spirit

Let me get more specific about what I mean about a person's "spirit." It can be explained this way. When you meet someone for the first time, you interact with him on three levels—first with your spirit, then with your soul, and finally with your body.

Imagine with me that I walk up to a person at one of our seminars and meet him for the first time. Before ever we spoke a word, the first thing that would "touch" would be our *spirit*. I'm defining the "spirit" of a person as the innermost, intangible part of our being that tells us if there is any natural connection or friction between us. It's also that part of us that relates to God at times when words aren't enough.

Next, is the *soul* (the Greek word for soul is "psyche"). The soul is made up of three inseparable parts: the intellect, the will, and the emotions. When we communicate with a person, we engage at all three of these levels. For example, with the person I met at the seminar, we would no doubt exchange words when we meet. Later, if we come to know each other better, we would exchange ideas or even dreams. In that way, our "souls" would have touched or interacted.[6]

If our relationship entered the third level, and if it were appropriate, we could physically touch. For example, you and I would probably shake hands if we met for the first time. Now we've had a complete relationship—body, soul, and spirit. Granted, at this point it's a shallow relationship, but at least it has all the elements of a "total" relationship.

In our seminar, I use my hand to illustrate the open and closed spirit concept. To make sure you understand this principle, hold out your own hand right now.

Look at the palm of your hand, with the fingers spread wide apart. Let's say that the fingers wiggling around freely are the spirit of a person. They're the first thing to reach out and touch others. The semicircular ridge where the fingers meet the palm of the hand could represent the soul where people meet intellectually. And the very center of the palm could stand for the body.

When you are happy and all is well in your relationship with your mate, child, or friend, those fingers are wiggling and happy. The palm is open and exposed—ready to reach out and even to lovingly hold someone else's hand. An open hand could have represented the woman whose story we told at the beginning of this chapter. When she first married, she was open and eager for love.

If I offend a person or provoke him to anger, however, that open hand can begin to close. Take time to give yourself a living object lesson. Close your hand slowly and notice what happens. The spirit begins to close over the soul and the body. If it is allowed to tighten up all the way, what do you have? A closed fist—the world-wide symbol of anger and defiance. In short, you have what that man had when he called me in the middle of the night—a wife who was so deeply hurt and so "closed" to him that she lashed back with the force of a rock-hard fist.

As long as everything is healthy in a relationship, the hand is open, the fingers wiggling and happy. The spirit is open and responsive. But hurtful words and actions—allowed to grow into a bitter spirit—can one day lead to our being shut out of someone's life completely.

How Do We Close a Person's Spirit?

While there are probably hundreds of ways to offend someone—and close his or her spirit—we consistently see several that top the list. To repeat just a few, we can close a person's spirit by—

- Speaking harsh words
- Belittling a person's opinions
- Being unwilling to admit that we're wrong
- Taking a person for granted
- Making jokes or sarcastic comments at the other person's expense
- Not trusting a person
- Forcing a person to do something he's uncomfortable with
- Being rude to that person in front of others
- Ignoring a person's genuine needs as unimportant or not nearly as valuable as our own

That's just a sample of the "hit list" of actions that can close a person's spirit.[7] Our loved ones could probably make up their own list. We may not even be aware of what we do to deposit anger into their lives. When it comes to relationships, an important rule of thumb is, *whatever dishonors another person usually closes his spirit.*

While it wasn't my intended goal, I got an early start in closing Norma's spirit. When we were first married, I spoke at a number of youth groups. We were still in college, and we had no children, so Norma always went along with me to these meetings.

I thought I was quite funny at the time, and I would crack jokes at Norma's expense, totally unaware of how it was affecting her spirit. I would say things like, "Oh, it sure is great being married to Norma. She treats me just like a god! Every morning she serves me burnt offerings."

That would get big laughs. So then I'd follow up with something like, "Being married to Norma is just like being married to an angel—she's always up in the air harping about something and she never has an earthly thing to wear!"

And if I was really on a roll, I could always tell the kids about the time I pulled up to the airport with Norma and a sky cap asked, "Can

I help you with your bag?" And I said, "No, thanks, she can walk." Later, in the car, you can guess what would happen.

Norma would often say, "I really didn't appreciate your jokes, Gary." To which I'd impatiently wave my hand, and say, "Oh, lighten up. You're *sooooo* sensitive!" I didn't realize it at the time, but each sarcastic comment was beginning to close her spirit to me.

Once again, part of the problem lies with the differences between men and women. Men are usually not aware that God has created most women with a highly sensitive spirit to sarcasm and criticism. I know I wasn't aware of this very important natural difference— particularly during that first important year of marriage.

My Own Valentine's Day Massacre

Six months or so after our wedding, Valentine's Day rolled around. It was our first Valentine's Day as a married couple and Norma had spent hours preparing a fancy meal just for me. In her mind as she was laboring over a hot stove, she was thinking thoughts like . . .

"It's Valentine's Day, and my new husband is going to be coming through the door any minute. He'll have a romantic card for me, and then we'll enjoy a memorable time together!"

What I did was certainly memorable—but it produced the kind of memory I'd like to forget. I called at two o'clock in the afternoon and said "Hon', I forgot to tell you something this morning. I've got a basketball game I'm going to play in tonight."

I could sense the surprise in her voice as she responded,

"But this is Valentine's Day!"

"I know, I know, but this game is really important."

Then Norma said,

"But I've already made this special dinner, and I've got the new tablecloth on, and candles set out, and . . . and . . ."

"Norma, I have to go to this game. I gave some of the guys my *word* that I'd be there." (Which meant that I wasn't about to embarrass myself by calling up my friends and telling them I had to stay home with my wife instead of playing basketball.)

For a long time, there was only silence on the other end of the phone. Although I'm ashamed of it now, do you know what I thought at the time? *Oh, no. I have a strong-willed woman on my hands!* I mistook a closing spirit for a strong will.

Right then I decided I might as well take advantage of this

tailor-made opportunity to straighten her out. So, in a controlled, but firm, voice, I said, "Now, Norma, you know that I'm going into the ministry, *right*? One of the very important things that the Bible says is the wife should submit to her husband. . . ."

I'm sure you know how well my lecture went over. Her spirit began to close on me that very moment because of my total insensitivity— only I didn't realize it at the time. I was so blinded by my own self-interest, I couldn't see the negative writing on the walls of her life, though I would one day be forced to read it.

Bit by bit, month by month, I did more and more of these "little," insensitive things until I knocked the sparkle right out of her precious eyes. It's difficult for me, even after all these years, to think about how unaware I was of her spirit—and how insensitive and wrong I was.

The tragedy is, the more a man steps on the spirit of his wife, the more resistant she becomes toward him. The more resistant she becomes to him, the more he closes his spirit toward her. Soon, you have a vicious circle of two people in the same home who have made a public vow to love each other—now living under a private pledge to have a closed fist, not an open hand. As I close my spirit to another person, what happens? It closes up my soul and my body as well.

"But how do I know that I'm actually closing someone's spirit?" The state of a child's spirit is the easiest to recognize, because children are not as practiced at hiding their real emotions. When children become closed to us in their souls, they disagree with everything we say, lose their desire to be "with the family," and seem to love to argue. Physically, they stop touching us, or they even resist our touch under any and all circumstances. They may even turn their backs on us when they see us.

To us, our remark may mean nothing. We may not even remember it. To us, our words may seem as light as a pebble. If I dropped a pebble on my spouse's or child's foot, I might think it should bounce right off without their notice. But for our loved ones, what is a "pebble" to us might be a ten-pound weight. And we just dropped it right on their barefoot toes!

Common Marks of a Closed Spirit

Because it's difficult for many of us to recognize when we've closed a family member's spirit, it's worth taking a moment to learn four common warning signs.

①Warning sign number one is *a feeling of tension between you that you can't explain away*. That may be the spirit closing.

②Warning sign number two is *an argumentative attitude*. They may resist discussing just about anything. They might avoid you, never ask for your advice, or criticize you for little or no reason. Before long, you can say the moon comes up at night and the sun in the day, and they'll find a way to disagree.

Some of us have worked for a boss who has deeply offended us. We know what it's like to disagree with anything he says—even before he says anything! If I have my spirit closed toward someone, I can have negative thoughts whenever I see that person.

The same thing happens when you step on the spirit of your children. Typically, they become resistant. It's the basic attitude of a persistently strong-willed child. Almost all toddlers (and most other kids of various ages) can go through "stages" of being strong-willed. If you win the battle early, then you can avoid facing many battles later in life.[8]

There is a major difference, though, in a child who is going through the normal "stages" of challenging mom and dad, and one who is retaliating out of anger by being stubborn or "resistant." You can tell a closed-fist child to take the trash out, and he won't be "typically" slow about it—he'll be blatantly defiant. "No, I'm *not* going to do it. You do it yourself or make someone else do it."

③Warning sign number three is *a loss of physical intimacy*. Hugs and kisses? Forget it; your loved one probably won't want to get within a block of you. Almost all children go through times when "hugging" mom and dad isn't "cool" (or "hot," or "rad"). But even during these times, if parents are persistent and creative, they can fill up their child's "touch" bank with quick hugs and playful wrestling (with the guys). If, on the other hand, his or her spirit is closed to you, it'll be like an armed guard in front of the bank!

Close a spouse's spirit, and watch the romantic feelings all but evaporate. I've had a number of women tell me that emotionally they felt like prostitutes when their spirit was closed to their husbands and they were involved sexually anyway.

I've heard husbands growl, "That woman is totally uninterested or unresponsive!" Yet he may be the primary cause of her low level of sexual response as the one closing her spirit. Physical intimacy for a woman is spirit, soul, and body, not just body alone. All three levels have to be interrelated, otherwise any sexual response, for both men and women, is, at best, mechanical and, at worst, dysfunctional.

Warning sign number four is *negative nonverbal signals.* If a person's spirit is closing toward you, his facial expressions may even be more negative than his words. Physically, he may pull away from you, leave the door to his room shut consistently for "privacy," or even turn his back on you in the middle of a conversation. If your children resent being at home—especially being alone with you—that too may be a sign of a closed spirit.

A Window of Hope

My purpose in writing about a closed spirit is not to heap guilt on spouses or parents who may find themselves battling a fist rather than an opened palm. It is, rather, to give people hope. As I have tried to share in detail, things I've done to both my wife and children have closed their spirits to me for a short time, but the key to maintaining strong relationships over the years is to be able to reopen a loved one's closed spirit. It reminds me of what I had to do with my oldest son, Greg, when he was just a young boy

Five Attitudes That Can
Help to Open a Loved One's Heart

In my parenting book, *The Key to Your Child's Heart*, I tell about my son Greg when he was about five or six years old. At the time, I worked for a large Christian organization, and I was often on the phone with pastors across the country. This also meant that I would have to take calls at home from a number of Christian leaders at times, so I made a rule in our home that couldn't be violated—nobody screams when I'm on the phone!

One evening I was in my bedroom on a long-distance phone call to a distinguished senior pastor. Suddenly, my son, Greg, let out a blood-curdling scream from the bathroom. He came running into the bedroom, screaming so loudly that I couldn't hear the person on the other end of the line.

"Hush!" I signaled to him emphatically, putting my hand over the mouthpiece of the phone, "Can't you see I'm on the phone?"

But Greg continued screaming, so I quickly ended my phone conversation, telling the person I'd have to call him back later.

When I hung up the phone, I grabbed Greg by the arm. "Why are you screaming and running around the house?" I demanded. "Couldn't you see I was on the phone?"

Without waiting for an answer, I hustled him down the hall and said, "You get into your bedroom right now." Still crying, Greg hurried into his room. Once we were inside, I picked up the little ruler that the kids had all helped to decorate (they affectionately named it the "teacher"). For breaking my inviolate rule, I swatted him on the bottom.

It was our practice after a spanking to hold the child and hug away any resentment, but this time, something took place that startled me.

"Come here so I can hug you," I said.

"No," he said, still crying, and the look in his eyes said, "I hate you." He backed away from me to let me know that he didn't want me to touch him at all.

Then after all that had happened, it hit me.

"Greg, why were you crying?"

With his little voice heaving with his sobs, he said, "I fell in the bathroom and hurt my ear and when you pushed me on the bed, I hurt it again."

He was hurt. That's why he was crying! Why hadn't I asked him earlier? Now I not only felt awful, I also felt like a child abuser. I knew I had closed Greg's spirit tightly at that moment, and if I didn't do something, it could leave an emotional scar on our relationship.

Convicted to my very heart, I got down on my knees.

"Greggy," I said in the softest voice I could. "I'm so sorry that I didn't ask you what was wrong or why you were screaming. You didn't deserve a spanking. I'm the one that deserves to be spanked." I held out the little stick to him, but he dropped it and backed up. It was obvious that he still didn't want any part of me.

So I said, "Greg, I was so wrong. Maybe you can't do it right now, but I wonder if you could forgive me? Would you?" Then it was as if his little heart melted, and he rushed into my arms. I fell back onto the bed with him in my arms and just held him tightly as his sobs slowly turned into regular breathing.

After a long time, I asked him again to be sure, "Greg, are you sure you've forgiven Daddy?"

He just patted me and said, "Oh, Daddy, we all make mistakes."

Do you know what that told me about Greg? It told me that Greg was opening his spirit to me. He was touching me. We were talking. His feelings were coming back. His body, soul, and spirit were re-opening.

What was happening between us as we held each other was the

result of five attitudes that work together to help open the spirit of a person. Let me state clearly, *these are not steps.* You can't mechanically go down the list and expect to wipe away every hurt or draw out all the anger in a relationship. With Greg, it took only a half-hour to reopen his spirit and put us back into harmony. With Norma, it took almost two years of consistently applying these attitudes to reverse all the closing of her spirit I had done.

The important thing is not the time it takes, but the decision and commitment to do whatever it takes to come back into harmony with a person *to release as much anger as possible.* For years now, I have practiced these same attitudes with my wife and each of my children. They have been a tremendous help in making sure anger is drained out of our home each day. I know they can be an encouragement in your home as well.

Five Attitudes to Reopen a Person's Spirit

1. Become soft and tender with the person

Proverbs says, "A gentle answer turns away wrath" (Proverbs 15:1). My whole problem with Greg started when I became harsh and unreasoning. Things began to turn around when my tone of voice softened along with my spirit. My attitude, nonverbals, and voice said I cared about him. Sometimes softness alone can open a person's spirit. That's the whole message of Chapter 5.

2. Understand, as much as possible, what the other person has gone through (remember, listen to what is said; do not react to the words used)

I would have cried if I had fallen in the bathtub, too. Then to get a spanking on top of that? So I showed Greg by my words, as best I could, that I understood what he felt. I talked with him about how awful it must have been, all the time being careful not to "react" to something he said defensively.

3. Acknowledge that the person is hurting, and be sure to admit any wrong in provoking anger

"Greg," I said, "I was so wrong." As a parent (or a spouse), it can be very hard to say those words at times, but as it did with Greg, it can work wonders. Admitting we are wrong (when we clearly are) is like drilling a hole in our loved one's "anger bucket" and allowing that unhealthy emotion to drain away. Once they hear us admit it, the anger has a way to escape from their lives.

Sometimes we may not think we are wrong, but our attitude might be. Or, it may be the way we've done something that's offensive. If my attitude is harsh and angry when I tell my wife about a legitimate problem, I'm still wrong. ". . . Man's anger (or that of a woman) does not bring about the righteous life that God desires" (James 1:20). Stopping short of admitting we were wrong leaves a dangerous gap between you and your child or mate that may not mend quickly—or at all.

4. Touch the other person gently

If you step on your mate's spirit at ten o'clock at night (or in the morning) and then you get into bed and expect to be amorous, what's likely to happen? Your spouse may move way over to the other side of the bed. That's when you'll hear that she has a headache, it's the wrong year, or she just doesn't want to be touched. The nonverbal message, "No touchie the toes," may mean, "My spirit is closing to you."

If you try to touch someone with a closed spirit, you will find out just how deep the hurt is. If a woman has only been touched in anger or to meet her husband's sexual needs, she may resent *any* touch and pull away, or be stiff and unbending. But persistent softness—expressed in meaningful touches apart from any demands for sex—can go a long way toward draining anger and negative feelings from a relationship.

5. Seek forgiveness—and wait for a response

Say something like, "Could you forgive me? I've disappointed you so many times. I know I don't deserve to be forgiven, but could you try?" or "I don't want you all tied up in knots, not responding to me at all. I know I have a million miles to go before I get everything together in my life, but I love you very much, and I ask you to forgive me. Will you forgive me?"

Try to get a positive response from the person before you quit, but if you need to, start with the first loving attitude of being soft and work your way back down to forgiveness again. Remember, too, *don't just respond to your loved one's words*. In the heat of battle, or if

you've deeply hurt someone, that person may say something in retaliation to hurt you: "That's right," they might respond. "You *don't*
deserve to be forgiven. I really don't know how I live with you when
you mess up so often."

For many people, men in particular, hearing words that may hit
below the belt can set off a defensive lecture—or even be an invitation to another round of angry retaliation. But those men and
women who are wise enough to reopen a person's spirit have to
learn to listen beyond the words to the hurt feelings behind the
words.

There have been times when I felt something Norma said to me
was unfair, even though I was trying to be soft and ask her to forgive
me. Perhaps she misinterpreted my motives or even questioned my
character in the process, but when you're asking another person to
forgive you, it's not the time to get into a lecture on the precise
wording of the problem. Your focus should be on draining away the
anger and not on compounding it.

The senior pastor at our home church is an exceptional individual.
One of the many things we've learned from Darryl DelHousaye is a
biblical admonition on dealing with anger. I've found it to be uni-
versally true in relationships. Time and again, Darryl has said from
the pulpit, concerning anger and the need for forgiveness, "Biblically,
the stronger person always initiates the peace." Are you willing to
be the "strong" one who seeks to set things right in a relationship?
Sometimes it takes a strong act of the will not to react to someone's
words. Remember—in most cases it was hasty reactions that helped
to close that person's spirit in the first place.

> Biblically, the stronger person
> always initiates the peace.

Untying Our Own Knots

There is an important reason why forgiveness plays such a pivotal
part in opening a person's spirit. It has to do with the very way the
Bible defines the word. In the original biblical language, remember,
the word for forgiveness means "to release, set free, to untie."

With that picture in mind, when we say or do something offensive to other people, we are actually helping, emotionally and spiritually, to tie them in knots. Perhaps what we've done has come as the result of knots someone else has left in our lives.

Do you know why most "difficult" people are so ill-natured, people who don't like themselves, who are resentful, or who feel rejected? Such people battle forgiving others—or feeling forgiven themselves. The way they tell us that they're tied up is through their negative, obnoxious actions. That's one reason why the Scriptures say we are to love our enemies. Their negative reactions are warning signals that their lives are tied up in knots.

What about my own knots, though? someone may be thinking. *How can I get the knots out of another person's life when I'm all tied up myself?* In the Lord's Prayer, Christ answers this important question.

If we could paraphrase a few verses, using the literal definition of forgiveness, it could read like this: "If you are willing to untie the knots of the one who offended you, then God will untie your own knots (forgive you). If you refuse to untie their knotted lives, then God won't untie yours." One major reason why forgiveness is so necessary is that anger blocks the working of God's spirit.

Can you see now that leaving someone angry is allowing them to be in "darkness" and tied up in "knots"? Not only are we damaging a person emotionally when we provoke anger in them, but we are also cutting them off from God's light. There is, however, an antidote to unhealthy anger.

If we are attaching value and honor to the people around us, then we will do our best never to do anything that ties them up in knots. If we do, we will try to untie them. "Do not let the sun go down on your anger" (Ephesians 4:26 RSV).

In Chapters 13 and 15, we'll share specifically about untying the knots that may be in your life. For now, though, keeping harmony in a home comes from understanding the attitudes that can reopen a loved one's life and love to us.

Never . . . Never Give Up

There is one final question we must raise. What if we try our best, and they still don't respond?

Gently persist . . . gently persist . . . gently, lovingly persist.

Near the end of his life, Winston Churchill was asked to give a commencement speech at a noted university in England. His car arrived late, and the jam-packed crowd suddenly hushed as one of the greatest men in British history made his way slowly, painfully to the podium.

Churchill's speech lasted less than two minutes—but it drew a standing ovation. It comprised only twelve words, but it has inspired decades of men and women ever since. What he said is the best advice I can give you when it comes to being persistent in love to open a spouse's or child's spirit. What did he say?

With his deep, gruff, resonating voice, he said, "Never give up . . . Never, never, give up . . . Never, never, never give up."

End of speech, but not the end of the message. If the man who called me at midnight had given up on being persistent in love, he would have sent a wife and family away tied up in knots and still in darkness.

I'm not sure if I have ever heard a more hostile woman than the one I called that morning. Yet a little less than a year later, she called me back and said, "Gary, I just wanted you to know that I'm back together with my husband. . . ."

I'll have to admit I was floored when I received her call. From every human angle, their relationship was dead in the water that fateful evening when she locked her husband out of the house. Obviously she had thought the same thing.

"A year ago," she said, "if you had even *suggested* that there was a possibility we would be back together—that I would even *like* him, much less love him again—I wouldn't have believed you. The amazing thing," she continued, "is that I do love him again. I actually want to be around him. That fascinates me all by itself. . . ."

What happened to bring about such a change? Because this man recognized that he had let anger ruin his home—and learned how to drain it out of his wife's life—he reopened her spirit, and he did one thing more. His commitment to allow God to change him and his attitude toward his family made him never, never give up—even when she said she hated him and never wanted to see him again.

If I had given up any one of a hundred times of working to get the anger out of Norma or one of my children's lives, I probably wouldn't be writing this book now—or enjoying the strong relationships we have at home. What I and my friend learned about opening a person's spirit can work for you too—as it has in my family—to help us all avoid a major destroyer of families.

Now we head into one of my favorite subjects: the tremendous value of a man. For God has given a man exactly what he needs to be a great lover and leader of his home. We men come to the marriage relationship equipped to contribute four essential ingredients that lie at the heart of a rock-solid relationship. Let's discover what those ingredients are.

7
The Tremendous
Value of a Man

JUST PICTURE THE scene. Norma and I are getting ready to begin one of our evening marriage encounter groups—an important part of the early work we did on a church staff: Everyone has been walking around, smiling, drinking coffee, catching up on small talk. Now they're all settling comfortably into the chairs we've arranged around the living room. Then, suddenly, the peaceful atmosphere is shattered.

With a bang, the front screen door swings open. In walks one of the couples from the group. The husband darts ahead of his wife and takes over the couch. Without a word, he crosses his arms and glares at everybody. His wife's eyes are red and puffy, and she walks right past him and sits down across the room, next to one of the other wives.

Only a few seconds had passed, and the evening had gone from easygoing to explosive! Since I was the leader of the group, I decided to get started, thinking that would help.

I opened with a prayer, then looked at the man again. He was still sitting with his arms tightly crossed, looking like Mount St. Helens just before it erupted. Thinking it might relieve some of the tension, I started off with him.

"How's it going this week?" I asked.

"*Terrible!*" he snarled.

"Okay," I said. "What's so terrible?"

"If you really want to know," he replied, leaning forward in his chair and looking me right in the eye, "I've been thinking about getting out of this marriage group.

"No—I'll tell you what," he continued, raising his volume level up a notch, "I've got a better idea. What I'm really thinking about is getting out of my marriage! I *can't stand* that woman over there, and I don't know if I can live with her any longer." His words ripped through the air as he sat back in his chair, a look of defiance on his face.

It was interesting to see what happened the instant he stopped talking. All the women immediately glared at him, and then went over to comfort his wife, and every man in the room instantly did the same thing, only for him. We all looked at each other and thought, *What do we do now?*

As the leader of the group, I knew I had to take charge, so I said, "Why don't we close in prayer?" And that's exactly what I did. It was probably the shortest marriage group meeting on record. As everyone filed into the kitchen, I was able to pull the man aside and asked, "Listen, why don't we get together for lunch tomorrow before you do something drastic?"

Reluctantly, he agreed.

The next day, as we talked at a restaurant downtown, we both discovered something fascinating. In fact, it's something I've used to strengthen my own marriage and have shared with hundreds of men since.

Self-Inflicted Wounds in a Relationship

"Why do you want to leave your wife? What bothers you the most about her?" I asked.

"Gary, there isn't enough time over lunch for me to tell you everything that gripes me. It'd take all afternoon!"

"Just try to hit the high points then," I said. In a few minutes, he had shared five things about her that were particularly irritating.

"She's a sloppy housekeeper . . . she's on the phone all the time . . . she's with her mother constantly . . . she won't take any trips with me . . . she never initiates when it comes to sex."

As the list piled up, his attitude became harder and harder. I threw up a quick prayer for wisdom and then I did something I'd never done before. I began by taking each one of his "gripes" in order and asking him specific questions about them. Questions like: "When it comes to her housekeeping, do you ever encourage her? For instance, do you ever praise her for the good things she does around the house?"

"No," he replied. "She never *does* anything good around the house for me to compliment."

"At least give me an example of what you might say to her when her housekeeping skills don't measure up to where you want them," I went on.

"Well," he said, his tone softening just a little, "the other day I got up and started vacuuming the house at six o'clock in the morning. When I started down the hallway toward our bedroom, she got out of bed and said 'What are you doing?' and I said, 'I'm sick and tired of living in this pig pen! We're cleaning up this place, and we're doing it *now!*'"

"Do you think that motivates her to keep the house clean?" I asked.

"No, I guess it doesn't. But that still doesn't solve the problem of her being a slob," he retorted. Ignoring his barbs, I continued through his list, asking questions.

"After work and on weekends, how much time do you spend actually talking to your wife about something important to her?"

"Well, frankly there's not a lot of time left over in my week. I've got a crushing schedule at the office. I play racquetball three days a week, and then we have to fit in *your* group which takes another night," he said, making sure I knew how much effort he was expending just to be in the group. "And I've got to do something to relax on the weekends, so I usually play golf with some of the guys from work. . . ."

"Do you spend any time talking to her during dinner?" I asked.

Reluctantly he replied, "I usually watch television during dinner. Basically, that's the only time I have to catch the news. But Gary, you've got to understand. In my line of work it's crucial for me to know what's going on, nationally and internationally, to see how it might affect my business."

I said, "Okay, the news may be important, but do you spend *any* time with her during the week, just the two of you, talking together about your lives? About what's important to her, not just your business?"

"No," he said in an emotionless voice, "not really."

I said, "Then it's no wonder she's on the phone day and night and always over at her mother's. A woman comes equipped with a tremendous need for meaningful communication—particularly with her husband. If that need is blocked, she'll find someone else to talk to."

"Oh," he said, a series of tiny lights beginning to switch on inside his mind, "I never thought of it that way."

"You've got your own company now, but in the past have you ever worked for a guy who was very critical?" I asked.

"You bet I have," he said, without pausing even a moment to think about it.

"I had one boss I really hated. He was the kind of guy who couldn't *wait* to come into my office to criticize me. He'd point out anything that was going wrong or even could go wrong in my department. Then he'd yell at me to 'Shape up! Do this! Do that!' After his tirade in front of all the other people I worked with, he'd go back in his office and drink coffee while I worked my head off."

> God has built into every man
> the natural ability to be the very
> loving leader his family needs.

I said, "How did that make you feel?"

"How did it make me *feel?* I hated working with him," he answered. "I couldn't wait until the end of the day just to get away from him."

"Would you like to go on a vacation with him?" I asked.

"*A vacation?* Are you kidding?" he said incredulously. "That'd be the *last* thing I'd want to do."

I said, "Don, do you realize that you're treating your wife the same way that boss treated you?"

His eyes widened, and he sat straight up in his chair as he took in what I said.

"It's no wonder your wife doesn't want to go on a trip with you, or even to respond to you physically. The way you've been treating her, it's as if she's living night and day with your former boss."

After a long silence, he grudgingly said, "You've got a point there."

We went through all five areas he'd mentioned and made an amazing discovery. With each and every problem he had with his wife, he was at least partially responsible for creating the very attitudes and actions that were so irritating to him.

"What do I do now?" he asked, plaintively.

It's not that this man's negative contributions to his marriage in any way justified his wife's negative behavior, but in many ways, his behavior helped support her actions. Basically, he had no idea he was adding to the very things he didn't want to see in his home. Now that he realized it, he didn't know how to begin to change.

Would you describe this man as a lover? Not really. Would you describe him as a nurturer? Not likely. Could he (and did he) become both? Definitely.

Unlocking a Man's Natural Strength

I am convinced that most men, if they have a plan and know what to do, are willing to take the steps to build a loving, lasting relationship.[1] The problem is that the average man doesn't know intuitively what it takes to do so—nor does he realize the incredible benefits that a strong relationship at home brings to nearly every area of his life.[2]

Remember the women's "built-in marriage manual" we talked about in Chapter 4? In that chapter, we shared how by nature, God seems to equip a woman from birth with important skills a man tends to lack. In part, that is the reason for the special title she bears as a man's "completer" and "helper" (Genesis 2:18).

For some people, a woman's natural edge in relationships can be used as ammunition for blasting men and a man's place in the home. Some people have even read some of my earlier books and felt that I was jumping on the "men-bashing" bandwagon. However, I'd like to set the record straight.

While it is true a man doesn't speak as many words or may not be as naturally sensitive as a woman, that doesn't mean he is incapable of being a great lover in the home. In fact, it seems that *God has built into every man the natural ability to be the very loving leader his family needs.*

Saying that God has designed a man to be the lover in a home may sound a bit strange after all we've said about a man's conquering, logical, fact-driven nature, but that very nature is the foundation for my conviction.

Why? Because the kind of love that lasts, the kind that can grow and thrive apart from feelings, is the kind that comes from a decision. And as I mentioned in Chapter 3, *love*—stripped to its core—is just that, *a factual decision that doesn't have to depend on our feelings.*

There are times in life when we may not feel like doing something that's important, but we still need to do it. We need to give our two-year-old the medicine she needs when she flatly refuses to take it. Or we may have to stay up late to finish the report that has to be done on time—no matter how it bends our schedule or robs us of sleep. Or perhaps it's getting up an hour early each day to exercise and spend time in the Word and in prayer. Whatever the situation, there are times when all our "natural" instincts may say "no," but God's Word or another person's best interest demands we say "yes."

When it comes to family relationships, that same hard-driving, conquering nature that can cause a man to get ahead in his profession, can cause one of two results at home. In many cases, it can create emotional strain and tension if a man tries to blast through his family relationships like so many projects at work. Take that same drive and harness it by giving a man a specific plan of action for the home—and it can be the driving force to bring about the very relationship a woman longs for.

If the truth be known, that man in my marriage group came into his marriage with tremendous *liabilities.* He didn't have a loving father as a child, and the two communication skills his parents modeled for him were anger and silence. Yet, though he didn't know it at the time, in spite of the poor example he'd grown up with, he still possessed a God-given *ability* on which he could draw— anytime—to develop a strong marriage. Namely, once he knew what it took to have a fulfilling relationship, he could tap into his natural drive and desire to "win" and use it to strengthen his marriage.

It's hard for many women to understand how in an intimate relationship, a man is often more motivated to communicate if he puts facts in front of feelings. Normally, a woman will feel something, and then do it. For example, she'll feel an emotional need for communication, and then seek out her husband to meet that need. That's simply not the case with most men.

Usually a man is not driven by an emotional need to relate. Rather, he'll be much more motivated to do something relational (like spending a half-hour in conversation) once he's made a factual decision that it's right. For a man, actions are primarily what dictate feelings, not the reverse.

In large part, I feel that a man's unique ability to blend fact and feeling is a major gift God has given him in order to carry out his responsibility of being the loving leader in a home. When a man is given the right information, told what is right to do and how to do it, he can draw on his natural force of will to make a decision that *stays* while his feelings may come and go.

A Biblical Blueprint for
Loving Leadership in a Home

For a man, the first place he should check when it comes to building a strong family is a blueprint found in Ephesians 5. In this important chapter, the man is called to be the "head" of his wife—the primary lover—just as Christ is the head of the church and the lover of the church.

Nowhere does it say that a man is to "lord it over" his wife. In fact, Christ specifically commands that "lording it over" another person has no place in a Christian's relationships. Rather, the Scriptures tell me I am to love my wife as Jesus loves His church.

How did Christ lead in love? By serving, by committing Himself to our best interest, and by doing so regardless of the cost. The greatest among us are simply following a pattern Christ set down—namely serving those He loved and for whom He laid down His life.

Yet let's take the command for a man to be a loving leader in the home, and move it down to the shoe-leather level. What does it mean to be the "leader" in a home?

When it comes to "leadership" and headship in the home, one very specific guideline is found in verses 28-29, ". . . husbands ought to love their wives, as their own bodies. . . . (for) no one ever hated his own body, but he *feeds* and *cares* for it, just as Christ also does the church" (emphasis added).

If we are following the biblical pattern for family leadership, we men are to nurture and cherish our wives (and children). We do so just as we nurture and cherish our own bodies—and as Christ nurtures and cherishes the church.

When a husband makes that first important decision to truly honor those entrusted to him, he takes the first step toward being the loving *nurturer* God meant him to be. As a result he can see his relationship begin to blossom before his eyes and grow.

Growing a Strong Marriage

What does it actually mean to "nurture" one's wife?

The Greek word for "nurturer" means "husbandman."[3] For those of us who haven't grown up on a farm, that's a tiller of the soil, a professional gardener. A nurturer is one who helps things grow, who provides a "greenhouse" atmosphere where the plants are shielded and protected.

In short, that's what I'm called to be as a husband. Like the top gardener at your local nursery, I am responsible for understanding what ingredients cause my marriage to grow and flower—and then for providing them on a consistent basis. The psalmist puts it this way. "Blessed are all who fear the Lord. . . . Your wife shall be like a fruitful vine within your house; your sons like olive shoots around your table . . ." (Psalm 128:3).

Can you imagine what would happen if that gardener at your local nursery went by guesswork when it came to caring for his plants? No wonder in many marriages we see a "Under New Management" or "Gone Out of Business" sign up in the front yard. No less skill is required of the "head" of a marriage. He is called to be a skilled nurseryman, a caretaker of sorts. He is to be the first one to recognize and supply the ingredients needed for growth and well-being in the family and the first to spot and pull any weeds that threaten to do it harm.

In short, *my role as a "nurturer" is to be a fact-finder*. I should interview each member of my family with my fact-finder mind to see what needs should be met that day and then discover how best to meet them. When I do, I nurture, cover and protect them—and get the privilege of watching them grow. In my own life, one word picture has helped to cement this concept of nurturing in my memory.

A Man Has a Natural, Relational "Green Thumb"

After we bought our first little home in Rockford, Illinois, I decided to plant a victory garden. I had heard that the ashes from burned leaves helped the soil, so I gathered a huge pile of leaves from all over the yard. My leaf pile burned all night long, and that's not all. At one point the wind shifted and I nearly burned down my neighbor's garage as well.

Barely escaping disaster, the next day I spread out all the ashes in the back part of the yard where I was planning my garden. I didn't really know what I was doing, but it looked great! The earth was dark and moist, and a few weeks later, the results were even better than I expected. Whatever we planted came up looking like the pictures on the seed packet covers.

Everything grew. In fact, the pumpkins became so enthusiastic about the soil that they grew along the fence and up into a tree and hung down everywhere like Christmas ornaments. After my one experience of gardening in Rockford, I felt that I was gifted with a permanently green thumb. However, one day I discovered that the green on my thumb was disappearing ink.

We had moved a thousand miles away, and I decided to unleash my gardening talents on the Lone Star state. From the first spade of soil I turned, I could tell things were going to be different in Waco, Texas. There the ground was a white, rocky, clayish dirt, not the deep brown I had been used to in Rockford.

Without consulting any of the local nurserymen or gardening books, I simply made the decision that what the soil must need was additional fertilizer. With that in mind, I went out and bought the biggest sack I could find with a label that said "For Gardens" on it. The picture on the sack looked just like the results I'd gotten in Rockford, so I figured this was exactly what I needed in Waco.

Spring came around, we put all the seed into the ground, and sure enough everything came up just like in the pictures. After a short time, the picture began to change radically. The beans started browning around the edge, the tomatoes were rotten in the middle, when we picked them, and our carrots were always spongy and wilted. It was obvious something was very wrong with this garden, but I didn't know exactly what to do.

Take Time to Talk to Your Garden . . .

At the time, I didn't realize that by dumping loads of fertilizer on soil that was already high in nitrogen, I was burning up my plants! Do you know what would have helped immeasurably, were it possible?

If only my garden could talk back to me, it could have let me know exactly what I was doing wrong—and what I could do to correct things. It may seem a little far-fetched, but I could say to my garden for example, "Good morning, down there, how are y'all doing?" And right off, the beans would speak up.

"How are we all doing down here? *We're dying!* That's how we're doing!"

"Come again?" I'd ask.

"We're dying down here! We're choking to death!"

"Hey, what's the problem?"

Then they'd say,

"Mr. Smalley, you know all those white things you poured around our roots? Well, now there are thousands of them, and they're killing us. Didn't you know how much nitrogen is in this soil already, and now you're dumping pounds of it all around us!"

I'd say, "No kidding? I didn't know I was hurting you. I never even thought to check the soil. What can I do to try to solve the problem?"

And they'd say, "Go down to the store and get some chemicals and neutralize this nitrogen. You've got to hurry, Mr. Smalley, we've only got a few days left!"

"Good idea! I'll take care of that." So I start to race off to the nursery when I notice my carrots, and I say to them, "Oh, look at your leaves, they're just wilting all over the place. Bless your pea-pickin' hearts!"

"Mr. Smalley," they cry out, "forget the peas. They're done for, but you can help us if while you're at the nursery, you pick up a nylon mesh to put over us to keep us cooler. Then we could really firm up."

"I never knew that!" I would say. "Listen, you sweet things you, I'll take care of everything, don't you worry."

If only I could have talked to my garden in Waco, I could have solved my green thumb problems in a few hours. Who knows? I could have even landed in a Miracle-Gro commercial. Unfortunately, my garden was for the birds—literally. Because I never took the time or had the wisdom to ask someone what the plants needed in my area, I ruined an entire summer's crop.

I suppose I could have taken a different approach to my "talking" garden. For example, I could have walked down early in the morning, taken one look, and said, "Hey, what's this mess? Look at all your leaves—they're browning out around the edges. Hey, you plants! Any more brown leaves on any of you and I'm going to jerk you up by the roots! Now shape up, all of you, and I mean *now!*"

Would my yelling at the plants have changed things around my garden? In actuality, I had caused much of the damage that my garden now displayed because I relied on wishing, not wisdom.

After almost twenty years of working with couples and families, I can testify that many husbands nurture the priceless relationships in their homes using the same principle that I employed in my gardens—*guesswork*. A husband often enters marriage with a picture of a great home in his mind, but relies on wishing, not hard work and wisdom, to see it come to reality. Unfortunately, when many men wake up to the damage they've done to their families, the summer's crop has almost been wasted and a bitter cold winter is fast setting in.

In short, that's why God calls the husband to be a wise "gardener" of his family. Each season of life, a man needs to prepare the soil of his family's lives, to protect them from the elements, and to mend the damage after any natural crisis. The better a man learns to be the nurturer in his home, the more it will look like the "picture" the Scriptures paint of a successful relationship. Wives and children, like the plants the psalmist talks about, reflect how well they've been gardened.

Going to a Plant for Lessons in Gardening

"Wait a minute," I can hear some men saying. "This nurturing business sounds like it puts all the responsibility on the man. What about the responsibility of a woman, or even the children, to make the home all it can be?"

Whenever I hear this argument, two things come to mind. First, it is true that a man is called to be the nurturer of his family, not a woman. In fact, the Scriptures never tell a woman to "love" her husband, but a man is specifically commanded to "love" his wife.

Throughout the Scriptures, a woman is pictured as the "responder" or reflector of her husband's and God's light. In the Song of Songs in the Old Testament, the bride of Solomon makes this important comment about their relationship, "Draw me after you, and let us run together!" (1:4, NASB).

Can you see the balance in this perspective? The man initiates the loving actions (drawing her after him); the woman responds (let us run together); and then the two of them grow together as a result. As we saw in Chapter 3, a woman's natural calling is to be a completer, a helper, a responder to his love. In addition, she is called to honor her husband (Romans 12:10; 1 Peter 3:1). When it comes to who wears the nurturing shoes in the family, biblically they come in men's sizes.

"But how can I know specifically what my wife needs, so that her life and our marriage blooms and grows?" you may ask. "I barely have time to finish everything I've got going at work. How am I going to learn all it takes to care for her in the way I should? Isn't that asking a lot?"

You're exactly right. It is asking a great deal to see that a marriage becomes successful. Without a doubt, a husband has a high calling in taking on the role of the nurturer in a home, but the task isn't impossible. In fact, it's far from it.

What are those non-negotiable ingredients to a successful marriage? After years of counseling, researching, and interviewing couples throughout the world, it's apparent a healthy relationship needs at least four things.

As we've mentioned, by nature a woman tends to manifest these actions—and to desire them deeply. But if a husband understands these needs in the home (needs his wife and children have on an everyday basis), then makes the decision to apply them consistently in his marriage, it's almost impossible for healthy growth not to take place. What are these four non-negotiable ingredients that can form a handbook for a committed nurturer—*man or woman!*

At the heart of "nurturing" our loved ones is providing . . .
   1) Deep-seated security
   2) Meaningful conversation
   3) Emotional/romantic times
   4) Positive physical touching

In almost all my books, I've talked about these four factors—and the only consistent power source that underlies each one. But as I speak, study, and talk to people across the country, my understanding of them deepens each year. These four needs are so essential that we'll take several chapters to highlight them all (and then two chapters at the end of the book in particular that talk about where we find the power to grow a love that lasts).

To begin with, let's take a look at the first ingredient in causing a husband, a wife, or child's life to bloom and grow. It's an ingredient that is so essential that with it, a family can experience fulfilling relationships. Without it, they often find nothing but frustration and constant bickering.

8

The First Aspect of Nurturing: Adding the Sunlight of Security to Your Relationships

IN SOME COUNSELING sessions, trying to get a couple to open up about the real issues they're struggling with is like trying to twist the lid off an old honey jar. When all else fails, there's a method that works every time. In fact, it's as effective as holding that honey jar under steaming, hot water.

All you have to do is invite God's little spies—their children—into the counseling session, and it's amazing how they can pop the lid off "hidden" problems in an instant. That's just what happened when Dr. Trent asked the young six-year-old daughter of one couple, "Honey, what makes you feel the worst when Mommy and Daddy argue?"

The little girl frowned and said in a small, hesitant voice, "It's when Daddy takes off his wedding ring and throws it away."

The husband quickly defended himself by saying that he didn't "actually" throw his ring away. Rather, it was only an unusual way of demonstrating his anger during a fight with his wife.

When this couple got into a heated argument, if he wanted to end the discussion he would take his wedding ring off and throw it across the room. As it pinged off the walls and rolled across the floor, the wife and his little girl would watch in silence. Later, someone would pick up the fallen ring and leave it on the counter. Eventually the husband would put it back on.

For this man, "throwing away" his wedding ring provided an immature emotional release from his frustration. For his wife and child, it caused a deep sense of insecurity and fear.

As the people who depended so much on him saw his ring go flying across the room, they saw their security level flying away as well.

He didn't actually need to say the words that he was leaving. He let a flying gold band do the talking for him. Each time the ring flew through the air it shouted out, "If things don't go the way I want around here, I'll throw you right out of my life too."

Living Life on an Icy Street . . .

Have you ever endured an ice storm in your home town and then tried to walk down the street? It can be done but there's always the internal tension of knowing a terrible fall is right around the corner.

What many husbands and wives don't realize is that an absence of security in a relationship is like sentencing a person to live on an ice-covered sidewalk.

You're never free to truly relax in a home where insecurity has frozen the relationship in an icy state. It's impossible to enjoy a marriage when you're always fighting to keep your footing.

Unfortunately, in more and more homes across the country, it is always winter and never spring. There are months at a time when the cold January clouds of insecurity are never penetrated by the warm sunlight of security. Yet there is an antidote to living life under a dark cloud cover.

You can warm up your relationship in a dramatic way. In fact, you can actually do something *today* that is like turning the full force of a July sun right on your marriage. What is it? It's providing this first crucial aspect of nurturing our loved ones—unconditional security.

The Warmth to Thaw out a Relationship and Help It Grow

Security is like providing warm, invigorating sunlight to a plant. Leave a plant in the icy darkness of insecurity, and soon its leaves will wilt and turn brown. If a relationship has just been planted, the cold shadows of mistrust can keep any growth from ever sprouting above the surface. A plant must have sunlight if it's to ever be healthy and flourishing. In a marriage, the same thing is true.

Security results when a man and a woman say to each other, "You're so valuable to me that no matter what happens in life, I'm going to commit myself to you. You're so valuable, I'm going to spend the rest of my life proving to you my pledge to love you." In short, it's a reflection of the kind of security we have in our relationship with Christ. Look at Romans 8 for example:

"Who shall separate us from the love of Christ? . . . For I am convinced that neither death nor life, neither angels nor demons, neither the present nor the future . . . nor anything else in all creation will be able to separate us from the love of God that is in Christ Jesus our Lord" (Romans 8:35-39).

> ## Every enduring marriage involves an unconditional commitment to an imperfect person.

God also goes to great lengths to assure us that the plans He has for us are grounded in His security and His protection. "'For I know the plans that I have for you,' declares the Lord, 'plans to prosper you and not to harm you, plans to give you a hope and a future'" (Jeremiah 29:11).

Now, that's security! And the better able we are to reflect the same level of security that we have in Christ to our loved ones, the more we bathe them in much needed sunlight. That goes for mothers who want to see their children feel confident in friendships and later in dating relationships. It's true for fathers who desire these same kids to do well in school and later in their professions. It's especially true for a husband or wife who want to live with the green leaves of a healthy marriage—not the brown leaves of a dying one.

Every enduring marriage involves an unconditional commitment to an imperfect person. This means we can gaze at each other's imperfections and say, "Those brown leaves do irritate me, but I'm going to find out what caused them, and see if I can help. No matter what shape you're in—I'll be around and help you grow." Without this kind of commitment, we're more likely to say, "I can't stand all these brown leaves. They've bothered me for years! That's it! I'm leaving."

If you're in a second marriage, I realize that talking about commitment "no matter what" can be an invitation to guilt feelings. Study after study exposes the long-term negative effects of insecurity that often follows a divorce. However, this still doesn't mean that genuine "security" is somehow out of reach in a remarriage situation.

Men and women who have, biblically and personally, dealt with their divorce and who have remarried have an equal or even greater need to build security in their present marriage. Like love, security is a decision we make on an everyday basis. (For those who may be struggling with guilt or fear from a past relationship, in Chapters 13 and 14 I'll look at ways God can use even something as traumatic as a divorce to make us more loving.)

For all of us, security is an essential prerequisite, not an emotional elective. Let's be even more specific in discussing how we can help our loved ones grow by providing the sunlight of security for their lives. There are at least three things that every man and woman can begin to do to build a secure marriage on an everyday basis.

They can start by 1) building their own "hallway of honor" in their home which in itself can help steer their mate or children away from the doorway of dishonor. Then they can 2) look to the Lord for the strength to make an unconditional commitment and sacrificial choices. Finally, 3) they can become students of their spouses' interests as a tangible way of expressing their commitment.

All are important ways to build security in a home, but the first has a dual benefit. It not only builds positive things into the relationship, it can also help to keep tremendous pain from the people we care about most.

1. A Hallway of Honor . . .

In the hallway of our patio-home, there is a plaque hanging on one wall that proclaims: "In assurance of my lifelong commitment. To Norma, Kari, Greg and Mike. Christmas 1976." Hardly a week goes by that I don't remind those four special people about those words and the commitment behind them.

I realize that words can be cheap. I've spoken with many hurting spouses and children who "believed" the words of commitment of a man or woman whose promises held as much weight as thin air. For them, their spouse walked out on the family leaving a doorway of shame, not a hallway of honor.

I fully realize the only things that will transfer the words of this plaque onto my spouse and children's hearts are my everyday actions and words over the years. Each time I match those words with my demonstrated commitment, I'm adding on to a "hallway of honoring acts" in my home. As a result, I'm leaving a daily legacy of love to my wife and children,[1] not a hurtful inheritance of emotional pain.

A marriage or family can't grow in a healthy way if security is constantly shifting in a home, but loved ones can live without perfection. In fact, the more genuine security a wife or child feels, the more room they allow a person to fail. It's a bit like the farmer who goes to his banker and says, "I've got good news and bad news. . . ."

"Give me the bad news first," the banker says.

"Well, you know all that money I borrowed to buy that farm? I'm not doing well, so I don't have any money to pay you for it."

"Oh?" the banker says.

"Second, you know that money you loaned me for all that equipment, the tractor and everything? I can't pay for that either. . . ."

"No . . ." the banker moans.

"And third, all that money you loaned me for all the seeds? I can't pay that back either. I can't pay you anything."

"Well, what is the good news, for heaven's sake?" the banker wails.

"The good news is, I still want you to be my banker!"

My family knows I'm not perfect; they know I'll lose my temper at times—and they know I'm not always as sensitive as I should be. But one thing that helps them be patient with my imperfections is the knowledge that I'm 100 percent committed to them. I "still want them to be my banker," and I'm trying hard to be the kind of father and husband I should be. With each act of commitment, they see me with hammer and nail, adding on to a hallway of honor in our home.

For your wife or husband, a plaque in your hall may not spell security. But sometimes a loving symbol of our commitment acts like a wedding ring. The ring itself doesn't commit a person to marriage, but it shows to the world that the commitment has been made.

Perhaps for your spouse, security is a special event like a romantic dinner or going to a helpful marriage seminar like Campus Crusade's "Family Life Conference."[2] It may even be something as small as sending a card or calling home from the office each day just to see how your loved one is doing.

Norma has told me often that the way I "date" our kids makes her feel secure. I make it a practice to take my daughter Kari out on a special outing about once a month to show my commitment to Norma. The children are such an extension of her that simply knowing I am spending time with each child individually makes Norma feel secure in the strength and love I hold for our family.

Again, like a wise gardener, ask your spouse, "What is security to you?" Then take careful notes of what he or she says. Security may be spelled, "Let me have a say in the financial decisions," or "Take the time to have family devotions," or "Call me each day when you have to travel."

If you understand what "security" is to them, then you can begin making deposit after deposit into their love bank. This accrues high interest in your relationship. Just begin with a few simple questions like, "On a 1 to 10 scale, one being very *'insecure'* and ten being very *'secure,'* how confident do you feel in my love?" or "What could I specifically do over the next few months that would raise the level of security in our relationship?"

By seeking to build security into your spouse through small, positive acts, you do even more than add positive marks to the marital ledger. You also can help them (and yourself) to guard against the temptation to walk through a doorway named "dishonor."

The more security and honor we build into our homes—the tighter we help to shut the doorway to temptation for our loved ones. Interestingly, it's also the tighter we close the door to temptation for ourselves.[3]

The more "single minded" we are in our commitment to Christ, the less the distractions of the world pull upon us. The more "single minded" we are in building a "hall of honor" for our loved ones through honoring acts, the less room we leave for insecurity to dwell in our homes.[4]

There's a second way to develop security in a marriage that calls for the courage to make and keep an unconditional commitment to one's spouse. That commitment is often best seen in the sacrificial choices we may have to make if necessary.

2. Sacrificial Choices Are Also a Part of Providing Security

Betty waited in a little examination room in the doctor's office, her head lowered. Here it was, only two weeks before their only daughter's wedding, and she'd had another "lock-up" with her arthritis.

Once, Betty had been a cheerleader in the West Texas town in which she grew up. But you could never tell it now. Her heart and bubbly spirit were the same, but today (at fifty-five) they were trapped inside a body that was so crippled, she couldn't walk as well as most ninety-year-olds.

The constant pain from her joints flaring up had been bad, but the "lock-ups" were worst of all. Whenever she had a reaction to one of the "experimental" medicines prescribed for her, it was as if every joint in her body froze in place, and the pain and discomfort were almost unbearable.

Betty was a brave woman, but as she sat in the privacy of the doctor's office, tears rolled down her cheeks. She thought of her marriage to Rusty and all their dreams. She remembered all the plans they'd made for their retirement years . . . that would always remain as dreams. She thought of all the places they wanted to travel . . . but now never could. In her heart she knew that her arms were so battered by arthritis she'd never even be able to hold her first grandchild—the pain would simply be too great.

The door to the room opened, and her husband walked in from talking with the doctor. Looking over at his wife, he could see her chin trembling as she fought to regain her composure.

Try as she might, she couldn't help breaking into sobs.

"Oh, Rusty, please leave me," she begged him. "I'm getting worse, not better. I'm a mess. It hurts too much for you to touch me. I'm spending every cent we've saved toward retirement fighting this thing. I'm a burden to you and the kids and you know it."

Her tall, weather-beaten husband pulled over a chair and sat down beside her. Gently, he took her hand, twisted by arthritis, and said, "Sweetheart, it doesn't hurt to smile, does it? If you'll just smile at me now and then, that's all I need. I really don't even need that. I just need you."

Real love means a sacrificial, courageous commitment—especially when the other person may not be able to give back to you. None of our family members should have to feel what that little girl did when she saw her father's wedding ring bounce off the wall. Security should never be something you take on or off as you see fit. It's an abiding conviction that all is well with our commitment and all will be well— no matter what.

Sometimes sacrificial choices must be made in a marriage—but time and again they can heighten the security level in a home. Take Bill and Brenda for example.

Brenda had always wanted to be a veterinarian. However, she and Bill only had high school educations, and neither could really afford to go back to school. But Bill wouldn't let her dream die. He decided that she would go to school, regardless of the cost.

He knew what it meant to encourage her to get the training she'd need. He was looking at long hours spent on a second job in order for them to have the money for tuition. It took seven years of grueling work and sacrifice on both their parts for Brenda to become a vet, but the day finally came when she got her diploma. That meant her diplomas now outnumbered Bill's, three to one, but he couldn't have been happier—and neither could she. Their relationship didn't suffer because he had sacrificed his time and effort for his wife; it flourished.

Why does sacrifice add so much to a growing relationship? It should be obvious to those of us who live on this side of the Cross. That symbol of sacrifice is an unforgettable word picture of God's love for a lost world—and for each one of us who love Him.

Bill was simply following a biblical pattern when he built security into his marriage through sacrifice. After coming through the winter of a tough struggle together getting Brenda's degree, their marriage experienced an Alaskan summer where there's sunlight nearly twenty-four hours a day.

We've looked at building a "hallway of honoring actions" and making sacrificial choices to add sunlight and security to a marriage. There's a third way to raise the security level in a home, and that's to practice the kind of love that gets involved in another person's life in a very special way.

3. Building Security by Going Back to School

Recently, a close friend of ours, Jim Brawner, did a survey of several hundred teenagers at perhaps the top Christian sports camp in this country, Kamp Kanakuk in Branson, Missouri.[5] One of the first questions each boy or girl responded to on the questionnaire was: *"What is one tangible way your mother and/or father demonstrate that you're important to them?"* Can you guess what the number 1 response was, by far?

"I know they think I'm important because . . . they attended my games . . . my practices . . . my concerts . . . my open-houses . . . my band competitions . . ." In other words, with a teenager, security can be spelled with four words, *"Come and watch me!"*

While many men and women may not realize it, we never really outgrow the deep need we have for our loved ones to be excitedly supportive of our interests. What this means in a marriage is that the sunlight of security can shine on a marriage when we show an active interest in our loved one's life.

This was brought home to me in a tangible way when I first met a couple who became special friends. He was a huge offensive lineman for an NFL team when we first met, and his wife was perhaps 5'4" in heels. On the basis of size alone, there probably wasn't a more oddly matched pair. But in terms of their shared interests, this couple was only a heartbeat apart.

I met them at a Pro Athlete's Outreach Conference and was fascinated with a conversation we had at lunch one day. Out of curiosity, I asked this NFL wife how much she knew about the position her husband played on his team. I expected her to say something like, "Oh, he's paid to stand in front of other people." Instead, she gave me a ten-minute presentation on offensive blocking techniques.

Taken aback by her grasp of the sport, I asked how she'd become such an expert on her husband's position on the team. That's when she gave me a real-life lesson on what it does to become one's spouse's biggest fan—by becoming a graduate student of their likes and dislikes.

She explained that when they were first married, she resented the time he spent on the practice field, she resented all the team meetings and the travel. Finally, she grew tired of feeling so negative all the time, and she decided to go on the offensive. She would stop throwing spit-balls from the back row, and get up in the front row and learn about this career that she resented so much.

She began to ask her husband all sorts of questions about playing on the line for a pro team. She even cornered a few of the assistant coaches to learn more intricate details of the game. The more she learned and read, the more of an encourager she became. That's when a funny thing happened.

As her level of encouragement and interest went up, she noticed their marriage improving. While it wasn't her goal to get anything from her husband in return, he began showing more than a passing interest in her likes and dislikes.

What this wise woman had done was to push back the dark clouds of resentment to let the sunlight of security shine on her marriage. She didn't try to "coach" her husband, but her knowledge and interest in his life said clearly, "Because you're so important to me, your interests are important to me, too."

At the end of our conversation, my huge pro-football friend made a comment I've never forgotten: "Sometime I'll have to tell you how much my wife's taught me about refinishing antiques. I wouldn't be surprised if learning about one of her big interests is where I end up after football."

For this couple, being committed to each other meant showing interest in the things they individually valued. The message came over loud and clear that because of that attitude, they felt secure in each other's love and commitment. That security level showed clearly in their lives and the quality of love between them.

Like sunlight to a plant, the warmth of genuine security can be the first element a husband or wife gives to a successful relationship. In the next chapter, we'll look closely at a second crucial ingredient if intimacy is to grow. In fact, we'll introduce you to something we can do in our marriages that can act like life-giving water to our loved ones.

9
Meaningful Conversation: Life-Giving Water to a Relationship

MOST PEOPLE TAKE rain for granted—but not farmers. One of the most powerful black-and-white pictures I've ever seen is that of a dust-bowl farmer. He had waited over a year for rain, and now at last he had a chance. His face was turned up to the sky as the desperately needed rain poured down and mingled with his tears.

Every time I see this picture, it calls to mind what happens in many homes. In a marriage, meaningful words are like those raindrops. They can bring life-giving water to the soil of a person's life. In fact, all loving and meaningful relationships need the continual intake of the water of communication, or they simply dry up.

How many couples have I counseled who after fifteen or twenty years of marriage say, "What went wrong? Why is our marriage over?" Time after time, even casual conversation will show that instead of building a spring of consistent, meaningful conversation, they let the well run dry of encouraging words.

If that is the case—if meaningful, intimate conversation is like much needed water to a relationship—why is husband/wife communication often so difficult? Why do couples often learn what *not* to talk about, rather than what *to* talk about?

All too often encouraging words fall as infrequently as a dust bowl storm. Why? There are at least four natural roadblocks to meaningful communication that typically seem to emerge after the wedding day:

Roadblock # 1: Emotional Mind-Reading— or "Please Give Me a Clue!"

Because of a woman's natural sensitivity, nine times out of ten she will be the first one to spot a potential problem in a relationship. However, the problem can be so "obvious" to her that she can legitimately think, *Surely my husband is alert enough to see what the problem is. I'm not going to embarrass him by having to draw him a map.*

Yet, that's the very thing most men need! Give a man a road map of what issues are important to discuss, and often he'll be motivated to talk about them. But expect a husband to "sense" the subtleties (or even bold realities) of a marital or family concern, and often he won't see it as clearly.

Time and time again, I've been thankful for Norma's willingness to point out the "obvious" I've overlooked.

"Did you notice that Greg was acting a little down at the dinner table tonight?" she might ask.

"No, I didn't notice."

"Don't you think you ought to talk with him?" she'd persist.

"About what?" I'd ask. Like most men, I'm motivated to talk about facts. So far, Norma has been cluing me in on "feelings" and nonverbal behavior she's sensed that I've missed. I need "facts" to get really motivated about a conversation.

At this point, Norma could give up, throw up her hands and either go in and talk with Greg herself or chalk up another mark in the insensitivity column for me. But her love—and her knowledge of how to motivate me to communicate—doesn't let her stop here.

"Gary, I'm not sure if it's school, or the girl he's dating, or exactly what it is. But I can tell you that something is bothering Greg. Would you be willing to take your 'fact-finding' nature upstairs and *lovingly* find out how your son is doing?"

Rarely am I able to withstand Norma's call to go on the hunt for a problem to solve, and almost never has she been wrong in her sensitivity about one of the children.

The difference between mis-communication and meaningful communication often comes when a woman is willing to take the extra time to paint the obvious into a picture a man can clearly see or vice-versa. Mind-reading is never encouraged in the Scriptures, and while it may be part of an illusionist's act, it can wreak havoc in the realities of life at home.

Roadblock # 2:
"I No Speaka Your Language . . ."

In Chapter 4, you will recall we discussed the different "languages" that men and women often speak. In short, it seems that there is a "language of the heart" and a "language of the head" often spoken by women and men. Let me paint you a picture. Failing to tap into the unique conversational world of your spouse can cause this kind of frustration. It helps to illustrate a major mistake many women make in dealing with men. Namely, while trying to improve the level of meaningful communication in her home, a woman can inadvertently stifle the very thing she wants so much!

Let's say I walk into an auditorium where in a few short hours, Dr. Trent and I are going to give our "Love Is a Decision" seminar. I'm relaxed and looking forward to a great time with the couples and singles who'll be there, when all of a sudden I get one look at the room and nearly hyper-ventilate.

There's no doubt that this is the room and this is the night of the seminar—but there's also no denying that someone has made a major mistake! The chairs in the room are scattered all over, trash litters the floor, and the stage hasn't been set up. What's worse, with little time left before people begin coming early, I don't see anyone working to get things ready!

Frantically, I begin doing what I can to get the room in shape for the crowd that is bearing down on the auditorium. After ten minutes of going at a whirlwind pace, I notice a petite, bright-eyed woman sitting in a chair near the front row. Elated, I run over to her, and with a smile on my face and excitement in my voice I say, "Pardon me, but in a short time I'm going to be speaking at a conference in here, and I've got a real problem. If you don't have anything to do, could you give me a hand, please? Would you mind setting up some of these chairs while I pick up the trash and get the stage set up? Thank you so much for helping!"

She responds with a warm smile and nods her head, so I bound off like a big puppy, happy to have someone to help. The only problem is—two minutes later she's still sitting there. A little annoyed, I approach her again.

"Pardon me, Ma'am, but setting up chairs must not be your thing, so I'll tell you what. Could you help me with the stage, and I'll worry about the chairs and picking up the trash? Thank you so much for helping!" Once again she smiles and nods her head—but after another few minutes she's still sitting right in the same place.

Now I'm really irritated, and I come storming up to her and say, "Pardon me, but . . . are you a Christian?"

I could get really angry at this woman and speak unkindly to her. That is until she opens her mouth and the words come out, *"Perdoneme, Senor. Yo no hablo Ingles. Puedo ayudarle a usted?"*

If I found out that this woman didn't speak a word of English, it would be pretty insensitive of me to stay angry at her, wouldn't it? But here's the very thing that many women do without even realizing it.

What many women fail to keep in mind is that their husbands genuinely may not see or understand the concerns that they're sharing. In many cases, they simply don't "speak-a" the language!

Getting angry and frustrated with a man to "motivate" him to a deeper level of understanding rarely works. Actually, it can make the surface soil of misunderstanding rock-hard and tougher than ever to penetrate.

Roadblock #3: *Test the Soil of a Relationship to Determine Its Needed Moisture Level*

As we've said, meaningful communication is like water to a growing relationship, but how do you find out how much "water" is needed in a marriage for maximum growth? Just as we found out that "security" needs are like sunlight to your spouse in the last chapter, in this chapter we'll look at what a nurturing husband or wife can do to encourage his or her partner. We'll find out how much meaningful communication he or she needs to feel fully watered. But let me make an observation.

I've asked hundreds of women in over sixty cities this question, "How much time do you need in meaningful conversation *each day* to feel really good about your relationship with your husband?" And time and again, the average woman answers that she needs at least *one hour a day* in intimate conversation to keep her marriage alive, thirst-free, and growing.

"An hour!" I can hear many men groaning. This can be a mammoth roadblock for many men. "Where am I going to find an hour a day?"

Before you panic, it's important to realize that the hour need not be spent in one block of time. Fifteen minutes in the morning as you trade places in front of the mirror getting ready for work, five minutes on the phone during the day, twenty minutes after work, fifteen minutes after the kids are down, five minutes before bed and then praying together can all be ways to bring needed moisture to your marriage.

We're not suggesting you put a stopwatch on your conversations (as one CPA friend did with the kitchen timer: "OK, Honey. We've got ten more minutes to talk. Now let's talk!"). Exact time limits aren't important, but providing sufficient, consistent time to talk about important issues is.

To be accurate, I realize that an hour isn't necessarily the conversational need of every woman. One couple may be content with half an hour of talking, while another may need two hours to work through some difficult issues. Each couple must explore what best meets their needs, and consistently carve out the time from already overcrowded days to make sure their marriage stays a priority. The important thing to realize is that if communication is like life-giving water, a marriage will yellow and brown out if this necessary ingredient for growth is insufficient.

Why Try to Take the Road At All If There Are So Many Roadblocks?

At this point you may be saying, "What's the use? We're so hopelessly different, we'll never be able to understand each other or be able to reach any kind of intimacy."

That's not true. Time and time again, we've seen the natural "incompatibility" of the two sexes become the very grounds for a great marriage.[1] Rather than retreating into frustration, silence, or verbal explosions, why not take the time to master two specific communication skills that can re-vitalize your communication. These two particular skills help take conversations to a level many never dreamed possible.

The first of these skills is to employ the most powerful communication tool we know of in the Scriptures. We call these emotional word pictures, and without exaggeration, we've seen it turn forty-watt communication into a laser beam of words that hits both head and heart at the same time.

One Emotional Word Picture
Is Worth a Thousand Words

"An emotional word picture is a communication tool that simultaneously activates a person's emotions and intellect. In so doing, it causes another person to not just hear our words, but experience them."[2]

Some of the greatest communicators in history have used word pictures to inspire patriotism, lead nations, and direct the course of history. George Washington and Thomas Jefferson did so in our early history. Abraham Lincoln credited Harriet Beecher Stowe with the North's involvement in the Civil War, claiming that once it got a picture of what slavery was like, there was no turning back. The picture she used? *Uncle Tom's Cabin*.[3] Roosevelt and John F. Kennedy, even Ronald Reagan in more recent times, all salted their political and public speeches with word pictures. For all the good these have done, tragically, many evil leaders like Hitler and Jim Jones have also been masters at using this powerful form of communication.

Without question, the greatest use of word pictures is seen in the Scriptures. Throughout the pages of the Old and New Testament, we are taught the greatest lessons of faith the Bible has to offer through word pictures.

What could be more descriptive of what our attitude should be toward God than King David's picture, "As the deer pants for streams of water, so my soul pants for you, O God" (Psalm 42:1)? Or what could more graphically describe God's love for a stubborn, hard-hearted people than Hosea's relationship with the prostitute Gomer and how it represented God's love for the lost?

What's a clearer picture of the call to a life of faith than of an athlete, training diligently and running hard so as to win the prize (Philippians 3:14)? And, what Christian serious about caring for a lost world has ever casually glanced at the portrait of the Good Samaritan and not been convicted to reach out (Luke 10)?

There's no doubt that word pictures are a powerful way to communicate. They take our words right to another person's heart and also lock them inside their memory. For now, let's look at a few examples of word pictures illustrated in relationships. See if they don't grab your attention more than everyday words.

Let's say a woman usually finds herself saying to her husband: "I'm sick of being ignored around here. You're always watching television." To which he could reply: "Now, honey, am *I always* watching television. Did I watch TV *this morning?* Did I watch it anytime during the day *yesterday?*" (Remember, if you share feelings with a man—(the language of the heart)—you're likely to get an answer back in facts—(the language of the head).)

Instead of the same overworked phrases that really don't address the real concern (which is not he is "always" watching television but her feelings of being ignored), you could use a word picture to carry your words.

The wife could ask: "Honey, can we talk sometime soon, right now or tonight if it's better, about something that's been concerning me?" When they do sit down to talk in a quiet setting, the wife could *hand her husband the remote control unit* from the television set. Instead of the standard lecture, she could say:

"Do you know how I'm feeling right now? When you watch TV, you use the remote control device to skip past something you don't like and turn to something really interesting. For the past several weeks, I've been feeling like I'm one of the channels on your set—one of the ones you skip past when you're looking for something really interesting to watch.

"In fact, when my face finally does come up on the screen, you either click the remote to the next channel or put it on 'mute.' On the few times you do leave me on the screen, I feel as if I'm talking and talking to you, but you're just staring at me as if you can't hear a word I'm saying.

"What I want to know is what it would take to have you get your finger off the mute button so I could get some 'air time' to talk about some issues that I feel are very important."

Or instead of a man saying to his wife over and over: "That's it. I've had it with you nagging me. I'll tell you when I'm going to fix the fence. *When I'm good and ready, that's when!* That is unless you keep bugging me—in which case I'll put it off even longer!"

He could use a word picture to communicate his frustration:

"Sweetheart, we've got to talk. Can I ask you a question? How would you feel if you were with the two little ones at the grocery store, and every cash register had a huge line behind it? And not only that, after you finally picked a line, the check-out lady decides to go on a break when you're two people from the front. That means you have to go all the way to the end of another long line and wait all over again, and all the time you're waiting in line, the kids are acting up and arguing with each other and embarrassing you. How would that make you feel?"

Certainly, if she'd experienced such a day at the store she'd be very frustrated, and after hearing her response, he could say:

"Well, you may not realize it, but that's exactly what's going on at work lately. With the move coming up and my having to work with so many different departments and problems, I feel as if I've had to stand in one line to order new equipment, then get in another line to get the space in the new building to put it in. Then I find out that I can't have the space, and I'm back in line, having to start all over again. All the time there are people running around pestering me with little problems and making things really frustrating.

"Finally, after standing in lines all day, I come home from work, and you tell me there's another chore you want me to do. I know that the house and the fence are important to you, but right now, I feel as if I'm standing in so many lines at work, I just can't get in the 'fence' line until we finish our move in three weeks. Can I have a 'time out' from reminders to fix the fence until the move is done at work?"

Do Word Pictures Really Motivate a Person to Change His Behavior?

Word pictures can help make the hard work of a relationship easier by providing the initial motivating factor in getting the process of change started. My own family continually uses word pictures with me because they're so powerful. Recently my daughter Kari shared a word picture with me that motivated me to change an out-of-balance attitude I had with my youngest son, Michael.

We were driving home from a vacation in our rented motor home. We had been gone for about five days, and it was about ten o'clock at night as we finally headed back to Phoenix. Everyone else was asleep when twenty-two-year-old Kari came up to sit by me. It brought back special memories of old times, as it seemed that she was always the one who would "stay up and talk to Daddy to help keep him awake" when she was a little girl. Only this time, instead of talking about her dreams or dating, she said: "Dad, there's something I want to talk to you about. . . . But it can wait until we get back home."

"No, go ahead," I said. "We've got nothing but time."

"But I don't know exactly how to explain this to you," she said.

"Why don't you try to think up a word picture?" I suggested.

"Okay," she said. I jogged her thoughts by saying, "Pick some area that's very familiar to me." We drove on in silence for a few moments as she thought up a word picture.

"Okay, I've got one," she finally announced.

"Pretend that you're giving a seminar somewhere, and it's a really big one. I mean like 2,000 people in the conference. On the first night, you're really funny and warm, and everybody's responded well. They all can't wait for the next day.

"But the next morning when the seminar starts, you're not warm or funny at all. In fact, you spend the whole time criticizing them—even when a lot of them really don't deserve it. You say things like, 'I'm fed up with all of you. You go to church and read the Bible but you don't really love your family like you should!' Or you say, 'I'm so sick of the way some of you wives hound your husbands, it's push, push, push all the time!!! And you men, why don't you grow up and be the lovers you're supposed to be?'

"What would happen to the people in the audience, Dad, if you spent the entire morning criticizing them?"

I said, "Kari, I probably wouldn't have an audience very long. Undoubtedly some of the people would get up and leave as soon as I got started—and many more would begin leaving at the first break. They'd say, 'Why am I sitting here listening to this junk? Who does he think he is? He doesn't even know my situation. . . .'"

I thought for a moment—not realizing that I was digging myself a deeper grave—and said, "You know in Proverbs it says, 'Pleasant words are a honeycomb, sweet to the soul and healing to the bones.' I pray that God will help me speak that way. I don't want to come across harsh."

Kari said, "Dad, I hate to say this to you, but this is probably more true of you than you realize. You see, Michael lives at one of those seminars every day where you are criticizing people—only he's a captive audience. He can't get up and leave like those people when you criticize him."

I couldn't have been stopped any shorter if I had just hit a brick wall with the camper. Perhaps it's because Michael is so much like me, but I have had to battle a tendency to "pick, pick, pick" on little things he does. "Mike, chew with your mouth closed. Mike, don't drink out of that. Mike, don't. . . ." At the time of this writing, it's been a year since Kari hit me with that word picture, and I have yet to forget it.

Kari's word picture literally changed my behavior on the spot, because her words turned into a laser beam and hit me right in the heart.

The first thing I did when Michael woke up that morning was to ask his forgiveness. For a year now Kari's word picture has been my constant reminder that I'm to be his greatest encourager—not his strongest critic. Word pictures can be extremely effective, but just as with any skill, we have to learn the basics—and practice them.

Becoming an Expert One Step at a Time

When I first learned to ski, the instructor had to show us how to do it one step at a time. That was frustrating at first, because I saw all these expert skiers gracefully gliding down the slopes, and all the time I was feeling like a pigeon-toed duck with two left feet. He kept drilling us on different skills involved, and after a while I became so dejected that I never thought I'd be able to ski like everyone else, but I was wrong.

> Deep-seated problems don't vanish instantly without consistent work by the couple and relying on God's strength for daily endurance.

Bit by bit, as I practiced what he taught, I began to wed one skill to another. Pretty soon, I could get out on the slopes and not have to think, *Plant your pole, pressure on the downhill ski, lean into the turn, turn around the pole, slide the uphill ski alongside.* After practicing time and again, it just came naturally! Now I enjoy skiing more than I ever thought I could.

It's the same way with word pictures. At first, you may feel awkward and discouraged when you try to use them. Each step may seem tedious. But keep at it! You'll get the hang of it quicker than you think. Soon you'll be a master at using them.[4]

Time and again we've seen frustrated, tense relationships transformed as committed couples have used word pictures. This change in their lives doesn't happen by magic. Deep-seated problems don't vanish instantly without consistent work from the couple and a reliance on God's strength for daily endurance. But word pictures can and do bring change—particularly as people discover this powerful pattern of "picture talk" set down in the Scriptures.

If word pictures are the most powerful method of communicating we know, there is a second aspect to communicating that any healthy home shouldn't be without. This method has saved many a conversation from deteriorating into a distasteful argument. It works by slowing down what we say—in order to quick listen!

The Effectiveness of Slowing Down to Quick Listen!

During my morning run one day, I thought of something I could do as a loving act for Norma. I decided that since we were going camping that afternoon, I'd volunteer to pack the camper. She could go to breakfast with her good friend Helen and have a great time while I got our things stowed away.

I increased my pace, and when I got home, I said, "Hey, do I have a surprise for you!"

"What's that?" Norma asked.

"What do you think about calling Helen and the two of you going out to breakfast this morning? I'll do all the packing for the trip."

"Hmmmph," she said as she turned and walked away. It was not exactly the reaction I was anticipating.

"What's wrong?" I said, following her. That's when she said something that I couldn't believe I was hearing:

"You've been thinking for a long time how you could take over the packing, haven't you?"

I was stunned. "No!" I answered emphatically.

She responded by saying, "Then why do I get the feeling you think you can pack the camper better than I'm doing it?"

"WHAT?" At that moment, I wanted to tell her *she* could go ahead and pack the camper and *I'd* go to breakfast with Helen.

When the initial anger subsided, I realized she thought I was coming from a totally different direction, but before we got into a major blowout, I decided we needed to do a little *quick listening* to straighten things out.

"Why are you reacting to me like this?" I asked.

"Because I know that secretly you don't like the way I pack the camper."

"You mean you think I made up the thing about you going to break-fast with Helen so I could get you out of the way and pack the camper. Is that right?"

"Yes, exactly."

"Norma! That wasn't it at all. I was trying to think of something loving I could do for you today."

She paused. "You're saying that you were trying to do something *nice* for me?"

"As strange as it may seem, *Yes!*"

By doing some quick listening, I was able to clarify exactly what she thought the issue was, allow her the opportunity to see that I truly understood her, and then correct the misperception in our communication. By listening rather than reacting, I was able to avoid a major confrontation.

Quick listening is simply one technique you can use to help you understand what the other person is really saying. It slows conversation to a pace that both of you can manage. Surprisingly, in our high-speed world, putting thoughts in low gear can move understanding ahead more quickly.

It's a helpful tool to use when an argument is about to erupt, and it is also very useful in everyday conversation to clarify meaning and enhance understanding. It helps you talk through problems succinctly and more clearly, and forces you to make your statements fairly. There are just three simple steps in mastering the art of quick listening.

Three Steps to "Quick" Listening

1. Try to Recognize the Issue Behind the Issue

Let's say you and I are having a discussion and are having difficulty understanding one another. Using quick listening, I can honor you by giving you the opportunity to clarify what you're saying first. It lets you know that I'm genuinely concerned and interested in what you're saying—and that I'm making an effort to understand you. It relaxes you because you realize I'm more interested in comprehending what you say than conquering the discussion. It also allows me another opportunity to hear what you're trying to say.

With Norma, the issue wasn't breakfast with Helen. The issue that was at the heart of her hurt feelings was her sensitivity in thinking I was really criticizing the way she packed the camper. We could have talked all day about my words, but when we slowed the conversation down to talk about the issue *behind* the words and her reaction, we quickly came to an understanding of the real problem.

2. Restate What the Other Person Has Said in Your Own Words

After the other person has had the opportunity to summarize what they've said, I can respond, "Now let me repeat what you've said to make sure I understand." I can then verbalize what they've said to see if I've actually received the message *they* meant to communicate.

If I have it right, they'll say, "Yes, that's it." If not, they can say, "No." Then I can restate what they've said. Again, that's what I did with Norma. I had to slow things down and ask her specifically—by repeating her words—if she felt that I was criticizing her instead of helping her. It's my responsibility at that point to keep asking questions and rewording her statement until I get a "yes." When I do, it's my turn to tell her how I feel. That way we're both honored in what is said.

3. Lovingly Confine What You Say

Using too many words during an important discussion can actually break down intimate conversation. When we talk in long, rambling paragraphs instead of short concise statements, we increase the chances the listener has for reacting to what we say, without really understanding it. If we continue to add words without clarifying the issues and feelings we have, the other person can become so frustrated or bored that he'll tune us out altogether.

Learning to be brief isn't always as easy as it sounds. Not too long ago, I took an intensive two-day course in Los Angeles on how to be interviewed on television, radio, and for a newspaper. The first day I felt like a dismal failure. The instructors kept trying to get me to be brief and to the point, and I just couldn't do it.

"Now, Gary," one said, "you have to summarize the most important part of your message in one sentence." After years of being "wordy" by nature, I couldn't do it. She kept stopping the tape and making me try again and again.

"Gary, you said that in five sentences. I said *one*!" my coach would insist. "If you're going to get your message across on television, you've got to be brief People may like to read about details, but on television or in person they won't stay with you for five sentences."

By the second day, I was doing much better. When I concentrated on what I was saying, I was amazed that I could use half as many words and say twice as much. I love to talk, so, take heart—if *I* can slow down and summarize my conversations, *anyone* can!

Often, couples need to limit their words to increase their understanding of each other. Once, while counseling a couple where the wife rarely stopped talking to listen, I had to break in on her: "I'm sorry, but if you really want your husband to spend time with you, I have to be honest." We were close enough friends for me to say, "You've got to make a decision to confine yourself to saying things with a fewer number of words. I'm getting bored listening to you, and I'm the counselor! Remember that confining your words and listening to what he has to say is one of the most loving acts you can do."

God has endowed some of us with a love for the spoken word. That's tremendous, but sometimes we can get carried away! As did the wife mentioned above, we can lose our audience of one as a result.

Quick listening has stopped numerous arguments from flaring around the Smalley household, and I know it can make a difference in your family as well. We've made a conscious decision not to let our anger stay around longer than the sun going down and to make every effort to honor one another through greater understanding.

Proverbs 14:29 says, "He who is slow to anger has great understanding, but he who is quick tempered exalts folly." One of the keys to any healthy relationship is a willingness to say, "I'm more interested in understanding what you're saying to me than in thinking of what I'm going to say once you're done talking." Quick listening is one of the best ways I know to help others discover what you're thinking—and what they're thinking as well.

In the previous chapter, we looked at how a husband or wife needs to provide security as bright sunlight in which a relationship can grow. Now we've seen that meaningful communication is like a summer rain shower to encourage such growth. These are two of the four essential elements a loving "nurturer" needs to grow a strong marriage or family.

Now let's go on to discover a third important element of a loving home. It is every bit as important as soil is to a healthy root system. At the same time, we'll be uncovering a secret to keep courtship alive in marriage for years on end.

10
Keeping Courtship
Alive in Marriage

WITHOUT A DOUBT, this was going to be the most romantic evening of their entire marriage. Of course, they'd only been married a year, but Greg knew his surprise for Sharon would redefine the word "romance."

Unbeknownst to his wife, Greg had taken off work early to get ready for their anniversary. He knew his wife's favorite thing was to enjoy dinner at a place with a beautiful view, so he came up with the ultimate restaurant—*on top of a nearby mountain!*

Greg spent five hours carrying a table, chairs, a Coleman stove, ice, and drinks up to the pinnacle of a small peak near their home. In his mind's eye, he saw the two of them sharing a wonderful dinner together, complete with thousands of city lights sparkling below them like candles. And after a romantic dinner . . . *who knows!*

All that remained for him to do was to drive to his wife's work-place, surprise her, and make the climb to the intimate nest he'd created on top of the world. Greg had thought of everything . . . except his wife's interests and response. For from the moment he "surprised" her at work, his beautiful plan began to unravel.

First, she was so tired from a grueling day of fighting office politics that she wanted to stay home and rest—not go out for a long evening. Then when he pulled out her climbing boots, she said she was too tired to climb anything—and she wasn't really hungry anyway.

Greg didn't want to give away his carefully arranged surprise. (Besides, he knew they had an hour up-hill ahead of them just to reach the summit.) So he demanded that she "quit griping" and start climbing.

Reluctantly, she trudged up the mountain to where the wind had kicked up and blown over most of his campsite. Then the campstove wouldn't light . . . and the ice had melted . . . and the wind kept blowing dirt all over the table . . . and he'd forgotten the forks.

Finally, dinner was served but Sharon was so tired from climbing and nearly being blown off the mountain-top, she said she'd pass on eating. In total frustration, Greg ripped off the tablecloth, sending dishes flying everywhere. This only caused her to begin to cry and him to begin to fume.

Instead of walking down the mountain arm in arm in the moonlight that night, they stumbled down the now pitch-dark trail in silence (naturally, he'd forgotten a flashlight). The ice for their drinks may have melted up on the mountain-top—but the wall of ice between them was as thick as a brick wall as they drove home!

Greg had the right idea. He was trying to add an important element to their marriage that is missing for many couples. Unfortunately, he missed some important aspects of this third important way to nurture a marriage.

Keeping Courtship Alive in Your Marriage

During courtship, romance is something that seems to overflow naturally. Let the years of marriage pass, however, and often romance slows to a thin trickle. Yet romance is an essential ingredient of a strong relationship. Most women admit it is lacking in their home, and most men confess inability and failure in supplying it.

Actually, romance is not unique to our day. It has filled stories since the beginning of time, but with our Hollywood images of intimacy, for many of us it's difficult ever to experience the real thing. While it may not seem as important as meaningful communication or keeping a person's spirit open, romance is still an essential element to building the kind of loving, lasting relationships we've been discussing.

Romance finds its place in a marriage right between the chapters that illustrate love as a decision of our will, and the sexual relationship which involves our feelings and emotions. In many ways, romance is the bridge between the two. It's an important way we express honor to our spouse, and it provides the basis for a meaningful sex life.

Poetically, we could say that romance is the flame which glows on the candle of unconditional love; it's the act of honor that soothes and refreshes a marriage like a gentle spring rain; it's the fertile soil in which passion grows. But for those of us who didn't major in poetry, what is it in plain English?

Romance is the act of keeping your courtship alive long after the wedding day. Put another way, romance is an intimate friendship, celebrated with expressions of love reserved only for each other.

> ## Romance is the act of keeping your courtship alive long after the wedding day.

Ground Rules for Helping Romance Blossom

In some ways, romance breaks open the deepest feelings of a person. Greg had hoped that all his special efforts would show Sharon how excited he was that she was his wife. He had sought to create a natural setting that would open up her life to a deeper intimacy. Instead, his relationship took a fall from the mountain-top. Why? For the same reason that many couples struggle in keeping courtship alive in their marriage. They need to follow several practical ground-rules to keep romance on the right trail to intimacy.

The most common reason why romance dies in a relationship is that it gets inseparably linked to physical intimacy. Often this happens because that's the way television or movies paint the scene. It's as if any display of tenderness or emotional intimacy is simply a warm-up for the main act of physical intimacy, but while effective romance may *sometimes* lead to sex, our goal in being romantic shouldn't be sex.

God certainly created men to be goal-oriented initiators. He filled their bodies with a wonderful chemical that heightens their sex drive (see Chapter 11). Sometimes, though, we allow our natural enthusiasm to get the best of us and make the fundamental mistake of substituting emotional closeness with a physical experience.

If the only time I take my wife's hand is to say, "Let's go to bed," I'm ignoring her need for romantic times apart from the bedroom. For most women, it's almost as if God has wonderfully crafted them with a built-in "relational safety switch" that won't allow a few moments of pleasure to be a counterfeit for a meaningful relationship.

If romance is more than just making sure the hallway's clear to the bedroom, what is it? First, it's

Friendship, Not Foreplay

In his book, *Romancing Your Marriage*, Norm Wright quotes a couple who define romance this way:

> Romance is not a setting. . . . It's a *relationship* which can be taken into and out of a wide variety of settings.[1]

I like that! Romance is a *relationship*, not an event. It's not something we do occasionally to stoke the fires of passion. Rather, it should be an ongoing, foundational part of our relationship, something that doesn't come and go like the tide, but flows as steadily as a river. An inescapable aspect of romance is being "best friends" with your spouse.

In the Song of Solomon, Solomon praises his bride saying, "This is my lover, this my friend . . ." (5:16). During the ideal courtship, couples should have time to build their friendship to its peak. Why is friendship so closely linked to romance?

Can you think back to "your song" on the radio, your table at a favorite restaurant, your secret way of holding hands? During courtship, an entire nation may be listening to the same love song on the radio—but that same song creates a special bond between the two of you.

A key to blending friendship with romance is to take the time to explore each other's interests and then share them together. I recently saw a cartoon that captures this idea. The scene shows a couple walking happily hand in hand, looking deeply into each other's eyes, and obviously enjoying a conversation together. The caption reads, "Romance happens when . . . he asks about her potted plants and she asks about the football scores." As unromantic as "sunflowers" and "screen passes" may seem, that cartoon really captures the essence of one important element of romance.

If you're not growing a friendship based on each other's shared interests—I can almost guarantee you that the romantic soil in your relationship is lacking the essential nutrients it needs. I learned this the hard way one summer when a "romantic" getaway did nothing but push Norma away from me.

Missing the Forest for the Trees

For years one of the things that I thought would be a "10" romantically would be to take a long camping trip to the Colorado mountains with Norma. This would be a special, two-week trip where we took scenic back roads to the most beautiful places in the state, visited historic spots, and stayed in campgrounds or even out in the wild. After years of prodding, I finally convinced my wife it would be a great experience, so we loaded up and headed for the hills.

Less than half-way through the trip, Norma was beside herself. She finally broke down and said, "I don't know how much longer I can take this. There are no malls around, no cute shops, and no restaurants. I can't handle another day of this, much less another week. Can't we camp in the mountains close to a town so we could walk to it and see some other people or shop for the kids?"

At first I was angry that she was trying to ruin my "romantic" dream vacation. I even drove nonstop from Colorado to Flagstaff, Arizona, without saying one word to her on the way home. Later, I apologized for my actions, and I realized I had never thought of asking what would be a romantic trip for *her*. I wasn't interested in what she was interested in; I had my own romantic adventure in mind, even though it was hopelessly boring for her.

Fortunately, even if we feel helpless in picking a romantic experience, there's something a man or a woman can specifically do to help turn one's spouse into the hopeless romantic we'd like him or her to be.

What's Your Ten?

Contrary to popular opinion, close romantic times don't just happen. With our over-committed lifestyles, if we don't set our schedules, someone or something else will set them for us. Since the chances to make great memories together come and go so quickly, it's important to take advantage of opportunities for romance that come our way.

Planning is the key. I know, some of you are thinking, *But Gary! . . . Planning takes all the thrill out of it. Romance is supposed to be spontaneous!* No doubt spontaneity has its place; we'll look at that in a moment. For now, though, it's crucial we rid ourselves of the false notion that the secret to building a romantic relationship is the five o'clock phone call for a candlelight dinner at six.

By planning, what I mean is using the "twenty questions" method with your spouse. This is something we've done at seminars across the country, and it's amazing the amount of "romantic" information you can get in a short time. If you remember, Chapter 4 listed questions a husband can ask a wife that can revolutionize their relationship. Each question uses the "one to ten" scale to gauge the other's response.

The same is true here. Husbands and wives should begin blending their recipe for romance together with:

"Honey, on a scale of one to ten, what's a romantic ten to you?"

It's a good idea to have paper and pen ready, to jot down each idea that is suggested. Next, "milk" these answers for added information. By "milking" I mean try to find out as much information as possible about what your spouse has told you by asking more questions about the idea.

For instance, if your spouse says, "I think it would be a ten to go on a skiing vacation," then you could ask, "Where would you want to go? What time of the year? What kind of snow would you like best? Would you need new ski clothes? What colors and styles? Where would we eat? Where would you like to stay? Would we meet friends there or go by ourselves? Would we do anything else besides ski?" The list could go on and on.

Each question you ask makes you a more insightful romantic. The more you know about what would be a "ten" for your spouse, the more you'll be able to understand his or her interests, and become more fully involved in them.

Not too many of us are able to schedule a week's skiing as a vacation, which leads to a very important principle we need to keep in mind. *The success of romantic times together has very little to do with how much money we spend.* If successful, romantic relationships depended on the size of our bank account, most of us wouldn't even have a nodding acquaintance! Focusing on money as the secret to sharing one another's interests will rob us of some of the most romantic times we'll ever spend.

Steve Lyon, one of our invaluable staff members, recently had no money in his pocket and an open Sunday afternoon. Sensing his wife's, Brenda's, need to get out of the house, he loaded her and their baby girl into the car and drove to a downtown civic and arts center.

Sidewalk vendors were selling trendy T-shirts, jewelry, and ice cream; couples and families sat on a plush carpet of green grass listening to a brass quartet. Fountains flowed with the gentle sounds of bubbling water, and the art museum was open free of charge. They didn't buy *anything*—not even an ice cream bar or a glass of lemonade.

Two hours later, they were relationally richer and not a penny poorer. Brenda would later say, "That was one of the most romantic times we've had in months." Surprising, isn't it? Not to a man who knew his wife's love and interest in art and who took time that could have gone into a Sunday nap to create a romantic memory in her life.

So who cares if you can't jet to the Rockies and schoosh down a mountain? Spend a Saturday morning hunting down garage sales or going for a frozen yogurt. Your romance will never be better, even if your wallet isn't bulging with money! (Later, we'll share twenty-five low-cost ideas on keeping courtship alive.)

Why not sit down with your spouse and look at the year ahead? Find out each other's romantic tens, and schedule what you can into the calendar. It's amazing what anticipation does to heighten romance! Be sure to commit to making these dates a priority. If you don't, other things or other people will crowd them out of your schedule.

At our house, we sometimes know what we'll be doing a year in advance. Most families don't plan that far ahead, but my work requires me to plan so that other things don't choke the romance out of our relationship. Norma and I talk about special times we'll have together as a family (something I discuss more fully in Chapter 12), but we make sure we reserve some special time just for the two of us.

Developing a deep level of friendship through shared interests is the first essential ingredient in a romantic relationship. Discovering each other's relational "tens" and making plans to make them happen can also make a huge difference in the quality of our romantic times together. There's a third way of keeping the courtship alive with our spouse. It's found in learning to . . .

Celebrate the Moments of Your Life

Those who are wise romantics will realize that some special date or event every year can be used to fan the romantic flame. I recall one man who did put together a very special celebration for his wife to honor her for a sacrifice she had made for him.

It was the eve of his graduation from a long, grueling master's degree program. Four years of intensive, full-time study had finally found him about to receive his diploma.

His wife planned a special party where many of their friends were to come and help him celebrate the long awaited "day of deliverance." There would be cake, refreshments, banners, streamers, a pool nearby, croquet, and other yard games. Many people had already accepted her invitation to come, and it looked like it would be a full house. Her husband, though, had other ideas. He secretly contacted each person who had received an invitation and told them he wanted to make the party a surprise in honor of *her*. Yes, there would be banners, streamers, and all the rest, but they would bear her name, not his.

He wanted to do something special to let her know how much he appreciated the years of sacrifice she'd devoted to his graduation. Working full time to put him through, and putting off her dreams of a house and family, had, in many ways, been harder on her than the long hours of study had been on him.

When the day arrived, she was busy with preparations and last minute details, still convinced that all was going according to plan. He arranged to get her away from the party site, and while she was gone, he put up a huge banner with her name on it. During that time all the guests arrived as well.

She returned to be greeted with a huge "SURPRISE!!!" and when she realized what was going on, she could barely fight back the tears. Her husband asked a few people to share what they most appreciated about her. Then he stood before them and, with tender words of love and appreciation, expressed his gratitude for all she'd done for him. When he was through, they saluted her with an iced-tea toast.

The rest of the evening was a fun-filled fiesta of laughing, catching up with one another, water volleyball, yard games, and more food than anyone could eat. It was a celebration of an experience they both shared, and by commemorating it in a special way, this husband created a lifelong, romantic memorial to his wife's love and dedication.

Birthdays, anniversaries, or holidays can become more than simply a traditional observance. They can be a personal opportunity to let your loved one know they are very special to you—in ways they'll never forget.

Creative Romance: Surprise, Surprise, Surprise!

We've seen that building a friendship around shared interests and tapping into times of special celebration, can strengthen the romantic bonds in a relationship. There's another aspect of romance that, if not overused, can also be a real help in a home, for if it's true that the element of surprise has won countless battles, it's equally true that it has won the hearts of untold lovers.

A young man in our home church recently pulled off a romantic surprise that's one of the best I've ever heard. It's something his wife-to-be will never forget, and it will make a great story for his grandchildren one day.

It was a beautiful, clear desert morning. The sun was still minutes away from its grand entrance, but it teased the Eastern sky with a hundred shades of gold. The mountains kept their silent sentinel in the cold, crisp dawn, the brilliant stars shining behind them like silver sequins on black velvet.

"WHHHOOOOOOOSSSHH," the sound of the hot-air balloon's burner broke the desert's quiet with resounding force. In a few heartbeats, its brilliant blue and red canopy sprang to life and lifted off the ground. It floated upward, carrying a basket with Steve, Jan, and the pilot cradled inside.

Going up in a hot-air balloon was something they'd both wanted to do for a long time, and now they were in the air! In just a few moments, they were several hundred feet up, gliding along with the wind's gentle currents.

The scene was spectacular, and while Steve and Jan were busy enjoying the moment, the pilot was making sure the flight continued to go smoothly.

All at once, the incredible quiet was broken by the distinct drone of an engine. At first, Jan thought it must be the sound of a truck on the road below them, but then she realized it was getting louder. Startled, Jan looked up to see an airplane headed right for them! She was paralyzed with fear—but if she had looked at Steve or the pilot, she'd have seen them both smiling.

The plane Steve had hired to "buzz" the hot air balloon was right on time. When it turned close to them, a long tail appeared behind it revealing a message that read, in larger-than-life letters, "I love you, Jan. Will you marry me?"

When the words on the banner finally hit her, she was beside herself; she jumped up and down in the confines of the balloon basket like a six-year-old on Christmas morning. "Yes, I'll marry you!" she said, laughing and crying at the same time. For this couple, a special surprise was an indication that creative romance would stay a part of their relationship.

Surprising ways to say "I love you" aren't reserved for restricted air-space. They can be a note put in a lunch-box, a cassette tape with a loving greeting put in the car's tape player in secret, a frozen yogurt that arrives with you at your husband's office on a hot, summer's afternoon. Planning can make sure that romance stays a consistent part of your relationship. But surprises can make the moment a cherished one. These actions all say, *I'm thinking about you, my love for you is secure, you're important to me, we're together for life.*

But I'm Just Not Creative. . . .

I once had a friend who worked with high school students in Young Life. He was one of the funniest, most creative people I'd ever met. One day I asked him his "secret" for being creative, and he told me, "My definition of creativity is forgetting who I borrowed the idea from."

Now, that might not work in writing books, but it certainly points out that even if you're unfortunate enough to have come up with a "zero" in the ingenuity department—there's still hope. Just draw together ideas from the hopeless romantics around, forget where you borrowed them, and put them into practice!

It's not so much coming up with good ideas on your own, it's knowing where to find them and then knowing how to make them work. It's important to have a good resource for creative, romantic ideas. Let me suggest two:

Tapping into Creative Ideas for Romantic Times

The first source is your spouse. Sometimes we overlook this tremendous resource because it's so obvious. If you ask your spouse, "Honey, what's a romantic ten to you?" you can potentially receive a wealth of ideas. Most people have a list of things that will strike them as creatively romantic.

One of the cornerstones of creativity is this: *Ideas give birth to more ideas.* Something your spouse says may trigger an idea in your mind for a creative way to pull it off. Be alert to this possibility as you talk together. Whatever you do, be sure to *write down your ideas.* Try to keep your "Recipes for Romance" notebook within reach as much as possible.

The second is collecting lists of romantic ideas. These can be found in a variety of places, but several of them are right in your local Christian bookstore. *Four Hundred Creative Ways to Say I Love You* by Alice Chapin is a great resource.[2] So is a chapter entitled "Keeping Romance Alive," in *Romancing Your Marriage* by Norm Wright.[3] *Men, Do You Know Your Wife?* by Dan Carlinsky[4] is a helpful way to get to know things about your wife that will no doubt spark some creativity.

Let me add a few ideas of my own . . .

Twenty Creative, Romantic Ideas That Cost Under $20

1. Dress up for a meal you bring back from your favorite fast food restaurant. Take out a tablecloth, centerpiece, and a tape recorder of your favorite romantic music and dine to a "Golden Arches" delight.

2. Buy a half gallon of your favorite ice cream, go to the most beautiful park in town, throw a blanket on the ground, and eat the whole thing.

3. Visit a museum or art gallery. Talk with each other about the art you like and dislike. Use the "twenty questions" method to learn all you can about why your spouse likes or dislikes what you see. Concentrate on listening to the other person and learning all you can from what he or she says.

4. Go to a driving range together. Cheer each other's good shots.

5. Go bowling together. Come up with prizes you can give each other for winning games: i.e., a massage, a week's worth of doing dishes, a promise to paint the fence, etc.

6. Go on a hay-ride with four other couples, singing camp songs from a tape recorder or guitar. Plan a cookout under the stars afterward.

7. Write love notes to one another and hide them in unusual places like the freezer, a shoe, in the car's glove box, in the bathtub, in a makeup kit, or under the bed covers.

8. Go snorkeling in a lake.

9. Collect leaves and pine cones together on an autumn day. Take them home and make fall ornaments for the house.

10. Attend a free outdoor concert.

11. Buy a pass from the Forest Service, go to a National Forest, and cut your own Christmas tree.

12. Buy a modern paraphrase of the Song of Solomon and read it to one another.

13. Walk hand in hand along a nature trail.

14. Watch a sunset together.

15. Make "dough" ornaments together, bake them, and then color them with the kids.

16. Rent each other's all-time favorite movies and play a double feature at home.

17. Go to your favorite restaurant for dessert. Bring a child's baby book or your wedding album and relive some memories together.

18. Throw a party commemorating your spouse's graduation date.

19. Get the children together and make a "Why I Love Mom" and "Why I Love Dad" book, complete with text and illustrations.

20. Take your spouse out for an afternoon spent in her favorite store. Note the items under $20.00 she likes best. Return to the store the next day and buy one of those items as a gift.

Friendship, planning, surprises, and tapping into each other's creativity are all-important aspects of romance, but before we close this chapter, we need to sound one caution. Let's take a brief look at something that can kill a romantic experience faster than a duck can jump on a June bug.

Putting Romance in the Deep Freeze

Imagine the following scene. A man and woman are casually strolling arm in arm along a beautiful white sand beach. The waves gently wash ashore, and the sea-gulls dart back and forth overhead. A full moon glimmers in the night sky, and the sand seems like an endless strand of silver dust. It's a romantic ending to a perfect day, until . . .

If you look more closely, you will see the look on her face. It isn't one of peace and love. It's one of frustration and anger. Why? The setting is all right, but something he did is all wrong.

Ten minutes before, she told him she wanted to take a quiet walk on the beach and talk. He agreed to the walk which excited her—but he destroyed the romantic setting when he held her hand with one hand, and his fishing pole in the other.

"Hey, I've been casting for years," he told her. "I can talk and fish at the same time, *no problem*!"

This man broke two cardinal rules of romance. *1. Make sure the romantic activity you're involved in receives your full, undivided attention. 2. Make sure you're doing the activity for her best interests, not yours.*

Any time I send Norma flowers, or give her a card, or do something special, I'm saying, "I love you." At the moment it's spontaneous and unclouded by hidden motives, but I can quickly ruin it for her. All I have to do is ask a favor or tell her about my plans for fishing with the guys that weekend, or intimate that what I've done "deserves" a romantic response, and it's as if I walked into the house saying, "Gee, honey . . . you're sure looking bad today."

We've seen several ways in which the courtship aura can remain in a marriage. First, romance doesn't just happen "naturally" in a marriage; it's not simply an extension of physical intimacy. It takes work! Second, the winning recipe for romance is found in developing a friendship centered on shared interests—and carefully planned. Third, by using surprise, spontaneity, and creativity in romance, we can celebrate those special moments that bond us in a meaningful way. Finally, we need to make sure we give our full, undivided attention to our loved one during a romantic time. Each of these suggestions on keeping the courtship alive in our marriage can help to insure that this important area of our lives blossoms like flowers after a spring rain.

The key to being romantic, then, is to concentrate on being *relational*! When that happens, and your spouse truly senses you desire a deep, intimate friendship, then the stage is set to enjoy the wonderful pleasures of physical intimacy. Let's now examine what makes the sexual union meaningful and fulfilling for both the husband and the wife.

11
Sex Is Much More
Than Physical Intimacy

WITHOUT QUESTION, ONE of the most interesting topics to both men and women is sex. But does physical intimacy mean the same to a man as it does to a woman? Hardly.

What is the basic physical need of a man? In most cases, the sexual act, and then, coming in a distant second, nonsexual touching. What is the basic physical need of a woman? Meaningful communication, nonsexual touching, and then sex.

We've looked at three ways in which a man or woman can nurture a marriage and see it bloom and grow. Each one is an important part of establishing a successful relationship—but the three are incomplete without a fourth. Within the confines of marriage, God has provided a way to meet an important need in a man and woman's life—that of physical intimacy.

Meeting Each Other's Needs

Numerous studies have shown that 70 to 80 percent of a woman's physical need is simply to be touched and held.[1] Just the opposite is true for a man, especially during the first several years of marriage. For most men, until they move into their late thirties, you could paint a big "T" on their T-shirt. The "T" could represent the sex hormone "testosterone" which tends to drive a man sexually.

In laboratory studies, if researchers inject a female Rhesus monkey with the hormone testosterone, she will gather other female monkeys around her and try to reproduce. Then, once the hormone has worn off, she'll go back to her more natural behavior.

(Some men have heard about the effects of testosterone and driven straight to their local druggist to see if they can get a prescription for their wives. However, as a dangerous steroid, the physical side-effects would include her shaving and being able to out arm-wrestle her husband.)

Perhaps a word picture might help to explain the common difference between a man and a woman in the sexual area. When it comes to marital intimacy, men tend to be like microwave ovens—instantly ready to be turned on at any time, day or night, and also ready to hurry through the cooking experience. The average woman, however, is more like a crock-pot. She needs to warm up to the sexual experience and savor the process, and the thing that warms her up the most is a quality relationship.

To get an idea of your husband's sexual appetite, think about your own desire to eat. How often do you feel hungry when you're on a diet? If you're like most of us, it's three times a day—morning, afternoon, and night! The hunger drive hits a woman on a diet about as often as a man's sex drive naturally hits him—especially during the first years of marriage. That's why a man can slip into bed at 10 o'clock at night after not seeing his wife all day, reach over and touch her on the shoulder, and say, "What do you *think?*"

After a hard day at work, with the kids or both—and little or no meaningful relational time spent to prepare her—her response may well be:

"*What do I think!* You *animal.* Don't even *think* about what you're thinking!"

To most women, sex is much more than just an independent physical act. It's the culmination of a day filled with security, conversation, emotional and romantic experiences, and then, if all is right, sex. For the average man, you can reverse the order—or just skip everything that comes before sex!

In many ways, it's just as hard for the average male to initiate intimate conversations and plan romantic activities as it is for his wife to initiate sex. But these two different needs in the physical area can be met—in a fulfilling way—for both a man and a woman. This is true particularly if you're aware of several practical attitudes and actions that can help to fan passion's flame.

Meaningful Touching Outside the Bedroom Can Help the Touching Inside

Recently I read of a survey conducted among several hundred women.[2] In it, nearly 70 percent of the women responding claimed that if they were never again involved in the sexual act with their husbands, they wouldn't complain a great deal. What they would strongly miss was not being touched, held, and caressed. Every area of a woman's life is affected if she's not touched and held by the most important people in her life. As we mentioned earlier, eight to ten meaningful touches a day is really a minimum requirement for a woman to stay emotionally and physically healthy.

One man I know took his wife's need for meaningful touches so seriously that it got him in real trouble. As he was lathering up in the shower, he realized he'd forgotten a towel. Opening the shower door, he made a mad dash for the linen closet in the hallway. As he opened the closet door, he looked and saw his wife standing at the far end of the hall in the kitchen.

An impulsive thought crossed his mind, and he decided he'd give his wife one of those "meaningful hugs" she needed—right in the kitchen—and with soap and water added. So without a stitch of clothing on and dripping wet, he ran down the length of the hallway and burst into the kitchen to give her a great big bear hug—and that's when he saw the neighbor lady sitting at the kitchen table.

Proper timing might need to be taken into account when giving meaningful touches, but they are certainly one important way to grow a strong physical relationship.

Learning to Put Problems at Arm's Length

Do you know what are the two *least* talked-about areas in most marriages? Death and sex. I'm not sure what the relationship is between these two subjects, but I do know many couples don't see anything humorous about either one. Unfortunately, the lack of communication about the physical side of marriage can add to the problems a couple may have—not subtract from them.

To have a healthy sexual relationship, a couple needs to have the freedom to talk about this often "out of bounds" area, the freedom to share their likes, dislikes, expectations, and frustrations. We know of one couple who used the "word picture" method we talked about in Chapter 9 to open up this sensitive area. The method resulted in their becoming closer than ever before.

Darryl was a pro football player on a championship team that wasn't in the habit of losing. Yet when it came to the sexual area of his relationship with his wife, he felt that they were always having a disappointing season. In particular, he was frustrated about how seldom she would respond to his advances—and the negative fallout that would result from his desires being blocked.

Finally, he became so frustrated he decided to come up with a word picture to explain his feelings. So, after being rebuffed again after watching her get ready for bed, and trying to initiate an intimate time, he sat next to her and shared his word picture.

"Honey, we have *got* to talk," he said.

"Do you know how I'm feeling about our sexual life? I feel as if every night we're playing the shell game. Do you know what I mean? It's the game where there are three cups placed in a row upside down on the dresser.

"Under one of those cups is a bean, and if I can just pick the cup that has the bean under it—you'll be in the mood and we'll share some 'you know what!' But the problem is, I *never* pick the right cup. I feel like every day when I'm at practice, you shuffle the cups all around, and no matter which one I pick when I come home, it's always the wrong one. What I want to know is when are you going to quit hiding the bean?"

Darryl sat back, confident that his word picture would run loose through her mind like an all-pro running back. Certainly now that she understood his feelings, his word picture would score a touchdown for his desires. Undoubtedly, it would result in nonstop "availability" on her part. The only problem was that two can play at word pictures, and the one she shared with him in response reversed fields and scored points for her team.

"Darryl, since you asked, let me tell you the reason why we end up playing the shell game most nights. Let's say I'm your favorite fishing reel." Susan instantly had Darryl's interest when she mentioned fishing—one of his favorite activities in life.

"When we were first married, I felt that I was in beautiful shape, having come right from the factory and being wrapped up in a gift box. As soon as we were married, however, you threw me an old rod you had and took me right out and fished me in salt water. Then when you got home, you never washed me off or took care of me.

"When you first got me, you could cast me a mile because my line wasn't all knotted up, and I was oiled and well taken care of. But over the years with the way you've treated me, the reel has gotten salt-corroded and rusted, the line is all frayed, and the eyelets on the fishing rod are all bent and twisted. Now, whenever you have the impulse, you take me out of the corner of the garage where you've thrown me, and without ever taking care of me, expect me to cast as if I'm brand new.

"Can you see now why all you get is knots and backlashes when you try to cast me?"

Her husband answered, "Well, what in the world can I do?"

"You can either leave me in the garage and get the kind of response you're getting now, or you can fix me," she said. "Honey, if you would hold me and listen to me and quit lecturing me when I ask you a question—it would help me respond like a reel with a brand-new line and new eyelets."

That night, Darryl walked into a word picture that hit him harder than an NFL linebacker. For the first time he was able to "see" what the problem was in their sexual relationship in a way that he could understand.

> Meaningful touching outside
> the bedroom can light sparks
> in a marriage, and meaningful
> communication can fan the
> flames.

They ended up on the back porch talking for hours about a "fishing reel." But in actuality, they were talking about the most intimate area of their marriage. Darryl learned what it would take to "maintain" Susan in a way that could actually make her excited about responding to him. On the other hand, she was able to understand how frustrating the "games" they were playing by not talking about this very important area were.

As an unexpected bonus, they both ended up sharing one of the most romantic evenings in months. Why? Because a word picture can help to take even the most difficult subject and put it at arm's length where it can be more easily seen and talked about.

Like many couples, Darryl and Susan were so close to their problems, they couldn't see the forest for the trees. What a word picture did for them was to take them up in a helicopter to where they could get their bearings, see where they first went off the trail, and find the right pathway back to sexual intimacy.

Meaningful touching outside the bedroom can light sparks in a marriage, and meaningful communication can fan the flames. If a couple cares enough to explain their needs, frustrations, and enjoyments to one another, it can help to turn their relationship around. But there's still more that a couple can do.

Purifying Our Character
Increases the Passion Level in a Home

What do you think our "lovesick" society would say is the greatest "love story" ever told? Clark Gable and Vivian Leigh in *Gone with the Wind* during the '30s? Humphrey Bogart and Ingrid Bergman in *Casablanca* during the '40s? Burt Lancaster and Deborah Kerr in *From Here to Eternity* in the '50s? Ali McGraw and Ryan O'Neal in *Love Story* during the '60s? Barbra Streisand and Robert Redford in *The Way We Were* during the '70s? Or Kelly McGillis and Tom Cruise in *Top Gun* in the '80s?

Actually none of these would be right (or even close!). The greatest love story of all times is recorded right in the Scriptures. In fact if junior high kids realized that an entire book in the Bible talks specifically and explicitly about romance, sex, and intimacy, they'd turn to it in droves. (Of course, they would have to understand a little bit about Hebrew poetry.)

How do we know this love story is the greatest? Because we're told so in the title of the book. This book announces itself as "The Song of Songs" in bold letters. For a reader of Hebrew, something significant stands out. When biblical writers wanted to address something as "the very best, the highest, without equal," they repeated it. In other words, that's why we read statements like "the King of kings" and "the Lord of lords!" in reference to Christ. He is the King above all kings and the Lord without equal.

The title's repetition of the words, "The Song of Songs," then, tells us that this is it. It's the greatest love story of all times. It begins with a strong statement of passion.

"Let him kiss me with the kisses of his mouth!" Solomon's bride says to him in the first full verse of the book. For observant readers, that's *her* initiating an intimate response and *her* asking for him to kiss her—repeatedly!

For every man who was ready to inject his wife with testosterone, here is an example of a woman who didn't need any artificial prompting to want to kiss her husband. Interested in what prompted those words of passion from Solomon's bride?

If we look at the very next verse, we're given the reason— and it might surprise us. She tells us that it wasn't his charm or his good looks; it wasn't the expensive cologne or clothes he could afford to wear as the king; it wasn't even his prestige and power. What made his bride responsive to him was his character (Song of Songs 1:3). Her passion came as a direct reflection of the positive qualities in his life.

"May he kiss me with the kisses of his mouth. . . . *For your name is like purified oil*," she tells him.

Let's not confuse our modern-day techniques for purifying oil with the way it was done in biblical times. The process this woman is picturing involved taking several trays of different size rocks and layering them from large rocks to the smallest pebbles. By the time oil had dripped through all those layers of rocks and pebbles, all the impurities had been filtered out and only "purified" oil remained. To this bride, Solomon's life, his "name," reflected that same process of purification. All the rough edges of indifference and insensitivity had been filtered out, and his wisdom and character reflected purity of "name" and purpose.

What Solomon's wife is telling us is a truth about marital passion. The more purified my character, the more attractive I am to my spouse—and the more responsive she'll be to me as a result. Time and again I've seen this principle working in the relationships of people—for good or for bad.

I remember the case of a man who lost his job with an insurance agency primarily because he wouldn't do something that was clearly illegal. He knew if he refused to comply with the wishes of his superiors, he'd be instantly fired—but he also knew he'd lose far more if he lied.

On the day before he went in to his boss to tell him he couldn't "cooperate," he went home and told his family about what he had to do. Dinner got cold that night as he made it clear to his wife and daughters that losing his job could very well mean they would lose their house as well.

This living object lesson of standing up for the truth distinctly marked his daughters and actually brought the family even closer together in the weeks that followed. But the response from his wife startled him. Even though his dinner got cold that night, her response to him sexually was the warmest, most romantic that he'd ever experienced in fourteen years of marriage. He was totally shocked, but Solomon wouldn't have been. This man's wife had seen her husband's character ring true as a bell, and that promoted far more passion than any flowers or gifts could ever do.

Before we move on, there is another side to this principle to consider. For those who want to see the romantic spark doused with buckets of cold water—all it takes is exposing major impurities in one's character. 1 remember the case of another person who did this, and it came very close to ruining his marriage.

Bill was a social climber who had to have the best clothes and the best car—but he couldn't afford either. It's not that he didn't make money, it's just that he didn't make nearly as much as he spent. One day, that dishonoring fact came crashing down on his wife.

He and his wife were both working, in large part so that the children could attend an excellent Christian school nearby. With the fall semester beginning, she handed him her endorsed paycheck to cover the beginning cost of their tuition. Without telling her, he cashed the check and spent it on a "need" he had for a new suit.

He fully intended to "rob Peter to pay Paul" and pay the tuition from another account before anyone else was the wiser —but Peter came up broke. That's when the call from the school came to his wife's office. It landed like a bombshell.

It was the school secretary on the phone. Regretfully she informed the wife that her children wouldn't be able to attend class any more until their tuition was paid. The wife confronted her husband when he got home. He lied at first, still trying to cover his tell-tale tracks. Then he made up another lie to cover the first one. Soon his character looked so full of impurities to her that she didn't even want to see him—much less touch him in love. It took months of counseling about his spending problems and re-establishing a track-record of trust before she began to respond to him physically again.

The moral of the story? Our romantic relationship may never be called the "Song of Songs," but we can still sing the chorus with gusto. And a clear stanza from that very helpful song reads, "If you want to raise the passion level in your marriage—increase the purity of your character."

Passion Grows Where a National Average Doesn't

We've all read reports in newspapers or magazines that give an "average number of times" that the "average" couple has sexual relations each day/week/month/year/ or decade. I'm not really sure what the purpose of such averages is, except to increase the counseling rate.

Too many couples who struggle sexually let a phantom national average dictate their loving response. One or both spouses can be so busy chasing after a national average that they forget that the "goal" they're working so hard to achieve is just that—average.

How should couples interpret such figures? Frankly, I recommend that they don't keep track of them at all. In a normal marriage, there will be times of high sexual activity, and periods where it is very low. Trying to keep up with someone else's idea of what "average" is, is an invitation to sexual frustration, not sexual satisfaction.

What's the best marriage guide? The Owner's manual on wise living, namely the Bible. First Corinthians 7:3-5 gives us a healthy "average" to shoot for: "The husband should fulfill his marital duty to his wife, and likewise the wife to her husband. The wife's body does not belong to her alone but also to her husband. In the same way, the husband's body does not belong to him alone but also to his wife."

In other words, a desire to respond to each other in love and a consistent willingness to meet each other's legitimate needs is the best advice on when to be sexually intimate. Don't let anyone set a loving "schedule" for you from a book or newspaper. Look to the Book for the best advice on timing—and on increasing intimacy as well.

Keep "Performance" on the Stage and out of the Bedroom

There are two words that work well on the playing field but are absolute killers in the bedroom. What are they? *Performance anxiety.*

The Diagnostic Statistical Manual, Volume III, is an encyclopedia of psychological dysfunctions. In fact, it lists almost 200 pages of possible sexual problems. Do you know what one of the primary "treatment choices" is for all but a handful of these many disorders? "*Decrease* performance anxiety." In other words, if you can get acting and unrealistic expectations out of the bedroom, you can erase almost every sexual dysfunction that doesn't have a physiological basis, and you decrease performance anxiety by lowering expectations to realistic levels, focusing on genuine love, and seeking to meet the other *person's* needs, comfort, and pleasure instead of your own.

Often a man who has performance anxiety is one who judges the quality of his marriage by his sexual prowess. If, in the normal course of a marriage, he experiences some frustration in his sexual performance, fear can set in, and he can lose all confidence in this area. On the other hand, if a woman "performs" her way through the "act of marriage" by faking her real feelings or responses, genuine intimacy can be a long-forgotten experience. Couples need to stay clear of performance anxiety if they want passion to occur—and not be a memory from the past.

In a way, the sexual side of a relationship can be a barometer to the status of the marriage. In other words, if a wife is not responding to her husband sexually, 99 times out of 100 you can find the reason in their emotional or spiritual relationship. Some men may say, "Forget all these 'relationship' reasons for our sexual problems—I just married a frigid woman."

If you're one of these men, I suggest you honestly check the temperature of your relationship—the security level, the conversation, the sensitivity and romance, and the meaningful touching apart from the sexual act. In reality, *less than three per cent of all women are organically nonorgasmic or truly "frigid."* Of course, I can just hear someone saying, "It figures. I've got one of those wives in the three per cent." If that's your attitude, this is where honor needs to comes in.

Love Does Not Dishonor . . .

Dishonoring words that come up around the sexual area act like red lights to an intimate response. Take the man who would comment on his wife's need to "lose weight" just as she undressed to get into bed. Usually it's the same man who couldn't understand why she was cold and unresponsive. Or what about the woman who "teased" her husband about his sexual endurance until they had a major problem in his responding at all?

Solomon's bride knew she was deeply loved by her husband, but still she says, "Do not stare at me because I am dark . . ." (Song of Songs 1:6). Ever since Adam and Eve hid their nakedness from God and each other, there has been a natural insecurity around the sexual act. That level of insecurity can be multiplied by ten with poorly timed or insensitive words, but it's not only words that can be dishonoring and result in lowered passion. Actions can speak louder and more powerfully in this area.

Not too long ago, a man approached me as I was walking out to my car after a seminar. I could tell he was nervous.

"Gary, could I ask you just one question before you leave?" It was pushing eleven o'clock at night, following the first session of our seminar.

"I didn't want to ask this in front of anyone else," he said. "That's why I didn't come up to you inside. You see, I have a problem in my marriage. For years I've been making my wife do something when we're making love that she has hated doing, and now it's gotten so bad, she doesn't want to have anything to do with me at all. *Gary, isn't my wife supposed to submit to me, or am I reading the Bible wrong?"*

The answers to his questions were yes and yes. Yes, the Bible does say that a woman is to place herself under the loving leadership of her husband, and yes, he was reading the Bible wrong. Nowhere does it say that "submission" gives a man (or woman) the right to make a spouse do something they feel is wrong or terribly "dishonoring"— just to meet a selfish need.

I know that there are books written by Christian leaders who say that basically anything is legal in the bedroom, but I would have to disagree. As we discussed in Chapter 2, at the heart of love is a decision to honor a person—to count him or her as incredibly valuable. Forcing my wife to violate her conscience to please my sexual appetite is absolutely wrong and an invitation to sexual problems.

Regardless of the "no holds barred" pictures of pornography that are painted throughout our culture as being "acceptable," some forms of sexual behavior are dishonoring. To ask a spouse to perform a sexual act that is wrong or repulsive to him or her is to show at least a degree of insensitivity or even a lack of love.

Being "one flesh" in a marriage is a wonderful gift of a happy marriage. But it's only one part of a successful relationship. Security, meaningful communication, emotional and romantic times . . . and physical intimacy go together like pieces of a puzzle to make a nearly complete picture of a fulfilling relationship. As we'll see in the last two chapters of this book, there is still a "missing piece" when it comes to a marriage of true oneness. If a marriage is to really reach its peak, a couple must learn how to tap into the *only consistent power source* for keeping their love alive through each season of life. But before we turn to this most important aspect of intimacy, let's look at one final way to build a close-knit family.

12
Discovering the Secret
to a Close-Knit Family

NOT LONG AGO, John and I were doing our "Love Is a Decision" seminar right in our hometown of Phoenix, Arizona. Whenever they can, my family makes it a point to attend the seminar, so I wasn't surprised when my oldest son, Greg, told me he was coming. What did surprise me, however, was a special request he made.

"Dad," he asked, "could I take about five minutes and share something I think is really important for the parents to hear?"

Gulp! I was honored that Greg would ask, but I also knew all too well that he is the family clown. With his light-hearted nature, he is basically capable of doing or saying anything once he gets in front of an audience. Now he'd be in front of almost a thousand people, and the possibilities for disaster were endless. Then again, how often does your son ask to join you at a family conference? So I readily agreed.

Just for safe-keeping, I did schedule his five minutes during the afternoon of the second day. That way I figured if he did say something off the wall, it would come after a day and a half of positive input from Dr. Trent and myself.

As the time grew near for him to speak, I'll have to admit I became a little nervous. *They're about to hear some inside stories about the Smalley family*, I remember thinking to myself.

Greg began by saying, "I just want you to know what a privilege it is to be here with my dad and to share in this seminar. I really enjoy being with him during times like this, *because it's one of the few times he's sober . . . ."*

The audience roared, and of course I thought, *Yep, I shot myself in the foot all right. What's this son of mine going to say next?*

"No, no," Greg laughed, "I'm kidding. My dad doesn't even drink." Then he said, "I want to share with you parents for a moment." I had been talking to these people for almost two days, and for the most part they had stayed right with me. When my son began to talk, however, I could see people actually leaning forward to hear what he was going to say.

"I want to encourage you to make every effort to become best friends with your kids—and there's an important reason why. I know firsthand that it can make a big difference in their lives as they get older.

"I'm in college now, and there's temptation everywhere. I've seen many of my friends go to other people they know on campus for advice on sex, drugs, cheating, you name it! And the suggestions they are getting would make your blood turn cold. It's like the blind leading the blind! In many cases, I know why they're going to friends and getting bad advice. It's because very few of them feel that they can go to their parents to ask the hard questions.

"That seems odd to me, because I've always been able to talk to Mom and Dad. Sometimes, I'll call them at two in the morning from school to talk about something I'm struggling with. I'm never afraid to wake them up because I know they really love me, and they want to listen to what's happening in my life.

"If I wasn't confident in their friendship, I would not have been able to call them—and I know I wouldn't be open to their counsel. I can assure you that the advice you give your children will be far wiser than most of what they'll hear from people in their dorms at school. So, please, to make sure they'll listen to you when the time comes . . . do what it takes today to build a strong friendship with your children when they're young, so that they'll *want* to come to you when they're older. . . ."

I've been speaking for years, but I can't think of a time when I've grabbed an audience as Greg did that afternoon. I also don't know when I've ever been more proud of him or more humbled to be his father.

Greg struck a chord on what is one of the most crucial factors in developing and maintaining a loving relationship: *learning to be best friends with your children:* At its heart, a close-knit family is one that respects and honors each member and experiences a deep bond of intimacy.

Almost nothing strengthens a husband and wife's relationship more than when the whole family is united and best friends. The question is, "How does a family take on that kind of personality on a consistent basis?"

What's the Secret to a Close-Knit Family?

Years ago, when our kids were little, I started speaking at family retreats across the country. As I spoke, I'd pick out families who looked happy and seemed to respond well to each other. When I had the opportunity, I'd approach the husband and wife with several questions.

First, I'd ask, "You seem to enjoy each other so much and have a real love for one another! What do you think is the most important thing you do as a family that makes you so close?"

Almost without exception, each family I interviewed said, "We've made a commitment to spend quality *and* quantity time together regularly. We have separate interests, but we make sure we do things together as a family on a regular basis."

Then I'd ask, "What's the one thing you do more than any other that you feel bonds you together?" Time and time again, I'd hear an answer that I simply couldn't believe. What was the common denominator of almost every one of these "successful" families? *Camping!*

At that time, Norma and I had never camped together—by choice. But since learning this secret, we've camped together for over fifteen years. That gives me some authority to speak on the subject, and I can say with absolute conviction—camping is *not* the secret. Before I let our noncamping friends off the hook, though, I do need to say that camping is still the best method I know *to find* the real secret to a close-knit family. You'll see what I mean by looking at our very first camping experience.

Baptism by Lightning

The evidence became overwhelming—we needed to go camping. The kids were small, but old enough to travel, so we decided to give it a try. We bought a tiny, second-hand pop-up tent-trailer, packed our gear, and sped off into the sunset.

We had spent a few nights sleeping in our driveway to "test out" the trailer, but our first night of camping out was in Kentucky. There we discovered a beautiful campground with pine trees everywhere. We set up camp under the shade of the largest pine we could find. That night we built a fire, cooked hot dogs, roasted marshmallows, and had a great time together.

Soon after dark the kids fell asleep in the camper, leaving Norma and me alone to talk the evening away by a nice crackling fire. Finally, we called it a night and crawled inside with the kids. We lay there, peaceful and content. For the life of me, I couldn't think what it was that had kept me from the wonders of camping all these years—but I was soon to find out!

Without any announcement, the wind began to blow steadily. Before long, a row of dark clouds marched overhead, and a gentle rain began to fall softly on the roof. Still, it was only a tranquil "pitter-patter" on the pop-up trailer. I settled back to smell the wonderful fresh scent of rain on a summer's night, and to listen to the soothing lullaby that would send us into dreamland. . . .

Then without warning, Wham! The gentle shower turned into a violent storm. The rain began to come down in sheets, and the wind whipped up to gale force levels. Our little camper, once seemingly anchored on firm ground, began to shake and sway like a break-dancer on television. Within moments, the rain was coming down so hard that it soaked through the seams of the canvas roof and began leaking inside the trailer.

Far worse than the rain was what followed. "Round two" of the storm seemed to throw all its punches at once. Monumental lightning blasts crashed and roared all around us for a solid hour. Each bolt that darted from the sky lit up the night like a Fourth of July fireworks display. The first "near miss" lightning strike instantly blew out all the campground lights, leaving us alternating between blinding flashes of lightning and pitch-black, inky darkness.

About halfway through the thunderstorm, Norrna and I grabbed each other's hands. Finally, she whispered to me what we both had been fearing, "Do you think we're going to blow over?"

Knowing it was my job to remain calm and relax her, I said, "Naaaa . . . not a chance!" Truthfully, I didn't think we'd blow over. *I thought we were going to blow up!*

It's amazing what kind of thoughts go through your mind at a moment like that. I couldn't help thinking . . . *This is it! We're going home to be with the Lord tonight. When was the last time I told the kids I loved them? Who's going to take care of the dog when we don't get back? I wonder who they'll interview for my position at work?* I just knew that any moment, our shiny metal trailer was going to act like Ben Franklin's key on his kite and draw the next lightning blot right down on top of our heads.

Fortunately, our portable "lightning rod" didn't attract any shocking attention, and we made it through the night with little more than a lack of sleep and rain-soaked sleeping bags. Still the memories of that experience continue as vivid as the night it happened.

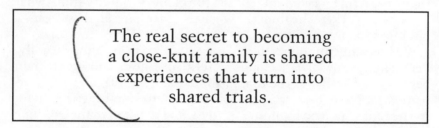

The real secret to becoming
a close-knit family is shared
experiences that turn into
shared trials.

Fortunately, not all our camping experiences have been as harrowing as that first one. After we'd gotten a few trips under our belt, a funny thing happened. Just like the couples we'd interviewed, we began to see a deepening bond developing in our home. Why?

Knitting Hearts Together

Going through harrowing experiences as a family draws people together like virtually nothing else. In other words, the real secret to becoming a close-knit family is *shared experiences that turn into shared trials.*

Have you ever noticed the way grown men on a football team will suddenly act like grade school kids, running around screaming and hugging each other, after a close, come-from-behind victory? Or have you ever stood at the Vietnam Memorial in Washington, D.C., and seen the closeness that veterans have there with one another after having gone through the horrors of war? The link people in those situations share is an inseparable relationship, forged from a common experience that stands the test of time.

I can think of one "trying" experience in particular that has marked my life forever—and my family's.

When our third child, Michael, was born, I have to admit I was a little upset. As terrible as it sounds, I wasn't sure I wanted another child. So, initially, I was ambivalent toward him and irritated with Norma for "talking" me into having another child.

I knew my attitude was dead wrong, but honestly, it was the way I felt at the time. During the first three years of his life, I just wasn't as close to Mike as I should have been. I wanted to feel close to him, at times I desperately tried, but nothing I did seemed to spark the emotional fires—that is until the spark of life almost went out of his life.

God's Mercy Creates an Unforgettable Bonding Memory

We were moving to Texas, enroute from Chicago, when Mike was a little over three years old. We had been traveling all day when we decided to spend the night at a motel—with a swimming pool.

It had been a long summer's day with five people stuffed into a tiny car, and the minute the kids spotted the shimmering water, they went crazy. I had to admit the water looked pretty good to me, too. We quickly checked in, dumped our bags in the rooms, and headed for the pool.

Norma took a quick dip and then curled up on a pool-side lounge chair with a *Good Housekeeping* magazine. In no time, the rest of us were in the water, really enjoying ourselves. Kari and Greg were old enough to swim, but Michael needed a small, round inner tube to keep him afloat.

After making sure he was "seaworthy" I turned my attention to the other two, who were screaming for me to play "toss me up," a game where I threw them up in the air and let them land in the water. After a few minutes with them, I looked back over my shoulder to see how our youngest was doing.

I saw the tube floating, but I didn't see Michael. At first, I couldn't believe my eyes. I thought Norma must have gotten him out of the water: Then I saw his tiny little body lying at the bottom of the pool. The only thing moving was his blond hair waving in the water. Instantly I swam underwater, grabbing him in my arms. When we broke the surface, his eyes were dilated, and he was coughing and sputtering.

When I got him on the deck, I began shaking him to get the water out of his lungs. In retrospect, Mike was probably in more danger from me trying to help him than he ever was on the bottom of the pool! After a couple of minutes he was back to normal, with all of us doting over him like a proud mother over a new baby.

When I first looked over and saw my son lying on the bottom of the pool, I was sure we'd lost Michael. During that instantaneous moment of emotion, something took place between us that has never left our relationship. There's something about seeing your three-foot-high son in five feet of water—knowing each second he's down there more life is draining out of him—that melts your hearts together like nothing else. That is, unless it's his first words after nearly drowning.

I'll never forget what Michael said to me when he was finally fully awake and breathing. "Daddy," he said looking at me with tears in his eyes, "I could see your legs, but I couldn't reach you!"

Instantly, my feelings of ambivalence toward my son were gone. I felt closer to him than ever before—and that bond has never been broken.

It was nearly a tragic mistake on my part that I had not kept a closer eye on Michael. As we realize now, it was God's grace that allowed me to go through that traumatic experience with my son. It shook me out of my passive indifference and replaced it with a special love for a very unique and valuable son. Michael has been, is, and always will be a living memorial of God's mercy to me. Each time any of our family brings up that harrowing experience, it unites our hearts in a bond of love and commitment.

Fast-Drying Bonds of Love

None of us would plan disasters just to make our family close knit. If your family is like mine, though, *you don't have to plan them*. They just happen! Because you never know for sure when the next one's coming, you've automatically got the perfect recipe for a "crazy glue" mixture that's perfect for family bonding.

"Crazy glue" experiences are what bond us to one another in the midst of unexpected crisis. When we're forced by circumstance to go through something trying with another person, the crazy glue gets set in place, and once it hardens the result can be life-changing.

Most of the time, being in the middle of a crisis doesn't find us saying, "Isn't this great! We're all feeling so close right now!" Normally, we're at each other's throats saying things that aren't nearly so positive. The secret is how we'll feel later.

In most cases it takes about three weeks for the "glue" of a shared crisis to set and permanent bonding to take place. Once set, though, it's usually so tight that virtually nothing can tear the memory apart. Let me give you a recent example of a family experience that has "stuck" like glue to our family's emotions.

Famous Last Words: "Trust Me"

We live in a small patio-home in a private subdivision in Phoenix. It's so private, in fact, that the homeowners' association even owns the streets! When Michael was fourteen, he asked if he could drive the car down the street a few houses and pick up some wood we could burn in our fireplace.

Since we lived on a private road, I didn't see any harm in it, so I gave him the go-ahead. But when Norma found out what I'd done, she was beside herself.

"Norma, relax," I said. "This is a private road. It's no problem. *Trust me.*"

A few moments later, we heard a tremendous "BANG!!!" Norma screamed and ran outside, with me just a step behind. When we got there, what we saw looked like something out of the new Disneyland-MGM Studio's theme park.

There was our van, looking as if the garage door had suddenly come to life and attacked it. When Mike started to pull into the driveway, he had accidentally pushed on the accelerator, not the brake. Ramming our van into the garage door made it look like a crumpled soda can. Because of poor judgment on my part, we had a pug-nosed van, one hysterical mother worried if her son was hurt, and one angry father ready to hurt his son's posterior if the accident hadn't hurt him. But there's more.

We'd only recently converted the garage into Greg's bedroom, and "typically," he was asleep inside at the time of the accident. When the van hit the garage door, it knocked a mounted fish off the wall, right onto Greg's head! Scared to death, he thought a massive earthquake had just hit Phoenix, so he jumped up and ran out of the house thinking the apocalypse had come.

At that moment, there was very little bonding going on around the Smalley household. Let's just say that as the neighbors began gathering to view the scene, not one of us felt like laughing. Several weeks later, though, something miraculous happened.

While we never thought it possible during the midst of our "van" crisis, in three weeks' time we'd all calmed down, and the garage door was fixed. Today, nearly a year later, it's one of the funniest stories we re-live with each other. Who'd have thought that a smashed garage door could have provided some of the best "crazy glue" for bonding a close-knit family that we've ever experienced? The Smalley family almanac is full of stories that have "crazy glued" us together. It's no wonder we're close.

To make sure the glue sets properly in a home, it's important to remember one thing: *During difficult times, it's vital not to do or say anything that will close the spirit of others.*[1] Harsh words and calloused actions in the heat of battle are the quickest way to dilute the glue.

That afternoon, I realized I had said several things in anger to Michael that I shouldn't have, and I had to apologize to him and ask his forgiveness. It's best when level heads and open hearts work together to cement family "disasters" into positive family memories that can hold you together forever.

Once you know the "stick 'em" power of a well-handled disaster, minor family crises can actually become welcome visitors in your home. While they may knock down the door like an unwelcomed guest at first, once the crisis leaves there is an opportunity for stronger, more intimate relationships.

How do I know this for a fact? Namely, because the same principle that helps draw a family together during times of trial, works in our bonding with our Heavenly Father.

Glued to the Father

One of the most amazing things I've learned is that the same bonding that happens to families in a crisis can happen in our relationship with God when a person of faith goes through trying times.

Have you ever been through a struggle and had to depend totally on the Lord? There's nothing like the helplessness of feeling there's no one on earth to turn to. As Christians, we may often *feel* that way, but the reality is that we can always turn to the most powerful, influential Person in the whole universe and totally depend on Him. Often He allows us to experience that kind of loneliness and desperation so we'll learn lessons about His great love and faithfulness we wouldn't discover otherwise.

Walking through those valleys, you can feel a bonding with God that the "good times" just can't produce. Lessons learned about His loyal love are what inspired David to write: "The Lord is my shepherd, I shall not want. . . . *though I walk through the valley of the shadow of death*, I will fear no evil; for thou art with me . . . " (Psalm 23:1,4 KJV, italics mine). Talk about bonding! David was a man whose heart cleaved to God's because he had faced the fires and yet God saw him through.

In the same way, when disastrous things happen to each of us, we can respond in thankfulness to Him, confident the experience will make us more trusting of Him. (This principle of looking to God to find value in trials is so important, we will take an entire chapter to talk about it.)

Making positive memories out of trying times is probably one of the most powerful ways to develop a friendship I know of today. Remember when Greg stood up in front of several hundred parents and urged them to become "best friends" with their children? Reflecting on past memories is one way to do it. This is especially true if you've suffered through some family crisis that you can look back on and laugh about. This very kind of disaster was one of the worst— but funniest—experiences of my life.

Just Hanging Around

It happened a few months before Christmas. Norma asked me what I wanted her to give me that year. I told her I'd been thinking about a pair of inversion boots, the kind you buckle yourself into and then use to hang upside down to stretch out all your muscles. I told her that before I made the request official, I wanted to try something first.

Norma left for the grocery store, and, thinking this was as good a time as any to try the "invention" out, I went to the garage. I drilled some holes in an old pair of boots, placed a metal hook in each one, and put them on. Then I got out my ladder, climbed up and hung myself upside down from my son's chinning bar. Actually the boots worked fine—my muscles certainly felt as if they were being stretched like never before. But I soon realized I had created a major problem with my new invention.

The problem was, now that I was upside down—hooked to the chin-up bar—I couldn't get down! I was stuck! What's worse, I didn't have enough strength to reach up and loosen the boots to free myself. To top things off, nobody was around. I was left to hang there helplessly like a side of beef in a meat freezer. I had visions of heart failure, and Norma opening the garage door, seeing me, and thinking, *Gary sure chose a weird way to commit suicide!*

The person who finally found me was Greg, the family clown! He had heard my cries for help, opened the door, saw me hanging there, and fell on the ground howling like a hyena.

There I dangled. Dear old Dad. The one who helped to change his diapers, who played ball with him in the park for countless hours, who worked long, hard hours to put food in his mouth and clothes on his back; and all he could do was laugh while I was dying!

Finally, Kari came in and urged Greg up off the floor and tried to help me. Even together, however, they were not strong enough to get me down. By this time, I knew I was going to die. I knew I was about to have a stroke that would finish me. Norma would have to fight the insurance company for years to prove that my death wasn't "suspicious."

At long last, Kari went to get some scissors and cut the shoe strings on my boots. This was certainly helpful in getting me out of the boots, but what they had failed to do was move the ladder I'd used. As a result, I fell onto it and onto the concrete floor and cut and bruised my head and hip.

The moment I hit the floor, the kids scattered—and for good reason. I can assure you, if I had been able to move just then, I would have "laid hands" on them!

It's been several years since my "upside-down" adventure, and just like our camping trips, the "crazy glue" of that shared trial has made this story one of our favorite family memories. It was a crisis that everyone in my family enjoyed, even me—after I got over the humiliation.

I have to be honest, though. That's not the end of the story. Two years later Mike and I were visiting some friends in a beautiful home in Seattle. I noticed they had a workout room with a *real* pair of inversion boots.

You know the rest of the story. I got stuck *again*. This time Mike got to do the honors of helping me down. Years after I've gone to be with the Lord, I'm sure my children and *their* children will still get together and talk—and yes, laugh—about "Dad and his boots."

Please Write on Our Walls

To add even more "bonding" glue to your memories, you can actually plan humorous things around your house that will build relationships and create happy times for your whole family as well. We know of a radio talk show host in our city who was a master at creating fun-bonding times when his children were young.

For example, when his son turned ten, he invited all the neighborhood kids over for the party—but not just *any* birthday party. He had saved for months and spent a small fortune in supplying an incredible surprise. Namely, 800 cream pies that he'd ordered for the biggest birthday pie fight that Phoenix has probably ever seen.

His son is grown now, but still recalls that party as one of the greatest highlights of his childhood—and almost every kid who participated does as well. It was terrific fun for everyone, and it created a special bond between father and son that still holds strong today. Still, that's not the extent of this creative man's talents.

As a radio celebrity, he was always being given "promotional" T-shirts when he would do commercials or "live" broadcasts. Even with giving many away to the Salvation Army, his shirt drawer soon began to bulge, and he came up with a creative idea.

When his kids were grade-school age, about once a month he'd pull out an old T-shirt that was ready for the trash (or one he'd been given that he knew he'd never wear). Then when he saw all the kids were home, he'd walk through the house yelling, *"I hope no kids are listening! I* sure hope there aren't any aggressive kids in their rooms that want to be destructive today and tear a T-shirt off of me. Because this T-shirt has a hole in it, and I'm ready to throw it away. . . ."

No sooner had he finished speaking than doors would burst open all over the house and voices screaming with delight would echo down the halls. From everywhere, his four kids would dive all over him and tear this shirt to pieces. He loved it, and they loved him for it.

How about one more example of a creative dad who knows that letting kids occasionally experience something "out of the ordinary" can build lasting, loving memories?

In every home, what is one rule that is always established as soon as a child begins testing his fine-motor skills? That's right. "Don't write on the walls." Just as in everyone else's home, this man's kids also had to obey this rule—until he decided that he'd make one "marked" exception.

One day, he and his wife were struggling over how to redecorate the guest bathroom when he came up with a very creative idea. He called the kids in (after talking to his wife, of course) and told them that whenever they brought home a friend, that child could sign his or her name on one of the bathroom walls. Of course, the wall signing had to begin by having the children put their names in what may have become the largest autograph book in Arizona.

Every other wall in the house was still "off limits" to writing, but soon this guest bath became a focal point of the entire neighborhood. It has stayed that way even now that the kids are all grown and out of the house. Today, when this man's children bring people over to their parents' home, the bathroom is still the first place they visit to have them see or "sign" the wall.

You may not know of many people who spend part of every "family reunion" all jammed into a guest bathroom . . . but now you do. This family loves to gather and look at years' worth of happy memories captured in the names of grade school, high school, and college friends of the kids—and the "grown-up kids" who are the parents' friends who also insist on signing the bathroom wall! One creative idea resulted in positive memories shouting from four walls that could have just held wallpaper.

Any kind of fun time you plan, even if it's just wrestling with your kids or playing leapfrog, is something that can bind you in special and significant ways. Don't let "tradition," or fatigue, or a busy schedule, steal all the fun from your family times. It's so important.

John and I have a very close friend named Bill Butterworth who is one of the most outstanding family conference speakers in the country.[2] Often, he asks his audiences this open-ended question: "If you could add anything to your home—what would it be?"

Do you know what answer he has received as the number 1 things many people wish they had more of inside their home? You guessed it—laughter.

Such an answer might surprise you—but then again, after reading this chapter, maybe not. In particular, it shouldn't shock Christians.

A very thought-provoking book came out a few years ago called *Desiring God*.[3] For many Christians, the Christian life can be something so cold and "humorless" it almost begs kids to look for a "cheerful heart" anywhere but in their home or church. Yet that should never be the case. In this author's book, he does a very good job of illustrating that "In the knowledge of God is fullness of joy." In other words, one clear hallmark of a Christian is a joyful life.

I fully realize that joking can sometimes be hurtful. Inappropriate humor can be sarcastic or disrespectful, but let's not leave joy out of a home if we want it to be marked as distinctively Christian. Your kids will always remember you for taking the time and creativity to add a sparkle of fun to the family—even if it costs you a T-shirt or two!

The Family That Decides Together, Bonds Together

Disasters can be great ways for family bonding to take place. For the faint of heart, however, it's also possible to plan times together as a family where neither hardship nor humor are the goals. These are special times for just being together, times that allow the opportunity for relationships to develop simply because you're with someone.

Family outings such as these generally don't happen without effort—particularly in our hectic, fast-paced world. So, the best thing to do is get the family together, talk about what you enjoy doing, and plan an event or activity everyone can enjoy.

But what if you're a group of "individuals" like my family and enjoy different activities? My family solved this situation by deciding to make it a priority to spend time together. That way, when it's time to plan a family activity, we're all open to talk about it.

"Okay, gang," I say, "it's time to plan this year's vacation. On a scale of one to ten, ten being the best, what would be a ten for you this time?" Each member then has the opportunity to share what would be a "dream activity" for them.

Kari and Norma will usually answer, "A cute beach where I can lie out in the sun, and probably cute little shops nearby." Mike and Greg typically respond, "Water, fishing, snorkeling, rock-climbing—anything adventurous." Then we put our heads together and try to come up with a place or activity that will fit our budget and still accommodate everyone's wishes as much as possible.

Sometimes, we have to make compromises, but that can be a valuable time for our kids to learn the importance of considering each other's needs and wants ahead of their own (Philippians 2:3-8). It may take time to hammer out a solution, but our commitment to doing things together as a family is a great help in urging all of us to bend enough to arrive at a decision everyone is satisfied with.

In the last few years, as our kids have moved through the teenage years, there's been stiff competition between family time and their team sports, clubs, and church trips. Sometimes, we decide *as a family* that we're already busy enough. Still, we try to plan times together as much as our schedules will allow.

It's also important to make a family decision to spend time alone with each of your children. A few years ago Greg and I went to Eastern Europe together on a speaking trip. If you want to bond with someone, just go through a few communist road blocks together as they search and re-search every stitch of you and your luggage! We'll always have the memory of staying in homes where people literally risked their lives to meet and to talk about Christ.

Taking mini-mission trips to your local Salvation Army to serve Thanksgiving dinner or help the poor can be a tremendous bonding time, or plan several years in advance to save up to visit one of your church's missionaries in the field. You can encourage and help them with a specific project or need they may have. Instead of just letting the youth leader get the advantage of all the bonding that goes on during a missions trip, go with the kids as a sponsor yourself. Usually the church is in such need of "sponsors" they may even pick up your expenses to travel with the kids! You'll lose sleep and possibly some hearing (if they're allowed to bring their tape players), but you'll never lose the closeness that can come from trips like these.

We can all waste time on television and movies, but we'll never waste one minute of time giving our children a picture of what God is accomplishing throughout the world.

Let me say clearly that it's not the distance or expense that counts but the personal contact you have with your children during the event. Over the years, Kari and I have made a habit of going out together for yogurt to talk. The warm, intimate father-daughter conversations we've had will always be dear to me.

When Greg got up to share at our conference that day, it made me very aware of—and very thankful for—all the hours we'd spent camping as a family. In many ways, we'd collected a twofold benefit. All the trials and family experiences we had have produced a loving bond with the children stronger and deeper than Norma and I could ever imagine. They've done something else as well. They've also given Norma and me more love for each other—and more positive memories to hold on to now that the kids are grown and moving away.

Whether you do all your "camping" at the nearest Marriott or deep in the heart of the Colorado Rockies, there's no substitute for quality time as a couple—or a family. A close-knit home, like our relationship with our Christ, grows and deepens as we share together moments of trial, tenderness, and laughter.

Now, finally, what I think are the most important chapters await us. I'll never write on more important subjects than the ones you'll find in Chapters 13 and 14, for they provide the insights for us to gain the desire and inner strength to do all the honoring and loving things we've written about in this book. Without these two chapters, this book would be just another "skill-building" book, but in today's world with the pressures we face—skills aren't enough. You need to be able to fully tap into the only power source for a love that lasts—if you want your love to last a lifetime.

13
Finding Fulfillment:
More Than Our
Cup Can Hold

ONE MORNING, A wife was desperately trying to get her husband up for church. She kept pushing and shoving him, trying to get him out of bed. "Get up, George!" she said repeatedly. "We're going to be late for church again!"

Finally, he rolled over in frustration and said, "I told you last night, I am *not* going to church and that's final. Now let me go back to sleep."

"But George," she pleaded, "it's important for you to be there." Finally, she decided to use another approach. "Okay, George. Give me two good reasons why you shouldn't go to church."

"Fine," he said, "I'll give you two reasons. Number one, I don't *like* those people. And number two, they don't like *me* down there either. That's why I'm not going."

There was a long pause as his wife thought over his answer. Finally he spoke up and said, "If you feel it's really so important I go to church, why don't you give me two reasons why I should go?"

"George," she said, "first of all you know that the Bible says it's important for you to go to church, and second, *you're the pastor!*"

Like anyone, pastors can get discouraged. I spent a number of years working at several churches, and I know what it's like to be discouraged. In fact, I know what it's like not to want to get out of bed.

When We Feel Like Never Coming out
from under the Covers

When I was thirty-five years old, there was a time I was so depressed from what I thought life had "dealt" me, that all I wanted was to crawl under the covers and never show my face again.

I blamed all my miseries on this job, and that person, and those circumstances. I can remember being so discouraged over a heartbreaking ministry situation that I lay upstairs in my daughter Kari's room, not eating for almost four days. Each of my children would come up and try to encourage me, but I'd just tell them to go away—I didn't want to face anyone or anything. Norma did her best to break me out of the doldrums as well, but for days I stayed in a darkened room, alone with my misery.

Finally, I remember telling my wife that I had made an important decision. I was getting out of the ministry. I didn't want any part of all the stress and broken promises I'd faced, and I was going to leave and get into some other kind of work.

Norma turned to me and asked, "What would you do?" That's when I realized that I didn't *know* anything else to do. I had been trained for the ministry and nothing else. I really became depressed when I thought about that! In my mind, I was on a dead-end street with no hope of ever finding a pathway that would take me away from my troubles.

During this time, I remember doing something out of desperation that turned out to be the greatest thing that has ever happened to me in my life. This period of personal darkness was the worst experience that had ever happened to me, but it turned into the greatest thing I ever experienced because of what it taught me.

I learned one biblical principle that taught me several important things I may never have learned otherwise. I discovered how to use my emotions—even the negative ones—instead of just being used by them. I learned something that led me to lasting freedom from worry, fear, anxiety, hurt feelings, and depression. I also learned how to take all the negative things that happen to me and actually find positive good and deeper love for others within the trial (I'll focus on this in detail in the next chapter).

Most of all, that terrible experience taught me the secret to experiencing continuing fulfillment in life. This is the very thing any individual or couple must discover if their marriage is to stay strong over each season of life.

Looking for Love, Peace and Joy in All the Wrong Places

What did I learn that had such a dramatic impact on my life? For years before that period of depression, I had spent a lifetime looking to any number of things to give me a sense of significance and security. But I was trying to find the right things in the wrong places.

I learned that we all have similar goals in life. If our lives were like a cup, each one of us would love to have it filled with wisdom, love, joy, and peace. We'd like to have our lives overflow with positive emotions and genuine fulfillment in life. At a very early age, we all begin to look around for what we think can fill up our cup with these positive qualities.

Unfortunately, what most of us do is to look to one of three sources, or all three, to give us the fullness of life we really want. Yet like a mirage, they shimmer with fulfillment, but offer only dust to our souls.

Looking to People to Fill Our Cup

The first place many of us tend to look is toward people. We think to ourselves, *if I'm really going to have my needs met, I've got to have another person in my life.*

Take the average single woman in her early twenties or even thirties. Often, she'll spend hours thinking and dreaming of how that "special" someone will come into her life and fill up her cup. For some women who come from a difficult family background, their personal cup may have so little love, peace, and joy that they long to finally be filled up. So in these cases, there can be a tremendous desire for a "Mr. Wonderful" to come along who can make up for the empty arms and missing love they've experienced.

In her mind's eye, this woman can come home at day's end and find "him" waiting for her. She wants someone who would hold her gently in his arms and spend hours at night in intimate conversation. She is looking for someone who is thoughtful and kind—and can fill up her cup to overflowing.

Many women enter courtship this way, but before a woman has been married a year, panic begins to set in. That's because she begins to discover almost immediately that her husband is not only failing to fill her cup—but often this "special someone" is drilling little holes in her cup by his small, insensitive actions.

Now, in addition to her cup not getting fuller, she's starting to lose whatever positive feelings with which she came into the marriage! Many women have actually told me that they experienced feelings of emotionally "drying up" when they realized that their husband would never fill their cup.

Then something happens. A light can go on in this woman's eyes as she comes to a startling realization. It isn't a husband who fills her cup. *It must be children!* Of course! God's plan. Little children running around the house. So they have little babies running around the house, and soon they discover something that all children have the capacity to do. That is, children can drill *big* holes in the cup!

Now this woman may really face a problem. Neither her husband nor her children are always filling her cup. They can be frustrating and irritating and drain away as much—or more—emotional energy than they give.

For those who look elsewhere, they'll ultimately find the same frustration in any other relationship. Friends can be a tremendous source of help and encouragement at times, but even they can disappoint us over the long haul. We can look to them as the source of positive emotions, but at times they too can punch holes in our emotional lives.

Tragically, some people have even turned to an affair to try to "fill their cup." The sweet taste of stolen waters may seem to fill up one's life, but it's actually like drinking ice-cold salt water. The burning aftertaste of sin can burn huge holes in our cup and leave us emptier and more miserable than we ever imagined.[1]

If people aren't the source that fills up our lives with the positive emotions we want so much, what is?

Looking to Places as the Source of Fulfillment

"We need a home! That's it, we need a place with a beautiful view and trees that are the envy of the neighborhood. If only we had the right place to live, *then* our cup will be full." Then we get that special home and live in it for a short while, and suddenly things begin to go wrong. In part that's true because the bigger our home, the more things there are to fix when they break.

Norma and I live in Arizona where grass front lawns are an exception, but for a period of time we thought, *We need a place that can be an oasis in the desert. We need a house that has a beautiful lawn.* Surely *that* would help our cup be full. Once we got our lawn in, though, we then discovered we were chained to it just to keep it alive.

One year I didn't water it enough, and the grass all died. The next year, I watered it too much and killed the grass again. In fact, there were numerous times when I was tempted to bulldoze the entire yard and pave it over, I was so frustrated with it!

We can put in a swimming pool, a fireplace, or even buy a mountain cabin, and those "places" don't fulfill us. Why? In part because no matter how pretty or fulfilling places look, they don't fit inside our personal cup. Instead they all have sharp edges that cut holes in our lives. What's more, the *people* we share our special places with are the same ones who continue to drain our cup as well!

But if people *and* places don't fill up the deepest part of our lives, where do we turn to finally find love, peace, and joy?

Looking to Things for Fulfillment

How about more money so that we can buy more things? Many of us feel that if we just had more money, we'd be happier in life. But study after study of people who "strike it rich" show this isn't the case.

The more money we make, the more wisdom we must have to handle it. Now I know that many of us wouldn't mind having to come up with that kind of wisdom. But to get money we normally have to pay a personal price. Thomas Carlyle once said, "For every person who can handle prosperity, there are a hundred who can handle adversity." Money alone, and all the things it can bring, can't fill up our lives with the kind of living water we desperately want.

I've met people all over the country who have little money and are miserable. And I've also met those with lots of money who are miserable. I've known people who have mountain cabins and third cars and aren't fulfilled. And some people I know barely have bus fare, but they also feel empty inside.

Most people who depend on "things" to "fill up their cup" end up looking for the one "perfect" job that will be the ticket to all their dreams. All jobs have one thing in common—work! And work doesn't always keep our cup full. It can positively drain us in terms of the people we work with, the place where we do our work, the equipment we must use, and so on.

Some of us try all our lives to get a key to a certain washroom, or a parking space with our name on it. When we get it, however, what do we have? The answer to being filled with wisdom, love, peace, and joy? Hardly. Just the opposite is too often true.

Coming up Empty in Life

At some times in each one of our lives, we run headlong into an inescapable fact. Life is not fulfilling. It's actually often unfair and exhausting. (Try reading the book of Ecclesiastes if you want a picture of someone who had everything, but everything wasn't enough.)

We can never pour enough people, places, or things into our personal cup to keep our lives filled and overflowing with the contentment we want so much. It's no wonder so many people lead lives of emotional desperation, and even consider suicide as a way out.

In fact, by focusing on people, places, and things, we not only miss the positive emotions we want . . . *we end up with the very negative emotions we've been trying all our lives to avoid!* This is true because hurt feelings, worry, anxiety, fear, unrest, uncertainty, and confusion come as a direct result of "expecting" life from a person, place, or thing.

If our ultimate goal in a marriage is saying to our spouse, "I need life from you. Will you cooperate, meet my needs, and fill up my cup?" we're asking for big problems and an empty life.

Many marriages find a husband and wife like two dry sponges, each waiting to soak up life from the other. While we're expecting wisdom, love, peace, and joy from our spouses on a daily basis, they can be sitting across the table expecting us to provide all their needs as well. Then we all come up empty, and major problems can develop.

Why do we get our feelings hurt in the course of an average week? If we're honest and look closely at our circumstances, it's because we've been expecting "life" from someone (or some-thing) who isn't cooperating, and there's one thing more. At the heart of our desperate longing for others to fulfill our deepest needs is a grabbing selfishness that says, "Me first, me first!"

My daughter Kari is a constant source of encouragement to me—and sometimes a loving source of correction as well. I can be frustrated with her over some minor matter and begin to get angry, but she'll always stay incredibly calm. I've often asked her to help me isolate why I'm feeling angry, and she'll say, "Now, Dad, you know that this thing is not really making you angry. It's just revealing your own self-centeredness!"

As much as I hate to admit it, she's generally right! A situation or person doesn't make me angry. I choose to be angry over whatever thing is blocking my goal or frustrating my plan.

We all face the temptation to look to people, places, and things to fill our cup. We're all selfish in wanting others to cooperate in meeting our needs right now. But it's only those who are wise who realize that there is a pathway to freedom from that unfulfilled feeling.

Freedom from Unfulfilled Expectations

Anger, worry, fear, hurt feelings—we wouldn't choose these emotions for anything. Yet we often end up with such feelings starring on our team.

For years, I carried around a great deal of worry and anxiety in my life. At least a part of it came from my background. A few years ago I began to learn what it takes to be completely free from most of the destructive emotions to which I once felt chained. Fear was one of my biggest problems. Here's how it sneaked up on me.

I grew up in a home that was very permissive. Primarily this was because my mother and father lost their first child not long after my mother had given her a spanking. The spanking itself didn't have anything to do with the child's death. A splinter led to an infection and complications that a country doctor and pharmacist in the early forties couldn't heal. Because of the emotional guilt, my mother made my father promise neither one of them would ever discipline us.

This meant that I grew up in a home with no rules. Take dating, for example. Because there were no boundaries in my home, I didn't actually begin my formal dating until the third grade. I did a lot of informal dating before then, but my formal dating started in third grade.

In a climate where "anything goes," my older brothers were left to come up with any "game" they wanted to tease and scare me. One brother loved to wake me up in the middle of the night and stand me up on a chair where he and his friends would laugh at me. He also loved to take his B-B gun and say to me, "I'll give you to *three* to get going." I'd take off as fast as I could because I knew he'd shoot me if I was still in range at the count of three.

He even used to take me out to the middle of a field with his bow and arrow and shoot an arrow up in the air and say, "Scatter!" I never knew where the arrow was coming down, and I was filled with fear and anxiety as I tried to run to safety. Later, every bush became a hiding place to "scare" me. Every time my parents were away was an opportunity to make me jump in some way.

It may seem that all these things were just "childhood games," but they left fearful memories inside my life. While it's hard for me to admit, I was so filled with fear that when I was twenty-four years old I still couldn't take a shower with my eyes closed. I couldn't even stay in a house alone because I'd think I was hearing people breaking in—and I was in graduate school at seminary at the time!

Today, though, it's been almost ten years since I had a fearful thought. Why? Because I've been learning something very specific from God's Word that has taken the fear right out of my life.

Envy, jealousy, comparison. I used to struggle with these emotions constantly, but rarely any more. Why? Because I'm learning how to take these very negative emotions and turn them into a flashing light that illuminates lasting fulfillment. Let me give you an illustration of what I mean.

Using Negative Emotions as Positive Warning Lights in Life

Let's say Dr. Trent and I have just finished our seminar and we've asked Bob, the local chairman, if he'd take us to the airport. As always, we're cutting it close, but if he hurries we'll make the plane just in time.

As we drive to the airport, Bob is having a great time, asking us questions and commenting on how the conference went. He's moving down the highway at a steady clip when suddenly the red light on the dashboard comes on and starts blinking, indicating there's an oil problem with the engine.

I see the light and point it out to Bob right away. After all, this is the last flight out for the day, and we're really anxious to get home to our families.

"Don't worry," Bob assures me. "That thing comes on and off all the time."

Now, though, the light is shining even brighter and is staying on, not flashing. "Bob, are you sure there isn't a problem with your car?" I ask, beginning to wonder if something is actually wrong.

"Naw, nothing to worry about," he says. Just then his engine freezes up, stranding us in the middle of the freeway and causing us to miss our plane.

Actually, Bob had several options when that warning light came on. He could have pulled over and checked the oil, or flagged someone down who could help him fix the problem or get us to the airport. He could even have done something like this:

When I asked him the second time about the red light on his dash, he could have said, "Gary, do me a favor. Reach into the glove box and hand me that little hammer that's inside there." When I handed him the hammer, he could have taken it and Wham! Wham! Wham!, smashed out the light. "There, now do you feel better? That light won't bother you any more!"

No intelligent person ignores a warning light. It's installed for a purpose. Rather than smash it, you should learn from it. It will alert you to a potential problem. Unfortunately, when it comes to experiencing negative emotions, many people try and "smash them" out of their lives instead of using them as positive warning lights.

Many people feel tremendously guilty when they experience anger, fear, worry, or hurt feelings. I've learned to use them in a positive way. These emotions are actually red lights flashing telling us our focus is in the wrong spot. We're expecting life from the wrong source!

You see, there's a fundamental problem with expecting fulfillment from people, places, and things. These are the *gifts* of life, not the *source* of life. Any time we expect the gifts of life to give us what only God can, we're asking for our cups to be drained of energy and life itself.

Now, when fearful thoughts come into my life, I don't degrade myself for feeling them. I simply say, "Thank You, Lord, for reminding me that you're the only One who can give life." Instead of resenting negative emotions, I can be thankful for their warning-light reminder that I'm looking for something other than the Lord to fill my cup. They can also be the prod that God uses to get us moving in the direction He has chosen for us. How can we learn to harness negative emotions to point us in the right direction?

> People, places and things are
> the *gifts* of life, not the *Source*
> of life. . . .

Seeking First the Source of Life

When the red lights of negative emotions fill my life, they are all ultimately tied into the same sensor. It's a spiritual sensor that is saying, "Smalley, you're expecting fulfillment from people, places, and things—not from the Lord." I'm focusing on the gifts of life and expecting them to be the Source of life.

Matthew 6:33 gives us a clear direction on what our Source of life should be. "But seek first his kingdom and his righteousness, and all these things will be given you as well." When I give God first place in my life, He promises to meet all my needs.

I try to love God with all my heart. In other words, He's the highest priority in my life. When I focus on Jesus Christ alone as the Source of my life, an amazing thing happens. Because He loves me and actually possesses the wisdom, love, peace, and joy I've always wanted—He alone can fill my cup to overflowing! That's exactly what He promises to do for His children. Ephesians 3:19-20 tells us that ". . . this love . . . surpasses knowledge—that you may be filled to the measure of all the fullness of God." Can you get any more filled than full? Absolutely not.

Do you understand now why very few people can hurt my feelings? Because I'm no longer expecting people to fill my cup, I'm not hurt when they don't respond in a particular way. Even if my wife or a close friend says something to hurt me, it is still a reflection that my focus was on what they could give or take away—not on what God gives.

Whenever those warning lights go off, I thank God for them. Then I pray and ask forgiveness for focusing on something that is less than Himself. Finally, I ask Him alone to fill my life. Psalm 62 says that we are to wait and hope in God alone. He's our rock, our salvation, our rear guard, our hiding place. He's everything we'll ever need!

Think of how many wives are manipulated by husbands from whom they "expect" life and vice-versa. The more we place our expectations on another person, the more control we give them over our emotional and spiritual state. The freer we are of expectations from others—and the more we depend upon God alone—the more pure and honest our love for others will become.

Tapping into a Limitless Source of Power

For twelve chapters we've looked at the various "skills" that can move a marriage from rock bottom right up at the top. We've also been careful to say that communication and intimacy skills alone aren't enough to build the kind of lasting love we all want. Why? Because if we really want a relationship "made in heaven," we must learn to appropriate the power of Heaven—and that power is available through prayer.

The key to powerful prayer is found in Luke 18. When I pray, I become a great deal like the little widow woman pictured in this parable of Jesus. He used her as an example to teach the disciples how to pray. Let me tell her story:

There was once a little old widow lady who went before a wicked judge seeking protection from people who were bothering her. The problem was, this judge had no respect for either God or man, and he repeatedly turned her away. Even with that kind of treatment, she never gave up.

Every day she got in line in front of that wicked judge. Finally, through sheer persistence day after day, she got the protection she was looking for. What was the point of this story? Jesus went on to tell His disciples that we have a God who loves us. "How much more will He hear and answer our prayers" when we line up every day with our requests.

That's how I pray. I line up every day before God and wait expectantly for His answer to my prayers. Of course, even before I pray, I make sure that I'm praying as I should. I always pray keeping 1 Timothy 6:3 in mind, checking to see that my petition is consistent with God's will and that it leads to godliness. If I'm careful that my request meets these standards, then I never get out of line—just like that widow woman. How does this apply to a marriage or having a strong family?

Remember John and Kay Hammer, the couple back in Chapters 1 and 3 who went through such terrible struggles? Kay learned all the "skills" I could teach her about how to have a strong marriage, but that wasn't all. She also learned how to tap into the one power source that could fill her cup to overflowing. That source was separate from anything John could ever do. Once her expectations for wisdom, love, peace, and joy were placed on her God and not her husband, she was finally free to love John. She also had the strength to keep persistently, expectantly praying for positive changes to happen in their relationship.

As she practiced the skills of growing a great relationship, she also prayed continually for a positive result in her home, in her own and her husband's lives. It was her attitude of prayer that gave her the power to keep going when all her feelings said, "Give up!"

Standing in line every day before God reminds me of the story of a man who died and went to heaven. The first place St. Peter took him was to a huge warehouse. It stretched for miles, and it was filled with millions and millions of presents.

"What in the world is this room?" the startled newcomer asked.

"This room is full of presents that were for God's children," Peter answered. "But they got out of line too soon."

I know many, many couples who began the work of forging a loving relationship—but they got out of line too soon. They weren't persistent enough. They ran out of strength to keep their relationship together, forgetting that "those who hope in the Lord will renew their strength" (Isaiah 40:31).

Whenever I wake up in the middle of the night and find my stomach knotted over some problem I'm facing, I've learned to do something that puts me right back to sleep. I've learned to thank God for my knotted stomach, because it's telling me that I'm focusing on one of the gifts of life for love, peace, and joy, rather than the Source of life. The level of my cup doesn't vary now from day to day, phone call to phone call, circumstance to circumstance, because His mercies are new every morning—a fresh full cup of life every day.

It's not Norma who fills my cup. It's not Kari, or Greg, or Michael. It's not my good friends or family members. They're "overflow," not my basic needs. John 17:3 says that to know God is life. Just knowing Christ is life. It's not knowing about Him, it's knowing Him. In 1 John 5:12 the apostle says, "He who has the Son has life; he who does not have the Son of God does not have life." It's as simple as that.

Is your life filled with negative emotions? Or all the fullness of Christ? As we close this chapter, let me share with you one example. I hope it will bring this concept closer to your heart. It did for me the first time I heard Linda's story.

A Single Place to Plug in our Lives

Linda was a young woman who had suffered terribly as a child. Her father adored her, but with his untimely death when she was only five, it seemed she was left without anyone to love her. Her mother resented her, and her brothers and sisters rejected her. All through her childhood, Linda could remember crying herself to sleep at night, wanting so much for things to be different, but they never were.

Linda's desires in life were the same as ours. She longed for others to highly value her. She wanted inner happiness, calm, and contentment. Yet growing up in a negative, non-Christian environment, she experienced only anger, bitterness, and defeat.

Up to this point, I've talked about the Lord filling our cup. Let me change the imagery to give us a different perspective. It was as if Linda's life were a lamp with a single cord.

She wanted desperately to see her life lit up with positive feelings and a warm, inner calm. She wanted the joy of knowing she was accepted unconditionally by her mother and loved by her brothers and sisters. Yet every time she tried plugging into her family, she received a terrible shock.

Over the years, Linda had been shocked so many times by her family, she sometimes felt like giving up. The very people who should have given her love and acceptance had given her only pain and hurt. Thus she often considered taking her own life.

Linda was so tired of darkness and being shocked, so desirous of light in her life, that she went to another extreme. She spent years plugging into anything and anyone she thought might bring her power and warmth.

She tried lighting her life by plugging into friends, dating, school, jobs, houses, even "recreational" drugs and alcohol. Every time she plugged into one of these things, they, too, left her trapped in darkness and afraid she would never see the light she longed for.

Do you know someone like Linda? Has a difficult background or even some present relationship left you searching for the light of love and peace, and full of darkness and fear? Like Linda, there is only one place where any of us can plug in our lives and find the satisfaction we so desperately need.

Plugging into the Source of Life

When Linda finally discovered that she needed to plug into the Source of Life, Jesus Christ, she saw her life light up for the first time. In His love she found unconditional acceptance (Romans 8:38-39; John 10:1ff; Hebrews 13:5). In His power she found the strength to be joyful in spite of her circumstances (Philippians 4:11-14; 1 Peter 1:6-9). Guided by His hand, she found a spiritual family at a nearby church. They loved her unconditionally. Through His Word and Spirit she received the inner peace that had always eluded her (John 14:6, 1 John 5:1ff).

Perhaps you need to ask yourself what your life is plugged into.

Many people try to carry around dozens of "extension" cords and plug them in to the Lord as well as many other people and things, but God has designed us with a single cord and only one place where we can plug it in to find lasting life and power—Himself.

One afternoon after a long conversation with a close friend, Linda made the most significant decision anyone can make. For the first time, she plugged her life into the Source of Life. For the next year and a half, she made a daily decision to look only to the Lord to light up her life.

Whenever she found herself angry with her husband or impatient with her children, she took time to realize that she was really plugging in to them, trying to use them for fulfillment or to meet an unmet need in her own life. Most importantly, whenever she thought about her terrible past and her light began to dim, she would immediately unplug from the hurtful memories and plug back into the positive words of Scripture to discover a special future her Heavenly Father had for her.

What happened when Linda found a single, unbroken source of life to plug into? Her life was never again the same.

Her marriage began to blossom as she finally stopped expecting her husband to make up for years of neglect she had experienced with her family. In her early fifties, she even called her estranged mother and began working to restore that relationship. Her mother was in her eighties!

Linda still met with the same painful, discouraging words, but somehow the shock had been turned off. She was finally free to love her mother because she wasn't expecting anything from her—and it made a major difference in their relationship. She never knew the joy of leading her mother to Christ, but at least Linda was free from the choking feelings of hatred and anger she had carried for years.

Are you expecting life from another person? Someone in the past, like your parents? Someone in the present, like your spouse? Are you struggling with forgiving them because they've "taken" something from you? Something only God could ever have given you in the first place?

For some of us, this single concept of plugging into Christ alone for wisdom, love, peace, and joy can be the most freeing experience in our lives. It certainly was for me.

For me, learning that the ministry, other people, and even my spouse would never fill my cup was the very thing that got me up out of bed when I was so depressed. Believing and practicing the fact that Jesus alone is the Source of life, wisdom, fulfillment, and purpose is what has kept me active and excited about life ever since. I've already accomplished more from a human perspective than I've ever dreamed possible—and in large part it's because I no longer look at life from a human perspective. I'm free to succeed or fail because Jesus Christ is the Source of my life, the fullness of my cup that can never be drained away.

There remains only one final area to discuss before we close this book. In many ways, it could be the most important. In addition to learning that Christ alone could free me from unrealistic expectations, I discovered something else during that difficult time. Even the very trials that led me to depression actually contained valuable gold for developing strong, lasting relationships.

14
The Source of
Lasting Love

SOME READERS MAY be thinking, *All this talk about having strong relationships and even "plugging" into Christ as my only Source of life is great, it's inspiring. I can even believe it works for other people—but not for me. There's no hope for me.*

I can hear you saying, "You've never met my husband! You've never met my wife! She's been unfaithful! He's left me before! My kids have turned against me! She's turned away from God! I'm a pastor's wife, and I can't tell anyone our problems! I've already been divorced twice! I've had five jobs in the last year and none of them have worked out! . . ."

In almost twenty years of working with individuals, couples, and families, I've heard terrible stories of heartache and tragedy. Many of these certainly sound like "exception" clauses to God's power to turn a terrible situation into something positive. Let me tell you Diane's story:

Diane came to one of our seminars. In her early sixties today, as a young girl she had lived in a very beautiful home in the Northwest. Her father was a well respected attorney in the community, but he was a terror to live with at home. Verbally and sometimes physically abusive, he was always critical and unreachable.

When she was nine years old, her mother caught her father in the midst of an affair. In a fit of anger, she threatened to expose her husband and ruin his reputation in their small town, but like a wounded lion, he turned on her and successfully sued *her* for divorce first—thoroughly slandering her name in the process. Their "soap opera" courtroom theatrics became so bad, other parents forbade their children to play or even talk with Diane or her older brother at school. Then, one day, circumstances turned from bad to far worse than Diane could ever have imagined.

When Diane and her brother came home from school, the movers were in the house packing all their things and getting ready to cart them away. Their father had won the divorce decree and had even gotten a court order evicting his former wife from the house.

As the mother wept, Diane's older brother became furious. He stormed into the house and up to his father's room, grabbing up a gun he knew his father always hid in his bedside drawer.

When he came out of the house, his grandmother was walking up the porch and saw him with the gun. In a burst of anger, he told her he was on his way to kill his father. She grabbed at him, trying to wrestle the gun away. But in the struggle the gun went off. In a terrible accident Diane's brother had killed his own grandmother.

Tragedy would follow tragedy that day. When the police came to the house, they tracked down the boy who was hiding in a neighbor's garage. A gun battle broke out, and an officer was critically wounded. Diane's brother was killed.

Can you imagine her feelings? Only nine years old, she had lived through the trauma of her parents' hostile divorce. She had lost her grandmother and brother in a single day. The community was blaming her because her brother had nearly killed a police officer. And now she was literally put out on the street after having lived in the lap of luxury.

There was nothing good about what happened to this woman or her family. The pain her father and brother caused will always be with her. And yet she told us, "It's taken many years, but I can actually say that God has used my terrible childhood to make me a much better person, especially with my own family. I've had to work through a lot, but I know God has made me a more loving wife and mother because of what I've been through."

Certainly, you say, her story is an exception. Exception*al* perhaps, but an exception? Hardly. Here is another story that may be even worse. We share it to underline that whatever we're personally struggling with, if God can turn a situation like this into something worthwhile, He can bring about a similar result in our trials.

Two Roads to the Same Destination

During the Vietnam War, two very different men were part of a Navy SEAL Team, an ultra-elite group sent on dangerous search-and-destroy missions. One was Dave Roever.

Dave would sit on his bunk and strum his guitar, singing religious folk songs and telling his buddies how much God loved them. The other man occupied the bunk above him. His name was Mickey Block, and along with another soldier, he gave Dave a hard time, constantly telling him to shut up and to knock off his preaching. In fact, as in many combat units, they gave Dave a nickname. During his tour in Vietnam, his handle would be the "Preacher Man." Dave came up with his own nickname for them, calling them Pervert Number One and Pervert Number Two!

One night, while on an ambush raid in their heavily armed patrol boat, another American vessel mistook them for the enemy and started firing. Mickey was hit over a dozen times by shrapnel and large caliber machine-gun bullets. His right leg was shot to pieces, and the top of his left hand was torn to the bone by a grenade blast.

The next year and a half, Mickey spent in and out of the hospital in tremendous pain. The doctors tried valiantly to save his leg, but they couldn't. The rest of his body was held together with pins and tubes for months. He found his only relief in getting high, and he stayed that way until he had become addicted to painkillers.

Life moved on at the front, and Mickey heard little about those he had fought with in his SEAL unit, but he did hear about Dave—and he knew he had to be dead.

Not long after Mickey was wounded, Dave was out on a combat mission with a squad of men when they were pinned down by enemy machine-gun fire. Dave pulled a phosphorus grenade from his belt to light up the enemy's position and stood up to throw it, but as he pulled back his arm, a bullet hit the grenade, and it exploded next to his ear.

Lying on his side on the bank of a muddy river in Vietnam, he watched part of his face float by. The rest of his face and his shoulder alternately smoldered and caught fire as the embedded phosphorus came into contact with the night air.

Dave Roever knew that he was going to die, yet miraculously he didn't. He was pulled from the water by his fellow soldiers, flown directly to Saigon, and then taken to a waiting plane bound for Hawaii. But his problems were just beginning.

In the months that followed, he would have dozens of operations—but he almost didn't make it through the first one. The Navy surgical team had a major problem during that operation. As they cut away tissue that had been burned or torn by the grenade, the phosphorus embedded in his body would hit the oxygen in the operating room and begin to ignite again! Several times the doctors and nurses ran out of the room, leaving him alone because they were afraid the flammable oxygen used in surgery would explode! Roever survived that first operation and was taken to a ward that held the most severe burn and injury cases from the war.

The real struggle for both men came after the war. Roever would start each day putting his wig on his bald head, adjusting his false ear, un-taping his eye which has to be taped closed at night since he has no eyelid, and staring at a face that shows the horror of burned flesh. Mickey, at the same time, was surviving skin grafts, amputation, traction, and plastic surgery only to acquire a bone disease and recurring abscesses and infection.

The two had pain and trauma in common after they came home, but beyond that their lives were very different. Mickey would sit in his house at night with a loaded gun in his lap, hoping someone would try to break in so he could shoot the intruder down. His marriage was ruined, and his addictions were getting worse.

Dave, on the other hand, had fallen back on his faith. Soon he was speaking across the country about his experiences. One special night, I heard him speak on national television, and he said: "I am twice the person I was before I went to Vietnam. . . . I wouldn't trade anything I've gone through for the benefits my trials have brought to my life. . . ."

I know what some of you are thinking now. *These people are crazy! How can a trial like this benefit us?* But before you put down the book, read what happened next.

About the same time that Dave Roever was telling how his trials had given him a better spiritual and family life, Mickey Block decided to kill himself. He sat in a chair in his bedroom and stuck his gun in his mouth. Even though he was not a "religious" person to say the least, he recounted that he suddenly felt as if he had seen a vision.

In his mind's eye, he saw the scene a moment after he'd pull the trigger, his brains and blood splattered over the wall behind him. He saw his children come running into his room after school. He tried to get up out of the chair and tell them not to look, but he couldn't! He saw the horror and fear in their eyes as they found his lifeless body slumped in the chair. . . .

As he sat there, a second away from death, he blinked away the terrible picture of what he had almost done and began crying for the first time since Vietnam. Then, also for the first time, he prayed. He thought back to all the "preaching" he'd heard from Dave Roever and other Christians he had known and finally surrendered what was left of his broken life to Jesus Christ.

What happened next, he would only explain as a peace settling over him. Nothing drastic changed that day. His marriage was still shattered, his leg was still gone. He still battled his addictions, but now there was hope in his life—and a deep inner knowledge that he was forgiven for a life turned against God. He was no longer alone with his problems. His wife viewed his conversion with skepticism but as the months passed, she knew he was a changed man.

Then the day came when a friend called who happened to be listening to a local radio program. "Hey, Mickey," he said. "There's a guy talking about God on the radio who was a member of the SEALs in Vietnam like you were. Do you think you know him?"

The Preacher Man? Mickey thought. It couldn't be. From the account he had heard from the men who put Dave's body on the helicopter in 'Nam, he knew he was dead.

He called the radio station, his hands trembling as he asked to speak to the Vietnam veteran who had just been on the show. After a few moments, a familiar voice came on the line and said, "This is Dave Roever. Can I help you?"

In a few moments of animated conversation, Mickey found out that the "Preacher Man" was in town to speak at a church that night. Dave warmly invited him to attend the meeting, and he agreed. Mickey hadn't been inside a church in years, but that night he went with his wife. By way of introduction he put a .308 caliber machine-gun bullet in the offering plate—the type of bullet they used on their patrol boats and that had torn off his leg.

When the bullet was given to Dave at the front, he stopped speaking and called for his combat buddy to come up with him. Mickey limped the length of the church to Dave's waiting arms, amidst the tears and cheers of the people in the church.

That night, two men stood at the front of that church. They had both lived through the same excruciating, horrible experience. Each had taken a different road to the same destination. One found a deeper faith through having his face nearly blown away. The other lost his leg and nearly his wife and family—but finally he gained everything worth living for. He had new life in Christ and new hope for his family.

Turning Wrong Around

Not one of us would want to experience the kinds of tragedies that Diane, Mickey, and Dave experienced. Yet in each case, these people became stronger in their personal and family lives as a direct result of their trials.

One of the greatest truths I know is that life is difficult and often unfair. What makes the difference between those people who experience difficulties and grow bitter—and those who find a better life produced by a similar or even more difficult trial?

I experience the joy of sharing all across the country that everyone who knows Jesus Christ as Lord and Savior can have the assurance that their trials will produce good in their lives. In fact, for the believer, I often say, every trial comes gift-wrapped with a treasure ready to be found inside.

When Trials Fall from the Sky

I once heard of a man who was walking along the sidewalk outside his high-rise apartment in New York City. It was very early on a bitterly cold winter morning, and he was hurrying to get out of the wind. Suddenly, from out of nowhere, he was hit on the shoulder by a heavy object and knocked to the ground.

For several moments he lay on the sidewalk, dazed, feeling to see if his shoulder was broken. Finally, he sat up and looked around. The street was deserted, so he ruled out a mugging. He looked up at the apartments above him, but he could see no lights on and no open windows. He glanced around the ground where he was lying and saw a shoe box next to him. It was heavily taped from end to end. He reached over to pick it up, but it was so heavy he had to use both hands.

He took the shoe box back to his apartment, got some scissors out, and cut through the tape. Inside were three fairly large cloth sacks. As he lifted out one of the sacks and opened it in the light he gasped. There were several small gold bars and dozens of gold coins! After a few more moments of gasping, he decided he'd better take this shoe box to the police station.

The police told him that more than likely the gold was stolen jewelry that had been melted down. Whether it had fallen from an apartment or from a plane overhead, they couldn't say. If he'd leave it with them for six months, they told him, it could be his if no one lawfully claimed it during that time.

The six months took forever to pass, but finally the day came. He hurried to the police station and there was the shoe box that had given him the sore shoulder. His shoulder didn't hurt anymore, and soon because of this treasure that fell from nowhere, his pocketbook didn't either.

> ... though apparent trouble may
> look as if it's destroying our home,
> it can actually turn into a benefit
> for us through God's power!

Most of us would gladly suffer through a sore shoulder to end up with a box filled with gold. Yet we may not realize that we have the same chance of benefiting every time we are hit by problems. For every trial is like a box containing valuable treasures. It may knock us to the ground and bruise us, but once we learn how to open the box, we can find a golden opportunity inside.

"Gary, you're either crazy or oversimplifying the problem of pain," some may say. "It's hard to believe that every problem can have a silver lining." After all, what good can come from some serious trial? A trial like having your face nearly blown away? Or from losing your leg and being on drugs? Or from being put out on the street at age nine?

As Diane, Dave, Mickey, Joni Eareckson Tada, Corrie Ten Boom, and many others can testify, trials are often devastating at the time. Yet in spite of the pain, they can produce a gold of sorts in our lives. Like a refining fire, each trial can work to make us more pure and sound. The Bible says God will "... bestow ... a crown of beauty instead of ashes ..." (Isaiah 61:3).

Don't misunderstand me. I'm not implying that God causes all trials (James 1:13). Neither am I saying that we ought to cause trials for others so that they'll gain from the experience (Romans 6:1-2). But I certainly do believe that in His sovereignty and love, God *can and does* take anything that happens to us and use it for good (Romans 8:28; Isaiah 61:7).

It isn't wrong to avoid painful situations when possible, but it is wrong to deny problems, ignore them, or try to explain them away. As Christians, we are left with a much more positive option than denial or trying to delude ourselves into thinking tragedies didn't happen. Of all people we have a promise that whether we get blasted in the jungles of Vietnam, or in the front yard of our father's home, trials can produce the very things that can make us the most like Christ—His love, peace, and joy.

It's never easy to "welcome" trials as friends, but trials can train us to become more Christlike, if they're experienced in the right light. I've learned to "treasure-hunt" with every difficulty I face. This attitude has been one of the most important tools we can give our children to help prepare them for the large and small trials of life they'll inevitably face.

How God Turns Trials into Triumph

I'm writing this chapter because I know that trials not only can defeat individuals, they can ruin entire families—especially if that family doesn't know how to handle the trials effectively. So here's a summary of this entire book in three sentences.

In Chapters 1 through 12, there's a practical plan we can follow to strengthen our relationships and develop the specific skills necessary to practice that plan. In Chapter 13, we looked at the only consistent power source—the Lord Jesus Himself. Only He can give me the strength to love my spouse as I should over a lifetime. *Now in this final chapter, we have the assurance that although apparent trouble may look as if it's destroying our home, it can actually turn into a benefit for us through God's power!*

That means all trials, over all seasons of the life-cycle. Let me give you a personal example. I'll take you on a treasure-hunting journey through three of my own personal trials and show you the benefits that God ultimately gave me through each one. We'll begin with a trial I faced early in life. It has left a lasting mark upon me.

Being Held Back Moved Me Forward

Until I was in high school, I had moved at least once every year of my life. I'm not proud to admit it, but between bouncing in and out of so many different schools, I flunked the third grade. A number of children are held back before or after kindergarten at an age when it's socially acceptable, but how do you explain to your friends that you're being held back in the third grade because you can't read well enough?

While it may not make anyone's list of all-time trials, I can assure you that at the time, it was one of the greatest traumas I had ever faced. Now, as I look back years later, what did I get from the experience? Humility, to begin with.

Not being promoted with my friends kept me humble for many years. To this day I am self-conscious about my spelling. That's especially true if I have to write a note to one of my children's teachers, because my atrocious spelling was one of the reasons I was held back. Humility may not sound like such a great benefit, but a valuable gift of gold can be added to our character as a result of being humbled. It's found in a verse that says, "God opposes the proud but gives grace to the humble" (James 4:6). While I didn't realize it at the time, God was actually giving megadoses of His grace to me during the third grade!

Flunking third grade also made it difficult for me to read aloud in front of people. One of my most embarrassing moments was the time I was not able to finish reading a section of Scripture at my church. As president of a large college group, I was humbled even more by that experience. It gave me a deep concern for those struggling with dyslexia and other spelling and reading disorders such as mine.

Also, because I was so embarrassed, to this day I am extremely careful to try not to embarrass people who attend my seminars. My experience of embarrassment increased my sensitivity. This is also a fundamental requirement for being a loving person.

At the time I didn't feel there was anything good about flunking a grade, but there was. I received more of God's grace and added sensitivity to hurting people. Two major benefits from one trial, and that's just one trial.

When Our Ship Came In . . . and Ran Aground

During our first few years together, Norma and I lived on the edge of poverty most of the time. My poor accounting skills didn't help.

One year, we had absolutely no money—but we could see our ship coming in any day! Especially since we knew that a tax refund of $2,000 was on its way to us in the mail. When the letter came from the IRS, I hurriedly ripped it open, certain that I'd find a check inside that would be a tremendous help to us financially. Instead, I learned that I had made a major error on our tax form and that we actually *owed* the government $1,700—and they wanted it *now!*

At the time, I couldn't think of a single treasure I was getting out of this particular trial. In fact, I was dying trying to come up with every cent of earthly treasure we had, just to keep the Federal agents away from our door. As Norma and I look back on that experience, however, the real treasure didn't go to the government to play catch-up with the deficit. We learned several lessons more important than money, and they have stayed with us until this day.

The first benefit was the reminder that money is not the source of life. We had focused on our tax refund so much, it had shifted our focus away from Christ. That experience took away everything we had monetarily in life, but God showed us that neither money nor anything money could buy could take away what was more important—our relationship with Him. Because we had to struggle so much to pay the tax bill, the whole family learned the value of trusting God to meet our needs. (Including things like saying "thank you" for care-packages of food that were delivered mysteriously by some close friends.)

Finally, the trial forced me to get professional help with my taxes so that I wouldn't get any "surprises" in the mail again. It also forced me to take a more serious look at the management of our finances. Trial number two, and this time three major positive benefits by nearly going broke! Actually, I could count even more benefits, especially the love we gained through the experience—remembering that we gain more of God's love in every trial (Hebrews 12:9ff).

A Matter of Life and Death

When it comes to my third example of treasure-hunting trials, to tell you the truth, I'm glad I'm still around to explain it. While it's not easy for me to talk about, for the last two years, my health has not been the best. Basically, at times I've felt I had one foot in heaven and the other on a banana peel here on earth.

You see, my brother died of a heart attack two years ago at the age of 51. My sister had a heart attack last year as well, and another brother had to have triple bypass surgery at age 51. For those who are believers in genetics, it seems that my father's background may have something to do with the hearts in our family giving out when they do. My father died of a heart attack at age 58.

With my family's health history in mind, something happened two years ago—when I was 46—that started me counting my days.

For years, I've jogged a short distance every day and carefully watched my diet, hoping that alone would keep me healthy and fit. Then one morning in Vail, Colorado, during a speaking visit, I walked out of my hotel for a morning jog. Before me were 50 to 60 people, all in running clothes, stretching out and pinning race numbers on their T-shirts.

Recognizing them as people from the convention I was addressing, I said, "Hey, what are you guys doing?"

"This is the annual three-mile race," several people said. "Why don't you come and join us? Everyone at the convention is invited to run."

"You're only going *three miles?*" I asked.

At the time I could do three miles without breaking a sweat in the near sea-level altitude of Phoenix. So I walked over to the sign-up table, got myself a number and joined in. However, I soon discovered that there was a slight problem. This wasn't the friendly three-mile jog I had envisioned. It was a flat-out sprint through two-mile-high Vail. I was a short-distance jogger, not a long-distance sprinter, but the male conqueror mentality inside me kicked in, and I decided I was not going to finish in last place if it killed me.

It almost did.

Before I reached the half-way point, there were small children and senior citizens passing me. It was as if all the breathable air had suddenly been sucked out of Colorado. As I struggled to reach the finish line, I could see that last place was either going to be me or to a woman wheezing alongside me who looked like she'd flunked out of Weight Watchers. So I gave it all I had at the end—and she beat me.

The moment the race was over, I knew something was terribly wrong. I was sick. I spoke that day, then got on the plane with chills and fever. Before I knew it, I was vomiting and bleeding internally. I spent two weeks in bed and even then my blood pressure and cholesterol levels didn't recover. My kidneys were secreting blood, and I was having massive headaches. They were so bad that one doctor wanted to do surgery on my sinuses to drill holes in them so they could drain. Something about the altitude, my health, and my sprint had turned my body inside out.

What good could come out of almost dying? Particularly when John and I had conferences to conduct and books lined up to write? All this required nonstop work.

In the last two years, I have been forced to learn how to balance my life—how to level out the "high-highs" and "low-lows." I have learned even more about healthy food, healthy eating habits, and healthy work habits. I learned what burn-out and stress can do to a body and how damaging out-of-control emotions can be on my system. I also learned how to seek the Lord in a way I'd never done before.

As I learned the concept I described in Chapter 13 (gaining my fulfillment from Christ), I also re-learned the "little widow lady" attitude of prayer. For months, I had to wait daily in that line for my own physical health and strength and to accept that I may not be able to walk through every door of "ministry" that's open to me. The treasure I've gained from that experience is a clearer understanding of how God does give His strength to the weak and of His faithfulness to those who seek Him alone.

These were three trials at different times in my life, some small and some large. Each resulted in similar gains in my store of God's love, peace, and joy. Herein lies the secret to successful treasure-hunting. We can gain a great deal through our trials or nothing at all— depending on our faith. It's not how *much* faith we have, but whether the faith we have takes God at His Word.

Great Faith or "Dinky" Faith

The secret to successful treasure-hunting is understanding two life-changing words: faith and love. The greater our faith in God's Word, the easier it is for us to treasure-hunt trials. The more we treasure-hunt, the more we'll be able to see the ways we're becoming more loving as a result of our circumstances. It all begins with faith, however. We have to take God at His Word. It's not more faith we need, but great faith. Here's what I mean.

Do you remember the story of the centurion who came to Jesus for the sake of his servant? It's one of the clearest descriptions in the Scriptures of exactly what "faith" entails. Read Luke 7 to see if I'm telling the story correctly.

The centurion was a powerful man who commanded an entire garrison of men. Yet one day he faced a problem he couldn't defeat on his own, and he pushed his way through a crowd until he stood in front of Jesus. Coming quickly to the point, he said, "Sir, my servant is lying paralyzed at home, suffering great pain." Even though the man made only a statement, not a request, Jesus answered, "I will come and heal him."

But do you remember the centurion's response?

"Lord," he said, "I am not worthy for You to come under my roof. I am a man used to giving and taking commands. Just say the word, and my servant will be healed." Amazed by the centurion's faith, Christ said to the people around him, "I have not found such *great faith* with anyone in all of Israel!"

Anyone! He was talking about a very religious country. This Roman soldier had greater faith than anyone Jesus knew? Even greater faith than the disciples who would one day die for Him?

"Have you ever wondered what the disciples must have thought about such a statement? Peter was probably saying under his breath, *Sure, Lord, embarrass us in front of our Jewish brethren!* There was no love lost between the Jews and Roman soldiers.

What had impressed Jesus so much about what the soldier had said?

The answer is like a picture-frame around the concept of faith. This soldier believed that Jesus had only to command it and his servant would be healed. "For I, too, am a man under authority," he said to Jesus, "with soldiers under me; and I say to this one, 'Go!' and he goes, and to another, 'Come!' and he comes, and to my slave, 'Do this!' and he does it" (Matthew 8:10). The centurion never doubted for a moment Christ's power and authority to heal his servant. Jesus had said it, and that settled it in his mind.

But why *didn't* he doubt? Problems in life are so quick to produce questions in most of our minds. Perhaps the centurion's faith came from facing the trials of spending many days, on many different battlefields. Perhaps it was a reflection of his own father's faith. We're never told how this man came about his great faith. In contrast, Christ's disciples showed theirs to be of "dinky" proportions almost immediately.

It had been a long day of speaking to the crowds and healing the sick, when Jesus told His disciples to "get into their boat and cross to the other side of the lake." Exhausted from the drain of the crowd, He lay down to take a nap.

When the disciples were halfway across the sea, a storm blew in. Waves crashed over the sides of the boat and the disciples panicked. In desperation, they woke Jesus and cried out, "We're perishing!" Jesus just sighed, stood up, and quieted the waves and the wind with a single command. Then, drawing on the living illustration of the centurion's faith, He said to His disciples: "Why are you so timid, you men of little faith?"

How did the disciples' faith differ from that of the centurion? Why did a Roman soldier have "great" faith and Christ's own disciples "dinky" faith? The difference was that in the midst of the storm, *the disciples forgot what Jesus had said to them.* They quit counting on His Word, and as a result they panicked and counted themselves in the "lost at sea" category.

Jesus specifically said to them before He went to sleep, "We're going to the other side," not, "You guys better hug everybody, because we're fish-food halfway across this lake." He had given them His word they would *all* cross to the other side. Yet they forgot His words when the water got choppy.

I'm not blaming the disciples—I'm too much like them. Many of us make the same mistake in our marriages and families, don't we? During difficult times. we forget that God promises we'll make it to the other side—He just never promises a smooth ride on the way there. *But as the waves crash around us, God promises He will produce maturity, righteousness, patience, endurance, and love in our lives.*

In James 1:2, the writer told us to "consider it pure joy . . . whenever you face trials" and in 2 Corinthians 5:7, Paul told us to "live by faith, not by sight." So questioning the waves and their effect on our trip through life is like saying, "God's promises don't apply to me. God doesn't understand my situation, so how can any good come out of all this suffering?" (Isaiah 40:27ff.).

We're Not the First to Be "Treasure-Hunters"

One look in the Bible shows story after story of gaining treasure from trials. How would you feel if you were hated by your brothers, sold for pennies into a foreign slave market, framed for adultery, thrown into jail without a trial, and then forgotten by the one person who could have saved you?

Joseph, in the Old Testament, knew what that felt like. Yet what did he say years later, when he, the Pharaoh's right-hand man, brought his brothers to Egypt? Even as he forgave them he said, "You intended to harm me, but God intended it for good" (Genesis 50:20).

Adam, Noah, Abraham, Isaac, Jacob, Joseph, Moses, Elisha, Elijah, Jeremiah, David, Solomon, Esther, Ruth, Isaiah, John the Baptist,

Peter, Paul, Mary Magdalene, James. . . . on and on the list goes. All these are people with whom we can identify. They all faced trials like we have. Even in cases of "failure" (remember, Elisha and Jonah ran away, Peter denied Christ, Paul persecuted Christ's followers, James deserted Him, etc.), God took tragedy and even "dinky" faith and turned it into eternal treasure.

Blocking Trials from Producing Love

I'll be the first to admit that there is a problem with experiencing trials. Namely, their worth to us often comes on a delayed basis. As the waves are bouncing us around, we are just like the disciples. All we can picture is surviving the immediate, not thanking God for how He's shaping us for eternity.

Remember how long it took the average family to turn disasters into "family glue" in Chapter 12? It often takes several weeks for the family to see those disasters in their true light and begin bonding as a result. The same is true with trials. It took time for Dave Roever to say he was a better man for having a hand grenade blow up in his face. Diane didn't stop crying herself to sleep for months after the tragedy she faced at nine years of age—but healing did come one fateful morning.

Experts say that it takes at least thirty days of consistent repetition before a habit becomes ingrained. In other words, don't give up on treasure-hunting when you're only a few feet from shore. When someone's experiencing a trial, it's natural to go through a stage in which anger or doubt takes over, but making a decision to remain angry or even to dwell on being a "victim" can block you from any positive effects the trial could have on your character.

If I wanted to, I could still be angry at my third grade teacher or my parents for not getting me the help I needed to pass the third grade the first time, but hanging on to resentment would simply act as a roadblock to any benefits God could bring me. I could blame Norma or the "Infernal" Revenue Service for a complicated tax system that nearly bankrupted our family—or I could admit my own mistake and look in faith to what God could teach me in what happened.

I could even hate my father's memory—and question God's wisdom—in giving me his genes that may put an early time limit on the years I have to serve Him. To do so, however, would be to kick and scream at a loving and sovereign—and—unfathomable God. (Remember from Chapter 5: Anger blocks God's working in our lives, so we're only cheating ourselves to hold on to feelings of being a victim.)

There's no earthly reason why Dave, Mickey, and Diane should be happy and fulfilled after what's happened to them—but there is a heavenly one. Solomon once said if we live long enough, we'll all see enough sorrow to knock the joy out of life if we let it (Ecclesiastes 12:1). Embracing the value of our trials and mining the constructive good God can bring from them is the only way I know to keep rejoicing for a lifetime.

Passing down the Faith to "Treasure-Hunt"

As I mentioned earlier in the chapter, there are important personal reasons for learning to treasure-hunt trials, but it doesn't stop there. For those of us who have children, it's vital that we begin teaching them lessons in centurionlike faith at an early age—especially if they seem destined to increase their sensitivity level by being slightly (or decidedly) accident-prone.

For whatever reason, my son Michael wins the "I've-experienced-the-most-natural-and-man-made-accidents" award in our family. When he was two weeks old, he almost died from severe stomach problems that required major surgery. For the next several years, he suffered through a series of childhood illnesses and came close to death again.

Once when he was three, I was digging in the back yard and unearthed a yellow-jacket nest. Where was my "award-winning" son standing? Right where the nest fell. He was stung repeatedly before I could get to him. Then in the same year, Mike nearly drowned in a motel swimming pool.

He's suffered through a retainer to enlarge his mouth and then braces to pull his teeth in tighter. At age thirteen, he was in a major car accident. He broke an arm and was showered with so much broken glass, it took the doctors two hours to take out all the glass slivers from the side of his face and from his eyelid. Soon he'll undergo an operation in which he will have to get his jaw broken and reset.

What do you say to a child who has gone through so many trials? Why not let him do the talking? When the doctor told Michael that there would probably be some pain involved in his upcoming operation, Mike said, "Oh, don't worry about it. I've had so much pain in my life that this isn't going to faze me."

When people go through painful experiences, it often seems to enable them to go through future experiences with less trauma, as if they understand the process and the refining fire. Michael had already been through so many things that the automobile accident wasn't that traumatic for him. Even during the two hours they worked to take all the glass from his face, he was calm and joking. A week after the accident, Mike's attitude was still positive when he learned that he'd have to go through the entire summer in Phoenix with a cast on his arm and unable to swim. The same will be true when he has his jaw operation. At age sixteen, he's already an avid, well-seasoned treasure-hunter—and he's needed to be!

Teaching Them to Look for Love in an Unusual Place

When you teach your children what God's Word has to say about troubled times, you're providing a true "lamp unto their feet" for the rest of their trial-ridden life. As John and I explain in detail in our book, *The Gift of Honor*, it all begins with your first reaction during a trial. Calmly comforting them at the beginning of a trial lays the foundation for them to find value in their difficult experiences. It teaches them they can be calm, too.

And how do we remain calm at such a chaotic moment? Calmness comes from our own deep inner confidence in God's abiding care. As we discussed in Chapter 13, it's a deep conviction that will work for good in God's time (Romans 8:28).

Watching Mike's positive attitude through his pain gave us an opportunity to praise him for the way he was handling the situation. Yet we made a mental note to keep tabs, as the months went by, on how he was responding (a bit like watching for aftershocks of an earthquake). By doing so, we'd be able to spot early warning signs like depression or anxiety that could grow into major problems later on. That is a good idea for all parents as they smooth the path toward finding the treasure of their children's trials.

Biblical principles are like powerful beacons that can light up even the darkest trial your children may experience. Teaching your children that Romans 8:28 and Philippians 4:1ff speak of spiritual benefits they can claim in faith is a precious legacy you can leave your loved ones. If you take God at His Word yourself, you'll verbally and nonverbally convey this message to your children as they watch your responses to your own troubles.

Great faith is confidently knowing that what God promises will come true. Great faith is the confidence even during a trial that it will one day turn out to our benefit. "Dinky" faith is complaining or "murmuring" during a trial that there is no benefit on the other side, we're doomed. . . . finished . . . beyond help . . . unrepairable. . . .

I firmly believe that the mark of a person who grows through trials is the degree to which he or she is willing to take God at His Word. That is called great faith in the love of God, and only possible for those who . . .

Don't Bail out of the "Love Boat" When Trials Hit

As we've mentioned, the most precious treasure we discover as we unwrap any trial is gaining more of Christ's love. Troubled times have a way of funneling the love and care of God to us, and the love of God *through* us, to others. Only those who desire God's best, His love, truly benefit from trials. Trials are coming to all of us, and it's crucial that we learn to use them for good, rather than let them get us down.

In the weeks after Mike's accident, I sat down with him several times and discussed some of the benefits that were a part of his trial. Because we've done this with so many of his trials, he jumped in quickly, telling me he could see the ways in which he had already become more sensitive. No longer could he pass an accident site and not begin praying for the people instead of just "looking" at what happened.

There's no question in our home about who is the most sensitive family member. No one feels the hurt of people or even animals as deeply as Mike does, and I believe it has everything to do with how much he has suffered.

Recently, on the way to a doctor's appointment, I asked Mike what he wants to do in life. Do you know what he said? "I think I want to try to help protect people somehow. Maybe I'll be a policeman or in some kind of service organization. Maybe I can be a secret service agent or something. I want to do something to help protect people somehow."

How often in our own lives has someone ministered to us during a difficult time with caring eyes and loving ways—and later we learned that person had been through the same kind of problem? One of the clearest treasures a trial offers us is to make us loving and sensitive in its wake. That wonderful sensitivity is, I believe, a major factor in genuinely loving others. We develop more patience, tolerance, sensitivity and overall we become better lovers of people (Romans 5:3-5).

The apostle Paul understood this mystery when he wrote his famous explanation of love: "Love is patient, love is kind. It does not envy, it does not boast, it is not proud. It is not rude, it is not self-seeking, it is not easily angered, it keeps no record of wrongs. Love does not delight in evil but rejoices with the truth. It always protects, always trusts, always hopes, always perseveres" (1 Corinthians 13:4-7).

These qualities of mature love are given to us through trials better and faster than any other way I know. Trials put us in a "love boat" with Jesus. As the disciples we're able to ride out the storm. Just as with them, it's our choice whether we're going to take Jesus at His Word and believe He'll take us to the "other side" of the trial—and gain more love for Him and others in the process. Or whether we'll wake Him up continually with our cries of mistrust and "dinky" faith—and hear His gentle reproof, "Oh, ye of little faith . . ."

I know I can't keep trials from coming. The Bible promises me that trials will show up on my doorstep (James 1:2ff.). Over the years, though, I'm finally coming to the place where I've quit fighting something the Bible says can "Purify you and make you lacking in nothing" (James 1:4).

> The qualities of mature love are
> given to us through trials better
> and faster than any other way
> I know. . .

Another way to look at trials is to treat them like long-term "interest-bearing" CDs. It may take time for them to mature and for God to produce a greater capacity to love through our trial, but there's a promise we can count on. We can take Him at His Word that we can cash in on that love one day. As the writer to the Hebrews says, no one enjoys trials, "No discipline seems pleasant at the time, but painful. Later on, however, it produces a harvest of righteousness and peace for those who have been trained by it" (Hebrews 11:11).

A Promise by Day and by Night

Faith is trusting that God's Word is reliable. If He promises, "We are going to the other side," then we are going to the other side. There are a number of promises in the Scripture that can keep us going, keep us searching for that buried treasure of love with a full and open heart. In fact, here's a quick list I offered in the book, *Joy That Lasts*[1] that contains just a few of the promises to remember as trials come to us day by day. I strongly urge you to memorize a list of scriptural promises like these, so that when the next trial hits—you'll stay in His "love boat" and be able to treasure-hunt more quickly when you reach the other side.

1. "And we know that in all things God works for the good of those who love him, who have been called according to his purpose" (Romans 8:28).

2. "Give thanks in all circumstances, for this is God's will for you in Christ Jesus" (1 Thessalonians 5:18).

3. "Consider it pure joy, my brothers, whenever you face trials of many kinds, because you know that the testing of your faith develops perseverance" (James 1:2-3).

4. "Our fathers disciplined us for a little while as they thought best; but God disciplines us for our good, that we may share in his holiness. No discipline seems pleasant at the time, but painful. Later on, however, it produces a harvest of righteousness and peace for those who have been trained by it" (Hebrews 12:10-11).

5. "Jesus replied: 'Love the Lord your God with all your heart and with all your soul and with all your mind.' This is the first and greatest commandment. And the second is like it: 'Love your neighbor as yourself.' All the Law and the Prophets hang on these two commandments" (Matthew 22:37-40).

6. "The goal of this command is love, which comes from a pure heart and a good conscience and a sincere faith" (1 Timothy 1:5).

7. "Dear friends, since God so loved us, we also ought to love one another. No one has ever seen God; but if we love each other, God lives in us and his love is made complete in us" (1 John 4:11-12).

8. Last, but certainly not least, is my favorite chapter in Scripture as I've gone through physical trials this year (Romans 5). To offer a paraphrase of these verses: "Therefore we have been made right with God through faith, peace with God through Christ, and enjoy the power of God in us through Christ. Not only do we have all we need in Him, but we can also be excited about our sufferings. Because trouble brings us endurance—the power to keep going—and endurance produces character (love), character brings hope, and we won't be disappointed (great faith) because God will pour out His love in our hearts through His Spirit!"

So the truth remains: No one likes trials, yet no one can escape them. We can let them ruin our lives, allowing ourselves to become bitter, angry, resentful. Or we can look for the treasure that will let us love and serve our family and others better. Again, the choice is ours. *For loving God—like loving one's spouse and children—is first, last, and always a decision.*

The Two Sides
of Love

We lovingly dedicate this book to our wives, Norma and Cynthia,
each an expert at giving both sides of love;
and to George and Liz Toles, faithful friends,
consistent encouragers and godly examples to us over the years.

Contents

1
Discovering Love's
Two Sides

DARRELL STOOD OUTSIDE the local pizza parlor, hesitating before he opened the door. He shook his head as if to clear away his last-minute doubts about this meeting. Finally, with a sigh, he forced aside his fear, pushed open the door, and walked into his son's favorite restaurant.

He dreaded this meeting so much that it took all his emotional strength just to walk inside instead of turning away. Little did he know that within a few hours, he would experience one of the most positive events of his life.

Darrell had come to meet his seventeen-year-old son, Charles. Though Darrell loved Charles deeply, he also knew that of his two boys, Charles was the most different from him.

With his older son, Larry, communication was never a struggle. They acted and thought so much alike that they didn't need to talk much. They just did things together, like hunting or working on their cars. Darrell had always treated Larry as he did the men at his construction sites—rough. And Larry had always responded well to—even thrived on—that kind of treatment.

But Charles was a different case. Darrell could tell early on that Charles was much more sensitive than Larry. Each time Darrell blasted this son to motivate him like his older brother, Darrell could hear an alarm going off deep inside himself.

Darrell had received major doses of discipline and distance in his life—the hard side of love—but only a scant spoonful of warmth and acceptance—love's soft side. And what little he had been given, he had also measured out to his sons.

It's my job to put clothes on their backs and food on the table; it's their mother's job to make them feel loved, he told himself over and over. But he couldn't quite convince himself that that was all there was to being a father. Darrell knew how deeply he had been hurt by his own dad. And he had seen that same hurt in Charles's eyes a hundred times.

Darrell knew what a major part of the problem was. Charles had expected—almost demanded—a close relationship with him over the years. It wasn't enough that they go hunting together. Charles wanted to talk while they were on the trip—even while they were hunting!

Only recently had Darrell realized that the sole reason he and Charles were getting along at the moment was that his son had quit talking to him altogether! Just as Darrell had done as a teenager with his own tough father, Charles had withdrawn to a safe distance and was doing his best to stay out of his dad's way.

Like many of us, Darrell had been on the run from close relationships. For years, his wife and son had been pursuing him. And for as many years, he'd been running away from them, trying to keep a "comfortable" distance between them.

Then one day Darrell got a clear look at himself during a men's retreat at his church, and the running stopped.

That day at the retreat, he came face to face with the fact that there are two sides of love. Like many men, he had become an expert on its hard side. He could hand out the spankings, but not reach out to hug his son. In a heartbeat he could call down a mistake Charles made, but words of encouragement came up only on a holiday or birthday—if then.

At that men's retreat, Darrell learned that as important as a mother's love is, children need more. They desperately need their father's wholehearted love as well.

Darrell was a strong man, both emotionally and physically. Yet as tough as he fancied himself, just one question the speaker asked pierced through to his heart: "When was the last time you put your arms around your son and told him face to face that you love him?"

Darrell couldn't think of a "last time." In fact, he couldn't think of a first time.

He listened as the speaker told him that genuine love has two sides, not just one. Instantly he realized he had been loving Charles only halfheartedly and that his son needed both sides of love *from the same person.*

What Charles needed most in a father was a real man who could show him how to love a wife and family wholeheartedly, not an insecure man who had to hand off all the warm and loving actions to his wife. Darrell had spent years hardsiding his son to gain his respect; what he had gained instead was his fear and resentment. And it was this realization that caused Darrell to talk his son into meeting him at the local pizza restaurant after football practice one afternoon.

"Hi, Dad," Charles said, shaking hands with his father, who had just walked in. Charles was six foot two and was used to looking down when he greeted people. But he was looking up to meet his dad's eyes. And although Darrell had turned fifty-one that same month, he had none of the middle-age spread that most men his age carry. Instead, he still possessed the athletic build that had made him a star on his high school football team.

Charles and his father were the kind of people that "all you can eat" restaurant managers hate to see walk in the door. That evening they kept their waitress running back and forth as they devoured three baskets of bread sticks and nearly as many pizzas. As their dinner progressed from appetizers to the main course, their conversation moved from small talk to the serious matter Darrell wanted to discuss.

"Charles," Darrell said, adjusting his glasses and looking down slightly as he spoke, "I've been doing a lot of thinking lately. It's been hitting me hard that this is your last summer at home. You'll be leaving for college soon. And along with the bags of clothing you'll be packing, you'll also be taking emotional bags that, for good or bad, *I've* helped you pack over the years."

Charles was normally the family comedian, but this time, instead of trying to "lighten up" the conversation, he sat quietly. It wasn't like his father to talk about their relationship. In fact, it wasn't like him to talk about *anything* serious. That's why he was all ears as he listened to his father.

"Son, I'd like to ask you to do something. Think back as far as you can—back to three years old even—and remember every time I've hurt your feelings and never made things right; every time I've made you feel unloved or inadequate by something I've said or done.

"I know we're different people. I can see now that I was always pretty hard on you. Actually, I was way too tough on you most of the time. I've tried to push you into being the person I thought you should be. Now I realize I've spent very little time listening to who you really want to become.

"Feel free to share with me anything I've done that's hurt you, and all I'm going to do is listen. Then I'd like for us to talk about it, and I want to ask your forgiveness for each thing you can think of. You don't need to be packing any extra, negative baggage that I may have given you. You've got enough ahead of you over the next four years in college without that.

"I realize there's been a lot of water under the bridge—a lot of wasted years." Taking off his glasses and wiping tears from his eyes, he sighed, then looked straight at Charles. "We may be here all night," he continued, "and I'm ready for that. But first, you need to know how much I love you and how proud I am of you."

Charles had seen the words "I love you" written on birthday and Christmas cards in his father's handwriting, but this was the first time he had heard them from his father's lips. He'd learned to expect his father's hardness. Now that Dad had added softness to his love, Charles didn't know what to say.

"Dad," he stammered, "don't worry about the past. I know you love me." But at his father's insistence, he put his memory on "rewind" and let his thoughts fly back across the pictures he'd accumulated from seventeen years of being with his dad.

Slowly, as Charles grew more confident that the conversational waters really were safe, he unloaded years of hurt right at the table. There were the seasons he spent becoming an outstanding football player to please his father, when all the time he would rather have been playing soccer.

There was the subtle resentment he had always felt that no matter how hard he tried, he could never quite live up to his older brother's accomplishments. And there were the many harsh comments his father had made to motivate him but that had actually been discouraging and hurtful.

As he recounted to his father each experience, large or small, Charles could see a genuine softness and sorrow in his dad's eyes. What's more, he heard words of remorse and healing for even the smallest thing that had left a rough edge on a memory.

Nearly three hours later, the fruitful conversation finally came to an end. As Darrell reached for the check, he said, "I know this was quick notice for you to have to think back on seventeen years. So just remember, my door is always open if there's anything else I need to ask your forgiveness for."

Dinner was over, but a new relationship was just beginning for them. After eighteen years of being strangers living under the same roof, they were finally on their way to finding each other.

Not long ago, television news cameras captured thousands of people cheering as the Berlin Wall came down after dividing the city for more than twenty-five years. And that night in the restaurant, we can just imagine that angels stood all around and cheered as the first hole in an emotional wall between a father and son was blown open.

It had been a moving night and an important one for both of them. But as they stood up, Charles did something that shocked his father.

Several people looked up from tables nearby as a big, strapping football player reached out and gave his equally strong father a warm bear hug for the first time in years. With tears in their eyes, those two strong men stood there holding each other, oblivious to the stares.

What Are the Two Sides of Love?

In many ways, on the football field and in the building business, Darrell was a warrior who had conquered any challenges put before him. But for all his success, he had never won the bigger battle for his son's heart until that night. How did it happen? While Darrell was at his retreat, he discovered the same things you will in this book.

It's essential that we learn to balance love's hard and soft sides every day if we want to communicate to others the deepest, most meaningful kind of love.

It's essential that we learn to balance
love's two sides if we want to communicate
the deepest, most meaningful kind of love.

What do we mean by "hardside" and "softside" love, and why is it so important to understand and communicate both of them to others? While it may seem an unlikely place to look, nature provides a classic illustration of the answers to those questions.

One of the most beautiful things in all God's creation is a rose. In our culture, roses signify love, hearty congratulations or other deep emotions. Roses have been bred to capture and show off the colors of the rainbow. There's great softness in them as well. Like the tenderness of a baby's skin, velvety rose petals beg to be touched.

But God knew when He designed the rose that the very softness that makes it a thing of splendor also leaves it easy prey to those creatures that would destroy its beauty. That's why, along with the softness, He also provided the hardness of thorns. They don't detract from its beauty but protect, preserve and enhance it.

What's true in the realm of nature is also true in the world of relationships.

Hardside love is doing what's best for another person *regardless of the cost.* Held in balance, it's the ability to be consistent, to discipline, to protect, to challenge and to correct.

It's the strength a mother needs to stand up to a defiant two-year-old instead of caving in to his immature demands. It's the courage of a father who risks his relationship with his daughter to point out how far she's wandered from the Lord. It's the power an elderly husband demonstrates every day he stays and cares for the wife of his youth who is smitten with Alzheimer's disease instead of giving up and walking away.

Like the thorns on a rose, hardside love is protective. But if left to grow unchecked and never cut back to allow for healthy softside growth, it can become a thornbush instead of a rosebush. Instead of drawing people to its beauty, it can be hurtful and even cause them to move and stay away.

Hardside love is essential. But it's also incomplete by itself.

Softside love is a tenderness that grows to be the same color as unconditional love. When held in balance, it manifests characteristics like compassion, sensitivity, patience and understanding.

It's the sympathy of a father who sits with his arm around his daughter as she cries over a lost boyfriend, and the dad doesn't even hint at a lecture or an "I told you so." It's the encouragement of a mother whose cheerful card arrives at the college post office the day before her son's medical school entrance exams. And it's the kindness of a man who still calls his best friend's parents each year on the day their son died in Vietnam—just to let them know he remembers and that their son is more than a name on a wall.

Softside love takes time to understand another's feelings and listens instead of lecturing. It shows itself in the willingness to reach out and warmly touch and hug someone. It's also the wisdom to ask "Will you forgive me?" or to say "I was wrong," especially to our children.

Like hardside love, softside love can be pushed out of balance. Without a protective hard side, it can become so emotional and unstable that all the soft petals end up withered on the ground.

Is such a view of love novel? Is trying to understand and balance these two sides of love an invitation to confusion? Hardly. It's actually the very way we were always meant to love others. For it's the way the greatest lover of all time loves us—God Himself.

The Source of Love

Have you ever wondered what God is like? Isaiah the prophet gave two closely connected word pictures to the people of Judah in anticipation of their being conquered by Babylon and taken into captivity for seventy years[1] At the end of that time, the weary refugees would experience God's presence again and finally return to the promised land. Get up on the rooftops and mountains, Isaiah told them in the first picture, because "the Sovereign Lord comes with power, and his arm rules for him" (Isa. 40:10). In Old Testament times, this signified a conquering warrior in all his strength. It was a clear picture of His hardside love.

But then we see the second picture in verse 11: "He tends His flock like a shepherd: He gathers the lambs in his arms and carries them close to his heart; he gently leads those that have young." God is a caring, loving shepherd who "gently" tends to those with special needs. That was a clear picture of His softside love.

The people weren't being told that two Gods were in view—just one. But our God does have two sides to His love: a hard side that's consistent, purposeful, protective and mighty with judgment; and a soft side that's compassionate, tender, forgiving and merciful.

If we're serious about what it means to love others with our whole heart, the place to begin is by looking to the greatest lover of all time, Jesus Christ. He loved a sinful world enough to take off the mantle of heavenly power and be born in a stable. What's more, He demonstrated that love to us in that while we were still His enemies, He died for us on the cross.[2]

Jesus had the ability to give softside love to Peter, warmly saying to him after his great confession of faith, "Blessed are you, Simon son of Jonah, for this was not revealed to you by man, but by my Father in heaven."[3] Yet just a short time later, He could draw on the healthy, protective, hard side of love to say to Peter, "Get behind me, Satan! You are a stumbling block to me; you do not have in mind the things of God, but the things of men."[4]

Christ wasn't being inconsistent in His love. Neither was He on an emotional roller-coaster ride, alternately critical and caring. Rather, He was demonstrating the same two characteristics Isaiah spoke about when he described God as both sovereign Lord and a tender shepherd.

As the visible expression of the invisible God, Jesus showed us that His love was soft enough to cry at the death of a friend, to hug children and have them sit in His lap. Yet it was hard enough to confront those opposed to God's way and to "resolutely set out for Jerusalem"[5] and the cross no matter what the personal cost.

> ## Jesus was always soft with people, yet hard on their problems.

If we want to love in a Christlike way, our love must have both hard and soft sides. Specifically, we need to remember that *He was always soft with people, yet hard on their problems.*

Jesus was soft with people like Peter, the rich young ruler and Paul. But He was consistently hard on their problems of pride, greed and hatred. He blasted the Pharisees who challenged Him, calling them white-washed graves and blind guides. Yet whenever one of these religious leaders turned to Him with a sincere faith—like Nicodemus, the rich young ruler or Joseph of Arimathea—His softside love was always there, ready to forgive, comfort, show mercy and point to the truth.

Christ used the hard side of love to confront wrong, but He also knew there are times when a person most needs softness. Under pressure from the Pharisees not to heal on the Sabbath, He rebuked their hardness of heart. He would always do what was loving, and at times that meant touching, healing and forgiving even when the Pharisees' rules forbade it.

What does this all have to do with a book on marriage, parenting and relationships?

Until we learn to love others the way God loves us—with both of love's sides—we'll never have the kind of relationships that reflect the nature of God.

As soon as Darrell, whose story opened this chapter, heard the concept, he knew he was a pro at being hardside with Charles. But when it came to expressing the soft side of love, he wasn't even on the course.

That dinner meeting with Charles was one of his first steps toward balancing the two sides of wholehearted love. It wasn't easy, and it didn't come naturally to him. But he learned the same things you will in this book—insights that can help you to add a loving softness or a healthy hard side to your life.

As Darrell put these ideas into practice, he saw major improvements in his relationships both at home and at work. In fact, all across the country we've seen many people experience these same benefits as they've understood and applied the two sides of love. Just what did they learn that you can as well?

- *You'll soon discover a method for identifying your personal balance point.* Is your love shifted to one extreme or the other? Do you find yourself at the North Pole and your spouse at the South when it comes to being hard and soft? As your spouse gets harder, do you find yourself getting softer (or vice versa) to bring some kind of balance into your home?

     All the warmth of love can be frozen in relationships that are out of balance, and discovering your personal balance point is the first way to begin to protect or repair a relationship.

- *You'll learn how your natural personality strengths can push you out of balance either hardside or softside.* Many books can help you discover your basic personality type, but it's not enough just to understand your natural bent. Even more important is recognizing how that natural bent can push you into an unbalanced relationship and rob you and your family of harmony and intimacy.

- *You'll see how you can identify and cut down on any unhealthy distance in your relationships.* Do you sense there's too much emotional distance in your marriage or between you and your children? Like Darrell, have you been aware of an inner alarm that's telling you, *We're not as close as we should be?*

     In the chapters to come, you'll learn what causes unhealthy distance in a relationship and how applying the two sides of love can move you closer to your loved ones than ever before.

- *You'll see how "emotional freeze points" can rob us of the ability to love wholeheartedly.* In many people's lives, some past event or season has frozen them into a particular way of relating to others, blocking the flow of love's two sides. And identifying and dealing with those freeze points is crucial in building and protecting strong relationships.

- *You'll learn ten ways a person who is too soft can add a healthy hardness to his or her love, and ten ways a hardside person can become softer.* Once you understand where you are today and how your basic personality may be pushing you to an unhealthy extreme, you'll discover twenty specific ways to balance your love and strengthen the bonds between yourself and others.

Taking the First Step Toward Balance

At the retreat he attended, Darrell came face to face with himself. But that weekend wasn't simply a time to look in the mirror and go away unchanged. Darrell took the time to ask hard questions of himself and to do something that helped him discover how far out of balance he actually was.

In less than five minutes, Darrell was able to pinpoint where he was in his most important relationships, both hardside and softside—the same thing you'll be able to do in a few pages.

In just a few moments' time, he saw a new side to himself. What's more, as he began to move toward balance, he won back something of immeasurable value—his son's heart.

Perhaps you don't have a relationship on the critical list. But you can still benefit from this book, because improving your relationship skills will directly benefit your marriage, friendships, family and work setting. By learning to give and receive the two sides of love, you'll see even strong relationships grow deeper and more committed.

It all begins with your taking a few minutes to pinpoint where you are today, either hardside or softside, in the way you relate to others. And after that important first step, we want to give you a number of practical tools that can put both sides of love well within your reach.

2
How Hard or Soft
Are You?

IN JUST A few pages, you'll find a short but important survey that helps you see your own tendency toward hardness or softness. You may be surprised by what you discover about yourself.

First, however, we have a confession to make. Out of all the books we've written, either together or separately, this is the one *we've* needed the most, both personally and with our families. Let us explain.

When we first decided to write this book, we sat down with our wives, Norma and Cindy, to have them sign off on the project. We involve them in all our publishing decisions because we respect their input, and also because the long days and nights that go with writing a book are not just demanding on us, but on the rest of our families as well. That's why we don't go forward with any writing project unless we're all in unity.

Normally, when the four of us sit down to talk over a book idea, it's a fun afternoon or evening of discussion. Then everyone agrees, often in writing, to go forward as a team with the project.

At least that's the way it's *supposed* to work. But when it came to discussing this book—well, we'll never forget what happened.

It was several years ago now that we first met with our wives to talk over *The Two Sides of Love.* As we had done in the past, we wrote up a short summary of the book and gave it to them in advance for their review.

Going into the meeting, we knew for certain that they'd be excited about this project. We could just see them jumping up from the table, giving us high fives, and shouting, "Go get 'em, guys!" As it turned out, things were jumping all right, but for a very different reason.

You have to picture the scene. We're on one side of the table in our conference room, grinning and talking excitedly about the need to get started writing this important book. Our wives are on the other side of the table, watching our excitement but knowing we're missing something crucial.

In a presentation worthy of any Fortune 500 company, we did our best to sell them on the central concept of this book. Finally, we grinned and leaned back in our chairs. All that was left was to hear their cheers and get their signatures on the dotted line. At least that's what we thought.

It was softside Norma who spoke up first—someone who normally avoids confrontation at all costs.

"Cindy and I have talked," she said, glancing over at her for support, "and we love the concept. We think you're right: there do seem to be two sides to love. What's more, we can see how important it is to be balanced in the way we love others. Giving only one side of love can cause real problems in a family, friendship or any other kind of meaningful relationship.

"We think it's a great idea. It's a ten. What's more, it's grounded in the Scriptures, and we think it can help a lot of people."

Up to this point, everything she'd said couldn't have sounded better. We *knew* they'd see things our way! We were ready to close the meeting and pick up the phone to call the publisher when Norma said, "But we can't sign off on this book—at least not yet."

"What?" we said in stereo, our mouths dropping open.

"You two have always told us that you only want to write books about things you've lived and practiced in your own homes, right?"

We nodded agreement, unaware of the trap we were walking into.

"Both of you are practicing a lot of what you've said you want to put in the book. But before you write it, there are a few things we feel you still need to finish.

"When it comes to marriage, you've both got the hard side of love down pat. But while the soft side is certainly there, too, we'd like to see it even more often with the two of us. What's more, even though you're both good fathers, we'd still like to see a better balance with the children at times."

I (John) looked to Cindy, hoping to hear her say to Norma, "Oh, that's not true about John! Gary, maybe, but not my husband." Instead, all I got was seasick from watching her head bob up and down in agreement.

They were right, of course. (How often they are!) But still we asked for examples. . . . We shouldn't have.

Fit to Be Tied

"John," Cindy said in her kindest voice, "I never doubt your commitment to Kari and me. But you're not quite balanced when it comes to giving us both sides of love."

"What do you mean?" I asked in genuine puzzlement.

"Sometimes you give me one side of love and Kari the other. What we really need is what you want to write about—the two sides of love."

"Give us a 'for instance,'" Gary said with a grin as I shot him a look that said, "Just wait till it's *your* turn."

"Take what happened after your last trip," Cindy offered. "Can you remember how you greeted me when you first walked in the door after being gone three days?"

Unfortunately, I did remember. The day I left on that trip, she had been very busy with our daughter and had forgotten to pick up some dry cleaning I was going to take with me. Naturally, I didn't think of the cleaning, either, until I was already in the air and realized I didn't have my only sportcoat along.

When did I let her know how inconvenienced I had been because she didn't pick up the dry cleaning as we had agreed? Regrettably, I chose to tell her as soon as I'd walked into the house.

"John," she said now, "you don't have any trouble giving me the hard side of love. But after you'd been away for several days, what I needed when I met you at the door was your soft side—a hug and a warm hello—not a lecture about forgetting your cleaning."

Right there in the middle of the conference room, I started looking for a hole to crawl into. And after she told me her next concern, I was ready to cover over the hole!

"That's not all," she continued. "There have been a number of times recently when you've given Kari just one side of love as well. Remember the other night with the dental floss?"

Once again, she had brought to mind something I was far more eager to forget.

"You do a great job of giving Kari the softside love she needs," she said. "But when it comes to being hard with her when she needs it, like following through on family rules . . ."

Cindy didn't have to say anything more. I knew exactly what she meant. We have a family rule that no one can pull out more than three feet of dental floss a night. The rule came into existence after Kari had pulled out seventy-five yards of the stuff one day.

Everyone in the family was clear on the rule—but I wasn't enforcing it. When it was my turn to help Kari get ready for bed, I would "look the other way" as she pulled out ten or twelve feet of the bubble gum-flavored string.

After all, I reasoned, it was cute watching her do it . . . and she would only be four once . . . and it was such a *small* rule. But it was beginning to have a much larger effect on my wife and daughter's relationship than I had ever dreamed.

"The other night, when you were on your trip," Cindy said, "Kari started pulling out yards of dental floss. When I told her she could only pull out three feet, immediately her lip went out and she told me in a defiant voice, '*Daddy* lets me do it!'

"'Oh he does, does he?' I said.

"'That's right. And you know what? I like Daddy better than you, Mommy.'

"'Why's that?' I asked.

"'*Because Daddy doesn't make me follow the rules.*'"

Cindy paused for what seemed like an hour before she continued, "John, Kari knows you love her, but there are times when you're too soft with her. When I keep the family rules and you don't, you make me look rock hard, but it's really you who's out of balance!"

She leaned over, took my hand, and said with a smile, "Honey, I'm not trying to be too hardside with you. I wouldn't trade you for any other husband or father in the world.

"But come to think of it," she added with a twinkle in her eye, "maybe it *is* a good idea for you to write this book. If it will help you learn how to be softer with me at times and harder with Kari, I'm ready to say yes today!"

My frown changed immediately to a grin when I realized Cindy was finished. *It's your turn now, Gary,* I figured. I was right.

"Gary," Norma said gently, "do you think you need more balance in the two sides of love?"

"Who, me?" I (Gary) asked.

To jog my memory, she said, "Remember the time with Mike and the banana?"

We were living in Texas at the time and had just returned from a long trip. I had driven for hours, trying to stay awake by talking on the CB and drinking coffee (which I hate). All I could think about was getting home and crawling into bed. Finally, well after midnight, I pulled into our driveway and had everyone pile out of the car.

"Come on, kids," I said. "Everyone to bed. Right now."

Michael, who was only about five at the time, then said the last thing I wanted to hear: "Daddy, I'm hungry. Can I eat something?"

"No way!" I said, my voice filled with frustration and the need for sleep. "We're all tired, and if you stay up and eat, everyone else will want to stay up and eat. Then it'll be another hour before we're all in bed. So go get on your pajamas, and do it now!"

"Gary," Norma said soothingly, "it's been a long trip. If he wants to eat some cereal, I'll stay up with him for a few minutes so you can go to bed."

Now I was irritated at Mike for wanting to stay up and at Norma for exposing my insensitivity. Out of pure frustration, I said, "You want something to eat, Mike? Okay!"

In a flash, I grabbed a banana off the shelf, peeled it, and shoved it toward him. Unfortunately, he moved toward me at the same time, and the banana hit him in the face *near* his mouth, but not in it.

As Mom rushed in to protect her son from the banana, chaos broke out in our home. My selfishness and lack of sensitivity had closed both my wife's and son's spirits and landed me in major trouble. I was so ashamed and upset with myself that I couldn't get to sleep that night anyway!

I asked for forgiveness from both of them right then, before we all went to bed, but it still took days for everything to thaw out. And now Norma was calling that scene back to mind.

"Gary, most of the time you're wonderful with the kids," she said. "They all know how much you love them and how proud you are of them. But occasionally—especially with Michael—you can be very critical. And when that happens, it's like you're pushing a banana into his mouth again!"

Once was enough for the banana incident. I could see exactly what she meant, and I knew that like John, I needed to give more-balanced love in my own home—and made the commitment to do so.

"I agree with Cindy," Norma added. "This is a good book idea. In fact, I'd like nothing more than to have you concentrate on adding softness to our relationship and home over the next few years." Then she said, "And when the book's done, I'll keep a copy next to the bed in case I need to get at it quickly!"

As you've obviously figured, since you're holding this book in your hands, Norma and Cindy finally agreed that we could write the book after we had been putting these concepts into practice for several months. That afternoon, they used the principles you'll learn here to help strengthen both the Smalley and Trent households. And the first thing they did was to help us identify our own balance points—the very thing we'll show you how to do next.

Finding Your Hard or Soft Tendencies

Later in the book, we'll be describing a number of specific ways you can balance the two sides of love and build strong, lasting relationships as a result. But as when we're beginning a trip, we have to know where we're starting from. Otherwise, the best road map in the world won't help us.

That's why we've provided a means for you to discover your personal balance point—today. You'll see for yourself where you stand with regard to balancing the two sides of love.

In relating to others day to day, are you shifted to one extreme or the other? Are you camped out in the far reaches of a hardside life, easily issuing commands and criticism but not given to caring actions? Is it easy for you to be hard on problems but too easy to be hard on people as well?

> ### In relating to others day to day,
> ### are you shifted to one extreme or the other?

Or do you rarely move beyond an unhealthy softside, unwilling to confront someone or take the lead? Do you hesitate to act, even when you know you should be firm and others need you to be strong? Is your softness with people pushed so far that you're soft on the problems facing you and your family—even serious problems?

Perhaps most important, *do you know for a fact how those closest to you view you on an everyday basis?*

By taking the self-evaluation below, you can discover your personal balance point. You may not see a need for such self-examination, but others close to you probably do. So for them, if not for yourself, take the next five minutes and follow the simple instructions for filling in this instrument.

Discovering Your Personal Balance Point

Twenty pairs of words are listed below. To take the quiz, begin by thinking about the person closest to you (your spouse if you're married, or a close friend or parent if you're single). Then circle the number that best represents how you act toward that individual. Be sure to respond according to how you *currently and consistently* act toward that person, not according to how you *wish* you would or *occasionally* do act.

We also highly recommend that you have that same loved one fill in the instrument based on how *he or she* sees you. Then the two of you can discuss the results, noting especially any differences of perception that arise.

One man who has a strong personality scored himself squarely in the center of the softness scale the first time he took this quiz. However, when his wife evaluated him, he came out more like Attila the Hun than Mother Teresa. It took some time for his shock to wear off. But as they talked about their different perceptions of how he acted at home, it turned into one of the most enlightening and helpful discussions they'd ever had.

For additional insight, you may want to take the quiz again based on how you respond to each *child* in your home. If they're old enough, have them use it to rate you as well.

As we've developed this instrument, we've had entire families (with grade school or older children) sit around the dinner table and take it as part of a family night. Time and again, when there is freedom to discuss each other's scores—and the feelings and issues behind them—we've seen this experience begin to mend relationship fences and pull the family closer together.

Finally, be careful to look at this instrument as a window into people's lives, not as a weapon with which to attack. If you do find your loved ones shifted to an extreme, be careful not to belittle. It's usually better to let them discover where they are by taking the evaluation themselves than to point out their shortcomings for them.

Keep in mind that regardless of where you score today, you can move toward a healthy balance. We'll go into detail later on ten specific ways you can grow softer if you're currently too hard. And we'll also describe ten ways you can become more hardside if you presently display an unhealthy softness. There's plenty of room for all of us to grow when it comes to giving both sides of love.

Finding Your Personal Balance Point

Example:

Takes the Lead   Follower

1   2   3   4   5   6   7

If you tend to take the lead in your relationship quickly and consistently, you would circle 1. If you tend to follow the other person's directions or wishes the majority of the time, you would circle 7. If you fall somewhere between the two extremes, you would circle whatever number best represents how you relate to your loved one.

A Hardside/Softside Evaluation

How do you tend to act in your relationship with

_____ ?

(Loved one's name)

1. Take the lead   Follow

    1   2   3   4   (5)   6   7

2. Forceful   Nondemanding

   (1)   2   3   4   5   6   7

3. Energetic   Reserved

    1   2   (3)   4   5   6   7

4. Strive to accomplish personal goals   Let others set your goals

    1   (2)   3   4   5   6   7

5. Be self-controlled   Lack discipline

    1   2   (3)   4   5   6   7

6. Make quick decisions   Hesitate in making decisions

    1   2   3   (4)   5   6   7

---

7. Want to hear facts   Want to share feelings

    1   2   3   4   5   6   (7)

8. Be a motivator   Respond

    1   2   3   4   5   6   (7)

9. Be highly competitive   Be noncompetitive

    1   2   3   (4)   5   6   7

10. Be possessive   Share

    1   2   3   (4)   5   6   7

11. Be assertive   Be shy

    1   2   3   4   (5)   6   7

12. Express anger to others   Hold anger inside

    1   2   3   4   5   6   (7)

13. Resist correction   Be very teachable

    1   2   3   (4)   5   6   7

14. Share your opinions openly   Hide your true feelings

    1   2   3   4   (5)   6   7

15. Function well under pressure   Function poorly under pressure

    1   2   3   4   5   6   (7)

16. Lecture when the person is hurting   Listen and comfort

    1   2   3   4   5   6   (7)

17. Hold grudges   Forgive easily

    1   2   3   4   5   (6)   7

18. Set rigid standards   Set flexible standards

    1   2   (3)   4   5   6   7

19. Be hard on him (her) as a person   Be soft on him (her)

    1   2   3   4   5   6   (7)

20. Be hard on his (her) problems   Be soft on his (her) problems

    1   2   3   4   5   (6)   7

Scoring the instrument:
The total of all the numbers circled = ___97___
Mark your total score with an "X" on the line below.

Hardside   **Intensity Index**   Softside

20   40   60   80   100   120   140

Application project:
We encourage you to discuss how close or far apart you were in your scoring with your spouse or close friend. Example:

Hardside   **Intensity Index**   Softside

20   40   60   80   100   120   140

Spouse (friend) viewed me   I viewed myself

Many people find themselves scoring in the 75 to 105 range. This often indicates an ability to give and take in expressing the two sides of love. Those scoring below 65 or above 115 typically express one side much more than the other. Regardless of where you scored, you'll find the material in later chapters very helpful in developing or maintaining the ability to express needed hardness or softness.

Remember that your score should be cross-checked by a loved one or close friend to see how that person views you. Time and again, we've seen people score themselves in the middle of the scale, while loved ones place them at one of the extremes.

If we're serious about building strong relationships, it's important to find our personal balance point. But that's just the first step in developing a wholehearted love. It's not enough simply to see where we are. We also need to know what brought us to that point and how to make changes if we're to balance the two sides of love.

In the next several chapters, we'll see that there's something else we need to discover that goes hand in hand with everything we've talked about so far. In fact, to be able to balance our love with others, we've got to understand what is perhaps the major factor that can push us toward either extreme.

We're referring to the particular personality strengths we all have as individuals. Some of us have a natural edge in being hardside with people when we need to, yet we struggle to show warmth and offer praise. For others, our natural style puts softness within easy reach, yet the hardness to face problems and take strong stands seems to slip through our fingers.

Clearly understanding our God-given temperaments brings to light common causes of family disharmony; provides practical handles for resolving long-standing friction in a home; dramatically increases our feelings of value for our loved ones and friends; and gives additional reasons to honor God. All this begins as we see how powerfully our natural strengths, pushed even slightly out of balance, affect our ability to give and receive the two sides of love.

3
Which Way Are
You Bent?

"**I** CAN'T BELIEVE it. My relationship with my daughter is so different now. We've had the best six weeks we've had in years! Even my husband can't believe it. If only I'd known earlier what Jessica really needed."

It was a cold Tuesday night, and a group was gathering for its weekly Bible study. Talking to me (John) was an attractive, blonde woman in her early thirties who had raced over the minute she arrived.

"Six weeks ago," she said, "I heard your presentation in another group about the need to give the two sides of love. I took the test you gave, and I could see that I'm good at being hard on problems. But that day I also saw how I was being too hard on people—especially my daughter.

"Jessica is eleven, and she turned out to have very different natural strengths from mine. When I saw that, I realized that all her life, I'd been putting pressure on her to go faster and do more, and she's gone slower and done less than I wanted. I finally understood how different she is from me. She has a deep need to do things right and finish one project before going on to the next, but until now, it's never been something I valued.

"You can ask my husband," she said, putting her arm around the man who had just walked up. "He used to be the referee in our home, keeping Jessica and me from each other's throats. But these past six weeks, I've stopped using a timer to hurry her up with her homework or telling her to 'Just write anything' on a thank-you note so we can mail it out. I've started praising her for being so precise instead of criticizing her for it.

"I finally feel like I understand her, and it's changed our whole relationship," she continued, beaming. "In fact, it's motivated me to go from a too-hardside person to softer than I've ever been!"

What made such a major difference in this woman's relationship with her daughter? She already knew (and the test she took confirmed) that she was extremely hardside by nature. But by taking the next step and discovering her basic personality strengths, she learned several things that helped bring her love into balance and caused positive changes in her daughter's life. And the truths she learned can make a real difference in your relationships as well.

- *You'll discover a major reason people are pushed out of balance either hardside or softside, and how to correct the problem.*

Children seem to come fully equipped with a God-given personality bent, and even as adults, we tend to express our bent clearly. For example, Proverbs 22:6 is a familiar verse that reads, "Train a child in the way he should go, and when he is old he will not turn from it."

In the original language of the Old Testament, that verse actually reads, "Train up a child *according to his bent. . .*" So pronounced are these natural bents that a man we highly respect, Dr. Ross Campbell, feels you can even spot them in a newborn![1]

In just a few pages, we'll show how you can discover your own personality strengths. We've provided a one-page test that can help you recognize and value another person's strengths, as well as your own, in a way you may never have before. In sharing this test with thousands of singles and couples across the country, we've seen the resulting insight bring many couples and families closer together instantly.

In addition to discovering your natural strengths, you'll see how, when taken to extremes, they can push you out of balance either hardside or softside. Of the four natural bents people display, two tend to push us out of balance toward the hard side. People with these bents tend to be hard on problems. Unfortunately, they can be very hard on people as well.

The other two types of people lean toward the soft side in relationships. Their natural strength is being supportive. But they're often much too soft on problems that demand a hardside response.

By taking the simple self-survey we've provided, you'll be able to see what your own and other people's natural strengths are. Then, aided by the chapters that follow, you'll be able to tell which way you have a natural tendency to drift. But those are only two benefits you'll gain by taking this survey. There are more.

**Many family conflicts are caused
by viewing another person's
natural strengths as weaknesses.**

- *Starting with the very next chapter, you'll be able to sense immediately what's at the heart of many family conflicts—and see how to solve them.*

It's incredible how many family conflicts are caused by viewing another person's natural strengths as weaknesses. A clear view of what naturally motivates another person can open the door to greater compassion, patience, compromise and caring. What's more, you'll see how people's natural personality strengths, just slightly out of balance, can become their biggest weaknesses and most irritating behaviors. Knowing that can be very helpful, particularly when there's stress or tension around the house.

Different temperaments handle tension in different ways. For example, the two natural bents that lean toward being hardside often become more controlling of people and the situation. If that fails, they're not above picking up their marbles and moving away from the problem altogether. However, the two bents that lean toward the soft side often either give in (or up) too quickly or become very verbal and emotional to try to get their way.

- *You'll gain a handle on dealing with your own weaknesses.*

Can you think of a past or present problem area in your life? If we asked you to write your three greatest weaknesses on a 3 X 5 card, could you do it? Many of us would just be getting warmed up if we listed only three! In fact, we'd start looking for legal pads to write them all!

Most people, particularly most Christians, are experts in understanding their weaknesses. But without realizing it, by focusing on their weaknesses, they're effectively blocking their ability to deal with those very problem areas. That's because *there is no way to overcome a weakness without first knowing our strengths.* Why?

Almost without exception, our weaknesses are simply a reflection of our strengths being pushed to an extreme. For example, a softside bent often includes the ability to listen closely and carefully to others. But pushed to an extreme, this positive trait can become a weakness. At times, our focus on listening can keep us from asking the hard questions we should. We can also listen so much to others' problems that we become over-burdened or never take the time to verbalize our own hurts and concerns.

Another person may possess the natural hardside bent of being a critical thinker. Held in balance, that talent can make him great at dissecting things or projects. But push that strength out of balance and the ability to take issues apart can be used to take people apart as well.

By using the personal evaluation form at the end of this chapter, you'll see your strengths more clearly or in a different light. In fact, we've seen many people, after taking this test, learn for the first time to value the way God uniquely created them.

• *You'll discover a major key to Christlikeness.*

Discovering more about these natural bents can also help us see the love of Christ in a clearer, deeper way. How?

For one thing, the way Jesus dealt with others demonstrated that He had the strengths of all four basic personalities held in balance. Seeing those bents in perfection in His person can both challenge us and draw us closer to Him than ever before.

Using Our Strengths to Balance Love

We know a number of good personality tests are available today. In all, we've examined more than thirty different instruments that can give you a helpful reading of your basic temperament.

For our purposes here, however, we're looking at personality types through a much different lens. That's why we came up with our own instrument to help you see clearly how your strengths specifically affect your ability to give both sides of love to your family and friends.

If, after taking our short survey, you want a more in-depth analysis of your personality, one instrument we recommend highly is the "Pro Scan" PDP survey. Dr. Mike Williamson, a committed Christian and close friend of Dr. James Dobson, helped create this extremely reliable test that provides a detailed, ten-page analysis. While it is geared primarily toward helping people identify their personality strengths and stresses in the workplace, it can also be adapted to the home situation. (For more information about how to obtain this and other personality surveys, see the Notes section at the back of the book.[2])

> ## Almost without exception, our weaknesses are a reflection of our strengths being pushed to an extreme.

In creating our survey, we tried to be sensitive to two important concerns. First, we feel strongly that behavior cannot always be neatly categorized and labeled. Personality types don't all fit into four distinct boxes. That's why we emphasize that each person is really a blend of all four natural bents. In fact, even though most people will have one or perhaps two primary personality bents, each of us needs to be able to tap into all four to build strong relationships.

People usually see themselves in one category, with a second bent as present but less dominant. Our goal, however, isn't to restrict behavior by labeling it. Rather, we hope the labels illustrate where we are today so that we can more easily use the strengths of all the bents tomorrow in providing others with both sides of love.

Second, we wanted to capture these natural bents in a way that would be easily understood and remembered. That's why we chose to picture them by using animals.

It was Corrie Ten Boom who inspired us never to teach without using objects. Again, as a way of staying away from restrictive labels, we like using animal names to breathe life into the different bents. If you dislike being pictured in a fun-loving way as one of God's furry creatures, feel free to change the descriptive titles to something with which you're more comfortable.

With all that in mind, we invite you to take the Personal Strengths Survey. In doing so, you'll see firsthand what your natural strengths are. What's more, you'll begin to see how you can blend your natural strengths with those of others in your home.

How to Take the Personal Strengths Survey

We've tried to make taking this survey as simple as possible, which isn't true of all tests. For example, one popular personality test has more than three hundred questions, asking things like "Do you smell things that other people don't?" and "When you watch television, do the people talk back to you?"

In the Personal Strengths Survey, all we ask is that you circle a few simple words describing yourself. Then, with that information, we'll show you specifically what your unique strengths are and why they make you such a valuable person in all your relationships.

To complete the instrument, just read through the four boxes on page 431 (the L, B, O and G boxes), and *circle* each *word or phrase that seems to describe a consistent character trait of yours.* Next, add up the number of words and phrases you circled in each box. Then there's only one more step: you *double your score* to come up with a total in each box. What could be easier?

If that's all the instruction you need, go ahead and take the survey. But if you're the type of person who thinks these things should be more complicated, here are some additional details.

As you'll notice, each box has fourteen words or word groups (like "Takes charge," "determined" and "firm") and one phrase (like "Let's do it now!").

In the first box (with an *L* above it), you might read each word or phrase and decide to circle only one word as representing a fairly consistent character trait of yours. On the other hand, you might decide that all fourteen words and even the phrase apply to you. In that case, you would end up with all fifteen choices circled.

Go through each box, circling as many words and phrases as describe who you are consistently. Then double the number of words you circled to come up with a total score for each.

Remember that if you don't circle at least one word or phrase in one of the four boxes, you probably don't have a personality! (And that's a problem beyond the scope of this book!)

Finally, take the total scores from all the boxes and transfer them to the graph below the survey. The last thing left is something that most of us enjoy doing: connect the dots!

As you take this short self-survey, keep two things in mind. First, circle your responses based on how you relate to the people in your family—the most important people in your life. However, you may also want to make a copy of this inventory and take it again based on how you respond to people at work. Why?

Many people tend to shift their actions and attitudes between home and work. We've seen many men, for example, who are extremely hardside at work but who go home and are out of balance softside. You may discover that having to be one way at home and another at work is the source of much of your personal stress.

Second, be sure to circle responses based on who you actually are and how you act toward others right now—not on how you *wish* you were or always *wanted* to be. Some surveys and testing instruments include elaborate "lie" scales to make a person be honest in taking a test. We haven't chosen to do that with ours.

Can you make yourself look "better" than you really are on this survey? Certainly. Should you? Not if you want an honest evaluation of who you are and how you relate to others. That's one reason we ask people to have a loved one or close friend fill out the survey based on how *they* see them; it's a way of getting a more-objective analysis.

The Personal Strengths Survey

Once again, in each box, circle every word or phrase that describes a consistent character trait of yours. Total the number circled in each box, then double your score. Next, take the total score from each box and put it on the graph. Take a few minutes now to complete the survey and fill in the graph before continuing.

After you've taken the instrument and transferred your scores to the chart, what does it all mean?

The four letters at the top of each section stand for the four basic personality types we'll describe in more detail in the chapters that follow. Each holds a key to whether we tend to be hard or soft in relationships. As you'll see, everyone is a combination of all four of these types. But for now, let's take a quick overview of the four animals.

Scoring high on the L line are those we call *lions*. Lions are take-charge leaders. They're usually the bosses at work, or at least they think they are! They're decisive, bottom-line folks who are doers, not watchers or listeners. They love to solve problems. Unfortunately, however, if they don't learn to use both sides of love, their natural hardside bent can cause problems with others.

Scoring high on the B line are those we call *beavers*. Beavers have a strong need to do things "right" and "by the book." In fact, they're the kind of people who actually read instruction manuals! They like maps, charts and organization. And they're great at providing quality control for a home or office.

Because rules, consistency and high standards are so important to beavers, they often communicate the hard side of love to others just like the lion. Beavers have deep feelings for those they love. But learning to balance the two sides of love usually involves adding the abil-

L

Takes charge   Bold
(Determined)   Purposeful
Assertive   Decision maker
Firm   Leader
Enterprising   Goal driven
Competitive   Self-reliant
Enjoys challenges (Adventurous)

"Let's do it now!"

Double the number circled _2_

B

Deliberate   Discerning
Controlled   Detailed
Reserved   (Analytical)
Predictable   (Inquisitive)
(Practical)   Precise
Orderly   Persistent
Factual   Scheduled

"How was it done in the past?"

Double the number circled _3_

O

(Takes risks)   (Fun-loving)
(Visionary)   (Likes variety)
Motivator   (Enjoys change)
Energetic   (Creative)
Very verbal   Group oriented
Promoter   Mixes easily
Avoids details   Optimistic

"Trust me! It'll work out!"

Double the number circled _6_

G

(Loyal)   (Adaptable)
(Nondemanding)   Sympathetic
Even keel   (Thoughtful)
(Avoids conflict) (Nurturing)
(Enjoys routine) Patient
Dislikes change   Tolerant
(Deep relationships) (Good listener)

"Let's keep things
the way they are."

Double the number circled _10_

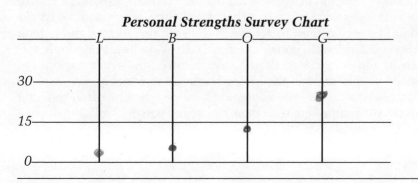

Personal Strengths Survey Chart

L   B   O   G

30

15

0

ity to communicate that softness and warmth in a way that's felt and clearly understood by others.

Scoring high on the O line are the *otters*. Otters are excitable, fun-seeking, cheerleader types who love to yak, yak, yak. They're great at motivating others and need to be in an environment where they get to talk and have a vote on major decisions.

Otters' outgoing nature makes them great networkers—they usually know people who know people who know people. The only problem is, they usually don't know everyone's name! They can be very soft and encouraging with others (unless under pressure, when they tend to use their verbal skills to attack). But because of their strong desire to be liked, they can often fail to be hard on problems and cause further problems as a result.

Scoring high on the G line are the *golden retrievers*. These people are just like their counterparts in nature. If you could pick one word to describe them, it would be *loyalty*. They're so loyal, in fact, that they can absorb *the* most emotional pain and punishment in relationships—and still stay committed. They're great listeners, empathizers and warm encouragers—all strong softside skills. But they tend to be such pleasers that they can have great difficulty in adding the hard side of love when it's needed.

With all these animals running around in families, churches and offices, life can be like a zoo! So how can we go about taming our own version of "The Wild Kingdom"? As you'll see beginning in the next chapter, the answer comes through learning how each of these personalities can give the two sides of love, as well as what can block them from doing so.

Let's look first at the two animals that display most naturally love's hard side, lions and beavers, and how they tend to respond in family and work relationships. After that, we'll turn our focus toward the two animals that tend to reflect love's soft side, otters and golden retrievers. Then we'll consider ten specific ways hardside people can learn to add softness to their lives, followed by ten specific ways softside people can add the loving hardness they need.

It all begins as we take a look at those people who often reflect a "king of the jungle" attitude in business and personal relationships—our lion friends.

4
Discovering the
Strengths of a Lion

LIONS POSSESS A number of admirable hardside strengths. They're decisive, purposeful and great at conquering nearly any challenge. As with the other personalities, however, if their strengths get pushed out of balance, those traits can become their greatest weaknesses.

We recently heard the life-changing story of an eight-year-old boy whose father had scored off the chart on the lion scale. This man was the service manager for his company, but he knew in his heart that one day he'd be the owner. His drive to accomplish things at work kept him away from the house most of every day, willing to hand out only emotional leftovers to his wife and children.

On a rare Saturday morning off, this man was seated in his favorite chair, reading his paper, when his son walked up.

For several moments, this young boy stood right next to his father without saying a word. His hardside dad tried his best to ignore him, putting on his sternest face. Finally, however, when he realized his son wasn't going to go away, he put down his paper and said roughly, "Now what do you want?"

His son smiled and held out a handful of crumpled dollar bills and assorted change. "Here, Daddy," he said, dropping them into his father's outstretched palm.

"What's this for?" the father asked.

"This is all I have in my piggy bank. It's eight dollars and fifty-four cents. Daddy, it's all yours if you'll just stay home and play with me today."

This lion father had spent all his days putting work ahead of his family. And when he wasn't working, he was resting to work. He didn't take time to play with his son because he didn't feel he was "accomplishing" anything by playing. But his son finally hit him right in his heart when he realized an eight-year-old was willing to give everything he had for some of Dad's time.

Traits of the Typical Lion

Not all lions are as hard as this man, of course. From a very early age, however, seven characteristics stand out in the typical lion's behavior. What's more, they tend to carry right into marriage and the workplace.

These strengths help lions to be naturally hard on problems. But the major challenge lions face is to add enough softness to their natural style to keep from being too hard on people in the process. What are these common characteristics of a lion?

1. Lions are born leaders.

Do you ever get the feeling that your son or daughter is letting you live at home? If so, you're probably the parent of a lion. From a young age, lions like to be in charge. As they grow up, they naturally gravitate to leadership positions in school, at work and at church. They definitely feel more comfortable if they're the ones calling the shots. As one lion friend told us, "Ever since grade school, I've never met a group I couldn't lead!"

Lions tend to be self-motivated and don't need a great deal to keep them going. In fact, like Peter and Paul in the Scriptures, they simply need to be pointed the right way! They're already headed in a specific direction, usually their own, and expecting others to follow.

Lions are so leadership oriented that they often resist being controlled by anyone else. As children, their parents often think about pasting their pictures on the cover of Dr. Dobson's book *The Strong-Willed Child*. And while this characteristic can help them be strong and independent in later life, it's crucial they learn that the best leaders know how to follow as well. If nothing else, they need to remind themselves that everyone has a boss, even if your only boss is God.

Over the years, we've met many Christian leaders. Can you guess whom you often find at the top of ministries and churches? Lions. They've taken their natural hardside strength of leadership and used it to charge ahead with a vision or to inspire leadership in others. But leadership isn't their only desire or strength.

> Lions feel very strongly that life
> is a series of problems they need to solve
> or challenges they need to meet.

2. Lions like to accomplish things with immediate results.

Some parents have told us that their lion children began issuing orders the moment they came out of the womb, and that may not be far off.[1] But lions like to take charge and be in control for a specific reason: *they feel very strongly that life is a series of problems they need to solve or challenges they need to meet.*

This powerful desire to accomplish something often means they can do the seemingly impossible. In fact, the easiest way to motivate lions is to tell them a job can't be done, then stand back and watch them accomplish it.

What does this strength mean when applied in a home setting? For one thing, most lions desperately need to learn that relaxation is not a crime. It's terribly hard for them to take it easy around the house. They usually have a demanding hobby or a challenging project they're working on. And if a project isn't at hand, they can choose their spouses or children as "projects" and begin trying to change or "motivate" them.

One young woman told her father, "Dad, every time you talk to me, I feel as if you're trying to change me or force me into becoming something I'm not. When are we ever going to talk without you giving me instructions the whole time?"

For most lions, even vacations can be something to attack! Take a vacation to the mountains, and instead of going to one or two of the sites, they want to hike every trail. Head for the beach, and they'll do anything except lie out in the sun. Why? Because lying in the sun doesn't *accomplish* anything.

This inner drive to accomplish tasks can help lions achieve great things. When pushed to an extreme, however, this strength can lead to elevating *projects* far ahead of *people* and laying the foundation for hardside workaholism.

3. A lion's time frame is *now!*

For the average lion, taking the lead in conquering projects or problems isn't enough. They have to be conquered *now.*

If you work for a boss who's a lion, she's capable of walking over to your desk, handing you a project, and saying, "I want you to do this now."

"But Boss," you might say, "you just gave me a project to work on."

"I know," would come the reply, "but that was twenty minutes ago. I want you to work on this *now!*"

Take this characteristic into a home setting, and dinner needs to be ready *now.* My diapers need to be changed *now.* Give me the remote control or change the channel *now. You* need to stop crying, take my advice, and grow up *now.*

What's communicated as people see lions' natural *now* orientation? Often it's hardside intensity. It's easy for lions to become so intense just working on a project (or simply thinking about the next important project) that they look mad to others, even if they aren't.

The average lion can radiate so much intensity that, as you'll see, golden retrievers and otters will learn to shy away from approaching or asking questions. They'll even avoid initiating important conversations because of the hardside nonverbal signals a lion can send out.

Sometimes lions will use this nonverbal intensity level as a shield from "stupid" questions or interruptions. However, if they're not careful, using their natural intensity to gain emotional "space" will quickly leave them isolated at best and resented at worst.

Speaking of resentment, we know of one lion on a church board who made a *now* decision that had major effects on a number of people far into the future. It all started with one of the most helpful times the church staff had ever experienced, but it wasn't to end that way. Even the word *disastrous* doesn't convey what happened.

For the first time ever, the senior pastor, all five of his associates and all their wives had gone to a neighboring city for a weekend together. With months to prepare for the trip, the pulpit and all the various class and counseling responsibilities had been farmed out to capable hands. At long last, an overdue opportunity to draw closer together as friends and ministry partners had taken shape—and they even had a weekend off!

Even the drive to the hotel helped bond these men and women whose ministries had become like six individual islands over the years. One car had a flat tire, requiring everyone to pitch in and get them back on the road. Another car (with the senior pastor's wife) set the record for most breaks in a fifty-mile trip by stopping at nine antique shops along the way.

When they all finally arrived, there was a scrumptious dinner awaiting them and a meaningful worship time that night in one of the rooms.

The time together went from being good to great the next morning. Following breakfast, they all gathered for an emotional meeting in which husbands and wives shared their pent-up feelings and frustrations. Apologies were offered and accepted, hugs asked for and given. The genuine spirit of love and restoration swept aside any cobwebs of misunderstanding, making everyone feel more like a team than ever before.

By the time each couple arrived home late Sunday evening, they were excited and enthusiastic about their various ministries. But that was soon to change.

Little did the pastors know that while they were gone, a purebred lion had been on the loose. In fact, the chairman of their elder board redefined the breed.

This man had been to a management effectiveness seminar for his business on the very Friday the pastors left for their retreat. Impressed with what he heard, in his mind's eye he saw what he thought were profound applications for both his business and the church. That's why, without hesitation or consultation, he had made up his mind what needed to be done.

While the pastors were out of town, he called in all the maintenance people, as well as several "starving student" movers. Then he set out to make the church more "effective" and "efficient," beginning with redesigning the church office.

What that meant in practical terms was that when the six pastors walked in on Monday morning, a surprise was waiting for them. When they put their keys in their doors and opened their offices, it was as if they had entered—The Twilight Zone.

The keys fit, and they were standing in front of the right doors, but they were no longer looking at their own offices. They shook their heads in disbelief as they stared at a different pastor's things all set up in what used to be their offices! Not only had every office been changed, but several secretarial relationships were also switched, splitting up some pastors and their secretaries who had worked together for five and six years.

The chairman of their elder board never thought of asking for a meeting to discuss the changes he wanted to make. It wasn't that he wasn't a good man. It was just that he saw what he thought was a problem, discovered a solution at his morning seminar, and the movers were at work that afternoon!

Lions will do well to make a consistent priority check on how much involvement they give their loved ones in decisions that affect them; it's an important part of softside love. They'll also do well to make sure their natural *now* tendency doesn't sacrifice a healthy future in their relationships.

4. Lions are decisive.

Tied in with their need to lead, control, accomplish and do things now, lions generally make decisions quickly—with or without the facts, and often without asking anyone for advice.

In the home, it's often great to have someone around who isn't afraid to make decisions, even difficult ones. But in some cases, that natural tendency toward being decisive can be pushed far out of balance.

We know of one wife who experienced something even worse than what happened to that church staff. Carol and her husband, Mark, had finally saved up enough money to make a down payment on their first house. They had picked out a small starter home they both liked, and the day came when they were to meet at the title company office to put down their deposit and sign the papers.

Carol was beside herself with excitement as she waited for the morning to drag by until their afternoon appointment. She was just starting to gather her things to meet Mark at the title company when she heard a horn beeping outside. Looking out the window, she didn't recognize the shiny, new truck that sat in the driveway. But as she stepped outside, she saw Mark behind the wheel.

"Where did you get that?" Carol asked in shock as she walked up to her grinning husband.

"Carol," he said almost flippantly, "I know we were going to use all that money for that house, but you'll never guess what kind of deal I got on this truck!"

That morning, Carol's lion husband had gone to the bank to withdraw their money and take it to the title company. But he had stopped at the local car dealership "just to look" on the way home. In a few minutes' time (and with a little pressure from a hungry salesman), he had made a decision to buy the truck instead of the house. And, it goes without saying, he made the decision without bothering to consult his wife.

When she pleaded with him to take the truck back, he told her, "Listen, I made my decision. It's not up for a vote, and that's final.

Besides, I wasn't all that hot on that house anyway, and you know I really needed a new truck for work."

Mark had his new truck that didn't bear a scratch or dent on it. But little did he know that as he drove off to work, he had just smashed his wife's heart and nearly totaled out his marriage by not involving her in a major decision.

When the pressure is on, one of the great hardside strengths of lions is that they can act quickly and decisively. We need such leaders; we have far too few of them in our churches and homes today. We sometimes even need people who can step out in faith without first gathering every possible fact. But leadership is more than being strong and forceful. It doesn't take an advanced degree in insensitivity to be considered a strong leader.

We encourage lions to read the final chapter in this book to see how the Lion of Judah balanced His purposeful decisiveness with compassionate, softside understanding.

5. Lions want *Reader's Digest*-length communication.

Perhaps it's their decisive attitude that makes most lions gag at small talk. One woman with a great deal of lion in her told us how frustrated she was with her golden retriever husband.

"When I ask him, 'How's your day been?' all I want is a one-page version of what happened. But every time I ask, I get the whole book of *War and Peace!*"

That same frustration is felt by many lion men. Often a wife will try to talk with her lion husband about something less "important" than nuclear disarmament or solving the federal budget deficit and be cut off in midsentence.

She may try saying something about one of the kid's days or her own and hear something like, "Honey, what are we trying to *solve* here?" Or if her spouse is really insensitive to the impact of his words, she may even hear something like, "Dear, I don't mind talking with you, but next time, let's talk about something important!"

For lions, meaningful communication usually equals short sentences, sticking to the point, and getting on to something more important than talking—namely, charging ahead and "doing" something rather than discussing it. Their natural desire for efficient conversation must be balanced with the time needed to generate softsided, relational communication. That means listening closely and with acceptance, not jumping in with a hardside lecture or solution.

6. Lions often feel challenged by questions.

Several years ago, a man and his wife went to an auction with some friends. Several hundred people were standing outside, ready to jam into the building holding the auction. The woman had a special need for a kitchen table and chairs, and she was looking forward to getting a great deal on an oak or maple set.

The doors finally opened, and in the rush of people going into the pavilion, the woman and their friends got separated from her husband. After trying hard to find him, at last they decided to sit down and watch some of the bidding.

Within a short time, the crowd began bidding on furniture, and one of the first items to come up was a dilapidated, green kitchen table and chair set. With its pea-green vinyl and rust-pitted legs, it had obviously seen its best days years ago. But strangely, the price kept going up and up as two men the woman couldn't see got into a bidding war over this nearly worthless dinette set.

When the final bid was made and the gavel slammed down, the woman leaned over and said to her friends, "I can't believe anybody would pay that much for that piece of junk!"

That's when the man who had just bought the green monstrosity stood up, and—you guessed it—it was the woman's husband!

"Henry," she said when they finally caught up with him, "that's the ugliest table and chairs I've ever seen! Why in the world did you buy that without talking to me? I wanted a *wooden* table, not a vinyl one. What were you thinking?"

The man instantly grew defensive. The only answer he gave her was, "You needed a table and chairs, I bought them, and that settles it!"

Asking a question of an out-of-balance lion is often interpreted as a personal challenge, not a reasonable request for information. Unfortunately, many lions marry people whom God has given a natural bent toward question asking—our golden retriever and beaver friends.

Denying those folks the right to ask questions is a great way to hardside them—to close their spirits and slam the door on meaningful relationship.[2] Lions need to slow down long enough to look at all sides of an issue. They also need to realize that developing a loving home is more important than simply demanding everyone's loyalty. Finally, they should make sure they don't interpret the deep need of a beaver or golden retriever for clarification as a challenge to their authority.

7. Lions are not afraid of pressure or confrontation.

As you may have sensed by now, in their quest for challenge and accomplishments, quick decisions and instant communication, lions can put a great deal of pressure on themselves and others. And while some people (like beavers and golden retrievers) are very uncomfortable with feeling pressured, lions thrive on tension.

A lion friend who owns a fairly large company confessed to us, "I get bored when things are going too smoothly around the office. In fact, my staff has often accused me of breaking things just so I can fix them!"

Put this tendency to pressure people alongside their natural lack of fear of confrontation, and *unless they're careful, lions can hardside and hurt other people's feelings without even realizing it.*

We once counseled a couple in which the man, a strong lion, was used to roaring at those at work and at home and always getting his way. He was extremely wealthy and owned his own company, so no one he employed was willing to question his pressure tactics. With three golden retrievers at home (his wife and two young children), no one there was willing to stand up to him, either.

In out first session together, we quickly saw by the way he treated his wife that he was an out-of-balance lion. He made a tremendous amount of money, but he kept her on a budget that wouldn't even get her through the grocery store checkout. And instead of being an encouragement to her or the kids, he came close to terrorizing them with his harsh language and attitudes.

Deep down, this man did love his family, but he didn't know how to show it. And it's no wonder. He came from a home where his own father used fear and intimidation every day, and he was simply passing down to his family the hurt he had felt as a child.

After listening for almost an hour to the story of his background and to his wife's concerns, I (John) made the comment that the primary way he communicated was by intimidating people.

Instantly he stood up, grabbed the edge of the table, and leaned over toward me. "My goal isn't to intimidate anybody!" he shouted, staring at me with venom in his eyes. "What do you know, anyway? You're just a *kid*."

I do have a youthful appearance, and that wasn't the first time I'd heard that comment. As a trained counselor, I knew how important it was to remain calm and understanding over such remarks. But something happened in that counseling office that has never happened before or since.

In the months that have passed, I've searched my heart to see if what I did was wrong. But in this case, I still feel the Lord was giving me the strength of a lion to deal with what was happening before me.

Without thinking, I stood up, grabbed the edge of the table in front of me, and leaned over toward *him*. "Your goal *is* to intimidate people," I said firmly. "And the problem is that it's worked for you. You've got everyone so afraid of you that they won't call you out or tell you you're wrong."

"Is that right?" he said, his voice dripping with sarcasm.

"That's right," I said even more firmly, looking at him eye to eye. "Now get this straight. You're killing your family with your words and your anger. Intimidation may have worked for you for a long time and kept you from being confronted, but it's not going to work in here."

"You think you can talk to me like that!" he roared, clenching his fists, standing up, and shifting his weight as if to draw back and take a swing.

I had fought a good deal in my non-Christian background, and I could tell that push had come to shove. He wasn't just mad; he was livid. I dropped my hands from the table, getting ready for the fight I knew was coming. At that moment, I fully believed we were going to get into a free-for-all right there in the counseling room, and I was ready. Gary's eyes widened and his jaw dropped as he watched us.

For what seemed like hours (but was actually only a few seconds), there was absolute silence in the room. We held each other's stare, refusing to look away and knowing what one move toward the other would mean. You could have cut the tension with a chain saw, as this man's wife and Gary sat transfixed at the table, not knowing if we were going to start throwing punches.

Finally, the man chuckled out loud, unclenched his fists, and sat down. "John," he said with a smile and a calm voice, "nobody has talked to me like that in years!

"You're right, you know," he continued, his voice softer than it had been all morning. "I've always been a bully. I probably don't know how to relate to someone other than by getting angry."

The tension had begun to ease in the room, and Gary and the man's wife were starting to breathe again, when suddenly the man sat forward, pointed his finger at her, and with his most-threatening voice said, "Why can't you learn to stand up to me like he does? Then we wouldn't be in this mess!"

All was not lost, however. That morning, they made a major break-through in their relationship. This man was very comfortable with pressure, and even with major confrontation. But he had finally learned that his natural hardside power could easily cross the line into intimidation, even when that wasn't his intent.

In cases like this, lions can be so strong that they win every verbal battle but end up losing the war and the prize of their family's hearts.

To review, we've seen that seven characteristics commonly surface in lions' lives. Namely:

1. Lions are born leaders.
2. Lions like to accomplish things with immediate results.
3. Lions' time frame is now!
4. Lions are decisive.
5. Lions want *Reader's Digest*-length communication.
6. Lions often feel threatened by questions.
7. Lions are not afraid of pressure or confrontation.

Lions can be so strong that they win every verbal battle but end up losing the war for their family's hearts

---

Lions' #1 Relational Challenge

One time we (John and Cindy) took our daughter Kari to the local zoo. To get an overview of what animals they had, we rode a tram that goes past all the exhibits. Not surprisingly, the largest crowd was assembled at the lion compound.

People are fascinated with lions of both the animal and human kind. The problem is that once lions roar, others can easily become afraid of them as well. Many lions are kept at an emotional arm's length because they seem distant, angry, unapproachable or all three.

In the midst of a war, we need field generals who can inspire and lead. With life and death in the balance, results and decisive action—even strutting and shouting at times—can become more important than sensitive relationships.

Unfortunately, some out-of-balance lions forget that their homes should normally be places of peace, and a few actually seem to declare war on their families. They demand unquestioned allegiance and expect others to follow their orders immediately. What's more, they view questions as a sign of disloyalty and, in some cases, as grounds for desertion. They desire "bottom line" communication without realizing that the real bottom line in a home is whether the other person goes away feeling loved and understood.

We're here to say that it's possible to become a sensitive lion without sacrificing the natural strengths God has built into a person. In fact, we've seen firsthand examples of it over and over. And we've seen that while people will follow any effective leader to a point, they'll go to the wall for a strong leader who loves them.

Every home, office and church needs the hardside strengths of a lion. But the Lion of Judah led in such a way that His hardside strengths didn't sacrifice His softside skill of giving unconditional love and acceptance to others (more about that later).

The challenge for lions is not to pull out all their claws. Instead, it's to balance their lion strengths with the love of the Lamb of God. Then they can see great things happen in their relationships.

We've looked at the first personality bent that leans toward being hardside. The second is that of our beaver friends, who like to "live by the book." Their strengths are many, but they, too, need to learn how they can give and receive the two sides of love.

5
Discovering the
Strengths of a Beaver

A S WE SKIDDED our bicycles to a stop in front of our house, my twin brother and I (John) looked up and saw the same thing. There it was—one pitiless eye staring right at us. Without a word being spoken, we both knew we were in major trouble—again.

As a child, I hated living on the street corner. It wasn't that our home wasn't nice. But owning the corner house meant the street light was planted right in our yard.

"Be home before the street light comes on!" was the ironclad law. No "fudge factor" was allowed. My grandfather would have scored at the top of the charts in the hardsided beaver category, and he lived life by the rules. All he had to do was look out the window and see if we'd made it home in time. And once again, we hadn't.

I know that for today's parents, the topic of spanking is often controversial. But when I grew up, there wasn't even a mild discussion. My grandfather had come to help my mother raise three rambunctious boys in a single-parent home, and he believed firmly in spanking. And in his rule book, being late for dinner was a two-swat offense.

My grandfather shared a number of characteristics with other beavers. They tend to be reserved in their relationships, playing their emotional cards close to the vest. They're detailed, cautious, and like to look at all sides of an issue.

As I grew up, I saw his attention to rules and emotional reserve as hardside weaknesses, not personal strengths. I often interpreted his tendency to be quiet and thoughtful as being cold and distant. But at least you were always sure of where you stood with him. You could depend on him to be predictable in his actions, emotions and attitude.

That's why, as I shuffled down the hallway to Grandfather's room, I knew exactly what was going to happen: two swats on the bottom with his old-style razor strap. Little did I know that one of the greatest times of blessing in my life lay ahead as well.

1. Beavers keep a close watch on their emotions.

After my spanking, my mother told me to go back down the hall and call my grandfather for dinner. While I didn't feel much like talking to him at the time, I didn't want to risk another spanking, either. So off I went to his room.

Many children grow up calling their grandfather "Gramps," "Grandpa," "Papa" or some other affectionate nickname. Not us. There were rules of respect to be observed in our home, and any time we addressed him, we were to call him "Grandfather" or "Sir."

What's more, it was a two-swat offense to enter his room without first knocking politely at the door and waiting outside until he gave us permission to enter.

I was about to knock when I noticed his door was already slightly ajar. That's why I broke the cardinal rule and gently pushed it open to look inside.

What I saw shocked me. My grandfather, a man who rarely showed any emotion, was sitting on the end of his bed, crying. I stood at the door in confusion, not knowing what to say. Suddenly, he looked up and saw me, and I froze where I was. I had no idea what was coming when he spoke to me.

"Come here, John," he said, his voice full of emotion. I walked over, fully expecting to be disciplined for not knocking. But instead of swatting me, he reached out and took me in his arms.

Grandfather hugged me closely, and in tears he told me how much he loved each of us boys and how deeply it hurt him to have to spank us. I had no idea why he always stayed in his room for a few minutes after disciplining us. Now I knew. He spent the time alone; sometimes crying, always praying that we would grow up to be the men God wanted us to be.

"John," he told me, seating me on the bed next to him and putting his big arms around me, "I want more than anything in life for each of you to become godly young men. I've done all I could to help you know what's right, and to encourage you to live your life by God's rules.

"I won't always be here to remind you. Besides, you're a young man now. I hope you know how much I love you, how proud I am of you, and how much I pray for each of you boys. I know you'll always be the man God wants you to be throughout your life."

I can't explain it, but when I left his room that night, I was a different person. As I look back today, that evening provided me with a meaningful rite of passage from childhood to young adulthood. For years afterward, recalling that clear picture of my grandfather's love helped to shape my attitudes and actions.

A few months later, in that same room, Grandfather died instantly and unexpectedly. I thank God that I didn't make it home that night before the street light turned on. I know now that the Lord allowed me to experience a time of blessing with the most important man in my early life.

Like others high on the beaver scale, my grandfather was reserved, cautious and controlled when it came to displaying emotions and affection. He was also sparing with his praise. But that night, I felt as if the veil had lifted. I got to see the soft side of his heart in a way I never had before. He let down his structured responses and tightly held feelings in a spontaneous act of emotion, and it made a major impact on my life.

It's not that beavers have a difficult time loving others. Their commitment to those they love can be just as strong as that of our loyal golden retriever friends. However, beavers often have difficulty communicating that softside warmth to others.

If you're a beaver and you find yourself standing back in relationships, you'll want to read Chapters 10 and 11 on developing a healthy softness. But for now, let's look at several other characteristics that describe this important member of the family zoo.

2. Beavers actually read instruction books.

Besides keeping a close watch on their emotions, people who score high on the beaver scale tend to have something else in common. They're the ones who carefully read instruction manuals instead of throwing them away. Not all animals in the family zoo have this same strong desire to do things "by the book," however—especially otters.

Cindy and I (John) had been talking about putting up a swing set in the backyard for our daughter. It was early on a Saturday morning, and as Kari stumbled into the kitchen for her pancakes, I made a typical, overly optimistic otter announcement.

Beavers are the ones who carefully read
instruction manuals instead
of throwing them away.

"Honey, Mom and I are going to get you a swing set this morning when the store opens, and you'll be swinging by lunchtime!"

It was in fact lunchtime when I finally finished putting together the three million bolts, screws, hex nuts, flying ring washers and horizontal stabilizers that came in the carton. Unfortunately, it was lunchtime three weekends later! And while the swing set was finally standing, it looked as if it had just withstood a major earthquake and could fall apart at any moment.

In classic otter fashion, the first thing I had done after opening the box was to toss aside the instructions. After all, I reasoned, reading instructions isn't fun. I knew it would be a snap putting the set together. What almost snapped, however, was my sanity as I "creatively" pounded and drilled new holes to fit the parts that had obviously been incorrectly shaped and drilled at the factory.

One last thing remained for me to do before Cindy would trust our daughter's life to the unusual-looking swing set I had created. I needed to anchor it into the ground so that when several children really got swinging, it wouldn't be pulled over.

Once again, however, instead of doing things by the instructions and anchoring it in concrete (as a good beaver would have done), I opted for a quicker and easier way. Namely, I bought four auger stakes to attach to each leg of the swing set. (Auger stakes are long, metal stakes that have a giant screw bit at one end.)

With a Herculean effort, I twisted each of the four stakes into the ground and then attached them to the swing set. At last it was finished, and Cindy gave Kari the green light to swing. She was swinging happily, and my creation actually looked as though it might work! But that's when I decided to do something funny while she was swinging through the air.

In Arizona, if you don't have some type of sprinkler system, you don't have grass. Thinking it would be entertaining, I walked over to the sprinkler box that was nearby to turn on the water for a moment.

I flipped the switch and—whoosh! Water began to spray all right, but not from the sprinkler heads. Instead, it was gushing out of the ground right where I had screwed in the auger stakes!

Had I stopped to check where the sprinkler lines were buried before anchoring the swing set? No! Would a *beaver* have checked to see where the plastic pipes were buried before driving four long, metal spikes deep into the ground? Yes!

Kari escaped with her life from the geysers I had created, but the swing set didn't. It was in such bad shape, I finally had to break down and call—a beaver. My good friend Jim McGuire came over the next day and helped me reassemble the set and patch the sprinkler system—correctly.

What's the first thing he asked for? You guessed it! The directions! And this time, as if by magic, we actually did have Kari swinging by lunchtime, safe and dry.

For beavers, stress is reduced in the home or on the job by having a manual to follow. Unfortunately, life is often unpredictable, especially in marriage and parenting. Much of what happens in relationships falls outside the pages beavers have memorized. For example, a beaver mother may plan her family's weekend to the half hour. But if she lives with lions and otters, things can change by the *minute*, causing her no end of frustration.

We've seen beavers in counseling sessions be as firm as any lion, but for a different reason. They're not trying to win for the thrill of victory. Instead, they become hard on issues, and often on people, because they're so committed to doing what they think is right.

Beavers' natural strength of doing things right can make them God's quality control experts in a home. Held in balance, that can make them a very valuable addition to a family.

3. Beavers like to make careful decisions.

It was Christmas Eve, and I (Gary) was driving home when I saw the flags waving and the freshly painted sign that announced a new patio home complex had opened. The words "Immediate sale" and "Price reductions" caught my otter eyes and pulled me off the main road and up to the sales office.

After all, I thought, we had been in the same house for nine years. I had moved every year of my life growing up. With the kids getting older, we certainly didn't need all the room we had now. We were overdue for a change of address, and perhaps a patio home was just what we needed.

It was certainly just what the saleswoman thought I needed. She proceeded to make me an offer I was sure Norma couldn't refuse—until I talked to her about it.

"Gary," she said in her patient, softside voice, "we've talked about moving, but not into a patio home. What if something happens and Kari decides to move home instead of living in the dorm at school? What if Greg decides to come back home to finish school instead of staying at Oklahoma?"

"Ha!" I said. "Fat chance. The kids are perfectly happy where they are, and I would be if we could just get this patio home."

Norma is a real blend of personalities. She has a great deal of a characteristic we'll talk about later, golden retriever. But she also has many beaver traits. I guess that makes her a beaver-retriever.

In her systematic way, Norma's natural beaver instincts told her that this wasn't the place or time to move. There was too much uncertainty about where the kids would be living to change from a medium-sized, four-bedroom home to a small, three-bedroom patio home.

Beavers are good at thinking through all sides of an issue. They normally have excellent instincts when it comes to decision making, and they aren't afraid to say no. But they do have a weakness in that they can let the enthusiasm of others talk them out of their well-thought-out plans.

Over the course of the next few weeks, I took the kids to see the new condo we "needed" so much. It was bright and freshly painted, and soon their enthusiasm and mine were beginning to wear Norma down.

Finally, in her desire to please everyone, she dropped her arguments, and we all agreed to move into the new home. But still she said, "Gary, I think we're going to be sorry. This patio home is too small, and we're going to regret it!"

Sure enough, everything worked out just as Norma said it would. For the first few weeks, our new home fit Norma, Michael and me like a glove. But within three months, we needed two more fingers in the glove. Unexpectedly, we added two kids and had half as much space to put them in as in our former home.

Who would have known that just before Kari graduated, she would want to move back home with us? And who could have foreseen that Greg would decide to leave the University of Oklahoma and move back home to finish his college? My wife, the beaver, could and did.

I had used all my typical otter persuasion skills (more about that in Chapter 6) to talk her into a decision that went against her natural grain. And once again, I learned I was wrong.

To take-charge lions and fast-paced otters, beavers can appear slow and overly cautious. Yet one of the great strengths they bring to a home is their ability to head off problems by saying no to bad decisions like the one I had made.

I finally listened to Norma's words of caution. Unfortunately, it was after we'd already bought the home. And after two years of putting up with cramped quarters, we finally moved back into a larger home just like our old one, except we had to pay more for it.

There are times when beavers can be so cautious that they fail to grasp an instant opportunity. One beaver husband we know could have bought a 1940 Cadillac convertible in mint condition for $2,000 from a business partner; the car eventually sold for more than ten times that amount at auction. But ninety-nine times out of a hundred, the beaver ability to make careful, thoughtful and correct decisions is a major strength.

4. Beavers like using their critical skills to solve problems.

The hardside ability to look at issues critically can be enormously valuable in problem solving. My (John's) "Aunt Dovie" demonstrated that truth vividly during World War II.

As the war raged in Europe and the Pacific, we had many heroes on the front lines. But there were also many hometown heroes who never got a medal and never went overseas. These were the men and women who rolled up their sleeves and went to work in defense plants that sprang up all over the country to support the war effort.

Aunt Dovie was one such woman. She stands all of five feet tall on a good day and probably weighs in at a little over ninety pounds. However, it was her beaver ability to take things apart that helped her track down a "Nazi saboteur" in the defense plant where she worked.

At Allison Division, General Motors, Indianapolis, they manufactured engines for the P-51 fighter plane—one of the most powerful fighters America provided her wartime pilots. The pistons of these engines were coated with silver, which was rationed and precious in 1944. My aunt was a section supervisor in the packing department.

As the pistons came off the production line, they went to packing, where they were immersed in oil, then heat-sealed in heavy-duty plastic wrap. Finally they were packed six to a prenumbered carton and shipped overseas to combat zones. As the supervisor in this area, Aunt Dovie was the last one to handle the pistons before they left for shipping. That's why she was one of the first people informed of a serious problem.

By the time the boxes of pistons arrived overseas and were opened, the silver plating was riddled with pinpoint holes!

The War Department wasted little time advising Allison, and the grapevine quickly began to buzz across the entire plant. The rumors raced from machine operator to machine operator. Foremen and supervisors began to cluster, holding somber discussions. "Pinpoint holes are showing up on the silver plate of our pistons. Engineering has called in the brass from Detroit. Quality control has tightened supervision of the plating department, but still the holes are showing up! There has to be someone—a saboteur—getting to the pistons at some point in the process."

Could someone be splashing acid on them somewhere on the production line? Or worse, in the final packing area? Would leaking the news at the plant be enough to flush out the culprit, or at least to make the saboteur fearful of further tampering?

That's when Aunt Dovie's beaver mind went to work. "G-men" trained to track down criminals were stationed in the plant. But never underestimate the power of a beaver when she starts taking problems apart!

Since my aunt was a supervisor as well as a beaver, she already knew every step of every job involved in inspecting and loading the pistons into packing cases. And in her determination to find the spy, she spent hours going through every possible place on the assembly line where acid could be applied. With her painstaking methods, she finally caught the perpetrator—or at least uncovered him.

It was lunchtime one day, and the break room at the factory was filled with people. Aunt Dovie was standing in line at the one snack machine they had. Suddenly, all her careful observations of every person in her department paid off. She saw the saboteur. Right before her was a culprit she never would have suspected. *It has to be!* she thought. *How obvious!* She marveled at why she hadn't seen it sooner.

After the break, she watched closely as everyone who had been in line with her went right back to work. That's when her suspicions were confirmed. Without a doubt, she had found the traitor.

You see, the "Nazi spy" who had been pitting the silver plating wasn't using acid at all . . . but salt! The culprit was none other than—the peanut machine!

The workers would eat a handful of peanuts, then go right back to work without washing their hands. The salt left on their hands was eating through the soft silver plating as the pistons traveled overseas. Leave it to a beaver to see that something as small and seemingly insignificant as salted peanuts was actually *the* thing causing major problems.

Beavers love to go into detail. They enjoy reading maps and drawing up diagrams. The only problem is that besides being so good at taking things apart, they're also very good at taking apart *people* with whom they're upset.

If beavers respect and appreciate you, they can be as loyal as a golden retriever. However, if they're unhappy with you, they can use their perfectionistic bent to become piercing, hardside critics.

Like lions, beavers can communicate an inner intensity level. What's more, they, too, tend to keep others at a safe emotional distance, erecting an invisible barrier that people can sense nonetheless. And while they may not be as verbal as a lion, they can become just as hardside in their positions and hold just as firmly to what they think is right in a given situation.

Where do they get the motivation to do things in such an orderly, by-the-book manner? From their deep dislike of being wrong and their strong desire to do things right.

5. Beavers live by the motto "Let's do this right."

"If it's worth doing, it's worth doing right." Do you live by that country proverb? Are your socks all rolled up and color-coordinated instead of just being thrown in a drawer? Is your side of the closet so well organized that you can find everything you need to get dressed in the dark?

If so, you probably scored fairly high on the beaver scale. Doing things right, with precision and accuracy, is very important to a beaver.

We've given our personality test to several thousand people all across the country. And in each group we give the test to, the members of one profession consistently score at the top of the beaver scale. Who are they? Surgeons. Of course this makes sense. We would much rather have a beaver surgeon operating on us, making sure everything was done just right, than a fun-loving otter surgeon who was more concerned about having a great time in the operating room!

This natural strength of spotting things that are wrong and wanting to make them right heads off many mistakes. We know of one mother who pushed this natural strength to an extreme, however, and made a major mistake with her son.

"We miss you, Son, and we love you," the voice on the phone said.

"Thanks, Dad. I miss you too," Roger said.

"And Son, one more thing. Could you spare the time to write your mother? I know it would encourage her."

Roger's father wasn't trying to be pushy. He knew that his wife and son had corresponded regularly when their boy first went away to an out-of-state college. She was genuinely interested in hearing about his life at school, and he could see that she loved getting his letters. But her son's letters had gradually come less and less frequently, and finally not at all.

Little did Roger's mother know that she was doing something to close his spirit and block his desire to write to her. She never would have dreamed that a common beaver characteristic was affecting her son the way it was.

There was a long pause on the other end of the phone before Roger spoke again. With emotion in his voice, he told his father, "Dad, I'm not writing Mom anymore. If she wants to talk to me, I'll talk to her over the phone."

"But why?" his father asked, obviously confused.

With a deep sigh, Roger said, "Because I'm sick of sending her letters and then getting them back with the spelling corrected. I've got enough people grading my papers here at school and giving me a hard time. I don't need to feel like a failure every time I write her a letter."

Roger's mother deeply loved her son. But her beaver tendency to do things right and be hard on even minor mistakes meant that if there was any kind of error in a letter, she just *had* to mention it. For her, it was only making wrong things right. But for her sensitive, golden retriever son, every red mark crossed out his feelings of being loved and accepted, not just the spelling mistakes on the page.

Every company and family needs a beaver. But like lions, beavers can get so wrapped up in the results of a project that they fail to see how dramatically they affect those working or living with them. Beavers need to make sure the details of a project or a letter don't become so important that they miss the message and people behind it. Without realizing it, they can come across extremely hard. The worst damage beavers do, however, is often to themselves.

6. Beavers tend to turn anger inward.

Out of all the animals in the family zoo, beavers are the most prone to times of depression and associated physical problems. Why? The reason can be found in the meaning of depression itself: anger turned inward.

While lions roar when they're angry and otters verbally attack, beavers tend to turn their anger on themselves. What usually fans the flames of their anger? Making mistakes.

Danny was only nine when his parents noticed a serious problem that was surprising in light of the strong beaver instincts he had exhibited since toddlerhood. While the other children in the family would throw their clothes and shoes in the closet, his shoes were always lined up and his little hangers hung in neat rows. He brushed his teeth carefully each night, while his otter brother usually just ran his toothbrush under the faucet so their mother would think he had brushed.

When school started, Danny always got high marks on his homework, and especially on citizenship—that is, until he reached the fourth grade.

A few months into the new academic year, Danny was struggling with school. He was withdrawing from friends and even beginning to shut out family members. He would sit for hours in his room with the door closed, ostensibly studying. But still his grades were suffering, and his attitude toward school was getting worse. He even began to fake illness to avoid having to go to class. And this from a boy who had nearly perfect attendance in the past.

What could bring such dramatic changes in only a few months? Danny had run into something no beaver can live with consistently without showing negative effects.

Mr. Ryan, Danny's teacher, was well liked by most of the parents and children. He had played pro football for one year and was a strong believer in challenging his students to do their best in sports and in the classroom. But there was one problem. What proved motivating to many students was emotionally killing Danny.

As we've mentioned, beavers like to have clear directions and to be able to ask informational questions. But there's something else they need as well: they need to feel a strong sense of support and be in a *noncritical atmosphere* to do their best work.

Mr. Ryan's way of challenging his students was to confront them. He knew Danny was a top student. So to motivate him, he would stand over him in the classroom and push him to do his best work. He would take mistakes Danny and others made and parade them in front of everyone.

While the teacher always smiled when he challenged Danny, this shy beaver youngster never saw any humor in his teacher's methods. All he felt was incredible pressure to be perfect so he could avoid being humiliated in front of his classmates.

It's important to understand that both golden retrievers and beavers tend to slow down under pressure. In fact, increasing the pressure on most beavers is like turning down the gas on the water heater when you want hot water.

As Danny became more afraid of failing, he started going slower to make sure he wouldn't make a mistake. As a result, the coach was constantly pushing him to go faster. "Come on, Danny," he'd say as he handed out an in-class assignment. "You're smart. You can finish this in twenty minutes."

Left on his own—or even better, with gentle encouragement and the freedom to ask questions—Danny *could* have finished in ten minutes. But faced with the pressure of loud challenges and the constant fear of having his mistakes pointed out in front of the class, he was taking twenty minutes just to read the instructions!

"I don't understand what it takes to motivate your son," Mr. Ryan told Danny's parents at the first parent-teacher conference. That was an understatement. While he saw the problem lying with their "unmotivated son," it was actually a reflection of his lack of understanding of the best way to motivate a beaver child.

> Beavers need to learn that it's all right
> to fail and that it's healthy to call
> for help when they're struggling.

Danny needed the calm reassurance and open-door policy that had always been there with his previous teachers. When he didn't get them, he didn't call out to Mom and Dad for help the way an otter child would. He didn't turn around and fight back like a lion. He was too intimidated to express his hurt and frustration toward the coach. What did that leave?

The only safe person to attack was himself. And in the short space of a semester, he had taken himself apart so many times that his self-confidence was in shambles. A former A student, he was now fully convinced that he was stupid and a failure, and he was heading right into a deep juvenile depression.

Parents of beaver children need to make sure they praise and encourage their children's character as well as their accomplishments. They also need to protect their children's character. And they can do that by taking the pressure off their kids to feel that life is only worth living if they get 100 percent right on every test.

Beavers need to learn that it's all right to fail and that it's healthy to call for help when they're struggling. Also, if there are other people in the home (particularly otters or lions), beavers need to guard against assuming that everyone will see the same problems or in the same way as they do.

For example, a broken slat on a wooden fence in the backyard might really bother a beaver. After all, someone might look in or, even worse, break in. But most otters, not being as detail-oriented, would probably have to see an entire section of the fence fall down before it caught their attention!

Finally, parents who are beavers need to value those children whose natural temperaments tend toward having a sock *room* instead of a sock drawer. That's not to say that parents shouldn't hand out chores, give room inspections, and expect their children to learn responsibility.[1] But with the average child requiring two to three hundred reminders before finally building a task into a habit, it's important that beaver parents allow their children to fail at something without considering themselves failures as parents.

Fortunately, Danny's story had a happy ending. Mr. Ryan was always teachable as a player, and he also had the wisdom to be teachable as a teacher. After his talk with Danny's parents, he learned what Danny needed to excel. Mr. Ryan decreased the hardside motivation and increased his softside support—more encouragement, more details on the homework or in-class assignments, more spontaneous hugs, and no more public displays of criticism.

We can help the beavers in our homes, offices and classrooms to feel more successful if we'll keep in mind their inner sensitivity to criticism. Being soft with them while hard on their problems is a must.

7. Beavers tend to focus on the past.

As a well-organized beaver, young Diane spent a great deal of time planning her future life. And for nearly thirty years, things went pretty much according to script.

She attended the college she had chosen years in advance and married a wonderful young man after graduation, just as she'd always planned. They saved enough money to put a down payment on a house, and then, after four years of "just we two," along came her first child—born only one day from the due date.

Like her mother, Diane got pregnant easily and had no problems carrying the baby—just as she'd expected. But then something hit her that greatly troubles many beavers: the *unexpected.*

Two years had passed since the birth of her son, and in Diane's mind, it was time for her little boy to have a little sister. But as weeks turned into months and then a year of trying and waiting, she finally had to face the possibility of infertility, and it knocked her well-ordered world out of its carefully planned path.

Diane would have scored near the top on the beaver scale. She took great comfort in following the same path her parents had. But now, for the first time, it was as if she had lost her map. Month after month she tried to get pregnant, and finally she broke down and went to a medical specialist. After that, there were the tests, the shots, the medications, the waiting and always the tears.

A beaver's primary time frame is the past. Beavers want a track record. They like knowing how something has been done before. And if it works, they'll stay with it. Beavers also tend to look to the past as a way of explaining present situations or problems.

Diane lay in bed for hours at a time, searching the past for some secret sin that could have brought on such a personal calamity. A hundred times a day, she would slam herself emotionally for not "starting my family earlier" or "not knowing" what she couldn't possibly have known.

Caught in the grasp of "What if. . . ," she was no longer free to enjoy her son or her husband, David, who deeply loved her. What's more, she couldn't enjoy her relationship with God anymore.

Her husband tried to encourage her by reading Bible verses on faith like this one in the book of Hebrews: "Faith is being sure of what we hope for and certain of what we do not see."[2]

"Honey, just have faith," he'd say, "We'll get pregnant."

For her otter husband, picturing a positive future was second nature. (More about that in Chapter 6.) The future was where he spent most of his time anyway. But almost by biblical definition, faith is more of a challenge for a beaver.

Faith focuses on the future. As the book of Hebrews puts it, faith is the assurance of things hoped for. It involves giving over all control of something important to someone else and still feeling positive about it. What pulled Diane through the three and a half years when she struggled with life's being "out of control" until God brought her another child by adoption?

"To be honest," she said, "I couldn't look into the future and feel as positive about things as David did. But I could look *back* at all the times God has been faithful to me in the past and draw strength from them."

Diane turned the corner in this faith-stretching time when she was finally able to use her beaver bent toward focusing on the past as an ally, not as an enemy to blast herself. Her faith in the present wasn't made stronger by trying to become a visionary like her husband. Rather, faith came by using her natural strength as a historian to bring reassurance that God indeed knew the best direction for her life.

We've now seen seven character traits that consistently show up in the lives of our beaver friends.

1. Beavers keep a close watch on their emotions.
2. Beavers actually read instruction books.
3. Beavers like to make careful decisions.
4. Beavers like using their critical skills to solve problems.
5. Beavers live by the motto "Let's do it right!"
6. Beavers often turn anger inward.
7. Beavers tend to focus on the past.

All seven of these characteristics help make these people exceptional employees, friends and family members. What's more, our Lord Himself had beaver traits. For example, did Christ like to do things "by the book"? Absolutely. In fact, He only did what was right and in His Father's will. Not one jot or tittle of God's law did He ignore.

Beavers have many great strengths, but like our lion friends, they can drift away from a healthy balance point. Without realizing it, they can let their personality or past push them into a hardside way of relating to others.

We've seen that a sensitive lion and a balanced beaver are among the most helpful, sought-after animals on this planet. But if they don't learn to add softness to their lives, their relationships often end up on the endangered species list.

If you have any lion or beaver characteristics in your life, be sure to read the next chapters that describe our otter and golden retriever friends. But you'll also get a great deal out of Chapters 10 and 11, where we'll give you ten specific ways to add a healthy softness to your love.

Next up is a look at the third animal in the family zoo, a specialist at having fun, being creative, motivating others—and getting kids to wear cereal!

6
Discovering the
Strengths of the Otter

Have you ever seen otters in the wild or in a zoo? Everything they do seems related in one way or another to having fun. Sea otters even eat by floating on their backs while they balance their food on their stomachs. How do their human counterparts act? Much the same way. People who score high on the otter scale are parties waiting to happen.

We've seen that the overriding drive for a lion is to conquer and accomplish something, and the major strength of a beaver is to do things right and in a quality way. We've also seen that left unchecked, they both tend to move toward the hard side of love. But the driving motivation for softsided otters is to have fun and enjoy life! That's just one of seven characteristics otters tend to share.

1. Otters just want to have fun.

If there's a way to have fun doing something, you can expect an otter to try it. We're both purebred otters, which probably explains the "funny" idea I (John) had one day.

When my daughter Kari Lorraine was two years old, she loved eating with her hands. Like many little ones, she tended to mash her food into unique shapes before eating it. And it was her lack of dining etiquette that got this otter into trouble one Sunday morning.

Time was running out in our race to get to church at least stylishly late. (Otters *enjoy* being stylishly late.) Kari and I were still sitting at the table, eating breakfast and watching "Sesame Street." I had poured her a small bowl full of a multivitamin cereal that should be renamed Post Soggies. The moment milk hits the flakes, they instantly turn into mush—the ideal thing for Kari to play in.

Picking up a handful of this glop, she let the milk run through her fingers. After squishing the cereal about a dozen times, she finally tired of the game and turned to me to ask, "Daddy, what do I do with this now?"

Ask a fun-loving otter what to do with soggy cereal? "Sweetheart," I said with a straight face, "you need to put it on your nose."

Was that a good thing to say to a two-year-old?

> # If there's a way to have fun doing something, you can expect an otter to try it.

Instantly her eyes lit up, and without hesitation, she broke into a big smile and smashed the cereal right into her face. We were both laughing hysterically when she reached down and—*pow*—mashed another handful all over her nose.

I should have been in control of the situation. Instead, I was laughing and rolling on the floor. We even went through a second bowl of cereal just so we could laugh some more at the incredible mess we'd created.

Two full bowls of soggy cereal and milk were all over us and the table. Cracker, the dog, was getting sick from slurping up this unexpected treat. And that's when Cindy walked into the room . . . and saw brown slime everywhere.

Cindy is a fun-loving person, but she's a beaver, and off-the-wall humor is not the goal of her life. Ten minutes before we were supposed to be at church, instead of being in the car, we were outside hosing down Kari and trying to get the breakfast nook cleaned up enough so we could leave.

Already I could tell I was in trouble, but it was the rest of the story that really sealed my fate.

My wife gently pulled me aside after we had dropped Kari off at her room at church. "John," she said, "you shouldn't teach her to play with her food that way. I work with her all week to teach her livable table manners for a two-year-old, and then you give her the green light to wipe out the kitchen!"

"Honey," I said good-naturedly, "lighten up." (*Lighten up* is a standard otter phrase meaning "Let's not get serious. Let's just have fun!") In my mind, I had experienced a great time of laughter and bonding with my daughter. But like many otters, I had forgotten a fundamental principle. Namely, we need to think through the consequences of our "fun" behavior.

After church, we were with some good friends (thankfully) at a local restaurant for lunch. Our food had just arrived, and we'd managed to get all the kids quieted down to say grace. We had just finished praying when I looked up and my heart sank.

There was Kari, a huge smile on her face and a massive lump of spaghetti in her hands. In my quest for fun, I had failed to consider that two-year-olds tend to repeat what they've learned—especially when it's gotten such a tremendous, positive response at breakfast.

"No!" I tried to say, but it was too late. Our entire section of the restaurant came unglued as the people watched my two-year-old wearing her spaghetti dinner and me trying to melt under the table. The look on my wife's face told me I was the one who had acted like a two-year-old. (It wasn't the first time I'd seen that look.)

If you're the parent of otters, expect them to come up with fun and creative ways to eat their food, take a bath, or do their homework. Marriage to an otter means getting used to surprises, spontaneity, and seeing a one-hour project in the yard turn into a three-hour, fun-filled adventure.

Beavers and golden retrievers appreciate and seek out an otter's fun-loving attitude. But it can become a source of frustration later in a relationship when they ask, "Do you *ever* get serious?"

Otters need to realize that while keeping things light is generally fine, they can't do it all the time. Avoiding serious discussions is like forcing their mates to live on a steady diet of icing instead of a complete meal of meaningful communication. Sometimes otters, too, have to tackle difficult topics and, especially, go deeper in relationships than light, surface-level humor. In short, that's why they need the ability to tap into the hard side of love.

My otter escapade with Kari produced little more than hurt feelings for me and the need for a new wardrobe for Kari. But there was a time for Gary when another otter characteristic nearly turned a fun time into a tragedy.

2. Otters are great at motivating others to action.

We Smalleys have enjoyed camping for years, and that's what led us to the beautiful, forested California Sierra mountains. At one place we stopped was a small waterfall. It would have been rushing with water in the spring, but this was late August, and the flow had slowed to a trickle.

The water didn't fall over a sheer cliff but down a steeply sloping hill. As I (Gary) climbed toward the top, I could see that the moss had formed a soft, slippery, green carpet that seemed to make a natural slide down to the pool below. That's when I had a great otter idea.

If I could get Greg, my older son, to climb to the top of the waterfall and slide down into the big pool, I could take the action shot of a lifetime. I was sure my new camera would capture just the right picture that would end up on the cover of our family album.

"Greg, come up here," I yelled down to where the rest of the family was seated at the base of the waterfall. He quickly climbed to where I was, halfway to the top, and I explained my idea to him.

"Dad," he said skeptically, looking at the slope and distance involved, "are you sure I won't get going too fast and miss that curve down there on my way to the pool?"

As I looked to where he was pointing, I could see what he meant. The slide went down a fairly straight path until the last possible moment. There it angled to the left before dropping into the deep water below.

"Trust me," I said. *(Trust me is* another classic otter saying that means "Don't ask me questions as if you think I've actually thought through all the details. It'll work out. Let's just go for it!")

"Greg," I said, "if it will make you feel any better, I'll position myself right where the slide turns so I can catch you if need be." Actually, I was thinking that from that position, I could get a great shot of him coming down the slide, and then I could turn around and get an incredible picture of him falling into the water.

I could see, however, that my words didn't make my son feel much better. But otters can be awfully convincing, and I kept talking. Before long, off he went to the top of the falls and the ride of his life.

With many accidents, things happen so fast that they seem to go at a speed all their own. Through my camera lens, I saw Greg push off the top, begin sliding down the hill, and pick up momentum. The grade was much steeper than I had realized (having never climbed all the way to the top), and before he had gone halfway down the hill, he was already traveling much too fast.

I gave up trying to focus my camera and started to put it down so I could catch Greg when—*zoom*—he shot right by me before I could even move. Need I say, he never made the turn! Instead of falling into the pool below, he bounced down the hill and disappeared over a small cliff!

As I turned, I saw Norma's face below. Her eyes were open wide with terror, and she screamed as she saw what I couldn't see yet. I ran to the edge of the cliff, and as I looked down, I watched Greg bouncing off rocks and finally lying still at the bottom of the hill.

My first thought was, *I've killed my son! As* I scrambled down the hill, I couldn't believe what I'd done. *Why didn't I think this through? Why did I talk him into it?* I scolded myself over and over.

Thankfully, this story has a happy ending. By the time I reached the bottom, Greg was already sitting up. He was slightly shaken, but he had kept his head when he first hit the ground and had slid on his seat until he came to a stop.

It was beaver/retriever Mom who was shaken up the most. In fact, we were going through some old family pictures recently and came across slides of that infamous waterfall trip. Norma leaned over to me and said, "Gary, that's the one time in my life when if I could have reached you, there's no telling what I would have done to you!"

Otters are excellent motivators. They can captivate an audience or encourage someone who is fainthearted. Many otters use their verbal skills to become preachers or teachers. And all of them seem to have a natural gift of gab that can provide a home or office with extra energy and drive.

3. Otters tend to avoid the fine print.

As a single parent, my (John's) mother played "Mr. Dad" in many ways, taking my brother and me camping and encouraging us in sports. But one thing we did miss out on was learning the skills of using tools.

> Otters are excellent motivators.
> They can captivate an audience or
> encourage someone who is fainthearted.

My lack of mechanical abilities was never a major issue until I got married. That's when my Cindy discovered how unmechanical I am and began to encourage me to improve in that area.

I'll never forget (or live down!) one incident. We were sitting at home, watching television, when a commercial came on for a particular brand of motor oil. As a novel twist, the commercial featured a trained monkey changing the oil to show you how easy it was. The monkey unscrewed the oil plug underneath, took off the old filter and put on a new one, then poured in fresh oil. "What could be simpler?" the commercial implied. "John," Cindy said with a smile, "I'll bet you could go out and change the oil in our car after seeing that!"

Change the oil. . . I thought. "You bet I could!" I said, and I jumped up from my chair, enthusiastic about saving us major dollars and protecting the engine like never before. As it turned out, the car should have had someone protecting it from me.

I was motivated (one otter characteristic), and I was ready to have fun (a second), but did I read any instructions before setting out to change the oil for the first time? No (our third otter trait).

Not having any tools, I went next door and borrowed a neighbor's wrench. With that, I was all set. I got under the car with my plastic pan ready to catch the old oil, and I managed to unscrew a large bolt that looked as if it was right beneath the engine. As soon as I removed the bolt, out came a gush of red oil.

Red oil? I thought to myself *It's a good thing I decided to change this stuff When oil gets old, it must turn really red, just like this.*

After letting all the "oil" run out, I replaced the bolt, put in the six or seven quarts of oil I'd bought *(After all,* I thought, *it's a big engine),* and was ready to go. Right? Wrong. I was ready to ruin the car.

If you haven't guessed already, I had unknowingly drained out all the transmission fluid, not the oil! I now had about twelve quarts of oil in the car instead of five, and not one drop of transmission fluid.

When did we make this exciting discovery? That night as we drove the car—when the transmission burned up in the middle of the Central Expressway in Dallas.

While my experience with avoiding details sent us to the transmission shop, in many cases an otter's ability to operate without instructions provides much more positive results. For example, many chefs, artists and musicians are otters who use their natural ability to "wing it" to create works of art. Trust otters to come up with an innovative way of doing something, but trust them to rarely do it by the book.

Otters share a fourth character trait as well. It seems that God has built within them an emotional escape elevator that can lift them above all but the most serious problems, a characteristic wrapped up in their view of time.

4. Otters focus on the future.

Otters rarely think problems are as serious as others seem to think, and that can be a real advantage. Why? Because otters tend to be incredibly optimistic, a trait that springs primarily from their view of time and can help keep them soft, even in trials.

For the average otter, the future is inseparably linked to the present. It's a view of life that easily looks down the road. And since 99 percent of all problems exist either in the past or in the present, focusing on the future, where everything can still work out, helps them stay optimistic.

We recently read a story that demonstrates beautifully the value of such optimism. It was the gripping account of an American pilot who was shot down by the North Vietnamese, captured, and imprisoned in the "Hanoi Hilton" for several years. We were fascinated to read about the skill many prisoners developed to cope with their confinement by mentally setting aside today's problems and focusing on tomorrow.[1]

In the confines of prison, these men designed and built homes and other structures all in their minds, even to the point of moving furniture into the rooms. Others set up imaginary baseball or football leagues, complete with regional rivalries, playoffs and college drafts. The ability to use the imagination to focus on the future helped them to face their present trials.

That same skill is consistently seen in otter individuals as well. Jean's daughter was born with a genetic birth defect. For many parents, little Diane's physical limitations would have looked like a closed door to a special future. But as an otter mother, Jean tapped into her natural strengths and lifted her eyes beyond that immediate barrier.

In faith, Jean kept believing and encouraging her daughter to become more than anyone else thought she could be. It took years of everyday hard work, but Diane eventually blossomed beyond everyone else's expectations because of her mother's ability to focus on a future goal.

The problem was that Diane's left arm had never developed below the elbow. At birth, only a fleshy appendage was present where her forearm and hand should have been. But her otter mother kept focusing on the future and telling her, "You can do anything you want."

All through grade school and high school, Jean stood beside Diane, encouraging her and instilling optimism. Then came college, and Diane decided to major in music at a very fine school in central Texas. The picture her mother had always given her of a positive future made her feel she really *could* do anything she set her mind to—even take piano as a minor, as all music students were required to do.

The happiest and proudest person at Diane's senior recital was her otter mother, someone who used her personal strengths to encourage and enrich the life of her daughter.

Optimistically focusing on the future can be a natural advantage, but it can be a weakness as well. That's especially true if otters push their natural strength out of balance and end up ignoring or explaining away their problems. That was clearly illustrated by one couple who came into our office for counseling.

Ray and Rochelle had been married for only a few weeks when they decided to divorce. In their minds, they had given the relationship a good shot. But before they actually filed papers, someone convinced them to come in for counseling.

The young man was an off-the-chart otter. Can you guess what he would say about all their problems? With his focus on the future, he'd been saying things to her like, "Just give it some more time." "Things are bound to get better." "Next month, you'll see." "Honey, give me a chance."

Unfortunately, Rochelle looked at life from the opposite vantage point. As an off-the-chart beaver, she focused on the past. She'd hear his pleas that the future would be different, but she wanted to see a history of success before she would believe it. And because things hadn't been good for the past six weeks or in the many months before their wedding, she made statements like, "It hasn't gotten any better yet" and "Our courtship was miserable, so why should I believe things are going to improve?"

Ray had failed in his courtship promise to change some habits Rochelle hated, and he minimized her growing feelings of despair after they were married. He had to realize in a hurry that in his situation, the future alone didn't hold the key to keeping his marriage together. It was only when he woke up to the harsh realities of the present and a wife who was about to leave him that he finally changed his focus.

Fortunately, they made it through counseling, and at last check, through five years of marriage. But they've both learned something vital about time. Namely, conflicting views of time in a marriage have to be addressed. The more an otter can respect the need other personalities have for a track record, the better.

Held in balance, otters' optimism based on a future focus is healthy. It can help build a positive outlook for themselves and others. But as you might imagine, their fun-loving, upbeat outlook on life can make it very difficult for them to face confrontation.

5. Otters tend to avoid confrontation at all costs.

As a newlywed, Dan was thrilled with both his new wife, Nanci, and his new job. At last he had been promoted to the very position he wanted in the advertising department of his company. He couldn't dream of things' being any better. He was right. Things were about to become a whole lot worse.

Dan had heard rumors of a hostile takeover of his company, but those rumors had been flying around for years. Then one day, people ran down the hallways, shouting out the news that they had been bought by a multinational corporation.

Dan told Nanci about the takeover. But he put off telling her the whole story: the new owners had their own ad agency, and it was very likely that his services would no longer be needed.

Dan wasn't trying to hurt Nanci. Just the opposite. With his soft way of handling problems, he thought he was doing the right thing in sparing her from knowing what "might" happen. But his interest in protecting her wasn't the only reason he didn't tell her. By not talking about his job problems with his bride, he put off facing them himself, at least for a short time.

Unfortunately, time ran out for Dan the day Nanci beat him home and found his pink slip in the mail!

If you scored high on the otter scale, expect to struggle at times with confronting others or tackling difficult discussions that demand a hardside stance. The guidelines in the chapters on adding a healthy hard side to your love (Chapters 10 and 11) will help you gain the balance you need in this area.

That's not to say that all otters will become manipulative or deceptive like Dan to avoid confrontation. But most otters are prone to avoiding explosive issues or procrastinating on having those hard discussions that aren't any fun.

6. Otters are tremendous networkers.

The sixth common characteristic of otters is one that makes them great employees or helpful friends. Namely, they seem blessed with the ability to put people together with other people.

Otters rarely meet a stranger. They know people who know people who know people. The only problem is that they don't remember everybody's name! They meet so many people, soon everyone they see can become "Old Buddy" or "Sweetheart."

My (Gary's) daughter, Kari Lynn, has a lot of otter in her and is one of the world's great networkers. At the time of this writing, she's in her first year of teaching at an inner-city school that historically has had poor attendance at parent-teacher meetings.

Rather than sit back and hope things might go better with her class, Kari took the initiative to schedule, on her own, a first-of-the-year potluck dinner for her students' families. And more than sixty people showed up!

What Kari had done is something most otters can do in a heart-beat—get people together for an event. She had heard about the low turnouts, but that didn't stop her. She knew that if she began calling the parents, and if she added the drawing card of food, anything could happen. And with all her phone networking and mentioning that so and so was bringing this, and so and so was bringing that, she had everyone from grandmothers to uncles come to get acquainted and enjoy dinner.

The principal was so impressed by Kari's enthusiasm for getting parents involved that he immediately asked her to help the PTA president plan several parent meetings throughout the school year.

We've seen that otters have many natural softside skills that can easily translate into friendships and fun relationships. But there's one problem these members of the family zoo share as well, and parents of otter children need to be aware of it.

Take the otters' deep need to be liked by everyone and be part of the group. Mix in their impulsive, creative tendencies with their love of excitement and adventure. Altogether you've got the perfect recipe for the personality that's most vulnerable to peer pressure.

7. Otters are very susceptible to peer pressure.

There's a man in the Old Testament who definitely lacked the playfulness of an otter but otherwise seemed to have many otter characteristics. Unfortunately, they were almost all pushed out of balance to the point of being weaknesses, not strengths.

When the Israelites demanded a king like all their neighbor nations, Saul was selected. Like many otters, he was concerned with how things looked to others. He was a head taller than anyone else and extremely attractive. But Israel's focus on the external in looking for a king compelled Samuel the prophet to say, "Man looks at the outward appearance, but the Lord looks at the heart."[2]

Saul also liked to be in the spotlight, particularly out in front of his troops. However, in typical otter fashion, he didn't think through the details of all the orders he gave his men. In fact, he once gave an impulsive order that none of his soldiers was to eat or drink during a major battle, and it cost Israel a great victory and nearly the life of Saul's son.

Under pressure, Saul reacted by attacking verbally those around him (something otters tend to do). But perhaps worst of all, he was terribly concerned with popular opinion. In fact, he was more concerned with being a people-pleaser than with pleasing God.[3]

Unfortunately, King Saul gave in to peer pressure and directly disobeyed God by letting his troops keep some of the loot from a major conquest. And as a result of his actions, God tore the kingdom from his hands.

None of us will lose a kingdom because we cave in to peer pressure. But that doesn't mean we won't lose someone's respect, a job or even our children to drugs or alcohol. And parents of otters need to make sure they build a strong friendship with their children to help them through the difficult times of adolescence, when peer pressure is so strong.[4]

Otters make popular leaders and personalities. However, they would do well to remember that the condition of the heart counts most, not the number of friends they have or how well they're liked.

Otters find it easy to be soft on people. What often is not so easy is being hard on problems. And the dangers of being a people-pleaser should be kept in mind amidst the fun, energy and excitement otters create.

In review, we've looked at seven traits otters tend to share:

1. Otters just want to have fun.
2. Otters are great at motivating others to action.
3. Otters avoid the fine print.
4. Otters focus on the future.
5. Otters avoid confrontation at all costs.
6. Otters are tremendous networkers.
7. Otters are very susceptible to peer pressure.

Otters aren't the only animals that have a natural softside bent. As you turn the page, you'll discover another group of people who tend to have an incredible capacity for deep, long-lasting relationships.

They're the ones with the sign on the forehead saying, "I like you. I'll be a great friend." Their nonverbal cues tell everyone they see, "Call me; I'd love to listen to you for hours." They're the ones who seem to come equipped with the most natural softside characteristics: our golden retriever friends.

7
Discovering the Strengths of a Golden Retriever

S EVERAL YEARS AGO, I (John) served as the staff counselor at a large church. After seeing numerous couples, I began to realize you can tell a great deal about people simply by watching the way they walk into the counseling office. When Dale and Diane first shuffled in ant then stiffened as I pointed for them to sit on the same couch, I knew their marriage was in big trouble.

"Well," I said, looking at their forms and letting them get seated as far apart as they could without falling off the couch. "It says here that you've been married for twenty-eight years. That's quite an accomplishment. It also says you're really struggling right now." Looking up from reading their case notes, I asked, "How long have things been rough?"

They glanced at each other as if looking for permission to speak, then turned and said in unison, "Twenty-eight years!"

Without ever giving them our personality test, I knew instantly that at least one of them was a golden retriever. Why? Because of all the animals in the family zoo, golden retrievers can absorb the most emotional pain and still maintain their commitment to another person.

How do they do this? By possessing at least seven God-given characteristics that plant them squarely on the soft side of love—qualities like making loyalty a top priority regardless of the personal cost.

1. Above all, golden retrievers are loyal.

The year was 1864, and in Edinburgh, Scotland, lived an old man named Jock. For years he had been a faithful shepherd, braving the elements and protecting his flocks. But the rugged highland hills had taken their toll. At nearly seventy years of age, he still had the skill and heart of a shepherd, but not the health. His legs could no longer make the climb to gather in a stray or chase off a predator. And though the family he worked for loved him, finances were so tight that they couldn't keep him on any longer. So, hobbled on the outside and hurting inside, he rode in a bouncing wagon from his heartland to his new home in the city.

Once there, Jock turned into a handyman and made many friends of the city's merchants. They liked Old Jock for his warm smile and needed him for his workman's skills. He was a wizard at odd jobs like fixing an unfixable chair and caulking a window so the wet, Scottish cold couldn't rush through a crack. But for all his friends, his family included only one: an orphan Skye terrier he had adopted by the name of Bobby.

> Of all the animals in the family zoo, golden retrievers can absorb the most emotional pain and still maintain their commitment to another person.

Jock and Bobby were inseparable as they made their way past the various shops, looking for work. Their routine was always the same. They began their day at a local restaurant where there was a small job in exchange for a warm meal. Then they'd make their way down the street, with a stop in each establishment to see if there was a need for the tinker's trade. Finally, at night, the two of them would go back to a run-down flophouse that served as their home.

It's said that many people have a feeling, or inner knowledge, when their time to die is near. And so it was for Jock. More than a year had come and gone since the old Scotsman had come to the city. Now it was late summer, and the heather was in full bloom in the hills. As the sun came up one day, instead of walking down to the restaurant with Bobby, he pushed his bed next to the only window in the room. There he lay, looking up to the towering hills and his beloved Scottish highland.

"Laddie," he said, stroking Bobby's thick, black hair with a hand that now held only the strength of love in it, "it's time for me to go home. They'll no be making me leave the countryside again. I'm sorry, lad, but you'll be having to find your own way in life now."

Only someone who has truly loved another could know how deep was the bond between these two. As the dying shepherd looked into the eyes of his closest friend, his own grew clouded. A chill swept over him, and Bobby, the little, black dog, snuggled closer to his master. He did his best to keep him warm one last time as old Jock slipped from life to eternity.

Jock was buried the next day in an unusual place for a pauper. Because of where he died and the need to inter the body quickly, he was laid to rest in one of Edinburgh's finest graveyards, Greyfriar's Churchyard. Amidst the mighty and most noble of Scottish history, a common man was entombed. But that's just where the story begins.

The next morning, little Bobby showed up at the same restaurant he and Jock had visited every morning. Then he made his rounds of the shops, just as he and Jock always had. This continued day after day. But somehow, Bobby would disappear at night, only to be back at the restaurant the next morning.

Concerned friends of Old Jock's wondered where the dog was sleeping, until at last the mystery was revealed. Each night, Bobby didn't look for the warmth of a fireplace, or even for a shelter from the biting Scottish wind and rain. He snuck into Greyfriar's cemetery to take up his position on his master's grave.

The caretaker of the cemetery would chase off the dog whenever he saw him. After all, there was a city ordinance against dogs in cemeteries. He tried fixing the fence and even putting up booby traps to catch the dog. Finally, with the help of a local constable, little Bobby was caught and impounded for not having a license. Since no one could claim legal ownership of him, it looked as if Bobby would have to be destroyed.

Friends of Old Jock and Bobby who heard of his plight actually filed suit on Bobby's behalf in the local court. Finally, the day arrived when their case came before the high tribunal in Edinburgh.

It would take nothing short of a miracle to save Bobby's life, not to mention making it possible for this faithful dog to stay near his friend's grave. That's exactly what happened, however, as an act unparalleled in Scottish history took place.

Before the judge could pass sentence, a horde of children from the streets came rushing into the courtroom. Penny by penny, these urchins had raised the seven shillings needed for a license for Bobby.

The lord provost was so impressed by the children's love for the animal that he officially gave the dog the "Freedom of the City," making him city property, with a special collar declaring this fact.

Now Bobby could run freely, playing with the children during the day. But each night, *for the 14 years until he died in 1879*, a loyal, loving friend kept his silent sentinel in Greyfriar's graveyard, right next to his master's side. Should you ever visit Edinburgh, you can visit the statue of Greyfriar's Bobby that's still in the old churchyard, more than 110 years since he died.[1]

Greyfriar's Bobby demonstrated something that comes naturally to the human members of the family zoo who score high on the golden retriever scale. In them you see the loyalty to stay at someone's bedside, to listen to others' problems for hours at a time, to lend a helping hand even on a Saturday or holiday.

That incredible kind of softside love and loyalty is being given in many homes today where golden retriever husbands and wives care for their families.

We think of Brenda, who held on for five and a half years while her husband was a prisoner of war in Vietnam and never once gave up loving and praying for him. Then there's Charlie, a rugged outdoorsman who hasn't been fishing in years as he takes care of his invalid wife's needs.

But golden retriever loyalty isn't seen only in dramatic examples like these. Many husbands and wives are unsung heroes, making strong loyalty to their families, their companies and their churches a hallmark of their relationships. What a strength that kind of loyalty is!

As we'll see in a later chapter, however, golden retrievers' deep loyalty can have a dark side as well. Terms like *codependency* and *negative enabler* can be laid at the feet of those who, in the name of loyalty, push their strengths into weakness.

Loyalty is the predominant characteristic of a golden retriever person, and in many ways, it acts like an umbrella above them all. Yet underneath that trait are six others that are just as important. The first we'll look at is a close cousin to loyalty. Springing from the retriever's strong sense of commitment to others comes an equally heartfelt need to know them on a deep, personal level.

2. Golden retrievers have a strong need for close relationships.

We've mentioned that otters and golden retrievers have natural strengths at building relationships. A big difference between the two, however, is the depth of relationships they enjoy.

Otters make friends easily with all types of people, often knowing a hundred different folks, but only about an inch deep. The goal isn't one incredibly close friendship but many not-so-deep ones. In fact, the average otter can easily have as many as ten to twelve "best" friends—a best friend in the neighborhood, a best friend from school, a best friend from work, a best friend at church, a best friend at the children's school, and so on.

Golden retrievers look at friendships through a different lens. They usually don't know nearly as many people. But with those they do count as friends, they want to go deep.

That's especially true in a marriage, where the average golden retriever expects the greatest depth of feeling and sharing. Thus, a lion's busyness with projects, a beaver's emotional reserve, or an otter's outgoing personality can become frustrating to the retriever spouse.

Both of our wives have strong golden retriever tendencies, and both of them tend to make friendships for life. Cindy still meets during the Christmas season with ten of her grade-school friends. I (John) can't even remember my grade-school *teachers*, much less ten of my classmates!

Norma has that same retriever depth of friendship. She recently celebrated a special birthday, and the kids and I (Gary) worked for months to put together a successful surprise party.

After Norma walked in the door to a chorus of "Surprise!" and "Happy Birthday!" we seated her in a chair in the living room. Unbeknownst to her, upstairs were several very special friends and relatives waiting to talk to her.

We have an intercom system throughout the house, but on this day it would carry voices from long ago, not music. Like the old television program "This Is Your Life," we'd have one person after another speak into the intercom upstairs and tell some personal story from Norma's past.

Norma could hear the voice, but she couldn't see the person. And each of them would close the story or comment with the words "Do you know who I am?"

Typical otters would be grasping for straws and hoping their natural sense of humor would cover their mistakes. But Norma's recall was perfect. She knew every voice long before the story was finished, and she called each one by name to come down. She didn't even stumble over the voices of three special friends who had been her high-school pals and whom she hadn't seen in many years.

For otters, having the same friends for three weeks is often an accomplishment. They enjoy moving from group to group and focus so much on the future that they don't usually look back. But golden retrievers' deep sense of commitment motivates them to latch on to their loved ones and do all they can to keep them close over the years.

Retrievers are naturally loyal and want deep, lasting friendships. And a third tendency they share is an instinctive expression of their lasting commitment to others.

3. Golden retrievers have a deep need to please others.

We had just finished teaching a section of our "Love Is a Decision" seminar on the various animal personalities when a young mother came up, nearly in tears. "Thank you for what you explained," she said with obvious emotion.

"I finally feel I can relax now. You see, our first child is exactly the way you described the golden retriever. He's loving, sensitive, longs to please us, and hasn't been a problem since I carried him in the womb. But when his brother, the lion, came along . . . It's been war ever since! Now I know why they're so different."

Many parents of golden retrievers share the same experience. They can see in their children a deep desire to please them and others— not in a people-pleasing fashion, as some otters do, but out of genuine best wishes for those to whom they're committed.

A classic example of someone who displays this golden retriever characteristic is Terry Brown, our national seminar coordinator. Terry had been the head of an extremely effective college discipleship program before coming on staff. And when he did come onboard, it was with only one goal in mind: to do whatever was needed to serve our ministry and help strengthen families across the country.

For almost six years, Terry has truly been the unsung hero of our ministry. Of the nearly thirty-three thousand people who will attend our "Love Is a Decision" seminar this year, very few will recognize his name. Yet all of them are attending as a direct result of Terry's tireless efforts to set up the host churches, arrange the seminars themselves, get out the information about the seminars, and manage the hundreds of details necessary to the success of such a ministry.[2]

If you have a golden retriever friend like Terry, you're as blessed as we are. Their uncommon willingness to set aside their own needs to serve others is a great virtue.

4. Golden retrievers have hearts full of compassion.

I (Gary) am currently involved in an accountability group of couples that meets every Wednesday. For an hour and a half, we go around the room and share the struggles and successes we've seen since the last meeting.

As a way of breaking down the barriers when we started the group, I had everyone take the Personal Strengths Survey you took earlier. And Shirley, a woman in the group, is a purebred golden retriever if ever there was one. How do I know that? Not just from her test score, but also from hearing what happened recently as she stood in a grocery store line.

Shirley suffers from the same syndrome I do. Namely, whatever line we get in at the bank or grocery store ends up being the slowest one. She was just getting a few things that day, so her junior high son had opted to stay in the car and listen to the radio.

As she patiently stood in line, Shirley smiled at the woman behind her. Perhaps it's the natural warmth that seems to come from golden retrievers or some way the sun reflects off their listening ears, but God seems to have put a clear mark on golden retrievers that lets others know they're His special counselors. And people who are emotionally hurting will spot that mark and start talking—even while standing in a grocery line.

The woman behind Shirley took her cue from the smile and began pouring out her heart. This complete stranger said her husband had left her recently after she had begged him to stay. He was verbally abusive to her and her children, yet she still wanted him back.

On and on went the story of her deep hurts, from her crumbling marriage to losing her job to her young son's catching the flu, which was what had brought her to the store for medicine. Anything that could have gone wrong in this woman's life seemed to have gone wrong.

Finally it was Shirley's turn at the checkout stand, but before she left, she got the woman's name and promised to pray for her. With her bag of groceries, she walked out to the car, put the sack in the back seat, and sat down behind the wheel.

"What took you so long?" her son asked innocently.

Sensitive Shirley looked over at him and burst into tears.

Her son was stunned by her emotion. "Mom, what happened in there?" he asked.

Between sobs, she retold the lady's story, using up two tissues in the process. When she finally finished and dried her eyes, her son shook his head and said, "Mom, *get real.*"

Not all golden retrievers are so sensitive that they wear their tears on their sleeves, but they all feel the hurts of others in their hearts. God has given them an incredible sensitivity.

A good friend told us a classic golden retriever story. Juli is a warm, attractive person who has one of the kindest hearts we've ever seen, and it's not surprising that people take advantage of her listening ear. Several years ago, she sat and listened to a neighbor pour out her sad tale of having to make a sudden move from her home state of Iowa to Arizona, and with a husband who didn't love her. Of all the things she'd had to leave behind, she missed her piano the most.

As Juli's neighbor explained how much that piano meant to her, Juli was deeply touched, and an idea sprang to her mind. She wasn't using the piano she had . . . Why not let this poor, hurting neighbor borrow it? Perhaps by making music she could melt away some of the troubles she faced.

Juli not only loaned her the piano, but she even helped the woman push it down the sidewalk to her house! The small sacrifice of not having her piano for a few weeks wouldn't hurt too much. But she hoped it would help her neighbor a great deal.

Several weeks went by, and Juli didn't hear anything more from her friend. So Juli decided it was time she checked in with her, and she walked down the street to the woman's house—or what *used* to be her home.

In the short time since Juli loaned her piano, the woman's husband had divorced her, and she had moved back to Iowa! With her went the piano Juli's father had given her for her thirteenth birthday! (She finally got her piano back, but with a broken leg.)

Most golden retrievers won't give you the piano out of their house, but they'll certainly give you the shirt off their back.

Over the years, I (Gary) have learned to accept it as gospel fact whenever Norma says to me, "Uh, oh. Greggie's really hurting" or "Oh, no. I can see Kari had a rough day at school." I might have just seen Greg or Kari, and they looked great to me! But sure enough, my golden retriever wife is so sensitive that she can spot the hurt lying just beneath the surface of our children's lives.

We should note right here that this sensitivity cuts two ways. *The same compassionate heart that can spot the hurts of others can be easily hurt by others as well.*

If you have golden retriever children, they'll be so supportive that they'll mother you if you let them. But don't let them take the full weight of the family's problems on their shoulders.

A loving way to live with golden retrievers is not to wrap them in cotton, but to recognize that they can be more easily hurt than some personalities. Words that may be an emotional pebble to a lion can be a ten-pound weight to a golden retriever's spirit. Respecting their deep capacity for caring and for being hurt themselves is one way to honor them.

> The same compassionate heart that can spot
> the hurts of others can be easily hurt
> by others as well.

Loyalty, deep relationships, a strong desire to please others, and a deep inner sensitivity. That's a strong list of softside character qualities. But the list goes on for this valuable member of the family zoo.

5. Golden retrievers define the word adaptable.

Dan was as near the top of the lion scale as you can get, and in a classic marriage of opposites attracting, he married Dana, a purebred golden retriever.

Over the years, Dana became an expert at adaptability. Repeatedly, Dan would walk in the door and announce, "All right, listen up. We're going to the cabin for the weekend, and we're leaving right now!" While all the children would cheer, Dana had to scramble to pack everything they'd need for an unplanned weekend outing.

There were also many times when Dan had a day off from his construction job or was between jobs for a week or more. Often when that happened, Dana would come home from her job and find he'd gotten bored again and gone to work on their house.

She'd walk in and find a wall blown out of one of the bedrooms to add a closet, or the kitchen in the midst of being remodeled. "Oh, Dan," she'd say as she suddenly had to adjust to living for weeks with a construction project underway.

And always she needed to flex around her husband's schedule when he went on summer hours. With the sweltering Texas heat, Dan would head off to the construction site at four o'clock in the morning and expect to be in bed at four o'clock in the afternoon. That meant breakfast had to be started at 3:30 A.M. and the kids kept quiet in the afternoon while he slept.

Being adaptable was a strength that helped Dana keep some kind of harmony at home. But we know that for some people, this positive golden retriever quality can become a terrible weakness.

In the chapters upcoming on developing hardside love, we'll mention a concept getting considerable attention these days called *codependency*.[3] In short, this term refers to someone who is an enabler, but not in the normally positive sense. These enablers are like the wife who "protects" her alcoholic husband by lying to his boss about why he's missed work; or the son who enables his mother to continue her tyrannical domination of his own wife and family by never being willing to confront her in strength.

If you're a golden retriever who has seen your strength of adaptability become pushed to an extreme, you've got the potential for a very serious and painful problem. That's why we strongly encourage you to read on and learn how to give *both* sides of love to the people in your home.

Thus far, we've seen five characteristics of golden retrievers. But they have two other traits that sound like exceptions to the rule of loving softness. The first we'll look at is that while they are indeed very adaptable on the outside, it comes at a high cost on the inside.

6. Golden retrievers often react to sudden changes.

If you have someone with strong retriever traits in your home, let us tell you four words that can help strengthen your relationship like almost nothing else. The four words are: Prepare them for change.

Lions and otters thrive on change. They can't wait to change something, even if it's for no other reason than just to put their mark on something. That's why these individuals have such a problem ordering from a menu. They want to be able to substitute a substitute for their substitute. And it drives beaver waitresses crazy!

Lions and otters don't just change menu selection, however. They're fully capable of making major changes without any warning—like coming home and saying, "Guess where we're moving, Honey?" or "Guess what job I took today?" And when they do this to the people they tend most often to marry—golden retrievers—at times they see something unexpected: their spouse's teeth bared in a snarl.

It hurts golden retrievers' feelings and their deep sense of fairness to be left out of a decision. It also makes them feel as if they're being used when they have to go along with something they had no part in discussing. Normally, they'll still fall in step out of their strong sense of loyalty, but they pay a high emotional price to do it.

A few pages back, we mentioned how thankful we are for Terry Brown, our ministry partner. Each month, Terry has to travel to our seminar site with two off-the-chart otters: us. And each month, he deserves a medal for putting up with our natural tendency to change things.

Several months ago, Terry finally reached his saturation point. He had put up with the way we talk every waitress into making a special order of everything—even toast. He hadn't complained when we changed rental car companies the minute we flew into a city, even though he had taken the time to reserve a car. He actually didn't mind too much our habit of changing hotels the way other people change socks. But we finally brought him to the end of his rope one day when we walked into the seminar room an hour before the program started and began to switch the location and arrangement of the book table.

For us, it was just the fun of having something else to change. But for Terry, who had spent hours figuring out the best place and the best way to display items and then setting up, it became a personal affront. We didn't see the problem—that is, until we closed his spirit so tightly that it became obvious we all needed to have a long talk.

Terry had done his best to put up with all the sudden changes, but our love of rearranging everything was actually very dishonoring to him. When we finally realized the negative message that changing the book table an hour before the seminar was sending him, we backed off and asked his forgiveness.

Those four words, "Prepare them for change," took on the form of a goal for us, and it led us to make some very real changes. Now if you were to travel with us to a seminar city, you'd see that we don't switch rental cars on Terry without letting him know well in advance. We've also learned to say, "Here's an idea to change the whole structure of the seminar—but not for a year or so. What do you think about it, Terry?" And we've learned to stay in the same hotel for more than one night.

Have we stopped using a menu as a starting point for negotiations? Well, we're not perfect! But at least Terry knows we're *trying* to honor him by preparing him before we change things, and that has gone a long way toward cementing our already strong relationships.

Do you have a golden retriever son or daughter who needs extra time to think about a major family decision or move? Do you have a spouse who doesn't need to hear, "Guess where we're going tonight?" but "Honey, I'd like us to go out tomorrow night. What do you think?"

Golden retrievers, of all the animals in the family zoo, are often the easiest to take advantage of. Their ability to love others deeply is what makes them vulnerable to someone who would exploit their softside strengths. But that's not to say they're emotional marshmallows.

7. Golden retrievers hold stubbornly to what they feel is right.

Don't draw the conclusion from what we've said that golden retrievers are wimps. They certainly are softer in attitude and action than the average lion, but many of them still possess incredible courage and strength.

Take a man from the Tennessee mountains named Alvin York, who reached manhood as World War I raged in Europe. In a dramatic way, after he was struck by lightning, he came to know Christ personally. As a result, he made a total about-face from his wild and rebellious ways to a solid commitment to Jesus. But then the war came along, and it reached into the hills of Tennessee and selected this newly transformed golden retriever for the draft.

York was a crack shot. He had won fame in a land of sharpshooters by winning all the local turkey shoots. He had fought and drunk with the worst of them in his non-Christian days, and he had come close to murdering a man who had tricked him in a business deal.

He was no coward. He wasn't any more afraid of going to war than the next man. But he had the Bible to deal with now, and it was the genuine fear of God that gave him pause. There was no denying that there were verses in the Bible that told him it was wrong to kill, and he had to deal with them before he could make a wholehearted commitment to the Army.

Reporting to boot camp, York quickly won the rank of corporal. But he struggled so much with his conscience that his commanding officer sent him back home to spend time in prayer and make up his mind. If he returned and asked for it, he would be granted conscientious-objector status. But if he returned with his inner questions answered, he would join his men who were waiting to be sent overseas.

Golden retrievers will follow all day behind a leader they respect. But try pushing them and they won't budge an inch. York's commanding officer knew his backwoodsman needed time to think instead of a push. And sending this new recruit home turned out to be the wisest thing he ever did.

Alvin York returned from Tennessee convinced in his heart and mind that he should join in his country's fight. And armed with that conviction, there was no stopping him. In fact, on October 8, 1918, in the trenches of France, he did something nearly unheard of in modern warfare.

York had been ordered to take a small patrol and reconnoiter a line of German machine gun nests. The enemy spotted their advance, however, and poured down small arms and machine gun fire, effectively trapping him and his men. Ignoring his personal safety, York crawled under fire to a flanking position and began firing round after round into the enemy troops.

With his expert marksmanship, he killed twenty-five Germans as he advanced down the trenches from machine gun nest to machine gun nest. Finally, in desperation, the next group of German soldiers threw up their hands.

A major was in the group he captured, and York then forced him to order all his men to surrender. With nearly thirty prisoners in hand, York began walking back to the Allied lines.

Along the way, other German soldiers saw the troops being marched under guard by the lone American. The sight of one man leading so many troops made them think their entire line had collapsed, and they, too, began surrendering to Corporal York in droves.

When this mountain man from Tennessee finally reached the American field headquarters, he had 132 prisoners in tow! And along the way, he had recruited only 3 other soldiers to bring them all in.

Corporal Alvin C. York was promoted to Sergeant Alvin C. York, and he also received the Congressional Medal of Honor for his bravery that day. French General Ferdinand Foch said of York, "The gallantry and courage exhibited by Corporal York was unsurpassed by any private soldier of all the armies of Europe."[4]

If you'd like to relive his incredible story and learn more about the stubborn strength of a golden retriever, we highly recommend you rent *Sergeant York*, a movie on videotape starring Gary Cooper in the title role. Cooper gives an Academy Award-winning portrayal of a genuine Christian hero. It's one of the few movies Hollywood has produced that's well worth watching. (Another, telling the story of golden retriever Eric Liddell, is *Chariots of Fire*.) Golden retrievers can hold as strongly to what they believe is right as anyone alive. And they're often the ones putting their very lives on the line to back up their convictions.

We've seen seven sterling qualities that capture some of what golden retrievers convey to others. Each makes them a valuable part of a friendship, family or work situation. Once again, those traits are:

1. Golden retrievers are loyal.
2. Golden retrievers have a strong need for close relationships.
3. Golden retrievers have a deep need to please others.
4. Golden retrievers have hearts full of compassion.
5. Golden retrievers define the word *adaptable*.
6. Golden retrievers often react to sudden changes.
7. Golden retrievers hold stubbornly to what they feel is right.

The Perfect Example

At this point, we've looked at all four animals in the family zoo
and seen that they fall into pairs when it comes to leaning toward
hardside or softside love. Lions and beavers tend to be hard on problems, but they're often hard on people as well. And otters and golden
retrievers tend to be soft on people, but too often they're also soft on
problems they face.

Is there any way to take the best of each of these personalities and
blend it into one person? There *is* for those who seek to pattern their
lives after the Savior's.

Jesus Christ had all the strengths of a lion. He was decisive and a
leader. As the Lion of Judah, He faced up to even the hardest of trials.
But He was also a beaver; doing things right, by the book, and in a
quality way that resulted in works and words that will stand forever.

Further, Jesus carried the strengths of an otter. He loved celebrations
(the first place He took the disciples was to a wedding) and motivating
others to godliness, and He was comfortable with crowds and initiating
contact with people He had never met. Yet He was also a golden retriever;
always going deeper than surface level with His disciples and followers,
faithful to keep His promises, and loyal all the way to the cross.

But is a balanced life that reflects both sides of love reserved only
for Christ? What about those of us with clay feet?

In the four chapters that follow, you'll discover twenty ways to help
you become more balanced in your love for others. First, we'll look
at ten ways in which hardside people can add softness to their lives.
Then we'll tackle an even harder task: we'll examine ten ways in
which softside people can add a healthy hardness to their love.

We can't be Jesus. But we're called to be like Him. *And it's in
discovering how to love others the way He did that we can grow even
closer to Him and our loved ones.*

Are you ready to see your love for others grow deeper and stronger
than ever before? That can happen as you turn the page and discover
a number of practical ways to increase commitment, affection and
closeness.

8
Increasing Softside Love

Part One

FEW THINGS DO more damage to a home than having one
member be far out of balance. And we're astounded at the way one
hardside event has the power to weaken instantly the bonds holding
a family together. That fact was brought home to me (Gary) dramatically several years ago.

It was the summer of 1982, and Norma and I had packed up our
kids, tents and swim wear and headed out to one of the many lakes
in the Chicago area. Some friends from our church, Charles and Pat,
had accompanied us with their three children, who were close to the
same ages as our own.

We pitched our tents on a grassy rise overlooking a narrow, sandy
beach, just yards from the lake. After breakfast that first morning,
Greg and Mike matched up with our friends' boys and trooped off to
explore the shoreline. That left the rest of us to clean the dishes and
set out what we'd need for lunch.

After straightening up the campsite, we all went down to the beach
to sunbathe and swim. The air was already warm and muggy as I waded
into the surprisingly cold water, preparing to do some snorkeling.

I remember looking over at our families on the beach as I adjusted
my mask. Nothing could have appeared more relaxed and peaceful.
Charles and his wife and daughter were spreading out their blankets
on the sand. And right beside them, Norma and my Kari were already
settled down, putting on suntan lotion.

With all the world seemingly at peace, I took a deep breath and
plunged underwater. After staying down as long as I could, I came
back to the surface, blew the water out of my snorkel, and swam in
a lazy circle for a few minutes. I watched the water get deeper as I
moved away from shore, and I enjoyed looking down at the waving,
green seaweed and few small fish that darted underneath me.

When I had completed the circle and come back to shallow water, I stood up, pushed up my mask, and wiped the water from my eyes. That's when I looked back to shore and saw a far different scene from the one of just a few minutes before.

Everything had looked like a Norman Rockwell picture when I submerged: calm, peaceful, relaxed. Now it looked like a nightmare scene that Stephen King would have scripted.

Charles and his ten-year-old daughter stood at the edge of the sand, screaming at each other. Then the scene got far worse. At the height of the shouting match, when his daughter refused to do something he asked, Charles slapped her with the back of his hand, sending her flying backward into the water.

Charles's wife and Norma immediately became hysterical, screaming at him and running to help his daughter. In an instant, an angry, hardside father had shattered everyone's relaxing weekend—but even more so his relationship with his daughter.

The Dark Side of Hardside Love

At the time of that incident, I hadn't met anyone who was harder on people, especially his family, than my friend Charles. But what happened that terrible morning became one of the keys that forced Charles to add softness to his life. As a result of the confrontation that followed, Charles not only apologized to everyone, but he also finally took the much-needed step of going into counseling.

For several years, he spent time in small support groups, dealing with his own background, which included parents who deserted him and major incidents of abuse with a step-family. It took time, tears of shame and a painful confrontation with the truth, but he finally saw his present anger as his own problem, not something he could explain away or blame on his parents or past.

Through the painful process of facing the truth, Charles did begin to change. In fact, he changed so much that he has learned to communicate even the hardest things to his daughter with the soft side of love.

Even the Hardest Can Learn

That day at the lake, Charles had struck his daughter for talking back to him and not taking his advice. Seven years later, he sat down with her to discuss something that was potentially just as explosive.

At age seventeen, like most young ladies, his daughter was looking forward to dating. One boy at school had been talking with her at length and was interested in taking her out. However, not only was he a non-Christian, but he had also earned the reputation of being one of the wildest boys in the school.

In times past, Charles would have put his foot down if his daughter had even brought up the subject of dating such a boy. But he had learned much over the previous seven years. He had discovered that having only one side of love isn't enough to sustain a relationship, much less cause it to grow. What's more, he knew there was far greater power to change others through adding softness to his love than in all his angry lectures combined.

With that insight, Charles took his daughter out on a date night (now a regular occurrence between the two of them). Over dinner, he did something that again brought tears to her eyes but this time for a different reason. At this meeting, instead of angry words, he used a softsided word picture to communicate his concern. (As we point out in our book *The Language of Love*, emotional word pictures are the best tool we know to carry hard or soft words right to a person's heart.)

Charles told her that she was like a precious diamond to him. And as they would do with a priceless gem, he and her mother were trying to keep her protected until her wedding day. He went on to tell her that he prayed each day that she would find the right kind of boys to date: young men who would realize what a treasure she was and wouldn't do anything to deface that priceless diamond.

He made sure she knew he didn't object to her dating. He pulled out the list of character traits they had all agreed should be a consistent part of her life before she began dating. Then he went on to tell her how she possessed each one and was certainly free to go out.

What concerned him wasn't her readiness but the character of this boy who was asking her out. To let her date him would be like handing over his precious treasure to someone who would put it on the concrete sidewalk and then use a sledgehammer to mar it.

By the end of his story, she was so moved by the picture of her father's love and saw so clearly his reason for saying no that she didn't even argue. She agreed this young man wasn't the kind of person she wanted to date, and she ended up having a meaningful talk with him about the Lord!

Charles is still a perfectionist and a consistent disciplinarian. He's still hard on problems. But to his natural hard side he has learned to add the other side of love with his daughter and others. He can now make his point without raising his voice or shaking his finger.

The Secret of Being Soft

Even for people as hard as Charles, it's never too late to learn the secret of being soft. You don't have to be born with a soft spirit to learn to display one.

As we pointed out in Chapter 2, neither of us is tender by nature. But we've learned to work at it. And in developing our own soft sides, as well as in counseling with others, we've found there are ten methods that, if put into practice, can help people add Christlike softness to their lives. Together, these methods can begin to take the cutting edge off hard personalities and draw us closer to others than ever before.

If you scored high on the beaver or lion scale, you'll find the next two chapters particularly helpful. The intensity and drive that most lions show, and the emotional reserve and desire to do things by the book that most beavers share, are indeed strengths. To the other animals in the family zoo, however, they can often project a hardside distance.

That's why it's so important to understand what balances the two sides of love if we're to see our affection for others really communicated. With that in mind, to add healthy softness to our lives, we must learn to do the following things.

1. Deal with emotional "freeze points" in the past.
Time and again in counseling, we've seen that something from a person's past is contributing greatly to out-of-balance relationships in the present. When we get to the heart of the person's problems, we find the free flow of balanced love blocked by what we call an emotional freeze point.

> Emotional freeze points reflect either
> a single event or a season of events that lock a
> person into giving only one side of love.

Emotional freeze points reflect either a single event or a season of events that lock a person into giving only one side of love. Consider what happened to Barbara.

Her father, Jim, sat at his desk at work one day. It was already late, time to be heading home. But that wasn't on Jim's mind this day. Instead, his hand shook slightly as he picked up the phone.

The call lasted less than two minutes. All it took was dialing seven numbers, issuing a few well-thought-out words, and bingo, he had accomplished what he wanted. As he hung up, he sighed in relief and then reached for his coat.

In his mind, he had simply closed the book on a bad story he had been living for too long. But at the other end of the line, it was as if a time bomb had just gone off . . .

Barbara was beginning to set up for the anniversary party later that night. She dragged the nice silverware from under the tablecloths in the china cabinet and began polishing the pieces at the dining room table. With her hands occupied, she let her mind flip back to the many pictures pasted in her memory.

Barb's father had never been physically abusive to her. But in some ways, his critical, hurtful words had hit just as hard as any blows he could have landed.

Barb shook her head to clear her mind of all the negative pictures and emotions that had flooded her thoughts. This wasn't the sort of day to be dragging up difficult memories. For all their problems, her mother and father had still endured twenty-five years together.

It was their anniversary! Soon a few friends and family members would be coming over for a small but carefully planned dinner party. As she finished putting up the last of the streamers, she had to smile. *If nothing else,* she thought, *at least they've stayed together.*

That one positive fact had always been an encouragement to her. Their willingness to stay married had acted like an anchor to help her ride out the emotional storms she saw blowing daily in their marriage. Little did she know that the fragile cable holding their commitment was about to snap.

It wasn't unusual for Barb's father to call from work and say he was running late. In fact, with guests set to arrive at any moment, she knew it was probably him calling as her mother walked over to pick up the phone. What she didn't know was that this call didn't come spontaneously as her father looked up at the shop clock. He had been planning for months what he was going to say and when he would call.

Barb couldn't hear the conversation taking place in the next room, but it was soon clear that a tragedy was taking place. After a few moments of stunned silence and interrupted sentences, her mother finally gasped and slumped into a chair near the phone. Tears streamed from her eyes.

"What's wrong, Mother? What happened?" Barb cried, running across the hall to her side. When she got no response, she said still louder, "Tell me what's wrong!"

Grabbing the phone that now hung limp in her mother's hand, she shouted into the receiver, "Who is this? What's going on?" The only answer she got was an impersonal, irritating dial tone.

"Mother," she said, grabbing her by the arms, "what happened?"

"It's your father," Barb's mom said in a voice just above a whisper. "He's not going to be at the party. He's not coming home—not ever."

"Why, Mother?" she asked, trying to make some sense out of what had happened.

"He's leaving me for another woman," she said, her face the picture of shock. "And he wanted to wait until today to tell me."

Never once in eighteen years had Barbara seen her mother lose her temper. But that night, as she got up from the chair and walked toward her bedroom, Barb's mother stopped at the dining room table, gaily decorated for the festivities.

With a fierce swing, she sent flying the beautiful centerpiece, a large, crystal vase filled with water and twenty-five long-stem roses. Shocked with herself and overcome by emotion, she ran crying into the bedroom, slamming the door behind her.

A shattered vase was the perfect picture of Barbara's world. Each time the doorbell rang that night, she had to relive and retell the heartache of her father's call to a confused, concerned guest. And each day thereafter, her heart was broken in pieces as she watched her mother go through an unwanted, ugly divorce.

End of the story? We wish it were. But one final tragedy slammed home a message to us like an iron fist.

As Barbara told us about what her father had done, she was looking back in time. Instead of being eighteen, she was now thirty-four, married and with a promising career.

At a Christian businesswomen's meeting where I (John) was teaching the concepts found in this book, Barbara came up afterward with tears in her eyes. "As you've been talking, I realized something important," she said. "The very night my father called home and said he was leaving, I made a major decision. I was looking into my mother's bedroom, watching her cry and seeing her whole world fall apart.

"That's when I said to myself, *I will never, ever, let anyone treat me like my father has treated my mother.* But what I was really saying was that *I would never be soft like my mother.* I would never let anyone get close to me and hurt me the way she was hurt."

Tragically, Barbara's decision to totally block the soft side of love was carried out with frightening efficiency. In tears she told me, "Now, after eight years of marriage, my husband just left me! After your talk, I know why. He's told me a hundred times. It's because I'm too hard with him. But after what happened with my mother, I could never be soft with him or anyone I love."

That's just one story out of a hundred we could have related about a traumatic memory in a child's life that locked that person into loving others halfheartedly. We've seen emotional freeze points caused by a divorce, death in the family, physical abuse, a difficult move, failing to get into a particular profession, or some other single situation that blocked off one side of love.

But emotional freeze points can't always be traced back to a single event. In Charles's situation (at the beginning of this chapter), it was a season of tragedies that froze his ability to give the soft side of love.

Charles's mother had dropped him and his brother off at an orphanage when he was five because she "just couldn't handle the stress" of raising them anymore. Both at the orphanage and in several difficult foster homes, he went through more instances of abuse than he wanted to remember. His mother's absence and each new incidence of abuse left unresolved anger in his life, freezing his heart harder and harder, blocking his ability to give or receive softside love.

If you struggle with giving others one side of love, especially its soft side, begin by taking two steps back and looking closely at your past. And as a way to help you do this, ask yourself questions like these:

Did you see a balance of softside and hardside love in your home? If not, toward what extreme was it shifted?

Are you aware of a specific situation or season in your parents' past that may have blocked them from giving you both sides of love?

Do you see yourself giving the same sides of love to your children that you received from your parents? Does that please or concern you?

Can you think of a specific time when you made an inner decision that you were not going to be soft or hard with others? What
prompted the decision?

How was God pictured in your childhood home? Did you receive
a balanced view of Him, or was He only a softside God of mercy
or a hardside God of judgment? How has this past view of God
affected your view of Him today?

Perhaps already, like Charles and Barbara, you can identify a situation or season that caused you to make an internal decision blocking one side of love. If you sense such a blockage in your life, you
need to do a little digging in your background.

Honestly facing the past is the beginning of thawing out from an
emotional freeze point. If your struggle to love others wholeheartedly today comes out of a reaction to your past, a number of resources
can help you in going deeper and gaining freedom. Take the time to
look up some of these helps in the Notes section at the back of the
book.[1] In addition, you can apply the remaining nine ways to add
softness to your life.

2. Recognize that certain personality bents can set up barriers to softside love.

One of the strongest desires we hear from women across the country is for closeness in marriage. They long for an intimate connection with their spouses, especially when it comes to sharing their
feelings, needs, hurts and desires. Yet there can be a natural barrier
to softside love growing out of the different ways the four basic personalities view distance and closeness.

Lions and beavers (and especially those who score high in both
scales) share certain characteristics. For example, they both like to
accomplish things and make sure they're done right. And in many
cases, they're also more comfortable with distance than with closeness. What do we mean by that?

Lions lean toward distance in relationships for several reasons. For
some, the tendency comes from a deep dislike, even fear, of being
controlled. Lions want to be in charge. They also know that the more
they share of themselves or give others a say in situations, the less
they determine the outcome of a conversation or decision.

Keeping themselves at a distance gives them a great deal of power in a relationship. One reason this is true is that the person who acts the least connected usually holds the most power cards. Think back to junior high for a picture of what we mean.

Remember the girl who was five inches taller than most boys in seventh grade but who stole their hearts anyway? Perhaps it was her perfume or her turned-up nose. But whatever the reason, the harder it was to win her attention, the more the boys tried to gain it. As long as she was cool toward their advances, they were kept on their toes. Her staying a distance from them kept them trying to please her by spending all their allowance on cards and presents she didn't really like.

If you add lions' desire for power, their natural inner intensity, and a lack of fear of confrontation, it's easy to see how they can look so strong and majestic. But for loved ones wanting to get close to them, they can appear to be isolated in their own fenced-in land, far from any personal encounters.

In short, lions are often comfortable with emotional distance because it gives them power in dealing with others Unfortunately, this distance can sometimes feel like an uncrossable emotional gulf for those who want a close relationship.

Beavers, too, can communicate a high degree of emotional distance, which in turn can convey a lack of emotional attachment and warmth. However, the breathing room they seek from others ties in with their reflective nature and deep desire to do things right.

Their critical bent is an unquestioned strength. However, if their critical skills are pushed out of balance, they can easily put people on the spot with their questions, causing them to draw back. Even more, their caution and emotional reserve can be like wearing a sign that says, "I'm too busy to talk with you now" or "I need space, so don't come any closer."

Even more than lions, beavers are comfortable with distance in a relationship. A woman named Sandy told us recently that after more than twenty years of marriage, she was ready to throw in the towel. She and her husband, Phil, had settled into a daily pattern of speaking ten words or less to each other. She longed not only for more conversation, but for more of him as well.

Talking to Phil revealed that there wasn't another woman, nor did he have an all-consuming job. He was simply an extreme beaver who *enjoyed* the distance between them. He liked being around her, but not being close to her. And he also liked the long periods of silence and felt threatened when she made efforts to draw closer.

We all need some degree of distance from others. But out-of-balance beavers can communicate, even unintentionally, an aloofness, a lack of need for others and a rigidity that nonverbally pushes people away.

Whom do hardsided lions and beavers tend to marry or have as children, however? That's right, softsided otters and golden retrievers. *And otters and golden retrievers have as strong a natural desire to move closer to others as lions and beavers do to move away.*

Otters can quickly share their hearts with people, even those they don't know well. Some otters are capable of making friends with strangers on an elevator if the ride is longer than three floors. And golden retrievers have an even greater need for a close connection with others. As far as they're concerned, no relationship is successful if it doesn't go any deeper than the surface.

What this means in many homes is that the race is on between otters and golden retrievers who are pushing forward, wanting that close connection with their spouses, while lions and beavers see them coming and pull back just as quickly.

What do distance and closeness have to do with developing the soft side of love? If people don't allow others to come close to them both physically and emotionally, they'll almost always fail at trying to communicate softside love.

> ## Otters and golden retrievers have as strong a natural desire to move closer to others as lions and beavers do to move away.

We can't tell you the number of now-grown children who longed for a parent to come closer. Nearly each week in counseling, we see a spouse who has tried for years to draw the other person into the relationship and been pushed back each time.

There is a way, however, to stop this distance/closeness dance, shrinking the gap between people and helping them gain the closeness they need for a strong relationship. It begins by first gaining a clear picture of the current distance or closeness between you and others.

Take a moment to answer the questions below. They'll help you to see how close or far away you are from others. Then share the results with your spouse.

Smalley/Trent Distance-Closeness Survey

Answer the following questions with particular loved ones in mind (e.g., your mate, child, close friend, parent). Fill in the blank with a number between 1 and 4, indicating your answer to each question as follows:

1 = never	3 = often
2 = seldom	4 = always

With your loved ones, do you . . .

- Give them the freedom to ask you questions without reacting or becoming defensive? __3__
- Seek to hear their real inner feelings without ridiculing them? __4__
- Freely express your own inner feelings and thoughts? __2__
- Know clearly their ideas and plans for the future? __3__
- Watch your everyday manners so as not to offend them? __4__
- Plan your schedule to include time with them? __3__
- "Light up" when they return from a trip? __3__
- Say "I love you" regularly and without conditions? __4__
- Share your personal problems and victories? __2__
- Laugh regularly? __2__
- Actively attend or support their hobbies or athletic events? __3__
- Regularly hug or kiss them? __4__
- Seek and value their opinions on family issues first? __3__
- Pray with and for them regularly? __3__
- Keep yourself well-dressed and manicured? __3__
- Build their trust by being consistently honest with them? __2__
- Actively listen to them by putting down the paper, turning off the television, or looking up from cooking? __3__
- Allow them to borrow your things? __3__
- Smile toward them regularly? __3__
- Seek their forgiveness immediately when you've offended them? __2__
- Attend church together regularly? __3__
- Keep their secrets if they want you to? __4__

- Keep your promises? __4__
- Show an honest interest in their friends and relatives? __4__
- Act cheerful and encouraging? __3__
- Make a genuine effort to be on time? __4__
- Watch your tone of voice? __3__
- Do your fair share of the housework? __3__
- Respect their personal property? __3__
- Avoid using negative nicknames ? __3__

The highest score you can get on this survey is 120; the lowest 30. If you're in the top third of the range (90-120), you can be fairly certain your loved ones are sensing your attachment and closeness. If you're somewhat in the middle, you may need to ask how connected your loved ones feel to you. However, our counseling experience indicates that if you scored at the bottom end of the distance scale (45 or less), *your independence from others is probably being perceived by them as unhealthy distance.*

Please understand that it's important to have a healthy degree of emotional distance. Some families are so close that if one member sneezes, everyone else reaches for a tissue. People need enough independence that they're able to stand on their own feet. But in marriage and as parents, we need to be close enough physically and emotionally to communicate warmth and love.

What's the answer to a distance problem in our relationships? Is it just to say, "That's the way I am! I'm not naturally a close person. My parents weren't close. My grandparents weren't close. My great-grandparents weren't close"?

Not if we're serious about giving others the two sides of love they need so much—or about reflecting God's kind of love.

We know it can be difficult to give up the protective comfort of emotional distance. It can be scary to get close to someone, particularly if we've been hurt in the past. But keeping others at more than arm's length can easily turn into a selfish distance that allows us to go our own way without making the kind of significant attachments for which our family members and close friends long.

If you've found yourself with far more distance than closeness in your family or friendships, increasing your softside skills can help you bridge the gap. And one of those skills is our third step toward building softness into your life.

3. Learn to give others a "softness sandwich."

My (Gary's) youngest son's football coach is one of the best in the area. But he became an even better coach this past year by learning to give his players what we call a "softness sandwich."

Jack, our coach, is a former professional football player. And like many coaches, he has a great deal of lion in him. That's understandable. There's nothing soft about taking a team through the rigors of two-a-day practices or making players run wind-sprints in Arizona in August to get them in shape for the season. What Jack has realized, however, is that hardness alone won't motivate every player on the team.

In Jack's first year here, he was really frustrated by his inability to motivate a number of players. Some of his top prospects even quit the team, leaving him with glaring holes in his lineup. Interestingly, the kids he was having trouble with were almost all golden retriever personalities.

After practice one day, he expressed his frustration to me. "I know I'm tough with these boys," he said emphatically. "But they've got to get motivated and intense. They need to get with it, or maybe they need to bag football and go out for some other sport."

"Coach," I said, "are you open to a suggestion?"

"Our season starts in three weeks," he said. "At this point, I'm willing to listen to anything."

That's when I gave him a two-minute explanation of the different animal personalities and told him about the softness sandwich that John and I teach in counseling.

"Coach, try an experiment for one week of practice," I said. "For every thirty seconds you spend getting on a player about a missed tackle or assignment, leave him with thirty seconds of softness as well. Look him right in the eye and tell him what he did wrong and how it might cost the team in a real game. But then put your arm around him, tell him you appreciate him, and tell him he's too good a player to make mistakes like that. Then send him back onto the field.

"Remember, thirty seconds of hardness surrounded by thirty seconds of being soft. *But make sure you leave with softness when you can.*"

Jack looked skeptical, and understandably. Most of the coaching done on anything but the most elementary level has become 99 percent hardside. The idea of sandwiching softness in with his hardside lectures obviously made him uncomfortable. But he was willing to try anything.

Old patterns are hard to break. In fact, at the end of the first practice where he tried this approach, he asked me, "Gary, when I talk with them and softly touch them, *can I be holding them around the neck?*"

Bue Jack did change, and so, dramatically, did the attitudes of many of the "problem" players on the team. He had a softside talk with each of the boys who had left the team, and he won nearly all of them back. He also came within one series and a missed field goal of winning the state football championship outright last year, settling for a tie and the title of co-champion.

Jack is an excellent coach, and adding softness only increased his success. Time and again, we've seen spouses and parents win a loved one's heart back by learning and practicing this same approach. Take Laurie, for example.

Laurie keeps the kind of house germs hate. As a very high beaver, she keeps her home so clean that germs don't even visit anymore. Unfortunately, her otter husband's idea of keeping things clean is straightening out his closet once a year whether it needs it or not.

During their early years of marriage, Laurie's natural hardside bent was pushed far into the critical zone. At least twenty times a day, she would find some reason to criticize her husband's behavior. He had put the bath mat fuzzy side up again, not fuzzy side down. He had taken a shower without wiping off the glass again. He had driven her car, and there were crumbs everywhere from his snack at the mini mart. On and on her list went.

The harder she became with her husband, trying to force him to change, the fewer results she saw. But when she began to practice the softness sandwich approach, she was shocked at the change that took place in him *and* in her.

"I made a decision that I wouldn't criticize Bill about something he'd done or failed to do unless I could say something positive to him as well," she said. "At first, I found myself not saying anything at all. It was so foreign to me to try to link a positive with a negative. I felt funny and two-faced. But in time, all I can say is that the change in both of us has been remarkable."

Why is softness such a key to decreasing conflict in a home? Studies have shown that the happiest couples are those who consistently do small acts of caring (particularly soft actions like a kind word, a gentle touch or an encouraging note), even during times of expressing concerns.[2] On the other hand, with the most unhealthy and conflictful couples, softside actions are next to nonexistent.

Thus, if we want to have the healthiest possible relationships, we'll learn to include a sandwich of softness with our hardside correction.

We've looked at three important ways of adding softness to our lives: spotting emotional freeze points from our past, recognizing and cutting down on the emotional distance in our homes, and learning how to use a softness sandwich when we need to correct someone. Each of these is important. But there are seven more powerful ways to increase this important side of love.

9
Increasing Softside Love

Part II

WE'VE ALREADY SEEN three keys to communicating love's soft side. A fourth involves looking at softness from the perspective of others.

4. Understand what softness means to the other person.

Varying personalities make it inevitable that people will view a given situation differently. And if a marriage or parent-child relationship is to flourish, we need to value each other's differing personality strengths and learn, in light of them, how best to communicate softness to the other person. *Conversely, the less we appreciate a person's natural strengths, the harder we'll tend to act toward that individual.*

Remember the story of Jessica and her mother that began Chapter 3? Jessica was a beaver by temperament and had to do things carefully. Her mother, on the other hand, was a lion who wanted everything done quickly and efficiently. But this wise mother learned to apply a powerful biblical principle that put more softness into her relationship with her daughter than ever before.

In the book of Matthew, Christ told us regarding our spiritual affections, "For where your treasure is, there your heart will be also."[1] What's true in the spiritual realm is also true in our families. The more we learn to treasure our loved ones' natural bents and talents. especially if they're different from our own, the softer our hearts will be toward them.

That's exactly what happened between Jessica and her mother. As this woman grew in her appreciation of Jessica's unique strengths, she wanted to learn what softness meant to her daughter. So she asked simply, "What are some ways in which I can be softer with you?"

Jessica immediately gave an answer that shocked her mother: "You can turn off the timer when I'm doing my homework."

Having to do her homework with the clock ticking in the background wasn't training Jessica to go faster; it was frustrating her into making mistakes and causing her to go even slower.

Jessica's mom liked working under the clock. It was a natural assumption that her daughter would, too. But God had given Jessica a different perspective on time, and problems began to develop when those two time zones crossed. The gift of unpressured time was one practical way her mother could demonstrate a softer love.

> # The less we appreciate a person's natural strengths, the harder we'll tend to act toward that individual.

Are you making demands on someone you love that are pushing the person away from you, perhaps hardening your own heart as well? Sometimes softside love comes wrapped up in the consideration to call before you bring a guest home to dinner. Other times it means dealing with procrastination and beginning your taxes before 10:00 P.M. on April 14. It may even mean being sensitive enough to make sure the dirty clothes go *inside* the laundry basket, not just on the floor next to it. And always it means a shoulder to cry on rather than a lecture.

In each case, learning to value others' differences, and especially *asking* what softness means to them, can give you insight into large and small ways to touch their hearts and soften yours.

5. Learn the secret of making hard decisions in a soft way.

All this talk about adding softness seemed like the last thing the Smiths needed to hear. After all, they were in the middle of a power struggle with their twelve-year-old son.

They had tried being soft with him, even to the point of bribing him to bring his behavior into line. But nothing seemed to work with their lion son short of bringing the hammer down in a harsh confrontation. Both mother and father were golden retrievers by nature, however, and having to hammer their son each day was breaking their own hearts.

Contrary to appearances, softness was actually the major thing this home needed. Why?

At the heart of many discipline problems is anger—often the immature anger of a child who wants his or her own way and rebels against any controls or boundaries. Unfortunately, in response to a child's anger, parents frequently decide to meet fire with fire, and the situation can escalate quickly to World War III proportions.

Until children grow to where they can stand shoulder to shoulder with Mom or Dad, parents can normally out-shout them and force them to follow the rules for a short time. But like tossing a bucket of gasoline on a small fire to try to put it out, the cumulative effect of anger in a home can cause even greater long-term damage.

We all know how easy it is to meet anger with anger. But what can turn away anger instead? The Scriptures tell us one thing decreases the presence of this damaging emotion in a home: softness.

Biblical paradoxes like "A gentle answer turns away wrath" and "A gentle tongue can break a bone"[2] are intriguing, but they're not always comforting, especially for a family like the Smiths. How can you add softness to a problem situation without handing over the home to an unruly child? What can help a mom and dad go back to being parents, not full-time police?

The Smiths and many other families need a tool for making hard decisions in a soft way—a method that increases a family's commitment to face a problem, task or goal together while decreasing tension at the same time. We've seen this method work in our own homes and in hundreds of others.

The method to which we refer is the family contract. Let's illustrate this tool with the example of the Murphy family, who faced the same problem many others do. Namely, they have the whole family zoo under one roof.

Ed, the father, is a lion and wants the family to run like a well-oiled machine. His son the otter, Sam, keeps throwing monkey wrenches into the machine. That leaves the mother, Doris, the golden retriever, constantly on call, trying to patch up things between the two men in her household. What about their daughter, Betty the beaver? She uses her critical skills to point out her brother's every fault while being close to perfect herself, starting the fireworks all over again.

Instead of suffering constant pandemonium and family friction, however, they learned to put even the hardest family rules into a soft enough form for everyone to swallow, including Sam—a mutually agreed upon family contract.

One evening, they all took stock of their situation. None of them was happy with the way things were going, but no one wanted to budge to make things better (except golden retriever Mom, of course, who had already bent herself out of shape trying to keep everyone happy).

Ed took charge of the meeting and had them all list what they wanted from their family. Once he had compiled everyone's lists, he boiled down their wants into three primary rules they all needed to live by. While each major category would have subcategories under it, the three rules they agreed to were:

1. Honor God.
2. Honor each other.
3. Honor God's creation.

Honoring God, they felt, meant regular church attendance, never using improper language or His name in vain, and a quiet time at least twice a week as minimums. Under "honoring each other" came the family rule that they weren't to talk back to their parents or dishonor any family member with their words And under "honoring God's creation" came the various chores to keep the house presentable, as well as taking care of the family pets.

All families operate by rules. The problem is that in most homes, the rules are unwritten. And while we can't explain it completely, we've seen that when a family's rules are put in writing and followed consistently, less confusion and greater harmony come to that home.

After writing out their basic rules, the Murphys began applying the three keys to making a family contract work. First, right next to each rule they drew two columns, one for a reward if it was fulfilled, and another for a penalty if it wasn't. *Then the children were allowed to write in their own rewards and penalties, with guidance.*

Betty needed help from her parents in fitting the penalty to the failure when she suggested, "If I miss feeding the cat, how about if I'm grounded for two weeks?" After some discussion, it was agreed that missing television for one night was more realistic.

Sam needed help in making the reward section more realistic. If he remembered to feed the dog each day during the week without being asked, his first suggestion was that he wouldn't have to mow the yard for the entire summer. After some discussion, they all agreed that keeping the rule meant he could spend two hours on Saturday afternoon at the local mall. Failing to keep it meant no mall that weekend.

Perhaps you can see already what was beginning to happen around the Murphy home. Now, instead of every rule's being "Dad's rule" or "Mom's thing," they were the children's rules, too, complete with their own set of rewards and penalties. As ownership of the family rules went up, the kids' grounds for defying Mom and Dad went down.

Fighting the rules soon became a way of fighting with themselves, and that wasn't nearly as much fun.

The second key to a successful contract was that *the children were allowed as much freedom as possible in meeting their specific responsibilities.* For example, the family members committed themselves to having at least ten minutes of "quiet time" twice a week. For Sam, this usually meant using the last ten minutes at night, reading some of the interesting stories and applications from *The Student Bible.*[3]

Of course, some rules were unbendable. There was no fudge factor if they used improper language or talked back in anger. However, flexibility about when the trash was taken out or when the dog was fed (any time before dark) again took away the need to nag. The children were also responsible for marking their own chores on the contract sheet if they wanted credit toward a reward that day. That put the responsibility back on the person whose chore it was, not on a parent to constantly remind Betty or Sam to get it done.

The third and most important key to an effective family contract system is something the best business leaders (and Ed and Doris) know: *You can expect what you take time to inspect.* The one meal the Murphy family could all count on having together was breakfast. So it was then that the parents took the contract sheet off the refrigerator to see what the children had checked off.

The first three weeks were a test for Mom and Dad and Sam. He missed doing his chores on several days, which meant he couldn't go to the mall that weekend. He even had to come home early from his cousin's birthday party when everyone else was headed to a movie at the mall. ("Miss feeding the dog, miss going to the mall—at all.") But after Mom and Dad held firm during that testing period, which they had been told to expect, soon many positive things were happening.

Ed found he had boundaries around his anger now. Instead of yelling, pointing his finger at the kids, or feeling he had to be dramatic to show how serious he was, he could point to the contract on the refrigerator. It also helped him to remember that in addition to giving penalties for rule-breaking, he could motivate positively by giving rewards for good behavior.

Doris, our golden retriever, found strength to be more lovingly hardside than ever before because of having the rules right in front of her. As she looked at the contract, she could see the positive things the children could gain, and she also knew there were limits to the discipline if they failed in their tasks. All this gave her the confidence to stand firmer in providing the unified parental front her children had needed all along.

Finally, Sam the otter and Betty the beaver also began to thrive under this system. In spite of himself, Sam liked filling out the chart, especially checking off what he had done with a big marker. After several months, he even found himself making habits out of several areas of responsibility he had once hated. And for Betty, a contract system was pure heaven. At last, the family was getting organized like her, and she was being rewarded for doing everything just right.

You might wonder if the positive things that happened to the Murphy family were a one-time phenomenon. But the Smalley family enjoyed the same results. That's because the contract system we taught the Murphys was the same one the Smalleys used for years. In fact, I (Gary) credit that system we used while the children grew up for much of the close-knit unity we're experiencing today.

As you'll see in the next chapter, the most important key to a family contract's success is the hardside love to hold another person accountable. But as tough as it was to inspect the contract each day, it brought incredible softness to our home through the reduction of friction and the addition of love and respect.

Bringing family rules to light and putting them down on paper is one way for everyone to win.

We know you may have a number of practical questions on using contracts that we're not able to cover here. If you'd like to go deeper in learning this helpful method, see Gary's book *The Key to Your Child's Heart,* or *Who's in Charge Here?* by Robert G. Barnes, Jr.

Now let's look at another way of adding softness that comes through awareness of a silent, hardside language.

6. Recognize the destructive power of nonverbal hardness.

The apostle James pointed out a way to be spiritually blessed by looking into a mirror. Wise people will look intently at who they are and make needed changes. But foolish people will look into that same mirror and walk away unchanged.[4]

How many times have you looked in the mirror today? This week? We may glance at our reflection ten times a day to help us look our best. But to act our best, we need to gaze into the mirror intently and even more often to see how others perceive us.

A counselor friend recently told us about a rather inventive wife. She just couldn't get through to her husband that one of her major concerns was not what he said to her, but the way he looked at her. She told the counselor that her husband rarely raised his voice, yet his angry and dishonoring gestures made her feel insecure and attacked. He could hold his tongue, but he couldn't control his gestures and sharp glances. When they were alone, his looks held an edge that could cut through cold steel.

Desperate to get through to her husband, she used a method we don't endorse because it could backfire, though it worked for her. She set up her own "Candid Camera," hiding their small video camera in the family room bookshelf and pointing it toward the kitchen, where many of their arguments took place. Then she turned it on the moment she heard his car in the garage.

> ## We'll never be truly effective at communicating the soft side of love if we don't take a hard look at what we're saying nonverbally.

That night, after another series of hardside looks and gestures, she again confronted her husband. And this time, she played back the tape so he could see what concerned her.

What he saw wouldn't have made the first cut on "America's Funniest Home Videos." But it could have won first prize on "America's Most-Strained-Out Couples." He was stunned as he watched how many times he rolled his eyes back, tossed out his hands as he tossed aside her words, and crossed his arms or turned aside when she talked to him. All he could say was, "Is that really me? Do I really look that way?"

Researchers tell us that the vast majority of what we say is nonverbal. From the tilt of our head to the narrowing of our eyes to slamming a door, we communicate volumes by what we don't say. *And we'll never be truly effective at communicating the soft side of love if we don't take a close look at what we're saying nonverbally.*

Learning to be softer with others begins with our eyes and mouths. If our brows are furrowed and our mouths are tightly drawn, our words may be as soft as a feather, but the person will be receiving a hardside message. That's because *in a mixed message of soft words and hard nonverbal signals, all ties go to the hard side.*

It's been said that one picture is worth a thousand words. And every time we talk to a person, our nonverbal clues are giving a clear picture of what we're really thinking.

The whole body gets involved in a frown. Take a moment and do this exercise. Put on your most disapproving face: eyes narrowed, teeth clenched, neck stiff—the kind of face you'd reserve for that teacher who always gave pop quizzes on Friday afternoon or the girl who broke up with you in ninth grade and wouldn't give back all the expensive stuff you'd bought her.

Now notice your breathing. Putting yourself in this nonverbal position will increase your heartbeat, make your breath become shallow, tighten your neck and stomach muscles, and in general put your whole body on the defensive.

Now try relaxing, and put on your widest smile. Can you feel your whole body relax? Your breathing automatically becomes deeper. If you could measure it, you'd also see that your pupils dilated slightly when you smiled, taking in more of your environment and assuming a warmer, more friendly appearance to others. "A cheerful look brings joy to the heart," the Bible tells us.[5]

The next time you're having a "serious" discussion with your spouse or child, try something that can help you as much as the most persuasive argument. Take a break from the intensity of the moment to smile and take a hand or give a hug, indicating that in spite of the issue you're facing, you still love the person.

We also need to be careful about our tone of voice. It rarely lies about what we're really feeling when we talk with someone. Ask your loved ones for a regular tone-of-voice check to make sure some negative embedded emotions aren't erasing the positive effect of your words.

Nonverbal softness is at its best, however, not when we're talking but when we're listening. We can be sure we're communicating softness if our shoulders are pointed directly at the person and we're leaning forward just a bit. Taking the time to turn and squarely face another person also communicates warmth and attention, as does getting down at eye level with a child. But turning to the side or facing the stove or television can communicate hardness, even if that's not our intent.

Finally, use the nonverbal hardness of others to spot tension in your home. Not too long ago, it seemed that something was wrong with Norma. So I (Gary) decided to look at her nonverbal signals to try to isolate the problem.

First, I noticed that when we spoke, she often wouldn't look at me. Our conversations seemed short and to the point. She'd also cross her arms or sit on the other side of the couch. But every time one of our children came around, her eyes lit up, and she was ready to talk at any hour of the day or night. Finally, when I reached out toward her, she resisted closeness and tensed up whenever we hugged.

I didn't need to be a missile scientist to realize her problem was with me! I finally found out that I'd been criticizing her over one particular area, and she'd had enough. She had never verbalized her frustration, but it was there to see in her actions.

Fortunately, by looking at her body language, I had quickly spotted her frustration. And by working at not being critical in that area, I soon had our relationship back on a positive note.

7. Become personally involved in helping others.

My (Gary's) daughter, Kari Lynn, is in the middle of her first year of teaching at an inner-city school. And while she has always had a compassionate heart, I've seen her develop an even deeper level of softness this year. Why? Because it's been a season of sacrificing for others, and it has really sensitized her heart.

Nearly all her students are Hispanic, and two of them started class speaking no English at all. I've watched her spend hours of her free time tutoring and encouraging her students to speak and read English better.

I don't say this to put a public spotlight on what she's done to help her students, but to point out the incredible way involvement with others softens hearts, even if it means sacrificing our time and resources. If you find your heart isn't as soft as it should be, ask yourself a question: Are you involved in a situation where you're serving others? Whether it's in the church nursery, taking a missions trip to Mexico, or at the local hospital, we can learn powerful lessons in softness by reaching out to others.

8. Allow tough times to mold us into soft people.

We know a couple on a church staff who have had to suffer the heartache of infertility. They've endured painful tests, various medications, and untold stress. For years, every toy store, every Sunday morning seeing all their friends' kids in the nursery, and every Christmas with only two stockings hung on the mantle were reminders of the emptiness they felt. But some of the most difficult times they experienced came at the hands of well-meaning church members.

On more than one occasion, the wife received notes from women who had children saying that she should accept and applaud "God's will" that they be childless. And often she was told how special, strong or blessed she must be for God to have given her such a burden. This couple didn't need lectures on God's will from people who couldn't relate to their pain, but sympathy, understanding and occasionally a shoulder to cry on.

Many people go through trials. but not all are trained by them. Physical pain or other problems can make us harder in our personal lives. Yet for this couple, and for many others who have gone through a season of difficulty, hard times can make soft people.

Some time ago, we had the opportunity to spend a week with Dr. Charles Swindoll and his church staff, speaking at their church's family camp. Since we were in the middle of our research on this book, it seemed a perfect time to ask one of the softest, warmest individuals we've met what his secret is to communicating so much genuine love for those in his flock.

Dr. Swindoll paused and wrinkled his brow. Finally, after a few moments, he gave a one-word answer: "Pain." Then he spoke of the pain of nearly losing his granddaughter, of doing funerals for too many close friends, of pouring his heart into people who wouldn't listen to biblical counsel, and of receiving unjustified criticism. Going through pain will make us either bitter or better. Charles Swindoll's trials have deepened and softened his love for Christ and for others.

Are trials making you harder, blocking softside love in the process? We believe that our response to pain and its effect on our ability to love is so important that we wrote a whole book about it: *Joy That Lasts*.

The apostle James told us that we're not to resent trials but welcome them as friends. And while that's not always easy to do, sharing in Christ's suffering is a sure way to gain a deeper sense of His love. It's also a powerful way of softening our hearts so that our love for others comes shining through.

9. Keep our hearts spiritually soft.

Without question, the greatest single way to soften our love for others is to increase our love for Christ. This is so important that we'll spend the entire last chapter of the book addressing it. But for now, we can do two things to keep our hearts spiritually soft.

First, we add softness by remaining open to correction from others. In the Scriptures we read, "A rebuke goes deeper into one who has understanding than a hundred blows into a fool."[6] In other words, wise people are soft and receptive to words of correction; fools are hardened to any attempts to point out their faults. And unfortunately, the less open we are, the more we harden our hearts toward God and others. Conversely, if we want to be wise, we need to remain soft toward what God can teach us through the correction of others.

Second, we add spiritual softness by not trafficking in those things that bring darkness to the heart. Romans 1 contains a long list of such things, including unrighteousness, wickedness, greed, evil, murder, strife, deceit, slander, hatred and especially sexual sin.

Without a doubt, the best way to add softness and keep darkness out is to live a godly life. Consider sexual sin, for example, which is epidemic in our society, One reason it darkens the heart is that it forces us to live two different lives. There's the public life of a devoted husband, wife, student or clergyman, yet there's also the secret life of trafficking in darkness.

The more we live as two very different people, the more we harden our hearts in a negative way toward God and others. Each time we push away the Holy Spirit's conviction of sin, refusing to repent, we invite our hearts to become more rock-hard. Time and again, we've seen that such an unfeeling heart can cause us to do and say things that would have been unimaginable only a few months before.

There's no question but that secret sins lead to a hardened heart. And all the time we're turning away from God, we're not really getting away with anything. As the psalmist said, "If we had forgotten the name of our God . . . would not God have discovered it, since he knows the secrets of the heart?"[7]

The more we walk in the truth, the less sin can act like slow-drying cement in our hearts and block our ability to give and receive both sides of love.

10. Make it your goal to be soft with those you love.

If you're a lion or beaver, goals feel as good as a hot towel right out of the dryer. When someone gives you a goal, the challenge fuels your fire. So with that in mind, we challenge you, here and now, to make it a goal to add softness to your love for others.

If you need to learn more about motivating your children based on their personality bents, we recommend the book *Tailor-Made Kids in an Off-the-Rack World*, by Jim Brawner. In this excellent resource, you'll see many ways to use both sides of love to inspire your kids.[8]

For the two of us, as of the time we're writing this, it's been almost two years since our wives sat us down and told us we needed to add more of this side of love to our lives. And for two years, it's become more and more of a conscious, daily goal. But such a decision comes at a cost. We still have the otter tendency to attack verbally when under stress. And our ideas of softness haven't always matched those of our wives and children. We've had to have family meetings to talk things out, and sometimes we've had to ask forgiveness for going back to what's comfortable, even if it is far out of balance.

We know it's not easy for a lion to take on characteristics of a lamb, but it's been done before. The book of Revelation is full of pictures of the Son of God who sits on His throne as both. And as we grow to be more like Him, we'll see softness increasing in our relationships with others.

Ten ways to add softness, and each has the power to enrich our relationships. But we also need the hard, protective side of love. And in the next two chapters, we'll look closely at ten ways to add more of that side if it's the missing part of a healthy balance.

10
Adding Hardside Love
in a Healthy Way

Part I

IT WAS PITCH-DARK as Steve stood in his daughter's room. *Perhaps I'm wrong*, he thought as he looked over the sleeping form of his daughter. *Everybody thinks I am. But Lord, I know I'm not. Please help me to stay strong.*

Steve would never be mistaken for a lion. It's not that he wasn't manly, but he was clearly at the far end of the golden retriever scale. He could be firm if he was pushed, but he was so flexible with others that he'd seldom had to use the hard side of love. Instead, he had always been the warm, supportive father who handed out more hugs and less discipline than the average dad.

As we've seen, softness is essential. Run down the biblical lists of the fruit of the Spirit and the character qualities of an elder or deacon, and half of them call for softsided love. But Steve needed now to apply the protection and correction of love's hard side. For a major problem had shown up at his door that softness alone couldn't handle.

In fact, Steve's worst nightmare had come true. While he had suspected it for several months, now he knew that his fifteen-year-old daughter, Robin, was doing drugs with her new friends at her new school. The guidance counselor had called in him and his wife when drugs were found hidden on top of the locker Robin shared. No charges had been filed because neither girl had been caught in direct possession, but an explosion went off in Steve's mind when he faced the facts.

He didn't know how involved Robin was, but he could no longer explain away her moody behavior and deceptive stories. He could tell he was losing his daughter to drugs, dead-end friends, and who knew what else, and he had to do something about it.

There are times when life calls us to take a stand, when strength has to be added to softness. In a move far out of character for Steve, he made several major decisions at once.

First, Robin would transfer to a different school. While drugs are on every high school campus, he felt strongly that she needed to make a break from this school. The same thing went for her newfound friends. She was to cut all ties with them, including phone calls or "accidental" meetings at the mall. (He chaperoned her to make sure of that.) Finally, they were going back to church, and she was to go into counseling, along with the rest of the family, beginning immediately.

You can imagine the impact these decisions had on the entire family. Robin was enraged and threatened to run away. Night after night, she refused to speak to him or even look at him unless forced to do so. Her younger sister, a golden retriever by temperament, responded to the hurt she saw in Robin's life and also attacked their father as being too harsh and cruel. Even his wife began to doubt him and wondered aloud if he had gone overboard with the whole situation.

Two months had now passed, and Robin was in her new school, away from the old friends. It was past midnight, and once again, Steve had been unable to sleep, tossing and turning with his stomach tied in knots as he struggled with conflicting emotions. *Am I being too hard? Have I gone overboard?* he thought. At last, he decided to do the only thing that seemed to give him any comfort; he was going downstairs to pray.

But this night, on his way to the stairs, Steve stopped by Robin's room. The door was half open, and he peered into the darkness. After a moment of letting his eyes adjust, he stepped inside and watched her sleep.

Emotions gripped him as he remembered all the nights he had stood there when she was young, looking down on her as she held her blanket or a favorite stuffed animal. He recalled how she used to smile whenever he walked into a room. But now he felt only hatred from her, and it was tearing his heart to pieces.

Tears filled his eyes as he started to turn away. And then his daughter spoke. "Daddy?" she said. "Is that you?"

He stopped where he was and turned slowly. "Yes, Honey," he said.

After a long pause, he could tell his daughter had begun to cry softly. "Daddy," she said, "thank you for loving me. I was stuck, and I didn't know how to get out. Thank you for being firm with me. . ."

Steve had paid a tremendous price to hear those words. There is no anger like that of a person who is caught up in darkness and then forced to look at the light. Steve even had to shoulder the anger of others who felt he was overreacting and cruel.

Tough love isn't easy, and it often doesn't bring rewards in just two months. We know other people who have had to be hard with a loved one and seen a child or spouse walk away for years. But one thing is certain: Had Steve decided to give only the soft side of love to his daughter, he would never have won back her love, and he might have lost her forever.

This chapter is for all of us who have struggled with being too soft in our love for others—people like Steve who lean toward the soft side, who need a healthy hardness to balance their love not just in a crisis, but every day.

It's our otter and golden retriever friends who tend to camp out on the soft side of love. Being naturally soft on people, they're often too soft on problems as well. To see just how well you fit that description, go down the following softness survey, answering yes or no to each question.

---

1. Do you tend to hold your feelings inside rather than express them to others? __Y__
2. Can you criticize a friend? __N__
3. Can you ask others for a favor or ask for help with a problem you're having? __N__
4. Do you have difficulty saying no to an added responsibility, even when you know you're overcommitted? __N__
5. Do you leave most of the discipline of the children to your spouse? __N__
6. When someone compliments you, do you feel uncomfortable or have to explain it away? __Y__
7. Are most of your times with friends spent listening to their needs and concerns, without voicing your own? __Y__
8. Do you feel that being aggressive and being assertive are basically the same thing? __N__
9. Do you often walk away from confrontations with your children and feel, deep inside, that they've won again?
   __Y__

10. Was it difficult for you to express anger in your home
    growing up? ___y___
11. Do you feel that your spouse is being too hard when he or
    she disciplines the children, even when you know the
    discipline is appropriate and justified? ___N__ y
12. If you say no to a friend's request, do you feel you may lose
    the relationship? ___y___
13. Do you find yourself being convicted by a message, Scrip-
    ture or book, but put off taking any steps to change? ___N___
14. Do you often think that something will "just happen" that
    will quickly turn a negative situation into a positive one?

    ___y___
15. Do you feel insecure in your spiritual life and growth? ___y___

If you had more yes answers than you have fingers on one hand,
this chapter is definitely for you. You're on the low side of the
hardside scale and will really benefit from what follows. But even
those who answered no fifteen times can learn a great deal about how
to be hardside in a healthy, balanced way.

Where do we begin? Just as in the last chapter, by blasting before
we build. For as important as it is to spot emotional freeze points that
can block softness, it's equally important to see how they can shut
off hardside love.

1. Recognize the effect of emotional freeze points.

The year was 1951, and Sergeant Davis's part of the Korean War had
just ended. When the war began, his reserve unit was one of the first
called into active duty. The Army had paid his way through college.
In return, for twelve months and eleven days, he paid the Army back
the hard way: fighting up and down the freezing mountains and hills,
often with fixed bayonet, near the thirty-eighth parallel.

Sergeant Davis was now just plain old Dad to Margie, his nine-
year-old daughter. But one night soon after his return from the war,
he put back on his stripes in an incident he would never forget.

It was bedtime, and Margie had asked for a glass of milk and some
cookies before turning in. She was laughing and clowning around in
the kitchen when she knocked over her glass, shattering it and spill-
ing milk all over the floor.

The late hour, the loud noise and his overwrought nerves from having recently been in a war zone combined to cause Margie's father to forget whom he was talking to. Instinctively, he reamed her out with a tonguelashing fit for a disobedient soldier. Shocked by his harshness and vulgarity, Margie burst into tears.

Unfeelingly, he shouted at her, "Get down the hall and get to bed." Then he stormed outside as she fled to her room.

"It was her that broke the glass, not me," he said defiantly to his wife when she came out later to talk to him. He refused to go in and apologize to Margie, ending the discussion with a halfhearted admission, "All right, I was a little hard on her. But she'll forget it." Only she didn't.

Later that night, terrible screams came from Margie's room. Davis rushed into her bedroom and found her sitting straight up in bed, soaked in sweat and crying uncontrollably.

"What's wrong?" he said, putting his arm around her as she shook with fear.

"Oh, Daddy, it was terrible," she said. "There was this bear, and he was attacking me. He kept clawing me, and he wouldn't stop."

It took nearly a half hour of gently rocking her before she was willing to try to go back to sleep. And even then, she insisted a small light be left on in the room. Just before he left, a thought struck Davis like a blow to the gut.

"I wasn't a Christian at the time," he said later, "but I felt even then that the Lord was forcing me to realize what I'd done." Turning to his daughter, he asked, "Honey, was the bear in your dreams Daddy?"

The nodding of her little head told him all he needed to know. He hugged her and asked her forgiveness for being so harsh with her.

Ex-Sergeant Davis, today Dr. Davis, later told us that night was a watershed event in his life. It would change the way he related not only to Margie, but also to each of the children who came later.

"As I reached the door and looked back on my daughter lying in bed," he said, "I couldn't believe what I'd done. I made a decision right then that I would never, ever, be harsh with my daughter like that. I would never make her feel like I was a bear again."

That decision became an emotional freeze point. The picture of his daughter, sitting up in bed and screaming in fear, was so vivid to him over the years that it pushed him far to the soft side of love. And while that was a positive outcome in many ways, it also had its drawbacks. By blocking off the hard side of love, he also pushed nearly all the discipline responsibilities onto his wife.

Dr. Davis isn't alone. Over the years, we've spoken with a number of people who have experienced an event or season that blocked them from expressing love's hard side. I (Gary) have also seen it in my own family.

I'm the last of five children, and just before I came along, my mother went through such a freeze point. I had an older sister named Lorna, who was five at the time. As my mother later told the story, Lorna had done something wrong and had been disciplined for it, including my mother's giving her a swat with a kitchen spoon.

While my mother didn't know it at the time, several days before, Lorna had picked up a splinter in her arm while playing outside. It was already sore, but soon an infection set in. And without the powerful antibiotics we have today, the infection spread too quickly for the doctors to catch, and Lorna died in my mother's arms.

The spanking had played no part in my sister's death, but never again would my mother discipline any of us children, nor would she let my father. She was devastated by losing her daughter, and the memory of her spanking Lorna just before she got so sick added a layer of guilt to the terrible pain.

I don't blame my mother for not being able to show this side of love. But I do know that the lack of discipline in my home affected me in several ways. For example, I had difficulty accepting rules for a long time because I never had to follow them at home. And it wasn't just me. I saw it affect my brothers, and especially my sister, in a negative way as well.

For many of us, however, our natural softside bent wasn't pushed to an extreme by something in the past; it's just always been there. We were the ones to take chicken soup to the sick or to be called for a favor in the middle of the night. If that description fits you, the next method of adding hardness will be important for you to see.

2. Allow a short time of distance to build a season of closeness.

In Chapter 8 (p. 495), we included a survey to help you see how close or distant you tend to be in your important relationships. Take a moment to review your results. Scoring high on the closeness scale can signal a very positive relationship. But it may also point out a possible problem when it comes to expressing the hard side of love.

By nature, otters and golden retrievers tend to be very strong at building relationships. But if those close relationships develop problems, they're apt to explain them away, "give them more time to work out," or try to ignore what's wrong altogether. Why? It's a classic case of people's strengths being pushed to an extreme and becoming their greatest weaknesses.

Time and again in this book, we've encouraged you to be hard on problems and soft on people. For many otters and golden retrievers, however, there's a basic problem in doing that. *They get so close to people that they can't separate the person from the problem. So they begin to equate legitimate correction with personal rejection.*

I (John) have certainly experienced this. My family was very close as I was growing up. However, in many ways, we were so close that I never learned to separate what people did from who they were. The focus was so much on personal acceptance (who we were, not what we did) that to attack a problem was to attack the person. And that inability to accept healthy correction proved to be a problem later on.

> ## The most insecure people are those who can't distance themselves from their loved ones far enough to discipline them.

After I married Cindy and our daughter was born, I found myself repeating the patterns I'd experienced at home. Much of what I passed on was good. But I also struggled with disciplining our daughter because somehow, deep inside, it felt as if correcting her was a way of saying I didn't accept or love her.

Thankfully, Cindy is a beautiful example of the balance I didn't grow up with. She loves Kari deeply, but she doesn't confuse disapproving of her actions with not accepting her as a person. She can be firm and put limits on her behavior, because she has enough emotional distance to separate the person from the problem.

That's one reason Kari loves Cindy so much and a large part of why she was an outstanding teacher for a number of years. Her students always knew they were deeply loved, but they also knew the rules. And they knew she was strong enough to keep them, even if that meant that for a short time there was some distance in the relationship.

The most insecure people are those who can't distance themselves from their loved ones far enough to discipline them. They fear that if they confront a child or spouse, they'll lose the relationship, or at least the *feelings* that go with it. Even if it's only for a short time and for the other person's good, they think confronting the person will be like pulling the rug out from under their relationship.

Actually, their fear is justified. As the Scriptures say, no child likes to be disciplined. After correction, there normally is a period of emotional distance between the parent and child. That's what makes it particularly hard for golden retrievers to confront. They can't stand being separated from their loved ones emotionally, even if it's only for a short time. But genuine love recognizes that not to lance a boil or give children the medicine they need—even if they don't want it or like us for it—isn't really loving at all.

Loving discipline may put an emotional distance between people for a few hours or, as in Steve's case, a few months. It's only natural and shouldn't be feared. If we balance that hardside correction with softness, we won't lose love. If anything, we'll enrich it.

Thus far, we've looked at two ways to increase hardside love. Now let's look at a third—learning a single word that can go a long way toward strengthening our most-important relationships.

3. Learn to use a word that can save your relationships.

It's hard to imagine the incredible power of a single word. We've seen people take or lose control of their lives simply by saying or failing to say this one hardside word: *no.* It's one of the first words we learn as children, and most of us become experts at using it repeatedly by the time we're two. But sometime between age two and our twenties, many of us lose the ability to say it.

Golden retrievers and otters have particular difficulty saying no. It's almost as if they have a genetic defect that doesn't allow their tongues to move away from the top of their mouths to complete the word. Instead, they start to say no, but it comes out, "Nnn—oh, okay."

We all know people who struggle with saying no. There's the loving mother who has to make at least one trip to the high school each day to bring her son something he's forgotten: his football jersey, his tennis shoes or his lunch. She understands she should say no to a senior who ought to be learning to be responsible for himself, but she just can't do it.

Then there's the person who can't say no to another volunteer job, even if it means missing time with the family, and the pastor who adds "just one more counseling session" to his packed schedule because he's called to the ministry, after all.

It's helpful to realize that Jesus said no. He said no when asked to come heal Lazarus. Instead, He waited right where He was for three days, and Lazarus died. Jesus said no to being crowned king by the mob, knowing His reign on earth would be at His next coming. He said no to His disciples when they asked to sit at His right hand, and He said no to His accusers when they baited Him to answer their unjust charges. Jesus said no often, and He had good reasons for doing so.

Of course, that doesn't mean we should say no to everything. If we really believe something is important, we may need to say yes, even if it costs us time and effort. But there are at least five reasons we should be able to say no, as Christ did, and draw on the hard side of love to do so.

Failing to say no can allow unwanted attitudes to take root in our homes. We hate to say it, but some parents in particular should be charged with contributing to the delinquency of a minor. By failing to say no to their children, they're building a learned helplessness and, to some degree, a level of irresponsibility within their kids.

Children are smart. If Mom or Dad will do it for them, why should they pick up their rooms, do their homework for themselves, learn to save money instead of spending it, or practice other responsibilities they'll need later in life? It's difficult to say no to kids and have them accept the consequences of their actions. But at times, they need the hard side of love to help them build positive habits and avoid negative ones.

Failing to say no can keep us from doing what's really important. Time and again, we've seen people who can't say no to what's important to someone else, and they end up sacrificing what's really important in their own homes.

Take Mark, for example. His otter need to be liked by others at work meant he spent a good deal of time helping them with their jobs. He took on so many tasks that should have been on other people's desks, never refusing a request, that he couldn't get to all that was on his own. He often had to take his work home just to stay caught up, robbing him of time that should have been reserved for his family.

People who can't say no usually get so caught up in the urgent needs of other people that they miss out on what's really important in their own lives—things like quiet times, time with their children and meeting household responsibilities.

Failing to say no can allow tension and resentment to build up. Doris was a new teacher, and for nearly a year, her "initiation" consisted of having her principal give her all the jobs nobody wanted. Feeling she had no say in the matter, she accepted the extra lunch, playground and bus duties that were laid on her. But while she took each additional assignment with hardly a word, inside she was screaming at herself and him and feeling used.

Finally, near the end of the school year, she blew up in the principal's office when he added yet another assignment. "Doris," he said with surprise written all over his face, "if you're overloaded, all you had to do was tell me. I'll get someone else to do it."

As a loyal golden retriever she thought saying no to her principal would be a personal affront to him. If she hadn't cared so much for the school and her job, it might have been easier to say no. But her natural depth of involvement made her accept anything handed to her until she finally reached the breaking point. It also made her so resentful toward her principal that it affected her sleep, her diet and her attitude toward work. Yet all the time she was carrying around such a burden, she never once expressed those feelings until she nearly snapped.

People who hold in their frustration and fail to be hard with others when it's needed pay a price—in some cases, much too high a price.

When I (Gary) was on the staff of a large organization several years ago, I supervised a man I'll call Dennis. He was an expert in his field, but he was just as much an expert at avoiding any kind of confrontation. He hated to say no to anyone, and he couldn't bring himself to correct those who worked for him.

Dennis had an employee who spent too much time socializing on the job. This employee was very likable, but he just didn't know when to stop talking and start working. To make matters worse, the head of our organization often saw him stop working and make small talk with anyone who walked by. After a while, it became so irritating to the boss that he brought it to my attention. He asked me to have Dennis, the man's supervisor, address the problem, which meant I had to call in "Never Say No" Dennis.

In a gentle way, I told him about the problem and gave him some suggestions for handling it. On several occasions when I brought it up again, he assured me he'd take care of it. But he never did.

Failing to say no can cut meaningful communication in half.

I tried everything I knew to help him deal with his fear of confronting this employee. We talked, we role-played, I encouraged, he promised, and still nothing ever happened. He just couldn't face the situation and say, "No, you can't take a break whenever someone walks by." This became such a major issue that it put his manager's job in jeopardy and subjected him to incredible stress.

As it turned out, Dennis developed serious health problems that were stress-related, according to his doctor. He soon retired, and he died as a result of those complications only a few years later. I'm sure Dennis wasn't aware at the time of the high price he was paying for failing to deal with problems. When he finally found out that bottling his fear and frustration inside was unhealthy, it was too late.

One of the biggest hurdles a softside person faces is being willing to confront others and say no. In fact, a number of top-notch Christian counselors have told us that *it's much easier to get a hardside person to become softer than it is to get a softside person to become harder.* It's almost as if there's an emotional trip switch that shuts down a softside person's attempts to confront, and especially to say no.

Failing to say no can cut meaningful communication in half. As Dennis's case shows, when people refuse to face a difficult situation (like telling a person no), they shut off the important discussion that can go with voicing their real feelings.

One reason people have difficulty saying no is that it begs questions in return. For example, if you tell your teenage daughter, "No, you can't go to that movie," what will you instantly hear? "But why, Mother? Everyone else is going."

What we often don't realize is that by not saying no, we miss some of the most important teaching times we'll ever have with others. We may avoid a heated discussion today, but we also lose the opportunity to say something that may affect the rest of their lives.

Not long ago, I (Gary) found it necessary to say no to one of our employees. He's so good at his job that other ministries and companies kept asking him to do work for them. Soon his talent was being used more for outside projects than for those within our organization, Today's Family.

As an otter, I like positive, friendly relationships, which is a nice way of saying I don't like to tell people no. I put off confronting him about what was happening for several months, thinking he'd see the problem himself or that the requests would just stop coming in. But he never did and they never stopped, and all the time I was growing more resentful.

While I don't struggle in being hard with my spouse and children, at the office I tend to be too soft with others. Finally, I realized *I* was the one paying the emotional price for not confronting him, and I brought him into my office and explained my concerns.

We had such a positive meeting that I couldn't believe I had been avoiding the conversation for months. He instantly saw the problem when I pointed it out and cut back nearly 100 percent on outside projects while we were so swamped with our own. By being willing to enter into a hardside discussion, I not only unloaded a ton of personal stress, but I also gained back a valuable employee.

Failing to say no can keep others and ourselves from the truth. Most of us are familiar with a term that current TV talk shows and self-help books have popularized: *codependency*. This word describes the way Martha learned to live with her alcoholic husband.

Martha was a perfect grandmother type: always there for the children, always ready to babysit their kids when they came along. Her only problem was that she was always making excuses for her husband's behavior.

Don was an alcoholic who maintained his job but who also put away several six-packs each night, and more on the weekend. If softside love alone could change a person, Martha's love would have changed Don. But it didn't. And as the years passed and his drinking became more of a problem, she found herself becoming an expert at uttering white lies.

She would tell her children about the "business that came up" so that their father couldn't make the family reunion; or that he "came down with something" and would have to drop by to see the new baby another day.

The only one Martha was fooling was herself, but the children pretended she was fooling them, too. It's not that Martha liked being a liar. But her out-of-balance softside love made protecting her husband and keeping peace in the family seem more important than the truth.

We've heard softside people say, "Sure, I'd like to go to that movie," when they really don't want to and know they shouldn't. We've seen others excuse a friend's behavior by saying, "Oh, he'll pay me back. He just needs a little more time." And much too often, we've seen people like Martha who, in the interest of protecting a husband, effectively prevented a cure.

These people don't think of themselves as liars, but their failure to give both sides of love to people who need both makes them so. The Gospel of John contains a verse that sounds soft and easy but can actually be very hard: "You will know the truth, and the truth will set you free."[1] Unfortunately, many people are missing the freedom of walking in the truth. They're afraid of exercising the kind of love that can face a problem, because they're afraid of saying, "No, this is wrong, and I need to deal with it."

We think we've made our case for the need to utter this small but incredibly important hardside word that can do so much to strengthen relationships. But how do you get a golden retriever to become more of a watchdog, or an otter to gain the strength of a lion?

Certainly it begins by practicing saying no. Dr. Howard Hendricks, a noted Christian educator and one of my (John's) seminary professors, had seen my natural otter bent toward pleasing people. And in a discipleship class I had with him, he gave me this excellent advice: "John, practice saying no to at least one thing a day. Even if it's just refusing a second piece of pie, get in a habit that can help you the rest of your life!"

So far, we've looked at three methods for adding hardside love to our lives. In the next chapter, we'll look at seven more ways, beginning with one that addresses perhaps the most common struggle of softsided people.

11
Adding Hardside Love in a Healthy Way

Part II

TIM KNEW HE was in deep trouble. Marcy wasn't just talking about leaving this time, she was doing something. The voice of a divorce attorney on their answering machine, returning her call, didn't change into harmless chatter no matter how many times he replayed the message. Sadly, it was an inability to tap into the hard side of love that had brought Tim to the brink of divorce.

Marcy had been attracted to his sensitive heart right off in high school, and they had married within a year of graduation. But as time went by, his softness became less and less appealing, particularly because whenever real problems came up, he lacked the strength to face them.

Tim bounced from job to job, always working beneath his abilities and bringing in far less than their needs. He was great at starting a new job, but he couldn't stay with one once it became routine. Marcy didn't mind working. But soon it was apparent that if she didn't work, even after the children came along, they wouldn't eat.

With each job change, Tim's self-confidence inched downward and his weight upward. Always he sought for some new thing, some opportunity that would instantly lift him out of his predicament. The state lottery drawing was always a high point in his week. He just knew that one day he would win the jackpot, and everything would change—even though his chances of winning were less than those of being hit twice by lightning.

That "something" he looked for to bail him out of having to change never came. And after nearly twenty years of marriage, they had finally reached rock bottom. Marcy had become so frustrated waiting for him to take the first step toward self-confidence and a decent job that she was ready to take the last step in contacting a lawyer.

Why could Tim, like so many people, see clearly what he needed to do, yet that first step seemed a mile high? Why couldn't he become more self-disciplined and spiritually strong, adding the hard side of love to his natural softness?

Tim was facing one of the greatest barriers to making needed inner adjustments. Whether the need is to take on the strength of hardside love or to become softer, the future of our relationships could well depend on our ability to make those changes. Yet it often seems as if a pair of giant arms holds us back until the opportunity for change has passed us by.

> ## When pushed to an extreme,
> as easily happens, procrastination has the power
> to put people out of work, freeze them in sin,
> and confine them to frustration
> and hopelessness.

That major barrier to change can be summed up in one word, *procrastination.* Overcoming it is the fourth way to add a healthy hardness to our lives. It may sound like an innocent problem on the surface. We all procrastinate at times, don't we? But when pushed to an extreme, as easily happens, procrastination has the power to put people out of work, freeze them in sin, and confine them to frustration and hopelessness.

That's why we can't afford to put off looking at the giant that procrastination can become. And while it certainly can strike a lion or beaver, softside people are particularly vulnerable to it. We'll look at procrastination from three different angles and see three practical ways to overcome it.

Take it from two authors who have spent years in personal research on procrastination and who put off working on this chapter until the last: learning to defeat this giant can go a long way toward enriching our relationships. And take it from Tim: if he could learn to defeat this problem—which he did—you can, too.

4. Face the heart of procrastination.

How would you like to wear the title "World's Greatest Procrastinator"? No, it's not a title your spouse can win! It doesn't even go to those men whose names were on the front page of our local newspaper recently, the ten worst procrastinators in the entire city when it comes to paying child support.

Those men may grab an unfavorable limelight for a short time. But that's nothing compared to the most publicized procrastinator in history, Felix. He was a Roman governor, and since his story is recorded in the world's best-selling book, the Bible, he's history's best-known procrastinator. We can learn a lot about the problem by looking at his experience in the book of Acts.

The apostle Paul had been captured by the Jewish leaders of his day and brought before Felix. They wanted Paul put to death, but Felix was interested in hearing what this man had to say, so he had him brought before him. "As Paul discoursed on righteousness, self-control and the judgment to come, Felix was afraid and said, 'That's enough for now! You may leave. When I find it convenient, I will send for you.'"[1]

Paul's words brought the conviction that Felix needed to change certain areas in his life. But then as now, *conviction only points out the changes we need to make. It doesn't make them for us.* And something short-circuited the change process. Did you notice it in the Scripture? After hearing about righteousness, self-control and the judgment to come, Felix *became frightened.*

The four-letter word that lies at the heart of procrastination is *fear.* And whenever we put off needed inner changes, at least six types of fear can be holding us back.

The first of these is *fear of discipline.* Tim feared becoming disciplined more than he feared doing nothing. He didn't want to hear about the need for self-control, because he knew it meant saying no to appetites he didn't want to stop feeding. That's true for many people who "can't" exercise, read the Scriptures, share their faith, or confront a problem person or situation. They fear becoming rigid or too rule-conscious, so they avoid the hardside discipline that can actually give them rest.

A second fear causing procrastination is *fear of failure.* For some people, the possibility of failure is so threatening that they never begin a project or try to make changes. This is particularly true of those who tend to be perfectionists. As far as they're concerned, it's better to do nothing and not face the risk of failure than to try and fall short. That was part of Tim's problem. While he looked and acted unkempt and unorganized, he actually scored high on the beaver scale. But he didn't want to try for a really good job and be found lacking.

A third fear that holds people back is the *fear of success.* Some people fear changing because success would put them in the spotlight, and they want to stay on the sidelines. Others are plagued by guilt or feelings of inferiority and think they don't deserve success. They find ways to explain or push it away even if it does come to them.

Still others fear that success will bring rejection. We know a bright young woman who won a scholarship to attend a local college. Yet after two semesters, she had stopped attending classes and flunked out. Why? She was the only one from her family to go to college. Deep inside, she feared that each step she took toward academic success was another step away from her loved ones.

Others fear success because they think that once a level of achievement is reached, it will mean there's another peak, just a little higher, that they'll have to climb next. And some fear success because they know that finally achieving a long-sought goal could leave them feeling empty and without purpose.

A few years ago, we were asked to counsel with an extremely successful person who had just won his industry's highest honor. Instead of thrilling him, it sent him into a deep depression. He had lived for this prize, but like living for anything less than the Source of life, once he had it, he was left empty and miserable inside.

A fourth fear leading to procrastination is *fear of finding out our limitations.* Procrastination allows people to take comfort in believing their ability is greater than their performance. It's more tolerable to blame themselves for being disorganized or lazy than to feel that they're inadequate or unworthy. Tim would have made an excellent support person or second-in-command. But he kept trying and failing to get the top spot with a company instead of admitting his skills lay in production, not management.

A fifth fear causing procrastination is *fear of commitment.* We spoke once with a man who didn't want help. He was a terrible husband and father, and perhaps the only positive thing we could say about him was that he was honest about why he was leaving his wife and children.

"Frankly, I *know* what it takes to have a strong family," he said, "and I'm not willing to pay that price." He knew that a commitment to his family would mostly take *time* for his wife and kids. And he was so totally consumed with career and financial success that he feared what such a commitment would cost him in dollars more than he feared losing his family.

The sixth fear is *fear of being controlled.* For Felix, and for anyone who procrastinates in response to spiritual challenges, this last form of fear is often the first in line. Many people rightly sense the loss of control that comes with putting themselves totally in God's hands.

And if the fear is strong enough, when God knocks on the door of their hearts, they slam it shut.

When we become frightened and put off changing, usually there's a moral problem we're struggling with, not an intellectual one. It's not that we don't understand what God is asking us to do, it's that we *do* understand. We just don't want to turn away from what we're pursuing and go in His direction. Felix wanted to hear about Jesus, but he didn't want Him to get close enough to change him. Tim rarely missed a Sunday morning at church, but he knew in his heart that his greatest fear was of giving himself totally to the Lord.

As you can see, two or more of these six types of fear can easily combine to block a person's ability to make needed changes—something we should know from reading the Bible. "Perfect love drives out fear" is a familiar statement from 1 John 4:18. But the reverse is true as well. Those who allow fear to control their lives actually become less and less loving.

What do we do when we realize we're putting off becoming more tough or tender?

The first thing is to face the fear. Pick an area you're procrastinating in right now. Perhaps you're a lion and you need to become more of a golden retriever with your children—more supportive of them and less demanding. Or you may be an otter who has started a hundred projects this year, but you need to add enough beaver qualities to finish some of them and save your job in the process. Perhaps you're a retriever like Tim who needs to stay put in one job rather than making monthly changes.

What's holding you back from making those changes? The first thing is undoubtedly fear. And facing which type of fear has a hold on you can be the first step in defeating it. What's the next step? It's actually the fifth in our series of ten steps toward adding healthy hardness to your life.

5. Avoid the trap of relying on instant change.

If fear is the fuel that causes us to put off needed changes, the hope of instant, easy change adds a turbocharger to the problem. Nearly every day, something or someone would convict Tim that he needed to become more assertive, more forceful, more consistent, more disciplined, more of a spiritual leader—all hardside traits. But he was never moved to action. Yet in the hope of instantly getting enough money to cover up his need for change, he couldn't buy lottery tickets fast enough. Likewise, codependent Marsha held on to the dream that one day her husband would wake up cured of his alcoholism instead of in a drunken stupor.

The problem with basing your life on such a dream is that one day you'll have to wake up—guaranteed. At any time during his twenty years of marriage, Tim could have taken a steady job and earned those things he wanted for Marcy one by one. But it was easier to hold on to the dream that one lottery ticket, one marketing scheme, one *something* would turn everything around—until his dream shattered when he heard the divorce lawyer's message on the answering machine.

We wish there were an easy way to change, but any hardside or softside trait we need to add will only make its way into our lives the old-fashioned way—by earning it in daily persistence.

Experts say it takes at least twenty-one days of repeating something before it becomes a habit. We don't just wake up one morning with a newfound ability to correct our children lovingly, stand up to a spouse, or confront a friend. These hardside skills come through the toughness of character that cements them, one by one, into the center of our lives. And a great way to start that process is with the next concept.

6. Allow yourself to become accountable to others.

When Cindy and I (John) were first married, I scored near the top in the otter scale and near the bottom everywhere else. My graph looked like an EKG chart with one spike. That meant I was basically friendly, funloving, soft on people—and much too soft on responsibilities like balancing our checkbook.

During the first years of our marriage, I took procrastination to new heights (or depths) as month after month I put off balancing our checkbook until the very last minute. Forget the fact that I was married to a beaver who could probably run her own accounting firm. I was the "Big Kahuna" of this family, and I wasn't about to let a few bounced checks stop me from my unsuccessful but easy method of accounting.

My method was similar to the one described by our good friends Chuck and Barb Snyder in their extremely helpful book *Incompatibility: Ground for a Great Marriage* (Questar, 1988). This (thankfully) little-used accounting procedure is to wait until the bank statement comes in and then simply cross off the balance in your checkbook, write in their balance, close your checkbook, and you're finished! (After all, the people at the bank have been to business school and have computers!)

Where this approach will lead you (besides the poorhouse) is into doing what I did regularly: change banks. That way I finally knew, at least for a short time, exactly what our balance was.

As you can imagine, my fiscal irresponsibility was causing great stress for my wife. And unfortunately, I couldn't print new money to get out of my problems the way our government does.

I'm happy to say I eventually stopped procrastinating in this area, and what made it possible is the most powerful method we know of defeating the problem: accountability. We've looked in the Scriptures and through every book we could find on the subject, and we've concluded that loving accountability is God's *primary* tool to stop a person from procrastinating and start making needed hardside or softside changes. Watch how it happened in my life.

Loving accountability is God's *primary* tool to stop a person from procrastinating and start making needed changes.

When we moved to Arizona from Texas, I joined a small group of men in an accountability group at our church. The group had three otters in it, including me, and one beaver, a man named Doug Childress.

When we started the group, we otters would all say the same thing about our spiritual and family lives: How was it going that week? Great! After a few weeks of the three otters meeting and high-fiving each other at breakfast over what a great job we were doing, Doug decided to do something beavers do best: inspect things.

I'll never forget the first night Doug called the house and asked to speak to—Cindy. That's when he asked her, "How's John doing as a husband and father?" and "Are there any areas he needs to work on that I could help hold him accountable for?"

You can imagine how much trouble I got in after that first call. But it wouldn't be the last. Doug was lovingly committed to me as a friend, so much so that he held me accountable week after week. And soon, in spite of myself, I found myself adding more beaver characteristics to my life—like balancing the checkbook the right way and seeing my relationship with Cindy improve as a result. I even started calling his wife, Judie, and asking how *he* was doing as a husband.

Is there someone who can be a Doug Childress to you, someone who can ask the hard questions, not to hurt you, but to help and encourage you? Remember, only the wise seek accountability, while fools resist correction. No one enjoys having a friend point out a weakness, but if it's done in a loving way for our best, even the strong arms of procrastination will begin to weaken. We all need someone who, "as iron sharpens iron,"[2] can chip away at the rough edges of our lives.

Dealing with procrastination isn't the only way of adding important hardside traits to our lives. The seventh method we'll look at taps into the natural strength of an otter and golden retriever to pave the way for our loved ones to accept our being hardside with them.

7. Build relational bridges to carry hardside words.

Otters and golden retrievers are great at building relational bridges. They enjoy closeness with others and can in no time build a secure environment of warmth and mutual respect. That skill is crucial to expressing the hard side of love to others. As a familiar Bible verse points out, "Faithful are the wounds of a friend, but deceitful are the kisses of an enemy."[3]

Have you ever met people who are so hard that they think this verse means wounding you *makes* them your friend? That's not what it means. Rather, it's in getting close to others that we can say the most difficult things and have them be taken in a faithful, loving way.

We can't encourage you enough to form strong, intimate relationships by using all the nurturing skills of the soft side of love. For in doing this, you'll be building the strongest bridge to carry loving hardside words when they need to be said. Lions and beavers especially need to work at this. And without question, the best way we know to convey hardside messages softly is to use word pictures. That's why we wrote an entire book explaining how they work (*The Language of Love*).

Otters and golden retrievers need to understand something important as well, however. Once those bridges of friendship have been built, we need to cross them when it's called for. Let us illustrate what we mean.

Shortly after I (John) graduated from seminary and had taken my first job as an assistant pastor, I was asked to do premarital counseling with a young couple. They were sure they were meant for each other, and they wanted me to perform their wedding. After meeting with them four times, I was sure I was being conned They may have felt ready for marriage, but they were immature and had serious personal problems. As I found out later, they were also practicing immorality in spite of assuring me they weren't.

But her father was a long-standing member of the church, the invitations had already been sent out, and the church had been reserved. So, to my shame, I let the pressure of the moment set aside my concerns about performing the service. I should have told the couple, "No, I can't do the wedding, and you shouldn't find anyone else to do it, either, until much time and counseling have passed." Only I didn't.

In our counseling sessions, I had definitely built a bridge of friendship and respect with this couple. But when it came to expressing the hard side of love as I needed to, I never crossed that bridge. And less than a year later, I learned from her father one Sunday morning that they were getting a divorce.

Pastors are not infallible, and it was, after all, the first couple I'd ever counseled. But I knew in my heart that those were just excuses for failing to be lovingly hard.

I learned a great deal from that experience. I still use my softside bent to build bridges with the many couples I counsel in the premarital class at our church. But I now force myself to cross the bridge and say the hard things I need to, even if it's, "I'm sorry, but you shouldn't get married."

8. Break hardside changes down into bite-size steps.

Debbie was the frustrated mother of a junior higher. She knew she needed to be more hardside with her daughter in several areas. But as a golden retriever, she had never been hard with anyone before.

We helped Debbie break down into concrete steps the changes she wanted to see in her daughter. First we asked her to pick one area where she felt she needed to be more hardside with her child. Instantly, she said she was tired of having the house look as if a tornado had hit it every time her daughter came home from school.

Next we asked Debbie to write down just what her daughter did before and after school that frustrated her in this area. After a week of keeping notes, she brought in a list of almost thirty things. We boiled that down to three things she really wanted the girl to do when she hit the door: take her books and clothes to her room; clean up any dishes or utensils she used when she had a snack; and keep the stereo below ear-piercing level.

At that point, it wouldn't have worked simply to tell Debbie, "Now be more hardside with your daughter about these things." Instead, all three of them were put into a written family contract such as we discussed earlier. It took some time and encouragement for both Debbie and her daughter to get used to this new system—and accountability in our counseling sessions—but soon softside Debbie was pointing to the consequences they'd written down instead of pulling out her hair. By breaking her hardside request into small steps, she was able to solve the problem with her feelings—and their relationship—intact.

9. Strengthen your spiritual confidence.

In the next chapter, we'll talk about the tremendous benefits of modeling our love after that of our Savior. Yet we want to make it clear in this chapter that being confident of what God has said in His Word is a powerful aid in expressing love's hard side.

Remember Steve, the golden retriever father whose story began our look at adding hardside love? What gave him the strength to be lovingly tough with his daughter was the confidence that what he was doing was right in God's eyes.

The more clearly we understand our God and His purpose for our lives, the easier it will be to provide whichever side of love our families need. Put another way, the more secure and satisfied we are with Christ as our provider and source of life, the stronger we can be in helping others be all God wants for them.

Where do we get such a confidence level? By studying the Scriptures first, and then any number of devotional and thought-provoking books that can help us deepen our spiritual walk. We especially like the work of authors such as Max Lucado, Ken Gire and Charles Swindoll.[4]

We've now seen nine ways of adding a healthy hardness to our love:

1. Spot emotional freeze points from the past.
2. Allow a short time of distance to build a season of closeness.
3. Learn to say no.
4. Confront what's at the heart of procrastination.
5. Avoid the trap of relying on instant change.
6. Become accountable in love.
7. Build relational bridges to carry hardside words.
8. Break hardside love into steps.
9. Build spiritual confidence.

All are important. And all lead to the tenth.

10. Set a lifetime goal of giving hardside love when it's needed.

Is it time you added more of this side of love to your relationships? It's easy to think of a hundred reasons why you shouldn't start today. But all those excuses may leave you with an empty life.

A current television commercial shows a close-up of a father talking to his son about the dangers of drugs. Suddenly the father breaks into tears and says, "Only, I didn't know I'd need to tell you all this when you were thirteen." Then the camera pans back and shows that the father is speaking to a grave in a lonely, windswept cemetery.

It's not just the fear of what drugs can do to our children that should prompt us to be lovingly hard with them, however. It's a side of love that needs to be part of all our lives. The writer of Hebrews tells us, "The Lord disciplines those he loves."[5] We need a healthy balance of love's hard and soft sides if we're to reflect the love of our heavenly Father.

By now, you should have a list of things you want to do to make your love more balanced. But you need to realize only one consistent power source can enable you to do those things as the years go by. We'll look at that in the last chapter.

12
The Secret to Wholehearted Love

W E'D LIKE TO say that loving others wholeheartedly is always easy. Unfortunately, it isn't. Sara learned that firsthand. She had to endure trials that most people will never face. Yet she discovered that even in the midst of incredible obstacles, there's an unending, unchanging power source that can sustain and enrich our love.

Sara was thrilled that the handsome young man was to be her husband. He was strong and energetic. And from the moment she met him, she was captivated. They enjoyed many blessings together in those early years, living in the beautiful countryside near their hometown of Rivas, Nicaragua.

First a son was born to Sara and Jose Angel Melendez. Sara would quietly rock her firstborn on the porch and read her Bible or a novel, enjoying the pleasures and challenges of a growing family. Soon she was pregnant with their second baby, and her heart was filled with an ocean of expectations. In a culture full of "religion," she came from a family that emphasized a personal relationship with Christ.

When early signs of her pregnancy were confused with flu symptoms, her uncle, a local physician, prescribed a new drug from West Germany to ease her discomfort. It was called thalidomide.

Unaware of the drug's drastic side effects, the Melendezes were unprepared for what they saw at the time of delivery. Little Tony, their new baby, was born with no arms.

While the doctors and nurses looked after Tony, his parents retreated to the recovery room, devastated. Sara looked for strength to deal with what had happened, and she found it when her mother arrived. The moment she entered the room, she wiped the tears from her daughter's eyes and said, "This is no time for crying. God has sent us this baby. And God knows what he's doing."

From that moment on, Sara found strength in her mother's faith. Her heart softened toward her new boy, so much so that she could pick him up tenderly and say, "Jose Antonio Melendez Rodriguez, . . . you are a beautiful baby. God has given you so much. You have a wonderful face with dark-brown eyes, a cute little nose, pouty lips, and two tiny, perfect ears. . . . You are almost perfect, Antonio. . . . You have . . . a strong, proud neck, broad shoulders, a wonderful chest. . . . You have all the working parts you need to become a strong, beautiful man. God has great dreams for you, . . . and he and I together will see that all those dreams come true."

As the years went by, Tony would learn the incredible softside love his mother brought to the family. Her constant prayers and supportive words ("Don't worry. God has something wonderful in mind for you. Trust him and he will take care of you.") were the guiding force in his life. But Tony also saw her model hardside love at a time when he and the rest of his family most needed it.

After Tony's birth, his father sacrificed greatly to make sure his son received everything he needed. Part of what he needed was medical attention unavailable in his homeland, so Jose moved the family from the comfortable, almost wealthy life they knew in Nicaragua to a dirty, run-down Los Angeles apartment.

Providing for his family meant trading his well-paying profession for dirty, meager jobs at less than minimum wage. It was always Jose's dream, though, to return to Nicaragua, to the life he knew and the land he loved, and raise his family there. The hope of that return sustained him through the indignities he faced as an immigrant trying to provide for his family. And provide he did.

Tony received every bit of attention and help he needed: surgery to correct a clubbed foot so he could walk, and the best education and physical therapy Jose could provide. Tony blossomed, developing his skills as an artist, musician, athlete and student. He even learned to play his father's guitar beautifully using his feet.

But as the years wore on, the father's dreams faded. He couldn't stand the thought of never being able to return to Nicaragua, and he couldn't bear up under the personal pressure he was putting on himself. In a vain attempt at escape, he started drinking.

By the time Tony was a teenager, alcohol had driven his father into a deteriorating pattern of anger and abuse. The situation was so bad that even their closest family friends suggested Sara take her children and leave. Jose was in a rapid tailspin and refused help, and it looked as if he would destroy the family as he went down.

Yet when times got tough, Sara drew on the hard side of love, which is consistent, determined and disciplined. Of his mother's dedication to his father, Tony would later write, "She refused to abandon the man she loved." She told Tony, "[H]e gave up everything he wanted for his own life in hopes of making our lives better. . . . He struggled against his illness, but it conquered him; and in his time of weakness I just couldn't walk away."

Jose Melendez died on May 24, 1983, of cirrhosis of the liver. He was an alcoholic, but he wasn't abandoned. His family was still together, and his son was still accomplishing things no one could have dreamed. In fact, Tony Melendez played the guitar with his feet for Pope John Paul II during the Pope's 1987 North American tour.[1]

Why Aren't Self-Help Books Ever Enough?

Where does love like Sara Melendez's come from? You may have seen already that it's going to take some real effort to provide the softness others need from you, or especially to become harder in a healthy way. Can't we just make a simple self-help decision and grab hold of the changes we need? For a short time, perhaps, but not for a lifetime.

Depending on our own power to give the two sides of love is like trying to push a car down the street instead of using its engine. We may be able to go a short distance, but each step further drains our energy and invites frustration.

Is there a better way? The truth is, there's only one way, one source of power to truly change our lives for good and maintain those changes for a lifetime. We begin to find it by focusing on a rugged hill outside a walled city. For on that hill stands the hardest—and softest—thing on earth.

> Depending on our own power to give
> the two sides of love is like trying to push a car
> down the street instead of using its engine.

On a Hill Far Away

There was a day when both time and eternity met. It happened during six hours on a Friday when the sky darkened, the wind howled, and angels wept. Nearly two thousand years ago, on a barren hilltop called Golgotha, the Son of God was crucified.

Christ's death on the cross was both the hardest and softest event in all of history. The cross represents the harshest judgment of sin— *our sin*—imaginable. Nothing could be harder than when God the Father turned His face away from His only Son and the sinless, spotless Lamb of God was scourged, mocked and nailed to a tree to die in our place.

But the cross is also a picture of the softest of all loves. That love was willing to forgive those who drove in the nails, who spit on Him and hit Him with sticks, and who refused to admit that they were killing the rightful King and Lord of glory. That love is the most important thing we'll ever know or experience.

Sara Melendez knew how to be hardside and softside with those she loved, but her strength to do so came from understanding and experiencing God's love.

A God of Balance, a God of Love

Being balanced between our hard and soft sides means accurately reflecting the character of Christ to the world around us. To do that, we've got to be wholehearted in our love for Him, which gives us the power and perspective we need.

Jesus was once asked, "Teacher, which is the greatest commandment in the Law?"

And He answered, "'Love the Lord your God with all your heart and with all your soul and with all your mind.' This is the first and greatest commandment. And the second is like it: 'Love your neighbor as yourself.' All the Law and the Prophets hang on these two commandments."[2]

Christ certainly knew what He was doing when He joined those two commandments together. The ability to love others is totally dependent on our ability to love Him. The more completely we love Him, the more balanced and complete our love for others will be.

A Man Who Knew

He was the envy of everyone who knew him. Educated in the best schools, he proved himself a worthy student early in life. Not only was he a brilliant scholar who mastered his studies, but he seemed particularly driven to make his knowledge a real part of his life. While others his age frittered away afternoons on boyhood games, this young student absorbed himself in his books. As the years passed, none of his contemporaries could match his zeal for knowledge.

As if that weren't enough, he also came from one of the finest families around. "Bred of good stock," admirers would say. "A fine boy. He's going to do well." His parents provided him with the best of everything. Unfortunately, they also bred into him an arrogant dislike for those things and people that seemed beneath him.

His self-appointed mission in life became the preservation of the heritage his parents left him. In the city where he lived, there were those who threatened to upend his life and culture with a radical philosophy that swept through the country. With the clever arguments of a skilled lawyer, the young crusader challenged any who held this heretical faith. And if they wouldn't listen to his arguments and deny their faith, he could call on the temple guards and a prison sentence or worse to teach them what was "right."

So strong was this man's conviction that one day, he and a group of associates were traveling to another city just to slap down the leaders of this upstart movement. They raced to arrest them—and ran headlong into a supernatural encounter.

> Christ's death on the cross was both the hardest and softest event in all of history.

In a split second of time, the man's entire life changed. In one brilliant flash of light that carried the image and words of the risen Lord, this young persecutor became a servant of the Savior. As they helped the zealot to his feet on that dusty road to Damascus, he was in for a name change—from Saul to Paul—and a lifelong adventure of learning the secret to balanced, wholehearted love for God and others.

Did Paul have a hard side? Absolutely! Of his former life as a persecutor of the church, Luke wrote, "But Saul began to destroy the church. Going from house to house, he dragged off men and women and put them in prison."[3]

But his years in the ministry, like hot steel in a furnace, bent his hard side back into balance. By coming to know God's character and learning how to love people, Paul learned when and how to be hard. And he had many opportunities to apply what he'd learned.

The Corinthian church was a real heartache for Paul. He poured everything he had into the people's lives, and they still lost themselves in divisive arguments, lawsuits against each other, drunkenness at the Lord's table, and tolerating perverted sexual sin in their midst.

Paul was so concerned for their well-being that he planned a personal visit to help straighten them out. First, however, he sent Timothy to try to bring the Corinthians to their senses. He didn't want to be hardside during his visit, but he was prepared to do that if that was best for them.

"Some of you have become arrogant, as if I were not coming to you," he wrote. "But I will come to you very soon, if the Lord is willing, and then I will find out not only how these arrogant people are talking, but what power they have. For the kingdom of God is not a matter of talk but of power. What do you prefer? Shall I come to you with a whip, or in love and with a gentle spirit?"[4]

Paul knew that if he wanted to do what was best for the Corinthians, he had to be willing to rebuke them for their unwillingness to follow Christ's example and teaching. He also knew he wouldn't win any friends doing that, but he was more interested in their relationship with God than he was in winning a popularity contest. He understood hardside love is often the best tool for dealing with sin, and he wasn't afraid to use it.

But God also used the years to breed a gentle softness in Paul. In writing to the Thessalonian church, he once said, "You know we never used flattery, nor did we put on a mask to cover up greed. . . . We were not looking for praise from men. . . . [B]ut we were gentle among you, like a mother caring for her little children."[5] Paul knew the value of tender, compassionate, understanding love. And he knew that one of its values is in encouraging the faith of people who have a sincere love for God.

Where's the Power?

Anyone who has witnessed the launch of the space shuttle knows it's one of the most awesome displays of power you can see. Perched on the launch pad, the shuttle stands eleven stories high and weighs 4.5 million pounds. As the sun creeps over the horizon and splashes its rays across the brilliant blue of an early Florida morning, the shuttle waits there like a silent, white eagle, ready to spring into the heavens.

As the countdown nears, the air grows thick with excitement. Systems are checked and rechecked. More than 143,000 gallons of liquid oxygen, chilled to minus 147 degrees Celsius, have been loaded into the giant external fuel tank. Then mission control gives the go-ahead for the final countdown: "Five, four, three, two, one, SRB ignition!"

For three seconds, 6.5 million pounds of thrust—roughly one-fourth the energy blast that leveled Hiroshima—heave against the combined weight of the shuttle and its tanks and boosters. Then the ivory bird seems to leap off the pad and streak into the sky. It's a sight that is the twentieth century's very definition of power.

For all the genius and technology that go into making the space shuttle, however, it's nothing but a whitewashed can of circuits and microchips without fuel to drive it into space. All that hardware means nothing if there's no power to make it work.

The same thing is true in being balanced with our hard and soft sides. We've come full circle, in a sense, and now we have the information we need to be more wholehearted in our love. But without the power to make it work, all you've got in your hands right now is kindling.

Where does that power come from? From God's Spirit as He takes up residence in our lives when we come to know Christ as Savior. "For God so loved the world [softside] that he gave his one and only Son [hardside], that whoever believes in him shall not perish [hardside] but have eternal life [softside]."[6]

Without God's power found in a personal relationship, a biblical hero like Abraham was a wandering nomad with no future and no family; Moses was a runaway slave with a speech impediment; Samson was another youth hooked on girls and lifting weights; David was another monarch with a wandering eye and no hope for forgiveness; Peter was a mixed-up fisherman who didn't know when to quit; Paul was a radical Pharisee who went off the deep end; and John was a lonely, forgotten old man with crazy dreams.

Making It Work

God's power, found only in that personal relationship with Jesus Christ, makes all the difference. But how do we apply that power in our everyday relationships? What steps can we take to make it active in our lives? We'd like to offer some practical suggestions.

First, admit you need it. Ted Turner was recently quoted as saying, "Christianity is a religion for losers. I don't need anybody to die for me."[7] But while that man may talk tough this side of his day of judgment, he *does* need the Savior, and so do we.

Have you ever acknowledged before God that you can't love others the way you should on your own? Even more important, have you admitted to Him that you can't love Him as you should? Each of us faces God's hard side, but He invites us to accept His soft side of never-ending life with Him.

George Toles is a close friend who helped us in many ways with this book. One of his insights speaks right to this point: Our relationship with God always *begins* with having to face His hard side. Think about it. If we recognize that God judges wrong and that we fall far short of His mark of perfection, we're all faced with judgment. But it is precisely His judging, hardside love that points us, urges us, toward His soft side—the way of escape—our Savior, Jesus Christ.

If you've never admitted your need for the Savior and asked Jesus to come into your life, we invite you to do so. Right now, in the quiet of your heart, you can let Jesus into your life and experience a love that is perfect and redemptive. To do that is to invite in all of God's softside love and to know for certain that His hard side will be exercised only in discipline, not judgment.

Simply go to God in prayer; you can use this as your prayer if you'd like: *Dear Lord, I know I've missed the mark in so many ways. I confess that I've looked at pictures of You on the cross all my life but never understood it was me You died for. I know I deserve only the hard side of Your love for all my sins, but I thank You for the softest, warmest love of all that forgives me and gave Your Son to die for me.*

Lord, I don't want to keep You at arm's length anymore. I humbly ask that You come into my life, cleanse my heart from sin, and live in my heart always as my Lord, my shepherd and my lifelong friend. Jesus, each day and in all my relationships, help me learn to walk worthy of Your high calling and great love. Amen.

Even after accepting Christ as Savior, however, we may still not ex-

544 The Two Sides of Love

perience the power of His Holy Spirit. Why? There's nothing wrong with God's ability to give us His power, but there's often something that causes us to reject or weaken it. Our culture makes that easy to do.

We live in a world that knows little of God and the power He provides through His Spirit. News reports don't begin with stories of how God's power sustained Christians in the latest catastrophe. Headlines don't read, "God's Power Revealed in Latest Congressional Session." No one talks about it, and few are even aware it's there. But it's the one thing we *must* have to be wholehearted in our love.

Christ told His disciples, "I am the vine; you are the branches. If a man remains in me and I in him, he will bear much fruit; apart from me you can do nothing."[8] Without God's power through abiding in His Spirit, we simply can't make the changes needed to be more balanced in our love. That includes maintaining our time in His Word, prayer, and with His people.

Second, confess your inability to live up to God's standards so you can maintain an open relationship with Him. The Bible calls that human inability *sin*, and sin has a way of clouding our vision and distorting our perception of God. Have you ever had a fight with your spouse and then tried to have a meaningful time with God? It doesn't work well, does it? Anger, guilt and sin act like hardening agents to a loving heart, and they also block a fellowship with the Lord.

Paul told the Ephesians, "'In your anger do not sin': Do not let the sun go down while you are still angry, and do not give the devil a foothold."[9] He understood that anger can harden into sin and weaken all our relationships.

It's not popular today to tell people that sin offends God, but it does. Like anger in a marriage, it drives a wedge between us, and between us and God. When we refuse to deal with wrong in our lives, we create an unhealthy distance in both our human and divine relationships. But confessing our sin or admitting how weak we are on our own clears the air with Him and allows us to develop the fellowship we must have to abide in Him, live in His power and genuinely love others.

Finally, take a step of faith, and trust God for the power to change. In seminars and counseling all across the country, we're often asked, "What do I do if I don't love my spouse anymore?" The answer is to *first put love into action, and wait for the feelings to follow.* In other words, don't wait until your feelings change for the better before you do something; take the right kind of action, and eventually your feelings will catch up with your loving deeds.

If you're a golden retriever or otter who needs to add some hardside characteristics, or if you're a lion or beaver who needs to develop a healthy softness, don't wait until you feel God's power and then try to change. There's no faith involved in that. *Start making the right changes, and trust God to supply the power as you need it.*

Corrie ten Boom used to tell how her father taught her what faith means. "When you go to the train station, do you buy your ticket before you get there or after?" he asked.

"After, Papa," she answered.

"In the same way," he explained, "God gives you the faith you need to face life *at the moment you need it*, not before."

The writer to the Hebrews tells us, "And without faith it is impossible to please God, because anyone who comes to him must believe that he exists and that he rewards those who earnestly seek him."[10] If we seek God wholeheartedly and trust Him enough to begin instituting changes, He will faithfully reward us with the power to make those changes a reality.

We've come to the end of our look at the two sides of love. Our prayer for you is that in the days to come, you'll discover more of God's love than ever before.

May you always be humbled by the hardness of love pictured in the cross, and thankful for His discipline when we need it. And may you also be thankful for the softness that sent God's only begotten Son to that cross—and would have done so even if you had been the only one without hope otherwise.

May the Lord bless you and keep you. May you come to know Him as both your mighty king and loving shepherd. And may all your relationships express what Jesus gave to others, the two sides of love.

Endnotes

THE LANGUAGE OF LOVE

Chapter 1

1. While some people may be more familiar with the expression "extended metaphors" or simply "figurative language," we like "word pictures" as a more descriptive term. The expression "word pictures" is found in articles like Carol Huber's, "The Logical Art of Writing Word Pictures," *IEEE Transactions on Professional Communication*, March 1985, 27-28.

Chapter 2

1. For a disturbing look at the damage caused by an angry father, see William S. Appleton's insightful book, *Fathers and Daughters* (New York: Berkley Books, 1981).

2. "When people use a figure of speech today, it is often met with the cry, 'oh, that is figurative'—implying that its meaning is weakened, or that it has quite a different meaning, or that it has no meaning at all! But the very opposite is the case. For a figure is never used except to add force to the truth conveyed, emphasis to the statement of it, and depth to the meaning of it." E. W. Bullinger, *Figures of Speech* (Grand Rapids: Baker Book House, 1968), 5-6.

Chapter 3

1. *Hunting Licenses and Federal Deer Stamp Sales as Reported by the Information Bureau of the Department of Interior July 15, 1941 through 1942* (Washington, D.C.: U.S. Fish and Wildlife Bureau, Federal Aid Office, 1942). Such a furor was caused by *Bambi*'s release that two major outdoor magazines of the day devoted full editorial articles to the issue. To see the movie's negative effect on the deer hunting industry, sée Donald C. Pettie, "The Nature of Things, *Audubon Magazine*, September 1942, 266-71. For a pro-hunting viewpoint, see *"Outdoor Life* Condemns Walt Disney's Film *Bambi* as Insult to American Sportsmen," *Outdoor Life*, September 1942, 17.

2. Cicero, *De oratore*, Trans. H. Ranckham, The Loeb Classical Library, 1942 (Cambridge: Harvard University Press, 1977).

3. Cicero, *De inventione*, Trans. H. M. Hubbell, The Loeb Classical Library, 1949 (Cambridge: Harvard University Press, 1976).

4. Aristotle, *"Art" of Rhetoric*, Trans. J. H. Freese, The Loeb Classical Library, 1926 (Cambridge: Harvard University Press, 1975).

5. Charles Lewis, *The Autobiography of Benjamin Franklin* (New York: Collin Books, 1962).

6. When Lincoln first met Harriet Beecher Stowe, he is reported to have said, "So this is the little lady who wrote the book that made this big war!" James Ford Rhodes, *History of the United States*, vol. 1 (1893); *Lectures on the American Civil War* (1913).

7. Winston S. Churchill, *The Unrelenting Struggle* (Boston: Little, Brown and Company, 1942), 95. For other examples of the many ways Churchill used word pictures, see Charles Eade (ed.), *Winston Churchill's Secret Session Speeches* (New York: Simon and Schuster, 1946) or *The End of the Beginning: War Speeches by the Right Honorable Winston S. Churchill* (Cassell and Company, 1943).

8. See Chapter 16, "The Dark Side of Emotional Word Pictures."

9. John F. Kennedy, "Inaugural Address," *New York Times*, January 21, 1961, 8.

10. Dr. Martin Luther King, Jr., *Letter from a Birmingham Jail & I Have a Dream* (Atlanta: The Southern Christian Leadership Conference, 1963).

11. Alfred A. Balitzer (ed.), A Time for Choosing: *The Speeches of Ronald Reagan, 1961-82* (Chicago: Regnery Gateway, 1983). Also see T. Marganthau, "Reagan Leaves the Democrats Mumbling," *Newsweek*, October 27, 1986, 29-30, or P. McGrath, "Never Underestimate Him!" *Newsweek*, April 19, 1982, 28-9.

12. S. L. Greenslade, *The Cambridge History of the Bible* (Cambridge: Cambridge University Press, 1973), 479. "The Bible has been read by more people and published in more languages than any other book."

13. John P. Eaton, *Titanic: Triumph and Tragedy* (New York: W. W. Norton & Co., 1986).

14. James and William Belote, *Typhoon of Steel: The Battle for Okinawa* (New York: Harper and Row, 1970), and Commander Herbert L. Bergsma, *Chaplains with Marines in Vietnam 1962-71* (Washington, D.C.: History and Museum's Division, Headquarters Marine Corps, 1985).

15. "Men of the Year," *Time*, January 3, 1969. Astronauts Frank Borman, Jim Lovell, and Bill Anders read Genesis 1:1-10 on Christmas Eve, 1968, during the mission of Apollo 8.

16. For the parable of the good Samaritan, see Luke 10:29-37. For

the reference to many mansions, see John 14:1-3. For the reference to faith like a mustard seed, see Matthew 17:20. And the story of the prodigal son is in Luke 15:11-32.

17. These word pictures are found, in order, in Isaiah 9:6; John 1:1; John 8:12; John 15:5; Revelation 5:5; and Revelation 22:16. God the Father is pictured as one who defends the righteous with a protective shield, Psalm 5:11-12; a rock, Psalm 28:1; a bird who spreads His protective wings over His own, Psalm 91:4; and a refuge and shield, Psalm 119:114.

18. Robert Hoffman, "Recent Research on Figurative Language," *Annals of the New York Academy of Sciences*, December 1984, 137-66.

19. Leonard Zunin. *Contact: The First Four Minutes* (New York: Ballantine Books, 1975).

20. L. D. Groninger, "Physiological Function of Images in the Encoding-Retrieval Process, *Journal of Experimental Psychology: Learning, Memory, and Cognition*, July 1985, 353-58.

21. G. R. Potts, "Storing and Retrieving Information about Spatial Images," *Psychological Review*, vol. 75 (1978): 550-60, and Z. W. Pylyshyn, "What the Mind's Eye Tells the Mind's Brain: A Critique of Mental Images, *Psychological Bulletin*, vol. 80, n. 6 (1973): 1-24.

22. Ibid., Pylyshyn, 22.

23. Among other studies, see A. Mehrablan, "The Silent Messages We Send," *Journal of Communication*, July 1982.

24. Louie S. Karpress and Ming Singer, "Communicative Competence," *Psychology Reports*, vol. 59 (1986): 1299-1306.

25. For an excellent resource on how to deal with differences in a marriage, we highly recommend Chuck and Barb Snyder's *Incompatibility: Grounds for a Great Marriage* (Phoenix: Questar Publishers, Inc., 1988).

Chapter 4

1. S. F. Witelson, "Sex and the Single Hemisphere: Specialization of the Right Hemisphere for Spatial Processing," *Science*, 193: 425-27, and Milton Diamond, "Human Sexual Development: Biological Foundations for Social Development," *Human Sexuality* (Baltimore: Johns Hopkins Press, 1981).

2. J. E. Bogen, "Cerebral Commissurotomy in Man: Minor Hemisphere Dominance for Certain Visuospatial Functions," *Journal of Neurosurgery*, 1965, 135-62, and John Levy, "A Model for the Genetics of Handedness," *Genetics*, 72: 117-28.

3. E. Zaidel, "Auditory Language Comprehension in the Right Hemisphere: A Comparison with Child Language," *Language Acquisition and Language Breakdown* (Baltimore: Johns Hopkins Press, 1978).

4. D. Kimura, "Early Motor Functions of the Left and Right Hemisphere, *Brain*, 97: 337-50.

5. Robert Kohn, "Patterns of Hemispheric Specialization in Pre-Schoolers," *Neuropsychologia*, vol. 12: 505-12.

6. J. Levy, "The Adaptive Advantages of Cerebral Asymmetry and Communication," *Annals of the New York Academy of Sciences*, vol. 229: 264-72.

7. See Chapter 16, "The Dark Side of Emotional Word Pictures."

Chapter 5

1. For the actual biblical account of this riveting word picture, see 2 Samuel 11-12.

2. 1 Samuel 16:1-12.

3. 1 Samuel 17; 2 Samuel 3:1.

4. 2 Samuel 5:1-25.

5. Noted Old Testament scholars Keil and Delitzsch comment on David's state of affairs, "These words went to David's heart, and removed the ban of hardening which pressed upon it. There is no excuse, no searching for a loophole, no pretext put forward, no human weakness pleaded. He acknowledges his guilt openly, candidly, and without prevarication." C. F. Keil and F. Delitzsch, *Commentary on the Old Testament in Ten Volumes: Vol. II: Joshua, Judges, Ruth, 1 and 2 Samuel* (Grand Rapids: William B. Eerdmans Publishing, 1975), 391.

Chapter 6

1. Francis Brown, S. R. Driver and Charles A. Briggs, *A Hebrew and English Lexicon of the Old Testament* (Oxford: Clarendon Press, reprinted edition, 1974), "aph," 60, and *The Compact Edition of the Oxford English Dictionary* (New York: Oxford University Press, 1971), "anger," 82.

2. Ibid., Brown, "kilyah," 480 and Oxford, "fear," 973.

3. 2 Samuel 12:1ff.

4. Gary Smalley and John Trent, Ph.D., *The Blessing* (Nashville: Thomas Nelson Publishers, 1986), 172-73.

5. For example, Christ used word pictures with certain groups of people who "had ears but would not hear, and eyes but would not see," Matthew 13:14ff.

Chapter 7

1. If you've just opened the book to this story, you'll need to go back to portions of chapters 5 and 6, which provide seven steps to creating emotional word pictures, for the steps Jim followed.

Chapter 8

1. Richard F. Newcomb, *Iwo Jima* (New York: Holt, Rinehart & Winston, 1965), 35.

2. Ibid., 229.

Chapter 10

1. Wilder Penfield, *The Mystery of the Mind* (Princeton: Princeton University Press, 1984), 148.

2. For a family vacation with a purpose, why not write to one of our favorite places for further information on their outstanding family retreats: Forest Home Conference Center, General Delivery, Forest Falls, CA 92339 or call 714-794-1127.

3. The Performax Personal Profile System (Performax Systems International, Minneapolis, Minnesota).

4. For information on the author's availability, write: Today's Family, Post Office Box 22111, Phoenix, AZ 85028.

Chapter 11

1. Gary Smalley, *If Only He Knew* and *For Better or for Best* (Grand Rapids: Zondervan Publishing, 1979); Gary Smalley and John Trent, Ph.D., *The Blessing* and *The Gift of Honor* (Nashville: Thomas Nelson Publishers, 1986 and 1987); Gary Smalley, *The Key to Your Child's Heart* (Waco, Texas: Word Books, 1984).

2. See Jim's word picture in Chapter 7, "The Well of Nature," and Susan's in the following chapter, "The Well of Everyday Objects."

3. *The Compact Edition of the Oxford English Dictionary* (New York: Oxford University Press), 485.

Chapter 12

1. Song of Songs 4:1ff.

2. Song of Songs 2:1ff.

3. William Shakespeare, *Romeo and Juliet*, Act II, Scene I (Oxford: Clarendon Press, 1986), 388.

4. Ibid.

5. Ibid., 396.

6. Elizabeth Barrett Browning, "Sonnets from the Portuguese."

7. Christopher Ricks, *The Force of Poetry* (Oxford: Cambridge

University Press, 1984), and J. R. Jackson, *Poetry and the Romantics* (London: Rouledge & Kegan Paul Ltd., 1980).

8. UCLA Monthly, *Alumni Association News*, March-April, 1981, 1.

9. For a challenging look at the origin and creation of affairs, see Willard F. Harley, *His Needs/Her Needs* (Old Tappan, New Jersey: Fleming H. Revell Company, 1986).

10. Marc H. Hollender, "The Wish to Be Held," *Archives of General Psychiatry*, vol. 22 (1970): 445.

11. S. R. Arbetter, "Body Language: Your Body's Silent Movie," *Current Health*, February 1987, 11-13.

12. See our definition of a word picture in Chapter Two, "Words That Penetrate the Heart."

13. Psalm 128:1,3, NIV.

14. See Gary Smalley, *Joy That Lasts* (Grand Rapids: Zondervan Publishers, 1985). In this book, Gary talks of the importance of a dynamic spiritual life as the key to success in all we do. While *The Language of Love* speaks primarily of how word pictures can be used as an effective communication tool, we look forward to doing a book that addresses the incredible power of word pictures to enhance a person's spiritual life.

Chapter 13

1. James C. Dobson, *Dare to Discipline* (Wheaton: Tyndale Publishers, 1970); *Hide or Seek* (Old Tappan, New Jersey: Fleming H. Revell, Power Books, 1974); *Love Must Be Tough* (Waco, Texas: Word Publishers, 1983); Paul D. Meier, *Christian Child-Rearing and Personality Development* (Grand Rapids: Baker Book House, 1977); Richard Allen, *Common Sense Discipline* (Ft. Worth: Worthy Publishers, 1986).

2. James C. Dobson, *Parenting Isn't for Cowards* (Waco, Texas: Word Publishers, 1988).

Chapter 14

1. Gary Smalley and John Trent, Ph.D., *The Blessing* (Nashville: Thomas Nelson Publishers, 1986).

2. Robert Pandia, "Psychosocial Correlates of Alcohol and Drug Use," *Journal of Studies on Alcohol*, vol. 44, no. 6 (1983): 950; Mark Warren, "Family Background and Substance Abuse," *Psychiatric Research Review*, vol. 35 (1985): 25; Joanna Norell, "Parent-Adolescent Interaction: Influences on Depression and Mood Cycles," *Dissertation Abstracts International*, vol. 45, no. 4-A (1984): 1067; Frank Minirth,

Paul Meier, Bill Brewer, et al., *The Workaholic and His Family* (Grand Rapids: Baker Book House, 1981); Frank Minirth and Paul Meier, *Happiness Is a Choice* (Grand Rapids: Baker Book House, 1978).

3. Brian Lucas, "Identity Status, Parent-Adolescent Relationships, and Participation in Marginal Religious Groups," *Dissertation Abstracts International*, vol. 43, no. 12-B (1984): 4131; J. R. Heiman, "A Psychophysiological Exploration of Sexual Arousal Patterns in Females and Males," *Psychophysiology*, vol. 14, no. 3 (1987): 2266-74; J. V. Mitchell, "Goal-Setting Behavior as a Function of Self-Acceptance, Over- and Under-Achievement and Related Personality Variables," *Journal of Educational Psychology*, vol. 50 (1970): 93-104.

4. V. Cosi, *Amyotrophic Lateral Sclerosis* (New York: Plenum Press, 1987).

5. E. M. Goldberg, *Family Influences and Psychosomatic Illness* (London: Tovistock Publishers Ltd., 1987).

6. See chapter 6, "Creating an Effective Emotional Word Picture, Part Two."

7. Cathy Dent, "Facilitating Children's Recall of Figurative Language in Text Using Films of Natural Objects and Events," *Human Development*, July-August 1986, 231-5; Robert Verbrugge, "The Role of Metaphor in Our Perception of Language," unpublished speech presented at the Linguistics Section of the New York Academy of Sciences on January 14, 1980.

8. Deena Bernstein, "Figurative Language: Assessment Strategies and Implications for Intervention," *Folia Phoniat*, vol. 39 (1987): 130.

9. Proverbs 22:6.

10. For an excellent description of what training a child involves, see Charles R. Swindoll, *You and Your Child* (Nashville: Thomas Nelson Publishers, 1977).

11. Proverbs 6:6.

12. S. J. Samuels, "Effects of Pictures on Learning to Read, Comprehension and Attitudes Toward Learning," *Review of Educational Research*, vol. 40 (1980): 397.

13. William Looft, "Modification of Life Concepts in Children and Adults," *Developmental Psychology*, vol. 1 (1969): 445.

14. Gary Smalley, *The Key to Your Child's Heart* (Waco, Texas: Word Publishing, 1984).

Chapter 15

1. Psalm 103:19.

2. Isaiah 55:8.

3. Psalm 23:1-2.

4. Psalm 23:4.

5. Psalm 51:11.

6. Romans 3:12-13.

7. Romans 12:1.

8. Isaiah 53:7.

9. Isaiah 53:6.

10. Psalm 3:1, 3.

11. Psalm 18:1-2.

12. Psalm 1:1-3.

13. See Luke 18:1-8 and 11:5-13.

14. Isaiah 40:21, 23-24.

15. John 14:2.

16. Don Richardson, *Peace Child* (Glendale, Cal.: Gospel Light, 1974).

Chapter 16

1. Proverbs 18:21, RSV.

2. Theodore Abel, *Why Hitler Came into Power* (New York: Prentice Hall, 1948).

3. Norman H . Baynes, *The Speeches of Adolf Hitler, Vol. I and II* (New York: Howard Fertig Publishers, 1969). This speech was given in the Kroll Opera House in Berlin on March 23, 1933.

4. Philip Kerns, *People's Temple/People's Tomb* (Plainfield, New Jersey: Logos International, 1979).

5. Edwin Meuller, *Making Sense of the Jonestown Suicides* (New York: Cassel Publishing, 1981).

6. Vincent Bugliosi, *Helter Skelter* (New York: Bantam Books, 1975).

7. Walter Martin, *Kingdom of the Cults* (Minneapolis: Bethany House Publishers, 1985), and a book by a former satanic priest, Mike Warnke, *Satan Seller* (Plainfield, New Jersey: Bridge Publishing, 1987).

8. For a chilling picture of people addicted to verbally inflicting pain on others, see M. Scott Peck, *People of the Lie* (New York: Simon & Schuster, 1983).

9. C. S. Lewis, *The Lion, the Witch and the Wardrobe* (New York: Macmillan Publishing Co., 1950), 75-76.

LOVE IS A DECISION

Chapter 1

1. In the years ahead, our goal as a ministry is to produce small group follow-up materials that will provide families everywhere with

biblically based resources to strengthen their most important relationships.

2. "Even youths grow tired and weary, and young men stumble and fall; but those who hope in the Lord will renew their strength . . ." Isaiah 40:30-31.

Chapter 2

1. Gary Smalley and John Trent, Ph.D., *Hardside/Softside* (Pomona, CA: Focus on the Family Publishers, to be released Spring, 1990).

2. From a training booklet by Jack Hilger, *Training Married Couples to Work with Premarital Couples*, Prepare/Enrich, Inc., 1987.

3. Joan Druckman, David Fournier, Beatrice Robinson, and David H. Olson, "Effectiveness of Five Types of Pre-marital Programs," *Education for Marriage* (Grand Rapids, MI, 1979). Gerald Cossitt, *Effects of Feedback on Idealism in Premarital Couples*, Doctoral dissertation, University of Alberta, Edmonton, Canada.

4. The biblical concept of "honoring" God and others is so important, Dr. John Trent and I wrote an entire book on the subject called *The Gift of Honor* (Nashville, TN: Thomas Nelson Publishers, 1987).

5. Reading books like Frank Peritti's *This Present Darkness* (Westchester, IL: Good News Books/Crossway Publishers, 1988) can help you believe that there may be a satanic cover-up of honor!

6. William F. Arndt and R. Wilbur Gingrich, eds., *A Greek-English Lexicon of the New Testament and Other Early Christian Literature* (Chicago: University of Chicago Press, 1957), 119.

7. Ibid., 120.

8. Men are motivated by the "awe" principle both negatively and positively. One major reason for the creation of affairs is that a woman outside the marriage will show a man "ah-h-h-h-h," and it draws him after her. See Proverbs 5, 6:20-35, and Chapter 7 for a picture of the adulteress who "flatters with her words" in working her destruction.

9. *The Gift of Honor*, Chapter 3.

10. For more on the tremendously damaging effects of negative word pictures, see Gary Smalley and John Trent, Ph.D., *The Language of Love* (Pomona, CA: Focus on the Family Publishing, 1988), Chapter 15, "The Dark Side of Emotional Word Pictures."

Chapter 3

1. For a long overdue look at the long-term negative effects of divorce on children, see the chilling book, Judith Wallenstein, *Second*

Chances (New York: Ticknor and Fields Publishers, 1989); Diana Medved, *The Case Against Divorce* (New York: Donald I. Fine, Inc., 1989), and especially, Gary Richmond, *The Divorce Decision* (Waco, TX: Word Books, 1988).

Chapter 4

1. Allen P. Ross, *Creation and Blessing* (Grand Rapids, MI: Baker Book House, 1988), 126.

2. Robert Kohn, "Patterns of Hemispheric Specialization in Pre-Schoolers," *Neuropsychologia*, 12:505-12.

3. James J. Lynch, *The Language of the Heart* (New York: Basic Books, Inc., 1985).

4. For a definition of "word picture," see *The Language of Love*, 17.

5. Arthur Bragg, "What's Holding Them Back?" *Business Insurance* (March 1989).

Chapter 5

1. Leprosy was such a dreaded disease that one rabbi taught it was all right to throw stones at lepers to keep them "a safe distance away," cf. Alfred Edershiem, *The Life and Times of Jesus the Messiah* (Grand Rapids, MI: William B. Eerdmans Publishing, 1971), 1:495.

2. See *aphieimi*, which has the basic meaning of "let go, send away, cancel, remit, pardon, leave, let go, tolerate," Ardnt and Gingrich, *Lexicon*, 125-26.

3. In *The Blessing*, we discuss the physiological benefit of elevated hemoglobin levels in both people involved in the meaningful touch. When elevated, the hemoglobin levels serve to carry more oxygen to our bodies and actually energize us. For more information, see Gary Smalley and John Trent, *The Blessing*, p. 40, and "Therapeutic Touch: The Imprimatur of Nursing," *American Journal of Nursing* (May 1975): 784.

Chapter 6

1. For a detailed description of the concept of "closing" or "re-opening" a person's spirit, see Gary Smalley, *The Key to Your Child's Heart* (Waco, TX: Word Publishing, 1984).

2. For a detailed look at the negative physiology of anger, see Paul Meier and Frank Minirth, *Happiness Is a Choice* (Grand Rapids, MI: Baker Book House, 1978).

3. Ibid., 23-29.

4. Albert A. Kurtland, "Biochemical and Emotional Interaction in the Etiology of Cancer," *Psychiatric Research Review* 35 (1978): 25.

5. "They can sit through sermon after sermon about forgiveness in church, never once misunderstanding what the pastor says, but still refuse to put their son's or daughter's picture back on the mantle." From Gary Smalley and John Trent, Ph.D., *The Blessing* (Nashville, TN: Thomas Nelson Publishers, 1986), 137.

6. We're using "soul" here in a nontheological way and especially not in the way some new-age people would call a "floating soul" touching another.

7. For a more complete list, see Gary Smalley, *If Only He Knew* (Grand Rapids, MI: Zondervan Publishing House, 1979), Chapter 5, "Climbing Out of Marriage's Deepest Pit," 82-86.

8. For an excellent resource on dealing with strong-willed children, see James Dobson, Ph.D., *The Strong-Willed Child* (Wheaton, IL: Tyndale House, 1979).

Chapter 7

1. There are, unfortunately, exceptions. See Gary Smalley and John Trent, Ph.D., *The Language of Love*, "The Dark Side of Emotional Word Pictures" (Pomona, CA: Focus on the Family Publishing, 1988), 150-62; and M. Scott Peck, M.D., *People of the Lie* (New York: Simon and Schuster, 1983).

2. We'll talk about this more later, but physically, emotionally and spiritually a man benefits by developing relationship skills.

3. From the Greek verb, *epitrepho*. Ardnt and Gingrich, *Lexicon*, 343.

Chapter 8

1. For a very helpful resource on leaving your children a legacy of love, see Tim Kimmel, *Legacy of Love: A Plan for Parenting on Purpose* (Portland, OR: Multnomah Press, 1989).

2. For more information on this outstanding conference, contact the Campus Crusade Family Ministry in Little Rock, AR, (501) 223-8663.

3. For an insightful, biblically based book dealing with sexual temptation, see Charles Mylander, *Running the Red Lights* (Ventura, CA: Regal Books, 1986).

4. Ibid.

5. For more information about our #1 favorite Christian sports

camp for any youngster aged eight to eighteen, please contact Kamp Kanakuk, Route 4, Box 2124, Branson, MO 65616, (417) 334-2432 or 334-6427.

Chapter 9

1. In fact, one of our favorite marriage books is by our good friends, Chuck and Barb Snyder. It's called *Incompatibility: Grounds for a Great Marriage* (Sisters, OR; Questar Publishers, 1988).

2. This is such an important concept, Dr. Trent and I have written an entire book about it called *The Language of Love* (Pomona, CA: Focus on the Family Publishers, 1988).

3. James Ford Rhodes, *History of the United States*, vol. 1: *Lectures on the American Civil War* (1913). On meeting her, Lincoln reportedly said, "So this is the little lady who wrote the book that made this big war!"

4. Even though you may not realize it, you probably have been using them all your life. Expressions like "I'm toasty warm," "His elevator doesn't go all the way to the top floor!" or "That went over like a lead balloon" are just three of the hundreds of word pictures that are a part of our everyday speech.

Chapter 10

1. H. Norman Wright, *Romancing Your Marriage* (Ventura, CA: Regal Books, 1987), 41.

2. Alice Chapin, *Four Hundred Ways to Say I Love You* (Wheaton, IL: Living Books, Tyndale House Publishers, Inc., 1981).

3. *Romancing Your Marriage.*

4. Dan Carlinsky, *Do You Know Your Wife?* (Los Angeles, CA: Price, Stern, and Sloan, 1984).

Chapter 11

1. Marc H. Hollender, "The Wish to Be Held," *Archives of General Psychiatry* 22 (1970): 445.

2. This survey of several thousand women was conducted by Ann Landers and its findings are recorded in "Is Affection More Important Than Sex?" *Reader's Digest* (August 1985).

Chapter 12

1. See Chapter 6 for more on "closing" a person's spirit.

2. If you're interested in contacting Bill to do a family enrichment

event at your church or business, you can contact him at P.O. Box 2929, Grass Valley, CA 95945, (916) 447-7738.

3. John Piper, *Desiring God* (Portland, OR: Multnomah Press, 1986).

Chapter 13

1. See Proverbs 7:1ff for a chilling description of the high cost of immoral relationships.

Chapter 14

1. Gary Smalley, *Joy That Lasts* (Grand Rapids, MI: Zondervan Publishing House, 1987).

THE TWO SIDES OF LOVE

Chapter 1

1. In Hebrew, the original language of the Old Testament, there's a very close grammatical and personal connection between the two figures of speech in this passage. Normally, two circumstantial clauses, like those found in Isaiah 40:10-11, would be connected by a Waw consecutive (similar to an English *and*). However, so close is the connection in this case that no conjunction exists between the two clauses.

In short, the "Sovereign Lord" *(Adonai Jehovah* in Hebrew) who comes in strength is directly linked with the picture of a compassionate shepherd. His "power" with which "his arm rules for him" cannot be separated from the great love out of which he "gathers the lambs in his arms" and "gently leads those that have young."

For further insight into these powerful figures of speech, see C. F. Keil and F. Delitzsch, *Commentary on the Old Testament in Ten Volumes*, vol. 7, *Isaiah* (Grand Rapids, Mich.: Eerdmans, 1975), pp.145-47; Edward J. Young, *The Book of Isaiah*, vol. 3 (Grand Rapids, Mich.: Eerdmans, 1972), pp. 38-40; E. Kautzsch, *Genenius' Hebrew Grammar*, rev. ed. (London: Oxford U., 1974), pp. 504-5.

2. Romans 5:8.

3. Matthew 16:17.

4. Matthew 16:23.

5. Luke 9:51.

Chapter 3

1. Ross Campbell, *How to Really Love Your Child* (Wheaton, Ill.: Victor, 1978), pp. 14-16.

2. For those who want to go deeper in understanding their personality, a number of popular tests are available, including the *Myers-Briggs* test, the *Keirsey Temperament Sorter* and the *Taylor-Johnson Temperament Analysis.* Our friend Florence Littauer has also written a helpful book called *Personality Plus.*

As mentioned in the chapter, we strongly recommend Dr. Williamson's "Pro *Scan" PDP Personality Survey* as well. After taking it, you get back an exhaustive, ten-page analysis that helps you identify your stress and energy levels, how you make decisions, how best to motivate yourself and others, and so on. For further information, write to Dr. Michael Williamson. CompuLink, 408 S. Santa Anita Ave., #13, Arcadia, CA 91006. To order the test, call 800-332-3291. The call is toll-free, but there is a reasonable fee for the ten-page analysis.

Another helpful test is the *Couple's Profile* developed by the Reverend Charles Boyd in conjunction with Performax International. It gives engaged and married *couples* a good look at themselves and their differences and is used extensively in Campus Crusade's Family Life Conferences. For more information, write to Boyd at #3 Diamond Pointe Cove, Maumelle, AR 72113. To order, send $12 per profile plus $3 shipping and handling. Specify whether you want the *engaged* or *married* version.

Yet another helpful test is the *Personal Style Indicator*, which is slanted primarily toward business use but offers strong insights and applications for a family as well. For more details, write to Terry Anderson, Consulting Resource Group International, #386-33255 S. Fraser Way, Abbotsford, B.C., Canada V2S 2B2 or #386-200 W. Third St., Sumas, WA 98295-8000.

Chapter 4

1 Ross Campbell, *How to Really Love Your Child*, pp. 14-16.

2. For an in-depth treatment of the concept of closing a person's spirit, see Gary Smalley, *The Key to Your Child's Heart* (Waco, Tex.: Word, 1984). Look especially at Chapter 1, "How to Overcome the Major Destroyer of Families."

Chapter 5

1. An excellent new book on establishing discipline and responsibility with our kids is *Who's in Charge Here?*, by Robert G. Barnes, Jr. (Dallas: Word, 1990).

2. Hebrews 11:1.

Chapter 6

1. For the heroic, inspiring account of what it was like to be a prisoner of war in North Vietnam for eight and a half years, see Everett Alvarez, Jr., *Chained Eagle* (New York: Donald I. Fine, 1989).

2. 1 Samuel 16:7.

3. C. F. Keil and F. Delitzsch, *Commentary on the Old Testament in Ten Volumes*, vol. 2, *Joshua, Judges, Ruth, I & II Samuel* (Grand Rapids, Mich.: Eerdmans, 1975), pp. 153-59.

4. An excellent book on peer pressure is Joe White's *Friendship Pressure* (Sisters, Ore.: Questar, 1989).

Chapter 7

1. Leonard Maltin, *The Disney Films*, rev. ed. (New York: Crown, 1984), section on *Greyfriar's Bobby*.

2. For information about how to bring the "Love Is a Decision" seminar to your city, write to Terry Brown or Norma Smalley at Today's Family, P.O. Box 22111, Phoenix, AZ 85028.

3. For a good perspective on this common problem, see Robert Hemfelt, Paul Meier and Frank Minirth, *Love Is a Choice* (Nashville: Nelson, 1989).

4. *World Book Encyclopedia* (Chicago: World Book, 1988), pp. 570-71.

Chapter 8

1. There are many good books that will help you deal with a hurtful past. Here are just a few we recommend: our own books *The Blessing* and *The Gift of Honor* (both from Thomas Nelson); *Healing for Damaged Emotions*, by David Seamands (Victor); *Unfinished Business: Helping Adult Children Resolve Their Past*, by Charles Sell (Multnomah); *The Missing Piece*, by Lee Ezell (Harvest House); *Unlocking the Secrets of Your Childhood Memories*, by Kevin Leman and Randy Carlson (Thomas Nelson).

2. See Richard B. Stuart, *Helping Couples Change* (New York: Guilford, 1980), especially "Caring Days: A technique for building commitment to faltering marriages," pp. 192-208.

Chapter 9

1. Matthew 6:21.

2. Proverbs 15:1; 25:15.

3. *The Student Bible* (Grand Rapids, Mich.: Zondervan, 1986).

4. See James 1:23-25.

5. Proverbs 15:30.

6. Proverbs 17:10, *New American Standard Bible.*

7. Psalm 44:20-21.

8. To get a copy of this important book, you can contact Jim Brawner directly at HCR4, Box 2212-A, Branson, MO 65616.

Chapter 10

1. John 8:32.

Chapter 11

1. Acts 24:25.

2. Proverbs 27:17.

3. Proverbs 27:6, *New American Standard Bible.*

4. Some of our favorite books by these authors are: Max Lucado, *No Wonder They Call Him Savior* and *Six Hours One Friday* (both from Multnomah); Ken Gire, *Intimate Moments with the Savior* (Zondervan); Charles Swindoll, *Come Before Winter, Rise & Shine* (both from Multnomah) and *The Grace Awakening* (Word).

5. Hebrews 12:6.

Chapter 12

1. Tony Melendez with Mel White, *A Gift of Hope* (San Francisco: Harper & Row, 1989), pp. 17, 19, 147-48.

2. Matthew 22:37-40.

3. Acts 8:3.

4. 1 Corinthians 4:18-21.

5. 1 Thessalonians 2:5-7.

6. John 3:16.

7. *Youthworker Update*, vol. iv, no. 5, January 1990, p. 8.

8. John 15:5.

9. Ephesians 4:26-27.

10. Hebrews 11:6.